GREEK TRAGEDY

GREEK TRAGEDY

BY

GILBERT NORWOOD, M.A.

A DRAMABOOK

 HILL AND WANG · NEW YORK

FIRST DRAMABOOK PRINTING FEBRUARY 1960
STANDARD BOOK NUMBER: 8090–0521–2

67890

PREFACE

THIS book is an attempt to cover the whole field of Greek Tragedy. My purpose throughout has been twofold. Firstly, I have sought to provide classical students with definite facts and with help towards a personal appreciation of the plays they read. My other intention has been to interest and in some degree to satisfy those "general readers" who have little or no knowledge of Greek. This second function is to-day at least as important as the first. Apart from the admirable progress shown in Europe and the English-speaking world by many works of first-rate Greek scholarship, in the forefront of which stand Jebb's monumental Sophocles, Verrall's achievements in dramatic criticism, and the unrivalled *Einleitung* of Wilamowitz-Moellendorff,—the magnificent verse-translations of Professor Gilbert Murray, springing from a rare union of poetic genius with consummate scholarship, have introduced in this country a new epoch of interest in Greek drama among many thousands who are unacquainted with the language. Even more momentous is the fact that the feeling of educated people about drama in general has been revolutionized and reanimated by the creative genius of Ibsen, whose penetrating influence is the chief cause of the present dramatic renaissance in Great Britain.

Two important topics have been given more prominence than is usual in books of this kind : dramatic structure and the scansion of lyrics.

It might have been supposed self-evident that the former of these is a vital part, indeed the foundation, of the subject, but it has suffered remarkable neglect or still more remarkable superficiality of treatment: criticism of the Greek tragedians has been vitiated time and again by a tendency to ignore the very existence of dramatic form. It is a strange reflection that the world of scholarship waited till 1887 for the mere revelation of grave difficulties in the plot of the *Agamemnon*. Examining boards still prescribe "*Ajax* vv. 1-865," on the naïve assumption that they know better than Sophocles where the play ought to end. Euripides has been discussed with a perversity which one would scarcely surpass if one applied to Anatole France the standards appropriate to Clarendon. Throughout I have attempted to follow the working of each playwright's mind, to realize what he meant his work to "feel like". This includes much besides structure, but the plot is still, as in Aristotle's day, "the soul of the drama".

Chapter VI, on metre and rhythm, will, I hope, be found useful. Greek lyrics are so difficult that most students treat them as prose. I have done my best to be accurate, clear, and simple, with the purpose of enabling the sixth-form boy or undergraduate to read his "chorus" with a sense of metrical and rhythmical form. With regard to this chapter, even more than the others, I shall welcome criticism and advice.

I have to thank my wife for much help, and my friend Mr. Cyril Brett, M.A., who kindly offered to make the Index.

GILBERT NORWOOD

CONTENTS

GREEK TRAGEDY

GREEK TRAGEDY

CHAPTER I

THE LITERARY HISTORY OF GREEK TRAGEDY

ALL the types of dramatic poetry known in Greece, tragic, satyric, and comic, originated in the worship of Dionysus, the deity of wild vegetation, fruits, and especially the vine. In his honour, at the opening of spring, were performed dithyrambs, hymns rendered by a chorus, who, dressed like satyrs, the legendary followers of Dionysus, presented by song and mimic dance stories from the adventurous life of the god while on earth. It is from these dithyrambs that tragedy and satyric drama both sprang. The celebrated Arion, who raised the dithyramb to a splendid art-form, did much[1] incidentally to aid this development. His main achievement in this regard is the insertion of spoken lines in the course of the lyrical performance ; it seems, further, that these verses consisted of a dialogue between the chorus and the chorus-leader, who mounted upon the sacrificial table. Such interludes, no doubt, referred to incidents in the sacred story, and the early name for an actor (ὑποκριτής, "one who answers") suggests that members of the chorus asked their leader to explain features in the ritual or the narrative.

At this point drama begins to diverge from the dithyramb. With comedy we are not here concerned.[2]

---

[1] See Haigh, *The Tragic Drama of the Greeks*, pp. 19 *sq.*
[2] It arose in a similar fashion to tragedy, from the phallic songs to Dionysus at his winter festival.

The drama of the spring festival may be called "tragedy," but it was in a quite rudimentary state. Its lyrics, sung by fifty "satyrs," would altogether outshine in importance the dialogue-interludes between chorus-leader and individual singers; the theme, moreover, would be always some event connected with Dionysus. Two great changes were necessary before drama could enter on free development: the use of impersonation in the interludes and the admission of any subject at will of the poet. The first was introduced by Thespis, who is said to have "invented one actor". The second was perhaps later, but at least as early as Phrynichus we find plays on subjects taken from other than Dionysiac legends. It is said that the audience complained of this innovation: "What has this to do with Dionysus?"[1]

Another great development is attributed to Pratinas —the invention of satyric drama. The more stately, graver features and the frolicsome, often gross, elements being separated, the way was clear for the free development of tragedy and satyric into the forms we know. But satyric work, though always showing playful characteristics and a touch of obscenity, was never confounded with comedy. Stately figures of legend or theology regularly appeared in it — Odysseus in the *Cyclops*, Apollo in the *Ichneutæ*—and it was a regular feature at the presentations of tragedy; each tragic poet competed with three tragedies followed by one satyric play. When the latter form changed its tone slightly, as in the work of the Alexandrian Pleiad,[2] it approximated not to comedy but to satire.[3]

---

[1] τί ταῦτα πρὸς τὸν Διόνυσον; (Plutarch, *Symposiaca*, 615 A).

[2] Pp. 39-41.

[3] These first paragraphs give a summary of the view almost universally held as to the origin of Greek tragedy. Of late, however, Professor Sir William Ridgeway (*The Origin of Tragedy, with Special Reference to the Greek Tragedians*, Cambridge, 1910) has combated current beliefs with great vigour. His belief is (p. 186) "that Tragedy arose in the worship of the dead, and that the only Dionysiac element in the Drama was the satyric play". Aristotle's evidence (see p. 4) he dismisses as mistaken, because "Aristotle was only interested in Tragedy as a fully developed art, and paid little heed to its early history" (p. 57). The present writer is bound

The Dorians claimed the credit of having invented both tragedy and comedy.[1] There seems little doubt that they provided the germ, though the glories of Greek drama belong to Athens. Arion, whose contribution has been described, if not himself a Dorian, worked among Dorians at Corinth, which Pindar,[2] for example, recognized as the birthplace of the dithyramb. Moreover the lyrics of purely Attic tragedy show in their language what is generally regarded as a slight Doric colouring.[3]

Aristotle[4] sums up the rise of tragedy as follows :

to confess that, after following and estimating to the best of his ability the numerous and heterogeneous statements put forward in evidence, he cannot regard Professor Ridgeway's contention as proved. It is undoubtedly true that many extant tragedies centre more or less vitally upon a tomb, but many do not. The mimetic ritual in honour of the slain Scephrus (p. 37) is real evidence, so far as it goes ; but the utmost it proves is that Greek tragedy *could* have arisen from such funeral performances—it does not show that it did. The most remarkable point in the book is the discussion of the well-known passage in Herodotus (V, 67) : τά τε δὴ ἄλλα οἱ Σικυώνιοι ἐτίμων τὸν Ἄδρηστον καὶ δὴ πρὸς τὰ πάθεα αὐτοῦ τραγικοῖσι χοροῖσι ἐγέραιρον, τὸν μὴν Διόνυσον οὐ τιμέωντες, τὸν δὲ Ἄδρηστον. Κλεισθένης δὲ χοροὺς μὲν τῷ Διονύσῳ ἀπέδωκε, τὴν δὲ ἄλλην θυσίην Μελανίππῳ (see Ridgeway, p. 28) : "The men of Sicyon paid honours to Adrastus, and in particular they revered him with tragic choruses because of his sufferings, herein honouring not Dionysus, but Adrastus. Cleisthenes gave the choruses to Dionysus, and the rest of the offering to Melanippus." It may well be that Professor Ridgeway is right in asserting that ἀπέδωκε means not "restored" but "gave"—that is, these tragic choruses were originally of the funereal kind which he suggests for all primitive Greek tragedy. This is excellent evidence for his contention, so far as it goes, But it only proves one example. Herodotus' words, on the other hand. imply that he believed tragedy to be normally Dionysiac. To sum up, we cannot regard Professor Ridgeway as having succeeded in damaging the traditional view.

[1] Aristotle, *Poetic*, 1448*a* : διὸ καὶ ἀντιποιοῦνται τῆς τε τραγῳδίας καὶ τῆς κωμῳδίας οἱ Δωριεῖς.

[2] *Ol.*, XIII, 18 *sq.* : ταὶ Διωνύσου πόθεν ἐξέφανεν σὺν βοηλάτᾳ χάριτες διθυράμβῳ ; *i.e.* as the context shows, the dithyramb appeared first at Corinth.

[3] *a* for η, and sometimes -ᾶν as the inflexion of the feminine genitive plural.

[4] *Poetic*, 1449*a* : γενομένη δ' οὖν ἀπ' ἀρχῆς αὐτοσχεδιαστική . . . ἀπὸ τῶν ἐξαρχόντων τὸν διθύραμβον . . . κατὰ μικρὸν ηὐξήθη προαγόντων ὅσον ἐγίγνετο φανερὸν αὐτῆς, καὶ πολλὰς μεταβολὰς μεταβαλοῦσα ἡ τραγῳδία ἐπαύσατο, ἐπεὶ ἔσχε τὴν αὑτῆς φύσιν. καὶ τό τε τῶν ὑποκριτῶν πλῆθος ἐξ ἑνὸς εἰς δύο πρῶτος Αἰσχύλος ἤγαγε καὶ τὰ τοῦ χοροῦ ἠλάττωσε καὶ τὸν λόγον πρωταγωνιστὴν παρεσκεύασεν, τρεῖς δὲ καὶ σκηνογραφίαν Σοφοκλῆς. ἔτι δὲ τὸ μέγεθος ἐκ

" Tragedy . . . was at first mere improvization . . .
originating with the leaders of the dithyramb. It advanced by slow degrees ; each new element that showed
itself was in turn developed. Having passed through
many stages, it found its natural form, and there it
stopped. Æschylus first introduced a second actor ; he
diminished the importance of the chorus, and assigned
the leading part to the dialogue. Sophocles raised the
number of actors to three, and added scene-painting.
It was not till late that the short plot was discarded for
one of greater compass, and the grotesque diction of the
earlier satyric form for the stately manner of tragedy.
The iambic measure then replaced the trochaic tetrameter, which was originally employed when the poetry
was of the satyric order, and had greater affinities with
dancing. . . . The number of 'episodes' or acts was
also increased, and the other embellishments added, of
which tradition tells."

We have but meagre knowledge of the drama before
Æschylus, whose vast achievement so overshadowed
his predecessors that their works were little read and
have in consequence practically vanished. Tragedy
was born at the moment when, as tradition relates,
THESPIS of Icaria in Attica introduced the actor. Arion,
as we saw, had already caused one of the chorus to
mount upon the sacrificial table or the step of the altar
and deliver a narrative, or converse with his fellow-
choristers, concerning Dionysus, using not lyrical metre,
but the trochaic tetrameter.[1] Thespis' great advance
was to introduce a person who should actually present
the character to whom Arion's chorister had merely

μικρῶν μύθων καὶ λέξεως γελοίας διὰ τὸ ἐκ σατυρικοῦ μεταβαλεῖν ὀψὲ ἀπε-
σεμνύνθη. τό τε μέτρον ἐκ τετραμέτρου ἰαμβεῖον ἐγένετο· τὸ μὲν γὰρ πρῶτον
τετραμέτρῳ ἐχρῶντο διὰ τὸ σατυρικὴν καὶ ὀρχηστικωτέραν εἶναι τὴν ποίησιν . . .
ἔτι δὲ ἐπεισοδίων πλήθη.   καὶ τὰ ἄλλ' ὡς ἕκαστα κοσμηθῆναι λέγεται . . .
Here and elsewhere, in quoting from the *Poetic*, I borrow Butcher's admirable translation.

[1] These narratives and conversations were naturally regarded as
interruptions in the main business, and this feeling is marked by the name
always given to the "acts" of a play, ἐπεισόδια (" episodia "), *i.e.* " interventions " or "interruptions".

made allusion: the action, instead of being reported, went on before the eyes of the audience. This change clearly at once begets the possibility of drama, however rudimentary. By retiring to the booth while the singers perform their lyric, he can change his mask and reappear as another person; by learning and discussing what has been said by his supposed predecessors, he can exhibit the play of emotion or the construction of a plan.

If this was done by Thespis, he was the founder of European drama. His *floruit* may be assigned to the year 535 B.C., the date of the first dramatic competition at Athens. But little is known of him. Aristotle in his *Poetic*[1] does not mention his name. Far later we have the remarks of Horace, " Diogenes Laertius,"[2] and Suidas. Horace tells[3] that Thespis discovered tragic poetry, and conveyed from place to place on waggons a company of players who sang and acted his pieces, their faces smeared with lees of wine: " Diogenes Laertius " says that Thespis " discovered one actor ". Suidas gives us the names of several plays, *Phorbas* or *The Trials* (ἆθλα) *of Pelias, The Priests, The Youths, Pentheus.* We possess four fragments alleged to belong to these, but they are spurious. Aristotle,[4] moreover, affirms that Tragedy was in the first place a matter of improvization. The conclusion seems to be that Thespis did not " write plays " in the modern sense of the phrase. He was much more like those Elizabethan dramatists who provided " the words " for their actors, and for whom printing and publication were only thought of if the play had achieved success upon the boards. He stood midway between Æschylus and the unknown actor-poets before Arion who improvized as they played.

The next name of importance is that of CHŒRILUS

---

[1] The text of the treatise is, however, incomplete. The author of the pseudo-Platonic *Minos* (321 A) speaks of the current belief that Thespis was the originator of tragedy.

[2] This is a mere name for a really anonymous collection of information on philosophical and other history.

[3] *Ars Poetica*, 275-7.

[4] *Poetic*, 1449*a*.

who competed in tragedy for the first time
the 64th Olympiad (524-1 B.C.) and continued
during the stage during forty years. He produced
written and sixty plays, and obtained the first prize
on times. Later generations regarded him as
th ally excellent in the satyric drama[1] invented by his
nger contemporary Pratinas. To him were attributed
e invention of masks, as a substitute for the wine-lees
of Thespis, and more majestic costume. We know by
name only one of his works, the *Alope*, which is concerned with the Attic hero Triptolemus. A fragment
or two reveal an unexpected preciosity of style; he
called stones and rivers "the bones and veins of the
earth".

PRATINAS of Phlius, in the north of the Peloponnese,
is said to have competed with Æschylus and Chœrilus
in the 70th Olympiad (500-497 B.C.). His great achievement, as we have said, was the invention of satyric
drama. Fifty plays are attributed to him, of which
thirty-two were satyric. Hardly any fragments of these
are extant, but we get some conception of the man from
a *hyporchema* in which he complains that music is en-
croaching upon poetry : " let the flute follow the dancing
revel of the song—it is but an attendant ". With boundless gusto and polysyllabic energy he consigns the flute
to flames and derision.

At length we reach a poet who seems to have been
really great, a dramatist whose works, even to a generation which knew and reverenced Æschylus, seemed
unworthy to be let die—PHRYNICHUS of Athens, son of
Polyphradmon, whose first victory occurred 512-509 B.C.
It is said that he was the first to bring female characters
upon the stage (always, however, played by men). The
following dramas are known by name : *Egyptians* ;
Alcestis ; *Antæus* or *The Libyans* ; *The Daughters of
Danaus* ; *The Capture of Miletus* ; *Phœnician Women
(Phœnissæ)* ; *The Women of Pleuron* ; *Tantalus* ;

---

[1] βασιλεὺς ἦν Χοίριλος ἐν σατύροις (Plotius, *De Metris*, p. 2633, quoted
by Haigh, *Tragic Drama*, p. 40).

Troilus. The *Egyptians* seems to have dealt with the same subject as the *Supplices* of Æschylus; so does the *Danaides;* these two dramas may have formed part of a trilogy. The *Alcestis* followed the same lines as the Euripidean play; it is probable, indeed, that the apparition of Death with a sword was borrowed by Euripides from Phrynichus. The *Antæus* related the wrestling-match between Heracles and his earth-born foe. The manner in which Aristophanes [1] refers to the play shows that the description of the wrestling-bout was still celebrated after the lapse of a century. The *Pleuroniæ* treated of Meleager and the fateful log which was preserved, and then burnt in anger, by his mother Althæa.

Two plays were specially important. The *Phœnissæ* (produced in 476), celebrated the victory of Salamis, had Themistocles himself for choregus, and won the prize; its popularity never waned throughout the fifth century. We are told that the prologue was spoken by an eunuch while he placed the cushions for the Persian counsellors; further—an important fact—that this person, at the beginning of the play, announced the defeat of Xerxes. The *Capture of Miletus*, less popular in later days—no fragments at all are to be found—created even more stir at the moment. Miletus had been captured by Darius in 494 B.C., Athens having failed to give effective support to the Ionian revolt. While the distress and shame excited by the fall of the proudest city in Asiatic Greece were still strong in Athenian minds, Phrynichus ventured to dramatize the disaster. Herodotus tells how " the theatre burst into tears; they fined him a thousand drachmæ for reminding them of their own misfortunes, and gave command that no man should ever use that play again ". [2]

---

[1] *Frogs*, 689 : εἴ τις ἥμαρτε σφαλείς τι Φρυνίχου παλαίσμασιν. The allusion in the first instance points undoubtedly to the famous *general* Phrynichus; but his political machinations are jokingly referred to as a "wrestling-bout" because of the celebrated description in his namesake the playwright.

[2] Herod. VI, 21.

Few lost works are so sorely to be regretted as those of Phrynichus. The collection of fragments merely hints at a genius who commanded the affection of an age which knew his great successors, a master whose dignity was not utterly overborne by Æschylus, and whose tenderness could still charm hearts which had thrilled to the agonies of Medea and the romance of Andromeda. The chief witness to his popularity is Aristophanes, who paints for us a delightful picture[1] of the old men in the dark before the dawn, trudging by lantern-light through the mud to the law-court, and humming as they go the "charming old-world honeyed ditties" from the *Phœnissæ*. In another play[2] the birds assert that it is from their song that "Phrynichus, like his own bee, took his feast, food of the gods, the fruit of song, and found unfailingly a song full sweet". One or two snatches survive from these lyrics, lines from the *Phœnissæ* in the "greater Asclepiad" metre which is the form of some of Sappho's loveliest work, and a verse[3] from the *Troilus* which Sophocles himself quoted: "the light of love on rosy cheeks is beaming".

It is clear that for most Athenians the spell of Phrynichus lay in his songs; succeeding poets he impressed almost equally as a playwright. It has already been mentioned that Euripides seems to have borrowed from the *Alcestis*. Æschylus, especially, was influenced by his style, and in the *Persæ* followed the older poet closely. Indeed the relation between the *Persæ* and the *Phœnissæ* is puzzling, but ancient authority did not hesitate to say that the later work was "modelled on" the earlier.[4] It is no question of a *réchauffé* to suit the

---

[1] *Wasps*, 220 (μέλη ἀρχαιομελισιδωνοφρυνιχήρατα).

[2] *Birds*, 748-51, reading ὥσπερ ἡ μέλιττα.

[3] λάμπει δ' ἐπὶ πορφυρέαις παρῇσι φῶς ἔρωτος. Notice the exquisite alliteration. Sophocles no doubt had this line in mind when he wrote *Antigone* 782.

[4] The writer of the Argument to the *Persæ* says : Γλαῦκος ἐν τοῖς περὶ Αἰσχύλου μύθων ἐκ τῶν Φοινίσσων Φρυνίχου φησὶ τοὺς Πέρσας παραπεποιῆσθαι. The late Dr. Verrall (*The Bacchantes of Euripides and Other Essays*, pp. 283-308) believed that not only is the *Persæ* modelled on the *Phœnissæ* but Æschylus incorporated a large portion of Phrynichus' play with little change (*Persæ* vv. 480-514 especially).

taste of a later age, like the revisions of Shakespeare by Davenant and Cibber, for the two tragedies are separated at the utmost by only seven years ; rather we appear to have a problem like the connexion between *Macbeth* and Middleton's *Witch*. Perhaps the soundest opinion is that the younger playwright wished to demonstrate his own method of writing and his theory of dramatic composition in the most striking way possible—by choosing a famous drama of the more rudimentary type and rewriting it as it ought to be written. Two features in the *Phœnissæ* seem to lend support to this view. Firstly, the prologue was delivered by a slave who was preparing the seats of the Persian counsellors. The *Persæ* expunges the man and his speech, presenting us at once with the elders in deliberation. Nothing is more characteristic of the architectonic power in literature than the instinct to sweep away everything but the minimum of mere machinery ; at the first instant we are in the midst of the plot. Secondly, the prologue at once announced the disaster. Nothing was left but the amplification of sorrow, a quasi-operatic presentation by the Phœnician women who formed the chorus. Here again the *Persæ* provides a most instructive contrast.

From the fragments, from ancient testimony, and from the recasting of the *Phœnissæ* which appeared instinctive or necessary to Æschylus, we gain some clear conception of Phrynichus. A lyrist of sweetness and pellucid dignity, he has been compared[1] to his contemporary Simonides ; the graceful phrases in which Aristophanes declared that Phrynichus drew his inspiration from the birds recall to us the " native wood-notes wild " of Shakespeare's earlier achievement. As a playwright in the strict sense he is, for us, the first effective master, but still swayed by the age of pure lyrists which was just reaching its culmination and its close in Pindar—so greatly swayed

[1] By M. Croiset, *Hist. de la Litt. grecque*, III, p. 49.

that the "episodes" were still little more than interruptions of lyrics which gave but a static expression
to feeling.

ÆSCHYLUS, the son of Euphorion, was born at
Eleusis in 525 B.C. At the age of twenty-five he
began to exhibit plays, but did not win the prize until
the year 485. The Persian invasions swept down upon
Athens when Æschylus had come to the maturity of
his powers. He served as a hoplite at Marathon[1] and
his brother Cynegirus distinguished himself even on
that day of heroes by his desperate courage in attempting
to thwart the flight of the invaders. That the poet was
present at Salamis also may be regarded as certain
from the celebrated description in the *Persæ*. He
twice visited Sicily. On the first occasion, soon after
470 B.C., he accepted the invitation of Hiero, King
of Syracuse, and composed *The Women of Etna* to
celebrate the city which Hiero was founding on the
slope of that mountain. Various stories to explain
his retirement from Athens were circulated in antiquity.
Some relate that he was unnerved by a collapse of the
wooden benches during a performance of one of his
plays. Others said that he was defeated by Simonides
in a competition : the task was to write an epitaph on
those who fell at Marathon. According to others he
was chagrined by a dramatic defeat which he sustained
at the hands of the youthful Sophocles in 468. A
fourth story declared that he was accused of divulging
the Eleusinian Mysteries in one of his plays, and was
in danger of his life until he proved that he had himself
never been initiated. These stories are hard to accept.
Possibly he wrote something which offended against

---

[1] This is asserted by his epitaph :—

> Αἴσχυλον Εὐφορίωνος Ἀθηναῖον τόδε κεύθει
> μνῆμα καταφθίμενον πυροφόροιο Γέλας,
> ἀλκὴν δ᾽ εὐδόκιμον Μαραθώνιον ἄλσος ἂν εἴποι
> καὶ βαθυχαιτήεις Μῆδος ἐπιστάμενος.

These verses are said to come from the pen of Æschylus himself. For
once such tradition appears to be true. No forger would have had the
audacity to omit all reference to the plays.

Eleusinian rule, and was condemned to banishment or possibly to death, which (as often occurred) he was allowed to escape by voluntary exile. We cannot suppose that he pleaded ignorance [1] seriously; a man of his genuinely devout temperament, and a native of Eleusis, must assuredly have been initiated. A second visit to Sicily was taken after he had again won the prize with the *Oresteia*. He never returned. Story tells how he was sitting on the hillside near the city of Gela when an eagle, flying with a tortoise in its claws in quest of a stone whereon to crush it, dropped its prey upon the bald head of the poet and killed him. He left two sons, Euphorion and Bion, who also pursued the tragic art—a tradition which persisted in the family for generations.

Æschylus is too great a dramatist to receive detailed treatment in the course of a general discussion; a separate chapter must be allotted to this. At present we shall consider only his position in the history of tragedy.

The great technical change introduced by Æschylus was that he "first introduced a second actor; he diminished the importance of the chorus, and assigned the leading part to the dialogue".[2] The two last statements are corollaries of the first, which describe a deeply important advance. It has been said above that the drama was founded by the man who "invented one actor"; at the same time it is easy to realize how primitive such drama must have been. The addition of another actor did not double the resources of tragedy, rather it increased them fifty-fold. To bring two opposed or sympathetic characters face to face, to exhibit the clash of principles by means of the clash of personalities, this is a step forward into a new world, a change so great that to call Æschylus the very inventor of tragedy is

---

[1] This, however, is certainly stated by Aristotle (*Nic. Ethics*, 1111*a*). On the other hand, Æschylus says in the *Frogs* (886) : Δήμητερ, ἡ θρέψασα τὴν ἐμὴν φρένα, εἰναί με τῶν σῶν ἄξιον μυστηρίων.

[2] Aristotle, *Poetic*, 1449*a*.

not unreasonable.   This meagre equipment of two actors
was found sufficient by two of the fifth-century masters
for work[1] of the highest value.   The further remark of
Aristotle that Æschylus "diminished the importance
of the chorus" follows naturally from the vast increase in
the importance of the "episodes".

Revolutionary as Æschylus was, he did not attain
at a bound to a characteristic dramatic form of his own
and then advance no farther.   In his earliest extant
play, the *Supplices*, the alterations mentioned above are
certainly in operation, but their use is tentative.   The
chorus is no doubt less dominant than it had been, but
it is the most important feature, even to a modern reader.
To an ancient spectator it must have appeared of even
greater moment.   The number of singers was still fifty,
and the lyrics, accompanied by music and the dance of
this great company, occupy more than half of our present
text.   We have left Phrynichus behind, but he is not out
of sight.

It is necessary at this point to give some account
of the life of SOPHOCLES and his position in dramatic
history, though a detailed discussion of his extant
work must be reserved for a separate chapter.   He
was born about 496 B.C., the son of a well-to-do citizen
named Sophillus, and received, in addition to the usual
education, more advanced training in music from the
celebrated Lampros.   The youth's physical beauty was
remarkable, and at the age of sixteen he was chosen
to lead the choir of boys who performed the pæan
celebrating the victory of Salamis.   Nothing more is
known of his life till the year 468, when he produced
his first tragedy.   One of his fellow-competitors was
Æschylus, and we are told[2] that feeling ran so high
that the Archon, instead of choosing the judges by

---

[1] The following plays were performed with two actors only: of
Æschylus, *Supplices, Prometheus, Persæ, Seven against Thebes;* of
Euripides, *Medea,* and perhaps *Alcestis.*

[2] By Plutarch, *Life of Cimon,* VIII.   Haigh (*The Tragic Drama of the
Greeks,* p. 128[2]) gives good reasons for rejecting the story.

lot as usual, entrusted the decision to the board of generals; they awarded the victory to the youthful Sophocles. For sixty years he produced a steady stream of dramatic work with continuous success. He at first performed in his own plays—his skill in the *Nausicaa* gained great applause—but was compelled to give this up owing to the failure of his voice. The number of his plays was well over a hundred, performed in groups of four, and he won eighteen victories at the City Dionysia; even when he failed of the first prize, he was never lower than the second place.[1] His genius seems even to have increased with advancing age; he was about ninety when he wrote the *Œdipus Coloneus*. Sophocles took a satisfactory if not prominent part in public life,[2] being twice elected general, once with Pericles and later with Nicias. He served also as Hellenotamias—a member, that is, of the Treasury Board which administered the funds of the Delian Confederacy. It is an interesting comment on the early part of the *Œdipus Coloneus* that the poet acted as priest of two heroes, Asclepius and Alcon. He had several sons, the most celebrated of whom was Iophon, himself a tragedian of repute. A famous story relates that Iophon, being jealous of his illegitimate brother, brought a suit to prove his father's insanity, with the intent to become administrator of his estate. The aged poet's defence consisted in a recitation of the *Œdipus Coloneus* which he had just completed, and the jury most naturally dismissed Iophon's petition. He died late in 406 B.C., fully ninety years old, a few months later than Euripides, and not long before the disaster of Ægospotami. The Athenian people mourned him as a hero under the name of Dexion, "The Entertainer," or "Host," and brought yearly sacrifice to his shrine.

The personality of Sophocles stands out more

---

[1] One of these occasions was that on which he presented the *Œdipus Tyrannus*.

[2] A fragment of Ion's Ἐπιδημίαι remarks : τὰ μέντοι πολιτικὰ οὔτε σοφὸς οὔτε ῥεκτήριος ἦν, ἀλλ᾽ ὡς ἄν τις εἰς τῶν χρηστῶν Ἀθηναίων.

definitely before the modern eye than that of perhaps any other fifth-century Greek. His social talent made him a noted figure whose good sayings were repeated, and of whom the gossips as well as the critics loved to circulate illustrative stories. He seemed the embodiment of all that man can ask. Genius, good health, industry, long life, personal beauty, affluence, popularity, and the sense of power—all were his, and enjoyed in that very epoch which, beyond all others, seems to have combined stimulus with satisfaction. Salamis was fought and won just as he had left childhood behind. His adolescence and maturity coincided with the rise and establishment of the Athenian Empire; he listened to Pericles, saw the Parthenon and Propylæa rise upon the Acropolis, associated with Æschylus, Euripides, Aristophanes, and Thucydides, watched the work of Phidias and Polygnotus grow to life under their fingers. Though he carried into the years of Nestor the genius of Shakespeare, he was yet so blessed that he died before the fall of Athens. Phrynichus, the comic poet, wrote : " Blessed was Sophocles, who passed so many years before his death, a happy man and brilliant, who wrote many beautiful tragedies and made a fair end of a life which knew no misfortune ".[1] Sophocles' own words [2] come as a significant comment :—

> μὴ φῦναι τὸν ἅπαντα νικᾷ λόγον.
> τὸ δ᾽, ἐπεὶ φανῇ,
> βῆναι κεῖθεν ὅθενπερ ἥκει,
> πολὺ δεύτερον ὡς τάχιστα.

" Best of all fates—when a man weighs everything—is not to be born, and second-best beyond doubt is, once born, to depart with all speed to that place whence we came."

Of his social charm there are many evidences. He gathered round him a kind of literary club or *salon*.

---

[1] Aristophanes, too, in the *Frogs* (v. 82), bears witness to his charm : ὁ δ᾽ εὔκολος μὲν ἐνθάδ᾽, εὔκολος δ᾽ ἐκεῖ· " Sophocles, on the other hand, is gentle here (*i.e.* in Hades) as he was in life."

[2] *Œd. Col.* 1225-8.

Some hint of the talk in this circle may be gathered from the fragment of Ion's *Memoirs* which tells how when the poet came to Chios he engaged in critical battle with the local schoolmaster concerning poetical adjectives, and quoted with approbation Phrynichus' line λάμπει δ' ἐπὶ πορφυρέαις παρῇσι φῶς ἔρωτος. He was a friend of Herodotus, from whom he quotes more than once, and to whom he addressed certain elegiac verses. With regard to his own art, we possess two remarks of deep interest. The first is reported by Aristotle : [1] " I depict men as they ought to be, Euripides depicts them as they are ". It is excellent Attic for "he is a realist, I am an idealist ". Nevertheless, he esteemed his rival ; when he led forth his chorus for the first time after the news of Euripides' death in Macedonia had reached Athens, he and his singers wore the dress of mourning. The second remark is a brief account [2] of his own development : " My dramatic wild oats were imitation of Æschylus' pomp ; then I evolved my own harsh mannerism ; finally I embraced that style which is best, as most adapted to the portrayal of human nature ". All that we now possess would seem to belong to his third period, though certain characteristics of the *Antigone* may put us in mind of the second.[3]

Apart altogether from his glorious achievement in actual composition, Sophocles is highly important as an innovator in technique. The changes which he introduced are : (i) the number of actors was raised from two to three ; [4] (ii) scene-painting was invented [4] ; (iii) the plays of a tetralogy were, sometimes at any rate, no longer part of a great whole, but quite distinct in subject ; [5] (iv) it is said [6] that he raised the number of the

---

[1] *Poetic*, 1460b : Σοφοκλῆς ἔφη αὐτὸς μὲν οἵους δεῖ ποιεῖν, Εὐριπίδην δὲ οἷοι εἰσίν.

[2] Plutarch, *De Profectu in Virtute*, 79 B : ὁ Σοφοκλῆς ἔλεγε, τὸν Αἰσχύλου διαπεπαιχὼς ὄγκον, εἶτα τὸ πικρὸν καὶ κατάτεχνον τῆς αὑτοῦ κατασκευῆς, τρίτον ἤδη τὸ τῆς λέξεως μεταβάλλειν εἶδος ὅπερ ἐστὶν ἠθικώτατον καὶ βέλτιστον.

[3] See Haigh, *Tragic Drama*, p. 162. [4] Aristotle, *Poetic*, 1449a.

[5] Suidas (*s.v.* Σοφοκλῆς) : καὶ αὐτὸς ἦρξε τοῦ δρᾶμα πρὸς δρᾶμα ἀγωνίζεσθαι, ἀλλὰ μὴ τετραλογίαν.

[6] In the Anonymous *Life*.

chorus from twelve to fifteen, was the first tragedian to use Phrygian music and to give his actors the bent staff and white shoe which they sometimes used.

The points named under (iv) are of small importance save the change in the number of *choreutæ*, but that is a detail which can scarcely be accepted. Æschylus during part of his career employed fifty *choreutæ*, and it is extremely improbable that the number sank as low as twelve, only to rise slightly again at once. The invention of scene-painting is clearly momentous; it became easy to fix the action at any spot desired, and a change of scene also became possible. Æschylus, of course, in his later years made use of this development. The other two points are vital.

Though the stage gained immensely by the introduction of a third actor, little perhaps need be said on the point. An examination of the early Æschylean plays, and even of the *Choephoræ* or *Agamemnon*, side by side with the *Philoctetes* or *Œdipus Coloneus*, will make the facts abundantly clear. In the crisis of *Œdipus Tyrannus* (for example) the presence of Jocasta,[1] while her husband hears the tidings brought by the Corinthian, does not merely add to the poignancy of the scene; it may almost be said to create it.

The last change, that of breaking up the tetralogy into four disconnected tragedies, is equally fundamental. The older poet was a man of simple ideas and gigantic grasp. His conceptions demanded the vast scope of a trilogy, and perhaps the most astonishing feature of his work is the fact that, while each drama is a splendid and self-intelligible whole, it gains its full import only from the significance of the complete organism. Sophocles realized that he possessed a narrower, if more subtle, genius, and moulded his technique to suit his powers. Each of his works, however spacious and statuesque it may seem beside *Macbeth*, *Lear*, or even *Hippolytus*,

---

[1] See Haigh, *Attic Tragedy*, pp. 139 *sq.*, where this excellent point is made.

shows, as compared with Æschylus, a closeness of texture in characterization and a delicate stippling of language, which mark nothing less than a revolution.

Tradition tells that EURIPIDES was born at Salamis on the very day of the great victory (480 B.C.); the Parian marble puts the date five years earlier. He was thus a dozen or more years younger than Sophocles. His father's name was Mnesarchus; his mother Clito is ridiculed by Aristophanes as a petty green-grocer, but all other evidence suggests that they were well-to-do; Euripides was able to devote himself to drama, from which little financial reward could be expected, and to collect a library—a remarkable possession for those days. He lived almost entirely for his art, though he must, like other citizens, have seen military service. His public activities seem to have included nothing more extraordinary than a single "embassy" to Syracuse. Unlike Sophocles, he cared little for society save that of a few intimates, and wrote much in a cave on Salamis which he had fitted up as a study. The great philosopher Anaxagoras was his friend and teacher; several passages[1] in the extant plays point plainly to his influence. It was in Euripides' house that Protagoras read for the first time his treatise on the gods which brought about the sophist's expulsion from Athens. Socrates himself is traditionally regarded as the poet's friend. Aulus Gellius[2] says that he began to write tragedy at the age of eighteen; but it was not till 455 B.C. (when he was perhaps thirty) that he "obtained a chorus"—that is, had his work accepted for performance. One of these pieces was the *Peliades;* he obtained only the third place. By the end of his life he had written nearly a hundred dramas, including satyric works, but obtained the first prize only four times: his fifth victory was won by the tetralogy which included the *Bacchæ,* performed after his death. His influence

---

[1] The most celebrated is the description of the sun as a "clod" (*Orestes*, 983). *Alcestis*, 904 *sqq.*, may very possibly refer to the death of Anaxagoras' son.

[2] XV, 20.

was far out of proportion to these scanty rewards.[1] On any given occasion he might be defeated by some talented mediocrity who hit the taste of the moment. When he offered the *Medea* itself he was overcome, not only by Sophocles, but by Euphorion ; yet his vast powers were recognized by all Athens. Euripides was married— twice it is said—and had three sons. Late in his life he accepted an invitation from Archelaus, King of Macedonia ; after living there a short time in high favour and writing his latest plays, he died in 406 B.C. He was buried in Macedonia and a cenotaph was erected to his memory in Attica.

Further light both on the career and works of Euripides has recently been provided by an interesting discovery. In 1912 Dr. Arthur S. Hunt published[2] extensive fragments of a life of the poet by Satyrus, from portions of a papyrus-roll found at Oxyrhynchus in Egypt by Dr. Grenfell and Dr. Hunt. Satyrus lived in the third century before Christ : our MS. itself is dated by its discoverers "from the middle or latter part of the second century" after Christ. The most striking points are (i) Satyrus quotes the fragment of the *Pirithous* dealt with below,[3] attributing it, as was often done, to Euripides, and saying that the poet "has accurately embraced the whole cosmogony of Anaxagoras in three periods" ;[4] (ii) there are new fragments, on the vain pursuit of wealth ; (iii) the poet was prosecuted for impiety by the statesman Cleon ; (iv) we read that Euripides wrote the proem for the *Persæ* composed by his friend the musician Timotheus ; (v) Satyrus, in discussing *peripeteia*, mentions "ravishings, supposititious infants, and recognitions by means of rings and necklaces—for these, as you know, are the back-

---

[1] A passage in his *Life* suggests that he was indifferent to the strictly "theatrical" side of his profession : οὐδεμίαν φιλοτιμίαν περὶ τὰ θέατρα ποιούμενος · διὸ τοσοῦτον αὐτὸν ἔβλαπτε τοῦτο ὅσον ὠφέλει τὸν Σοφοκλέα.

[2] *Oxyrhynchus Papyri*, Vol. IX, pp. 124-82.

[3] Pp. 29 *sq*.

[4] ἀκριβῶς ὅλως περιείληφεν τὸν Ἀναξαγόρειον διάκοσμον ἐν τρισὶν περιόδοις.

bone of the New Comedy, and were perfected by Euripides".

A discussion of Euripides' surviving work will be found in a separate chapter. Our business here is to indicate his position in the development of technique. Though he is for ever handling his material and the resources of the stage in an original and experimental manner, the definite changes which he introduced are few. That many of his dramas are not tragedies at all but tragicomedies, is a development of the first importance. Another fact of this kind is his musical innovations. The lyrics of his plays tend to become less important as literature and to subserve the music, in which he introduced fashions not employed before, such as the "mixed Lydian"; it is impossible to criticize some of his later odes without knowledge, which we do not possess, of the music which he composed for them and the manner in which he caused them to be rendered. Hence the loose syntax, the polysyllabic vagueness of expression, and the repeated words—features which irritated Aristophanes and many later students.

Another novelty is his use of the prologue. Since this is properly nothing but "that part of the play which precedes the first song of the whole chorus," [1] prologues are of course found in Æschylus and Sophocles. The peculiarity of the Euripidean prologue is that it tends to be non-dramatic, a narrative enabling the spectator to understand at what point in a legend the action is to begin. It is from Euripides' use of the prologue that the modern meaning of the word is derived.

Aristophanes in his *Frogs* makes a famous attack upon most [2] sides of Euripides' art as contrasted with that of Æschylus. But it is often forgotten that, damned utterly as the younger tragedian is, Æschylus by no means

---

[1] Aristotle, *Poetic*, 1452*b*.
[2] Not all. The elegance of his iambic style excited Aristophanes' admiration : indeed he confessed to imitating it, and the great Cratinus invented a significant compound verb εὐριπιδαριστοφανίζειν. See Meineke, *Frag. Comicorum Graecorum*, II, 1142.

escapes criticism. Many of the censures put into Euripides' mouth are just and important; it seems likely that Aristophanes is practically quoting his victim's conversation; the remark [1] about Æschylus that "he was obscure in his prologues," is no mere rubbish attributed to a dullard. That Euripides did criticize his elder is a fact. The *Supplices* [2] contains a severe remark on the catalogue of chieftains in the *Septem;* the elaborate sarcasm directed in the *Electra* [3] against the Recognition-scene of the *Choephorœ* is even more startling. Besides this, Aristophanes seems to quote remarks of Euripides on himself and his work: "When I first took over the art from you, I found it swollen with braggadocio and tiresome words; so the first thing I did was to train down its fat and reduce its weight". [4] His comment on dialogue is no less pertinent: "With you Niobe and Achilles never said a word, but I left no personage idle; women, slaves, and hags all spoke". [5] Finally, there is the perfect description of his own realism [6]: οἰκεῖα πράγματ' εἰσάγων, οἷς χρώμεθ', οἷς σύνεσμεν, "I introduced life as we live it, the things of our everyday experience". Such sentences as these reflect unmistakably the conversation of a playwright who was jealous for the dignity and the progress of his art.

Though during his own time Euripides was hardly equal in repute to his two companions, scarcely had his Macedonian grave closed over him than his popularity began to overshadow theirs. Æschylus became a dim antique giant; Sophocles, though always admired, was too definitely Attic and Periclean to retain all his prestige in the Hellenistic world. It was the more cosmopolitan poet who won posthumous applause from one end of the civilized earth to the other. From 400 B.C. to the downfall of the ancient world he was

---

[1] *Frogs*, v. 1122: ἀσαφὴς γὰρ ἦν ἐν τῇ φράσει τῶν πραγμάτων.

[2] vv. 846-54.　　　　　　　　[3] vv. 518-44.

[4] *Frogs*, 939 *sqq.*　　　　　[5] *Ibid.* 948 *sqq.*

[6] *Ibid.* 959 : σύνεσμεν may recall Grant Allen's famous sentence about taking Hedda Gabler down to dinner.

unquestionably better known and admired than any other dramatist. This is shown by the much larger collection of his work which has survived, by the imitation of later playwrights, and by innumerable passages of citation, praise, and comment in writers of every kind.) He shared with Homer, Vergil, and Horace the equivocal distinction of becoming a school-book even in ancient times. Nine of our nineteen plays were selected for this purpose : *Alcestis, Andromache, Hecuba, Hippolytus, Medea, Orestes, Phœnissæ, Rhesus,* and *Troades.* It is not easy to see what principle of selection prompted the educationists of the day : *Andromache* and *Hippolytus* do not strike a modern reader as specially " suitable ". Owing to their use in schools they were annotated ; these *scholia* are still extant and are often of great value. In the Byzantine age the number was reduced to three : *Hecuba, Orestes, Phœnissæ.*

Among the numerous lesser tragedians of the fifth century five hold a distinguished place : Neophron of Sicyon, Aristarchus of Tegea, Ion of Chios, Achæus of Eretria, Agathon of Athens.

NEOPHRON is an enigmatic figure. It would seem that he was an important forerunner of Euripides. Not only do we learn that he wrote one hundred and twenty tragedies and that he was the first to bring upon the stage "pædagogi" and the examination of slaves under torture ; it is said also that his *Medea* was the original of Euripides' tragedy so-named.[1] " Pædagogi " or elderly male attendants of children are familiar in Euripides, and the "questioning" of slaves is shown (though not to the audience) in the *Ion.*[2] As for the third point, we have three fragments which clearly recall the extant play—a few lines in which Ægeus requests

---

[1] Of these three points the first two come from Suidas (under the article Νεόφρων), the third from the argument to the extant *Medea* : τὸ δρᾶμα δοκεῖ ὑποβαλέσθαι τὰ Νεόφρονος διασκευάσας, ὡς Δικαίαρχός τε περὶ τοῦ Ἑλλάδος βίου καὶ Ἀριστοτέλης ἐν ὑπομνήμασι.

[2] γν, 1211-6,

Medea to explain the oracle, a few more in which she tells Jason how he shall die, and the celebrated passage which reads like a shorter version of her great soliloquy when deciding to slay her children. There is the same anguish, the same vacillation, the same address to her "passion" (θυμός). Such a writer is plainly epoch-making: he adds a new feature to tragedy in the life-time of Sophocles. The realism of everyday life and the pangs of conscience battling with temptation—these we are wont to call Euripidean. But some have denied the very existence of Neophron as a dramatist: the fragments are fourth-century forgeries, or Euripides brought out a first edition[1] of his play under Neophron's name. Against these views is the great authority of Aristotle,[2] who, however, may have been deceived by the name "Neophron" in official records. An argument natural to modern students, that a poet of Euripides' calibre would not have borrowed and worked up another's play, is of doubtful strength. Æschylus, as we have seen, probably acted so towards Phrynichus. The best view is probably that of antiquity. We may note that Sicyon is close to Corinth, and that a legend domestic to the latter city might naturally find its first treatment in a playwright of Sicyon.

ARISTARCHUS of Tegea, whose *début* is to be dated about 453 B.C., is said by Suidas to have lived for over a hundred years, to have written seventy tragedies, two of which won the first prize, and one of which was called *Asclepius* (a thank-offering for the poet's recovery from an illness), and to have "initiated the present length of plays".[3] This latter point sounds important, but it is difficult to understand precisely what Suidas means. For though the average Sophoclean or Euripidean tragedy is longer than the Æschylean,

---

[1] There is good reason to suppose that what we possess is a second version. The scholiast on Aristophanes mentions passages as parodies of lines in the *Medea* which we no longer read there.

[2] In his ὑπομνήματα, quoted by the Argument to the *Medea*.

[3] πρῶτος εἰς τὸ νῦν μῆκος τὰ δράματα κατέστησεν,

Aristarchus began work later than Sophocles and no earlier than Euripides. It has been thought that Suidas refers to the length of dramas in post-Euripidean times, but of these we have perhaps no examples.[1] Aristarchus' reputation was slight but enduring. Ennius two and a half centuries later translated his *Achilles* into Latin ; the same work is quoted in the prologue of Plautus' *Pœnulus*. A phrase[2] from another play became proverbial.

A more distinguished but probably less important writer was ION of Chios, son of Orthomenes, who lived between 484 and 421 B.C. A highly accomplished man of ample means, he travelled rather widely. In Athens he must have spent considerable time, for he was intimate with Cimon and his circle, and produced plays the number of which is by one authority put at forty. Besides tragedy and satyric drama, he wrote comedies, dithyrambs, hymns, pæans, elegies, epigrams, and scolia. He was, moreover, distinguished in prose writing : we hear of a book on the *Founding of Chios*, of a philosophic work, and of certain memoirs.[3] This latter work must be a real loss to us, if we may judge from its fragments. In the fifth century B.C. no one but a facile Ionian would have thought it worth while to record mere gossip even about the great ; for us there is great charm in an anecdote like that of the literary discussion between Sophocles and the schoolmaster, or the exclamation of Æschylus at the Isthmian Games.[4] Ion would seem to have been less a great

---

[1] Unless we except the *Rhesus* (996 lines).

[2] The original form of it seems to have been :—

ὥστ᾽ οὐχ ὑπάρχων ἀλλὰ τιμωρούμενος
ἀγωνιοῦμαι.

[3] The name is not certain. The book is variously called ὑπομνήματα ("notes"), ἐπιδημίαι ("visits"), and συνεκδημητικός. The first is not a "name"—it merely describes the book. The second was explained by Bentley to mean "accounts of the visits to our island of Chios by distinguished strangers". The third could mean something like "traveller's companion".

[4] Plutarch (*De Profectu in Virtute*, 79 E), no doubt quoting from Ion, tells us that at a critical moment in a boxing match Æschylus nudged Ion

poet than a delightful *belletrist;* the quality is well shown in his remark [1] that life, like a tragic tetralogy, should have a satyric element. One year he obtained a sensational success by winning the first prize both for tragedy and for a dithyramb ; to commemorate this he presented to each Athenian citizen a cask of Chian wine. He died before 421, the date of Aristophanes' *Peace*,[2] wherein he is spoken of as transformed into a star, in allusion to a charming lyric passage of his :—

> ἀῷον ἀεροφοίταν
> ἀστέρα μείναμεν ἀελίου λευκοπτέρυγα πρόδρομον.

"We awaited the star that wanders through the dawn-lit sky, pale-winged courier of the sun."

His tragedies,[3] though they do not appear to have had much effect on the progress of technique or on public opinion, were popular. Aristophanes, for instance, nearly twenty years after his death, quotes a phrase from his *Sentinels* [4] as proverbial, and centuries later the author of the treatise *On the Sublime* [5] wrote his celebrated verdict : "In lyric poetry would you prefer to be Bacchylides rather than Pindar ? And in tragedy to be Ion of Chios rather than—Sophocles ? It is true that Bacchylides and Ion are faultless and entirely elegant writers of the polished school, while Pindar and Sophocles, although at times they burn everything before them as it were in their swift career, are often extinguished unaccountably and fail most lamentably. But would anyone in his senses regard all the compositions of Ion put together as an equivalent for the single play of the Œdipus?"

and said : "You see what a difference training makes ? The man who has received the blow is silent, while the spectators cry aloud."

[1] Plutarch, *Pericles*, Chap. V.

[2] v. 835. To the scholium on this line we owe much of our information about Ion.

[3] One of them bears the curious title "Great Play" (μέγα δρᾶμα), but nothing is known of it.

[4] *Frogs*, 1425.

[5] XXXIII, 5 (Prof. Rhys Roberts' translation).

ACHÆUS of Eretria was born in 484 B.C., and exhibited his first play at Athens in 447. He won only one first prize though we hear that he composed over forty plays, nearly half of which are known by name. That he was second only to Æschylus in satyric drama was the opinion held by that delightful philosopher Menedemus [1] the minor Socratic, the seat of whose school was Eretria itself, Achæus' birthplace.

It has been suggested that the apparent disproportion of satyric plays written by Achæus is to be accounted for by his having written them for other poets.[2] He is once copied by Euripides and parodied twice by Aristophanes.[3] Athenæus makes an interesting comment on his style: "Achæus of Eretria, though an elegant poet in the structure of his plots, occasionally blackens his phrasing and produces many cryptic expressions".[4] The instance which he gives is significant :—

> λιθάργυρος δ'
> ὅλπη παρηωρεῖτο χρίσματος πλέα
> τὸν Σπαρτιάτην γραπτὸν ἐν διπλῷ ξύλῳ
> κύρβιν,

" the cruse of alloyed silver, filled with ointment, swung beside the Spartan tablet, double wood inscribed ". That is, " he carried an oil-flask and a Spartan general's bâton ". Aiming at dignified originality of diction Achæus has merely fallen into queerness. On the other side, when he seeks vigorous realism he becomes quaintly prosaic. In the *Philoctetes*, for instance, Agamemnon utters the war-cry ἐλελελεῦ in the middle of an iambic line.

A far more noteworthy dramatist was AGATHON the Athenian, who seems to have impressed his contemporaries, and even the exacting Aristotle, as coming next in merit to the three masters. Born about 446 B.C., he

[1] Diog. Laert. II, 133.
[2] Croiset III, p. 400 (n.), thus explains the strange words of Suidas, ἐπεδείκνυτο δὲ κοινῇ σὺν καὶ Εὐριπίδη.
[3] Haigh, *Tragic Drama of the Greeks*, p. 409.
[4] Ath. X, 451 C,

won his first victory in 416 and retired to the Court of the Macedonian prince Archelaus some time before the death of Euripides (406). From contemporary evidence we gather that he was popular as a writer and as a social figure, handsome, and given to voluptuous living.

Three striking innovations are credited to him :—

(i) He produced at least one play of which both the plot and the characters were invented by himself.[1] The name of this "attractive" drama is uncertain : it may have been *The Flower* (*Anthos*) or *Antheus*. Agathon, here as elsewhere, shows himself a follower of Euripides. The master had employed recognized myths as a framework for a thoroughly "modern" treatment of ordinary human interests ; his disciple finally throws aside the convention of antiquity.

(ii) Another post-Euripidean feature is the use of musical interludes. Aristotle tells us: "As for the later poets, their choral songs pertain as little to the subject of the piece as to that of any other tragedy. They are therefore sung as mere interludes—a practice first begun by Agathon."[2] Our poet then is once more found completing a process which his friend had carried far. Sophocles had diminished the length and dramatic importance of the lyrics, but with him they were still entirely relevant. Euripides shows a strong tendency to write his odes as separable songs, but complete irrelevance is hardly found. Plays such as Agathon's could obviously be performed, if necessary, without the trouble and expense of a chorus, which in process of time altogether disappeared. His interludes served, it seems, more as divisions between "acts" than as an integral part of the play. In this connexion should be mentioned his innovation in the accompaniment—the use of "chromatic" or coloured style.[3] His florid music is laughed at by Aristophanes as "ants' bye-paths".[4]

---

[1] Aristotle, *Poetic*, 1451*b*.
[2] *Ibid.* 1456*a* (Butcher's translation).
[3] Plutarch, *Symposiaca*, 645 E.   [4] *Thesm.* 100 ; μύρμηκος ἀτραποὺς.

(iii) Occasionally he took a great extent of legend as the topic of a single drama, and it seems likely [1] that he composed a *Fall of Troy*, taking the whole epic subject instead of an episode. Agathon is trying yet another experiment—it was necessary for a writer of his powers to vary in some way from Euripides, but this attempt was unsatisfactory. [2]

In the *Thesmophoriazusæ* Aristophanes pays Agathon the honour of elaborate parody. Euripides comes to beg his friend to plead for him before an assembly of Athenian women, and the scene in which Agathon amid much pomp explains the principles of his art, contains definite and valuable criticism under the usual guise of burlesque; that Aristophanes valued him is shown by the affectionate pun on his name which he introduces into the *Frogs* (v. 84):—

ἀγαθὸς ποιητὴς καὶ ποθεινὸς τοῖς φίλοις,

"a good poet, sorely missed by his friends". Plato lays the scene of his *Symposium* in the house of Agathon, who is celebrating his first tragic victory; the poet is depicted as a charming host, and, when the conversation turns to a series of panegyrics upon the god of Love, offers a contribution to which we shall return.

From these sources we learn as usual little about the poet's dramatic skill, much as to his literary style. But under the first head falls a vital remark of Aristotle: "in his reversals of the action (*i.e.* the *peripeteia*), however, he shows a marvellous skill in the effort to hit the popular taste—to produce a tragic effect that satisfies the moral sense. This effect is produced when the clever rogue, like Sisyphus, is outwitted, or the brave villain defeated. Such an event is, moreover, probable in Agathon's sense of the word: 'it is probable,' he says, 'that many things should happen contrary to probability'." [3] Agathon belongs to the class of playwrights who win popularity by bringing down to the customary theatrical level the methods and ideas of a genius who is

---

[1] Aristotle, *Poetic*, 1456a.   [2] *Ibid*.   [3] *Ibid*.

himself too undiluted and strange for his contemporaries.
Agathon's relation to Euripides resembles that of (let us
say) Mr. St. John Hankin, in his later work, to Ibsen.
Of his literary style much the same may be said.   He
loves to moralize on chance and probability and the
queer twists of human nature, with Euripides' knack of
neatness but without his insight.   Such things as

$$\mu\acute{o}\nu o\upsilon\ \gamma\grave{a}\rho\ a\mathring{v}\tauo\mathring{v}\ \kappa a\grave{\iota}\ \theta\epsilon\grave{o}\varsigma\ \sigma\tau\epsilon\rho\acute{\iota}\sigma\kappa\epsilon\tau a\iota,$$
$$\mathring{a}\gamma\acute{\epsilon}\nu\eta\tau a\ \pi o\iota\epsilon\hat{\iota}\nu\ \mathring{a}\sigma\sigma'\ \mathring{a}\nu\ \mathring{\eta}\ \pi\epsilon\pi\rho a\gamma\mu\acute{\epsilon}\nu a$$

"this alone is beyond the power even of God, to make
undone that which has been done," and even the celebrated τέχνη τύχην ἔστερξε καὶ τύχη τέχνην, "skill loves
luck, and luck skill," give the measure of his power over
epigram.   His easy way of expressing simple ideas with
admirable neatness may remind us of a much greater
dramatist—Terence, or, in later times, of Marivaux.[1]

Plato tells us that he was a pupil both of Prodicus[2]
and of Gorgias,[3] the renowned sophists, and we may
trace their teaching in the fragments and in the remarkable speech which the greatest stylist of all time puts
into his mouth in the *Symposium*—the rhymes, antitheses,
quibbles, and verbal trickiness of argument.   The parody,
both brilliant and careful, which Aristophanes presents
at the opening of his *Thesmophoriazusæ* is directed
chiefly perhaps against his music, whereof we have no
trace.   The blunt auditor, Mnesilochus, describes it as
lascivious.[4]   The words set to it read like a feeble
copy of Euripides—fluent, copious, nerveless, in spite
of the "lathe," the "glue," the "melting-pot," and the
"moulds"[5] over which his satirist makes merry.

---

[1] Such a sentence as that of M. Orgon in *Le jeu de l'amour et du
hasard* (I, ii.) : " Va, dans ce monde, il faut être un peu trop bon pour l'être
assez," strikes one as thoroughly Agathonesque.

[2] *Protagoras*, 315 E.

[3] *Symposium*, 198 C.   Socrates says of Agathon's panegyric upon
Eros : καὶ γάρ με Γοργίου ὁ λόγος ἀνεμίμνησκεν.   The whole speech of
Agathon is intended to show these characteristics.   Cp., for example, 197
D : πραότητα μὲν πορίζων, ἀγριότητα δ' ἐξορίζων · φιλόδωρος εὐμενείας,
ἄδωρος δυσμενείας κτέ.

[4] *Thesm.* 130 sqq.   [5] *Ibid.* 54 sqq.

Agathon, then, marks unmistakably the beginning of decadence. The three masters had exhausted the possibilities of the art open to that age. A new impulse from without or the social emancipation of women might have opened new paths of achievement. But no great external influence was to come till Alexander, and then the result for Greece itself was loss of independence and vigour. And the little that could be done with women still in the harem or the slave-market was left to be performed by Menander and his fellow-comedians.[1] Agathon made a valiant effort to carry tragedy into new channels, but lacked the genius to leave more than clever experiments.

On a lower plane of achievement stands CRITIAS, the famous leader of the " Thirty Tyrants ". Two tragedies from his pen are known to us, *Pirithous*[2] and *Sisyphus*, both at one time attributed to Euripides ; but he is too doctrinaire, too deficient in brilliant idiomatic ease, for such a mistake to endure. The *Pirithous* deals with Heracles' descent into Hades to rescue Theseus and to demand of Pluto Persephone's hand for Pirithous. Of this astounding story we find little trace in the fragments, which are mostly quasi-philosophical dicta. For instance :—

> A temper sound more stable is than law ;
> The one no politician's eloquence
> Can warp, but law by tricks of cunning words
> Full often is corrupted and unhinged.

In strong contrast to these prosaic lines is Critias' superb apostrophe to the Creator, which may be paraphrased thus :—

> From all time, O Lord, is thy being ; neither is there any that saith, This is my son.
> All that is created, lo, thou hast woven the firmament about it ; the heavens revolve, and all that is therein spinneth like a wheel.

[1] It is noteworthy that Socrates' famous " prophecy of Shakespeare " (*Symposium*, 223 D), "one who can write comedy can write tragedy and *vice versa*," is addressed to Agathon and Aristophanes jointly.

[2] The attribution of this play to Critias is not certain, but probable ; it is accepted by Wilamowitz. The new life of Euripides by Satyrus (see above, p. 18) attributes it to that poet.

Thou hast girded thyself with light ; the gloom of dusk is about thee, even as a garment of netted fire.

Stars without number dance around thee ; they cease not, they move in a measure through thy high places.

From the same hymn probably comes the majestic passage which tells of "unwearied Time that in full flood ever begets himself, and the Great Bear and the Less. . . ."

In apparent contrast to this tone is the remarkable passage, of forty-two lines, from the *Sisyphus*. It is a purely rationalistic account of religion. First human life was utterly brutish : there were no rewards for righteousness, no punishment of evil-doers. Then law was set up, that justice might be sovereign ; but this device only added furtiveness to sin. Finally, "some man of shrewdness and wisdom . . . introduced religion" (or "the conception of God," τὸ θεῖον), so that even in secret the wicked might be restrained by fear. The contradiction between these two plays is illusory : Critias combines with disbelief in the personal Greek gods belief in an impersonal First Cause. It is too often forgotten that among the "Thirty Tyrants" were men of strong religious principles. The democratic writers of Athens loved to depict them as mercenary butchers, but it is plain from the casual testimony of Lysias[1] that they looked upon themselves as moral reformers. "They *said* that it was their business to purge the city of wicked men, and turn the rest of the citizens to righteousness and self-restraint." Such passages read like quotations from men who would inaugurate a "rule of the saints," and if their severities surpassed those of the English Puritans, they were themselves outdone by the cruelty which sternly moral leaders of the French Revolution not only condoned but initiated. Critias was the Athenian Robespierre. But the one revolution was the reverse of the other. The *régime* of the Thirty was a last violent effort of the Athenian oligarchs to stem the tide of ochlocracy, to

[1] *Eratosthenes*, II.

induce some self-discipline into the freedom of Athens. They failed, and Critias was justified on the field of Chæronea.

The most successful tragic playwright of the fourth century was ASTYDAMAS, whose history furnishes good evidence that after the disappearance of Euripides and Sophocles the Greek genius was incapable of carrying tragedy into new developments. While prose could boast such names as Plato and Demosthenes, the tragic art found no greater exponent than this Astydamas, of whose numerous plays nothing is left save nine odd lines. There were, moreover, two Astydamantes, father and son, whose works (scarcely known save by name) it is difficult to distinguish. But it seems that it was the son whose popularity was so great as to win him fifteen first prizes and an honour before unknown. His *Parthenopæus* won such applause in 340 B.C. that the Athenians set up a brazen statue of the playwright in the theatre; it was not till ten years later that the orator Lycurgus persuaded them to accord a like honour to the three Masters. We learn from Aristotle [1] that Astydamas altered the story of Alcmæon, causing him to slay his mother in ignorance; and Plutarch [2] alludes to his *Hector* as one of the greatest plays. He was nothing more than a capable writer who caught the taste of his time, and probably owed much of his popularity to the excellence of his actors.

Only one fact is known about POLYIDUS "the sophist," but that is sufficiently impressive. Aristotle twice [3] takes the Recognition-scene in his *Iphigenia* as an example, and in the second instance actually compares the work of Polyidus with one of Euripides' most wonderful successes—the Recognition-scene in the *Iphigenia in Tauris*. It appears that as Orestes was led away to slaughter he exclaimed: "Ah! So I was fated, like my sister, to be sacrificed." This

[1] *Poetic*, 1453*b*. [2] *De Gloria Atheniensium*, 349 E.
[3] *Poetic*, 1455*a*, *b*.

catches the attention of Iphigenia and saves his life.
Polyidus here undoubtedly executed a brilliant *coup
de théâtre*.

During the fourth century many tragedians wrote
not for public performance but for readers. Of these
ἀναγνωστικοί[1] the most celebrated was CHÆREMON, of
whom sufficient fragments and notices survive to give a
distinct literary portrait. Comic poets ridiculed his preciosity : he called water "river's body," ivy "the year's
child," and loved word-play : πρὶν γὰρ φρονεῖν εὖ
καταφρονεῖν ἐπίστασαι.[2] But though a sophisticated attention to style led him into such frigid mannerisms, he
can express ideas with a brief Euripidean cogency : perhaps nothing outside the work of the great masters was
more often quoted in antiquity than his dictum " Human
life is luck, not discretion "—τύχη τὰ θνητῶν πράγματ',
οὐκ εὐβουλία.

The only technical peculiarity attributed to him
is the play *Centaur*, if play it was. Athenæus calls
it a "drama in many metres,"[3] while Aristotle[4] uses
the word "rhapsody," implying epic quality. It may
be that the epic or narrative manner was used side
by side with the dramatic in the manner of Bunyan.
Here is another proof that by the time of Euripides
tragedy had really attained its full development. Attempts at new departures in technique are all abortive
after his day.

A delightful point which emerges again and again
is Chæremon's passion for flowers. From *Thyestes*
come two phrases—" the sheen of roses mingled with
silver lilies," and "strewing around the children of
flowering spring"—which indicate, as do many others,
Chæremon's love of colour and sensuous loveliness. It
was his desire to express all the details of what pleased

---

[1] Aristotle, *Rhetoric*, III, 12, 2 : βαστάζονται δὲ οἱ ἀναγνωστικοί, οἷον
Χαιρήμων· ἀκριβὴς γὰρ ὥσπερ λογογράφος.
[2] " You know how to feel contempt before you have learnt wisdom," or,
to reproduce (however badly) the play upon words, " You practise contempt before using contemplation ".
[3] Athenæus, fr. 10 : δρᾶμα πολύμετρον.   [4] *Poetic*, 1447b.

his eye that led him into preciosity—a laboured embroidery which recalls Keats' less happy efforts. But he can go beyond mere mannerism. A splendid fragment of his *Œneus* shows Chæremon at his best : it describes the half-nude beauty of girls sleeping in the moonlight. One can hardly believe that Chæremon belonged to the fourth century and was studied by Aristotle. In this passage, despite its voluptuous dilettantism, there is a sense of physical beauty, above all of colour and sensuous detail, which was unknown since Pindar, and is not to be found again, even in Theocritus, till we come to the Greek novelists. In one marvellous sentence, too, he passes beyond mere prettiness to poetry, expressing with perfect mastery the truth that the sight of beauty is the surest incentive to chastity : κἀξεπεσφραγίζετο ὥρας γελώσης χωρὶς ἐλπίδων ἔρως :—

> Love, his passion quelled by awe,
> Printed his smiling soul on all he saw.

It is the idea which Meredith has voiced so magically in *Love in the Valley* :—

> Love that so desires would fain keep her changeless,
> Fain would fling the net, and fain have her free.

That Greek literature has progressed far towards the self-conscious Alexandrian search for charm can nevertheless be observed if we compare this passage from Chæremon with the analogous description in Euripides' *Bacchæ*[1] (which no doubt suggested it). There the same general impression, and far more "atmosphere," is given with no voluptuous details : θαῦμ' ἰδεῖν εὐκοσμίας—"a marvel of grace for the eye to behold" —is his nearest approach to Chæremon's elaboration. If, as has been well said,[2] one may compare the three Masters to Giotto, Raffaelle, and Correggio respectively, then Chæremon finds his parallel among the French painters ; he reminds one not so much of the handsome

[1] vv. 677-774.
[2] Symonds, *Studies in the Greek Poets*, II, p. 26.

sensuality of Boucher as of that more seductive *simplesse* in which Greuze excelled.

A curious figure in this history is DIONYSIUS the Elder, tyrant of Syracuse from 405-367 B.C. Like Frederick the Great of Prussia, not satisfied with political and military glory, he aspired to literary triumphs. With a pathetic hero-worship he purchased and treasured the desk of Æschylus, and similar objects which had belonged to Euripides, hoping (says Lucian [1]) to gain inspiration from them. The prince frequently tried his fortune at the dramatic contests in Athens, but for long without success, and naturally became a butt of the Attic wits, who particularly relished his moral aphorisms (such as "tyranny is the mother of injustice"!) ; Eubulus devoted a whole comedy to his tragic *confrère*. In 367 B.C. he heard with joy that at last the first prize had fallen to him at the Lenæa for *Hector's Ransom;* gossip said that his death in the same year was due to the paroxysms of gratified vanity. Little is known about the contents of his dramas, but we hear that one play was an attack upon the philosopher Plato. In other works, too, he appears to have discussed his personal interests. Lucian preserves the bald verse :—

> Doris, Dionysius' spouse, has passed away,

and the astonishing remark :—

> Alas ! alas ! a useful wife I've lost.

But one may be misjudging him. Perhaps by "useful" (χρησίμην) he meant "good" (χρηστήν) ; Dionysius had a curious fad for using words, not in their accepted sense, but according to real or fancied etymology.[2]

Ancient critics set great store by CARCINUS, the most distinguished of a family long connected with the theatre. One hundred and sixty plays are attributed to him, and eleven victories. He spent some time at the court of

---

[1] *Adversus Indoctos*, 15.

[2] Athenæus III, 98 D, reports, for example, that he called a javelin βαλλάντιον (properly "purse"), because "it is thrown in the face of the foe" (ἐναντίον βάλλεται).

the younger Dionysius, the Syracusan tyrant, and his longest fragment deals with the Sicilian worship of Demeter and Persephone. We possess certain interesting facts about his plots. Aristotle[1] as an instance of the first type of Recognition—that by signs—mentions among those which are congenital "the stars introduced by Carcinus in his *Thyestes*" (evidently birthmarks). More striking is a later paragraph:[2] "In constructing the plot and working it out with the proper diction, the poet should place the scene, as far as possible, before his eyes. . . . The need of such a rule is shown by the fault found in Carcinus. Amphiaraus was on his way from the temple. This fact escaped the observation of one who did not see the situation. On the stage, however, the piece failed, the audience being offended at the oversight." This shows incidentally how little assistance an ancient dramatist obtained from that now vital collaborator, the rehearsal. In the *Medea*[3] of Carcinus the heroine, unlike the Euripidean, did not slay her children but sent them away. Their disappearance caused the Corinthians to accuse her of their murder, and she defended herself by an ingenious piece of rhetorical logic: "Suppose that I *had* killed them. Then it would have been a blunder not to slay their father Jason also. This you know I have not done. Hence I have not murdered my children either." Just as Carcinus there smoothed away what was felt to be too dreadful in Euripides, so in *Œdipus* he appears[4] to have dealt with the improbabilities which cling to *Œdipus Tyrannus*. He excelled, moreover, in the portrayal of passion: Cercyon, struggling with horrified grief in Carcinus' *Alope*, is cited by Aristotle.[5] The *Ærope* too had sensational success. That bloodthirsty savage Alexander, tyrant of Pheræ, was so moved by the emotion wherewith the actor Theodorus performed his part, that he burst into tears.[6]

Two points in his actual fragments strike a modern

---

[1] *Poetic*, 1454b.   [2] 1455a.   [3] *Rhetoric*, II, 1400b.
[4] *Ibid.* 1417b, but the passage is obscure.
[5] *Eth. Nic.* 1150b, 10.   [6] Ælian, V.H. XIV, 40.

reader.   The first is a curious flatness of style noticeable
in the one fairly long passage ; every word seems to be a
second-best.   The opening lines will be sufficient :—

> λέγουσι Δήημτρός ποτ' ἄρρητον κόρην
> Πλούτωνα κρυφίοις ἁρπάσαι βουλεύμασι,
> δῦναί τε γαίας εἰς μελαμφαεῖς μυχούς.
> πόθῳ δὲ μητέρ' ἠφανισμένης κόρης
> μαστήρ' ἐπελθεῖν πᾶσαν ἐν κύκλῳ χθόνα.

To turn from this dingy verbiage to his amazing
brilliance in epigram is like passing from an auctioneer's
showroom into a lighthouse.   (The difference, we note,
is between narrative and "rhetoric".)   Such a sentence
as οὐδεὶς ἔπαινον ἡδοναῖς ἐκτήσατο ("no man ever won
praise by his pleasures") positively bewilders by its
glitter.   It is perhaps not absolutely perfect : its miraculous ease might allow a careless reader to pass it by ;
but that is a defect which Carcinus shares with most
masters of epigram, notably with Terence and Congreve.
More substantial is the wit of this fragment :—

> χαίρω σ' ὁρῶν φθονοῦντα, τοῦτ' εἰδώς, ὅτι
> ἐν δρᾷ μόνον δίκαιον ὢν ποιεῖ φθόνος ·
> λυπεῖ γὰρ αὐτόχρημα τοὺς κεκτημένους.

"I rejoice to see that you harbour spite, for I know that
of all its effects there is one that is just—it straightway
stings those who cherish it."   One notices the exquisite
skill which has inserted the second line, serving admirably to prepare for and throw into relief the vigorous
third verse.

THEODECTES of Phaselis enjoyed a brilliant career.
During his forty-one years he was a pupil of Plato, Iso-
crates, and Aristotle, obtained great distinction as an
orator (Cicero[1] praises him), produced fifty plays, and
obtained the first prize at eight of the thirteen contests
in which he competed.   Alexander the Great decked
his statue with garlands in memory of the days when
they had studied together under Aristotle.   That
philosopher quotes him several times, and in particular
pays Theodectes the high honour of coupling him with

[1] *Orator*, 51.

Sophocles ; the examples which he gives[1] of *peripeteia* are the *Œdipus Tyrannus* and the *Lynceus* of Theodectes. The same drama is used[2] to exemplify another vital point, the difference between Complication and *Dénouement*.

He was doubtless a brilliantly able man and a popular dramatist with a notable talent for concocting plots. But all that we can now see in his remains is a feeble copy of Euripides, though he was, to be sure, audacious enough to place Philoctetes' wound in the hand instead of the foot—for the sake of gracefulness, one may imagine. For the rest, we possess a curious speech made by some one ignorant of letters, who describes[3] as a picture the name " Theseus "—this idea is taken bodily from Euripides—and sundry sententious remarks, one of which surely deserves immortality as reaching the limit of pompous common-place :—

> Widely through Greece hath this tradition spread
> O aged man, and ancient is the saw :
> The hap of mortals is uncertain ever.

Mention should be made of DIOGENES and CRATES the philosophers, who wrote plays not for production, but for the study, as propagandist pamphlets. They may none the less have been excellent plays, like the *Justice* of Mr. Galsworthy. Very little remains on which an opinion can be founded. One vigorous line of Diogenes catches the attention: " I would rather have a drop of luck than a barrel of brains ".[4]

A more remarkable dramatist was MOSCHION, whose precise importance it is hard to estimate, though he is deeply interesting to the historian of tragedy. For on the one hand, he was probably not popular—nothing is known of his life,[5] and Stobæus is practically the only writer who quotes him. On the other hand, he is the

---

[1] *Poetic*, 1452a.   [2] *Ibid.* 1455b.
[3] " First there came a circle with a dot in the middle," etc.
[4] θέλω τύχης σταλαγμὸν ἢ φρενῶν πίθον.
[5] That he belongs to the fourth century is not certain, though extremely probable.

one Greek poet known to have practised definitely the historical type of drama. Moschion is of course not alone in selecting actual events for his theme. Long before his day Phrynichus had produced his *Phœnissæ* and *The Capture of Miletus*, Æschylus his *Persæ*; and his contemporary Theodectes composed a tragedy *Mausolus* in glorification of the deceased king of Caria. But all four were *pièces d'occasion*. Moschion alone practised genuine historical drama: he went according to custom into the past for his material, but chose great events of real history, not legend.[1] His *Themistocles* dealt with the battle of Salamis; we possess one brief remnant thereof, in which (as it seems) a messenger compares the victory of the small Greek force to the devastation wrought by a small axe in a great pine-forest. *The Men of Pheræ* appears[2] to have depicted the brutality of Alexander, prince of Pheræ, who refused burial to Polyphron.

These "burial-passages" include Moschion's most remarkable fragment, a fine description in thirty-three lines describing the rise of civilization. The versification is undesirably smooth—throughout there is not a single resolved foot. Like a circumspect rationalist, Moschion offers three alternative reasons, favouring none, for the progress made by man: some great teacher such as Prometheus, the Law of Nature (ἀνάγκη), the long slow experience (τριβή) of the whole race. His style here is vigorous but uneven; after dignified lines which somewhat recall Æschylus we find a sudden drop to bald prose: ὁ δ' ἀσθενὴς ἦν τῶν ἀμεινόνων βορά:[3] "the weak were the food of the strong".

It is convenient to mention here a remarkable satyric drama, produced about 324 B.C., the *Agen*,[4] of

[1] We have only one title (*Telephus*) which implies a legendary theme.
[2] Meineke suggests that the subject is an incident related by Xenophon, *Hellenica*, VI, iv. 33, 34.
[3] He might at least have written τοῖς ἀμείνοσιν.
[4] The meaning of this name is unknown.

which seventeen consecutive lines survive. This play was produced during the Dionysiac festival in the camp of Alexander on the banks of the Hydaspes or Jhelum, in the Punjaub. Its subject was the escapades of Harpalus, who had revolted from Alexander and fled to Athens. The author is said[1] to have been either Python of Catana or Byzantium, or the Great Alexander himself. No doubt it was an elaborate "squib" full of racy topical allusions. Were it not that Athenæus calls it a "satyric playlet"[2] we might take the fragment as part of a comedy. But about this time satyric drama tended to become a form of personal attack—a dramatic "satire". Thus one Mimnermus, whose date is unknown, wrote a play against doctors[3]; Lycophron and Sositheus, both members of the Alexandrian "Pleiad," attacked individual philosophers, the former writing a *Menedemus* which satirized the gluttony and drunkenness of the amiable founder of the Eretrian school, the latter ridiculing the disciples whom the "folly of Cleanthes" drove like cattle—an insult which the audience resented and damned the play.[4]

The third century saw a great efflorescence of theatrical activity in Alexandria. Under Ptolemy II (285-247 B.C.), that city became the centre of world-culture as it already was of commerce. All artistic forms were protected and rewarded with imperial liberality. The great library became one of the wonders of the world, and the Dionysiac festivals were performed with sedulous magnificence. Among the many writers of tragedy seven were looked on as forming a class by themselves—the famous Pleiad ("The Constellation of Seven"). Only five names of these are certain—Philiscus, Homerus, Alexander, Lycophron, and Sositheus; for the other two "chairs" various

---

[1] Athenæus XIII, 595 F.
[2] He uses the diminutive δραμάτιον.
[3] κατὰ ἰατρῶν (Stobæus, 102, 3). He was thus a precursor of Molière and Mr. Bernard Shaw.
[4] Diogenes Lærtius, VII, 173.

names are found in our authorities: Sosiphanes, Dionysiades, Æantides, Euphronius. Nor can we be sure that all these men worked at Alexandria.[1] That the splendour of the city and Ptolemy's magnificent patronage should have drawn the leading men of art, letters, and science to the world's centre, is a natural assumption and indeed the fact: Theocritus the idyllist, Euclid the geometer, Callimachus the poet and scholar, certainly lived there. Of the Pleiad, only three are known to have worked in Alexandria: Lycophron, to whom Ptolemy entrusted that section of the royal library which embraced Comedy, Alexander, who superintended Tragedy, and Philiscus the priest of Dionysus. Homerus may have passed all his career in Byzantium, which later possessed a statue of him, and Sositheus was apparently active at Athens.

LYCOPHRON'S *Menedemus* has already been mentioned. His fame now rests upon the extant poem *Alexandra*, in high repute both in ancient and in modern times for its obscurity. But SOSITHEUS is the most interesting of the galaxy. We may still read twenty-one lines from his satyric drama *Daphnis* or *Lityerses*, describing with grim vigour the ghoulish harvester Lityerses who made his visitors reap with him, finally beheading them and binding up the corpses in sheaves. Sositheus made his mark, indeed, less in tragedy than in satyric writing: he turned from the tendency of his day which made this genre a form of satire, and went back to the antique manner. SOSIPHANES, finally, deserves mention for a remarkable fragment :—

> ὦ δυστυχεῖς μὲν πολλά, παῦρα δ' ὄλβιοι
> βροτοί, τί σεμνύνεσθε ταῖς ἐξουσίαις,
> ἃς ἕν τ' ἔδωκε φέγγος ἕν τ' ἀφείλετο;
> ἣν δ' εὐτυχῆτε, μηδὲν ὄντες εὐθέως
> ἵσ' οὐρανῷ φρονεῖτε, τὸν δὲ κύριον
> Ἅιδην παρεστῶτ' οὐχ ὁρᾶτε πλησίον.

" O mortal men, whose misery is so manifold, whose joys so few, why plume yourselves on power which one day

[1] This point is made by Bernhardy, *Grundriss der Gr. Litteratur* II, ii. p. 72.

gives and one day destroys? If ye find prosperity, straightway, though ye are naught, your pride rises high as heaven, and ye see not your master death at your elbow"—a curiously close parallel with the celebrated outburst in *Measure for Measure*. We observe the Euripidean versification, though Sosiphanes "flourished" two centuries[1] after the master's birth, and though between the two, in men like Moschion, Carcinus, and Chæremon, we find distinct flatness of versification. The fourth-century poets, however second-rate, were still working with originality of style: Sosiphanes belongs to an age which has begun not so much to respect as to worship the great models. He sets himself to copy Euripides, and his iambics are naturally "better" than Moschion's, as are those written by numerous able scholars of our own day.

After the era of the Pleiad, Greek tragedy for us to all intents and purposes comes to an end. New dramas seem to have been produced down to the time of Hadrian, who died in A.D. 138, and theatrical entertainments were immensely popular throughout later antiquity, as vase-paintings show, besides countless allusions in literature. But our fragments are exceedingly meagre. One tragedy has been preserved by its subject—the famous *Christus Patiens* (Χριστὸς Πάσχων), which portrayed the Passion. It is the longest and the worst of all Greek plays, and consists largely of a repellent *cento*—snippets from Euripides pieced together and eked out by bad iambics of the author's own. The result is traditionally, but wrongly, attributed to Gregory of Nazianzus (born probably in A.D. 330). Its only value is that it is often useful in determining the text of Euripides. It would be useless to enumerate all the poetasters of these later centuries whose names are recorded.

In this chapter we have constantly referred to the *Poetic* of Aristotle, and it will be well at this point to

[1] His date is not, however, certain, and there is some reason to assign his *floruit* to the time of Alexander the Great.

summarize his view of the nature, parts, and aim of
tragedy. Before doing so, however, we must be clear
upon two points : the standpoint of his criticism and the
value of his evidence. It was long the habit to take this
work as a kind of Bible of poetical criticism, to accept
with blind devotion any statements made therein, or
even alleged[1] to be made therein, as constituting rules
for all playwrights for ever. Now, as to the former
point, the nature of his criticism, it is simply to explain
how good tragedies were as a fact written. He takes
the work of contemporary and earlier playwrights, and
in the light of this, together with his own strong common sense, æsthetic sensibility, and private temperament, tells how he himself (for example) would write a
tragedy. On the one hand, could he have read *Macbeth*
then, he would have condemned it ; on the other, could
he read it now as a modern man, he would approve
it. As to the second point, the value of his evidence,
we must distinguish carefully between the facts which
he reports and his comment thereon. The latter we
should study with the respect due to his vast merits ; but
he is not infallible. When, for instance, he writes that
" even a woman may be good, and also a slave ; though
the woman may be said to be an inferior being, and the
slave quite worthless,"[2] and blames Euripides because
" Iphigenia the suppliant in no way resembles her later
self,"[3] we shall regard him less as helping us than as
dating himself. But as to the objective facts which he
records he must be looked on as for us infallible.[4] He

---

[1] The most amazing example is that of the " Three Unities "—those
of Action, Time, and Place—of which such a vast amount has been heard
and which ruled tyrannically over French " classical " tragedy. It is difficult to believe that Aristotle never mentions the " Three Unities ". On the
Unity of Action he has, of course, much to say ; the Unity of Time is dismissed in one casual sentence. As to the Unity of Place there is not a
word. (It is signally violated in the *Eumenides* and the *Ajax*.)

[2] *Poetic*, 1454*a*.

[3] *Ibid.*

[4] See Wilamowitz-Moellendorff's magnificent *Einleitung in die
griechische Tragödie*, pp. 48-51 (*e.g.* "nicht mehr Aristoteles der aesthetiker
sondern Aristoteles der historiker ist der ausgangspunkt unserer be-
trachtung" and "unser fundament ist und bleibt was in der poetik steht ").

lived in or close to the periods of which he writes ; he commanded a vast array of documents now lost to us ; he was strongly desirous of ascertaining the facts ; his temperament and method were keenly scientific, his industry prodigious. We may, and should, discuss his opinions ; his facts we cannot dispute. The reader will be able to appreciate for himself the statement which follows.

Aristotle's definition of tragedy runs thus : " Tragedy, then, is an imitation of an action that is serious, complete, and of a certain magnitude ; in language embellished with each kind of artistic ornament, the several kinds being found in separate parts of the play ; in the form of action, not of narrative ; through pity and fear effecting the proper purgation of these emotions ".[1] Adequate discussion of this celebrated passage is here impossible ; only two points can be made. Firstly, the definition plainly applies to Greek Tragedy alone and as understood by Aristotle : we observe the omission of what seems to us vital—the fact that tragedy depicts the collision of opposing principles as conveyed by the collision of personalities—and the insertion of Greek peculiarities since, as he goes on to explain, by "language embellished" he means language which includes song. Secondly, the famous dictum concerning "purgation" (*catharsis*) is now generally understood as meaning, not "purification" or "edification" of our pity and fear, but as a medical metaphor signifying that these emotions are purged out of our spirit.

Further light on the nature of tragedy he gives by comparing it with three other classes of literature. "Comedy aims at representing men as worse, Tragedy as better than in actual life."[2] In another place he contrasts tragedy with history : " It is not the function

---

[1] *Poetic*, 1449*b* : ἔστιν οὖν τραγῳδία μίμησις πράξεως σπουδαίας καὶ τελείας μέγεθος ἐχούσης, ἡδυσμένῳ λόγῳ χωρὶς ἑκάστῳ τῶν εἰδῶν ἐν τοῖς μορίοις, δρώντων καὶ οὐ δι᾽ ἀπαγγελίας, δι᾽ ἐλέου καὶ φόβου περαίνουσα τὴν τῶν τοιούτων παθημάτων κάθαρσιν.

[2] 1448*a*.

of the poet to relate what has happened, but what may happen—what is possible according to the law of probability or necessity. The poet and the historian differ not by writing in verse or in prose. . . . The true difference is that one relates what has happened, the other what may happen. Poetry, therefore, is a more philosophical and a higher thing than history : for poetry tends to express the universal, history the particular."[1] Our imperfect text of the treatise ends with a more elaborate comparison between Tragedy and Epic, wherein Aristotle combats the contemporary view[2] that "epic poetry is addressed to a cultivated audience, who do not need gesture; Tragedy to an inferior public. Being then unrefined, it is evidently the lower of the two." His own verdict is that, since tragedy has all the epic elements, adds to these music and scenic effects, shows vividness in reading as well as in representation, attains its end within narrower limits, and shows greater unity of effect, it is the higher art.[3]

In various portions of the *Poetic* he gives us the features of Tragedy, following three independent lines of analysis :—

§ I. On the æsthetic line he discusses the *elements* of a tragedy : plot, character, thought, diction, scenery, and song. Of the last three he has little to say. But on one of them he makes an interesting remark. "Third in order is Thought—that is, the faculty of saying what is possible and pertinent in given circumstances. . . . The older poets made their characters speak the language of civic life ; the poets of our time, the language of the rhetoricians."[4] This prophesies from afar of Seneca and his like. As for character, it must be good, appropriate, true to life, and consistent.

Concerning Plot, which he rightly calls "the soul of a tragedy,"[5] Aristotle is of course far more copious. The salient points alone can be set down here :—

[1] 1451a, b.　　　　　　　　[2] 1462a.
[3] 1462a, b. (The phrasing in the summary above is borrowed from Butcher.) See further 1449b.
[4] 1450b.　　　　　　　　[5] 1450a.

(*a*) "The proper magnitude is comprised within such limits, that the sequence of events, according to the law of probability or necessity, will admit of a change from bad fortune to good, or from good fortune to bad." [1]

(*b*) "The plot . . . must imitate one action and that a whole, the structural union of the parts being such that if anyone of them is displaced or removed, the whole will be disjointed and disturbed." [2]   A tragedy must be an organism. It therefore follows that "of all plots and actions the episodic are the worst . . . in which the episodes or acts succeed one another without probable or necessary sequence". [3]   He is recommending the "Unity of Action".

(*c*) "Plots are either Simple or Complex. . . . An action . . . I call Simple, when the change of fortune takes place without Reversal (or Recoil) of the Action and without Recognition. A Complex Action is one in which the change is accompanied by such Reversal, or by Recognition, or by both." [4]   Reversal we shall meet again.   By Recognition Aristotle means not merely such Recognition-scenes as we find in the crisis of the *Iphigenia in Tauris* (though such are the best) but "a change from ignorance to knowledge, producing love or hate between the persons destined by the poet for good or bad fortune". [5]

(*d*) "Two parts, then, of the plot—Reversal and Recognition—turn upon surprises. A third part is the Tragic Incident. The Tragic Incident is a distinctive or painful action, such as death on the stage, bodily agony, wounds, and the like." [6]   In the words "death on the stage"—or "before the audience" (the phrase [7] has no bearing on the stage-controversy), Aristotle casually but completely overthrows another critical convention, that in ancient Tragedy deaths take place only "behind the scenes".   In the extant

---

[1] 1451*a*.   [2] 1451*a*.   [3] 1451*b*.
[4] 1452*a*.   [5] 1452*a*.   [6] 1452*b*.
[7] οἱ ἐν τῷ φανερῷ θάνατοι.

plays, not only do Alcestis and Hippolytus "die on
the stage" in their litters, but Ajax falls upon his
sword.

(e) The best subject of Tragedy is the change from
good fortune to bad in the life of some eminent man
not conspicuously good and just, whose misfortune,
however, is due not to wickedness but to some error
or weakness.[1]

(f) The poet "may not indeed destroy the framework of the received legends—the fact, for instance,
that Clytæmnestra was slain by Orestes and Eriphyle
by Alcmæon—but he ought to show invention of his
own, and skilfully handle the traditional material".[2]
This injunction was obeyed beforehand by all the three
Athenian masters ; it is especially important to remember it when studying Euripides.

(g) "The unravelling of the plot . . . must arise out
of the plot itself; it must not be brought about by the
Deus ex Machina, as in the Medea. . . . The *Deus ex
Machina* should be employed only for events external
to the drama—for antecedent or subsequent events,
which lie beyond the range of human knowledge."[3]
This vital criticism will be considered later, when we
discuss the *Philoctetes*[4] of Sophocles and the Euripidean
drama.[5]

(h) "Within the action there must be nothing irrational. If the irrational cannot be excluded, it should
be outside the scope of the tragedy. Such is the
irrational element in the Œdipus of Sophocles."[6]
Aristotle means certain strange *data* in the *Œdipus
Tyrannus*—the fact that neither Œdipus nor Jocasta
has learnt earlier about the past, and so forth.

§ II. On the purely literary line he tells us the
parts :—[7]

[1] 1453a.   [2] 1453b.   [3] 1454a, b.
[4] pp. 163-5.   [5] pp. 313-5.   [6] 1454b, 1460a.
[7] 1452b : ἔστιν δὲ πρόλογος μὲν μέρος ὅλον τραγῳδίας τὸ πρὸ χοροῦ
παρόδου, ἐπεισόδιον δὲ μέρος ὅλον τραγῳδίας τὸ μεταξὺ ὅλων χορικῶν μελῶν,
ἔξοδος δὲ μέρος ὅλον τραγῳδίας μεθ᾽ ὃ οὐκ ἔστι χοροῦ μέλος, χορικοῦ δὲ πάροδος
μὲν ἡ πρώτη λέξις ὅλη χοροῦ, στάσιμον δὲ μέλος χοροῦ τὸ ἄνευ ἀναπαίστου καὶ
τροχαίου, κόμμος δὲ θρῆνος κοινὸς χοροῦ καὶ τῶν ἀπὸ σκηνῆς.

(*a*) "The Prologos is that entire part of a tragedy which precedes the Parodos of the chorus" (see below for the Parodos). Thus a drama may have no "prologos" at all, for example the *Persæ*. The implications of our word "prologue" are derived from the practice of Euripides, who is fond of giving in his "prologos" an account of events which have led up to the action about to be displayed.

(*b*) "The Episode is that entire part of a tragedy which is between complete choric songs." "Episodes" then are what we call "acts": the name has already been explained.[1]

(*c*) "The Exodos is that entire part of a tragedy which has no choric song after it." The few anapæsts which close most tragedies are not "choric songs"— they were performed in recitative. Thus the Exodos is simply the last act.

(*d*) "Of the choric part the Parodos is the first un-divided utterance of the chorus: the Stasimon is a choric ode without anapæsts or trochees: the Commos is a joint lamentation of chorus and actors." It will be seen later[2] that by excluding trochees he probably means the trochaic tetrameter as seen in dialogue; lyric trochees are very common.

§ III. On the strictly dramatic line he tells us the *stages of structural development.*

(*a*) "Every tragedy falls into two parts—Complica-tion and Unravelling (or *Dénouement*). . . . By the Complication I mean all that comes between the begin-ning of the action and the part which marks the turn-ing-point to good or bad fortune. The Unravelling is that which comes between the beginning of the change and the end."[3]

(*b*) "Reversal (or Recoil, Peripeteia) is a change by which a train of action produces the opposite of the effect intended, subject always to our rule of probability or necessity. Thus in the Œdipus, the messenger

---

[1] p. 4.   [2] Chap. VI.   [3] 1455*b*.

comes to cheer Œdipus and free him from his alarms about his mother, but, by revealing who he is, he produces the opposite effect." [1]

Much might be written on this analysis of dramatic structure. One remark at least must be made. It is not plain how much importance Aristotle allots to the Recoil or Peripeteia. We have seen that he did not regard it as indispensable. At the most he seems to think it a striking way of starting the *dénouement*. It is better to look upon it, and the action which leads up to it, as a separate part of the drama—and it may be argued that every tragedy, if not every comedy, has a Peripeteia—to form, in fact, that middle stage which elsewhere [2] in the *Poetic* he mentions as necessary.

[1] 1452*a*.　　　　[2] 1450*b*.

CHAPTER II

THE GREEK THEATRE AND THE PRODUCTION
OF PLAYS

I. THE OCCASIONS OF PERFORMANCE

GREEK drama was looked upon not only as a
form of entertainment and culture, but as an
act of worship offered to the god Dionysus.
It was, in consequence, restricted to his festivals ; performances of a quite secular character are unknown.
Three Attic festivals are connected with the tragic
drama : the City Dionysia, the Lenæa, the Rural
Dionysia. The City or Great Dionysia were the most
splendid of the three, held in the precinct of Dionysus
Eleuthereus on the south-eastern slope of the Acropolis,
where the ruined theatre still lies. Tragedies, comedies,
and dithyrambs were performed, but of these tragedy
was the most important. The time was the month of
Elaphebolion (March to April). The Lenæa or
"Wine-Press Festival" which occurred in Gamelion
(January to February) was the great occasion for
comedy, though tragedies were also to be seen. It was
held at first in the Lenæon, a sacred enclosure, the site
of which is still uncertain, later in the same theatre as
tragedy. The Rural Dionysia fell in Poseideon (De-
cember to January), and were celebrated by the various
Attic townships, especially the Peiræus ; most of the
dramas performed were probably such as had been successful in Athens itself ; companies of actors travelled
about the country for this purpose.

Of these three celebrations the City Dionysia were

the most important for tragedy. The tyrant Pisistratus greatly increased the splendour of this festival and instituted the tragic contest. Each year during the fifth century three tragedians submitted each a tetralogy, and five comedians one play apiece. Tragedies were given in the mornings, comedies in the afternoon, and the celebration continued for at least five days.

II. The Buildings

Since the performance was a state-function, the whole nation was theoretically expected to be present, and in point of fact enormous audiences attended: the great theatre accommodated perhaps 30,000 [1] spectators. This fact governs the nature of the whole presentation. The theatre could not be roofed, and the acting therefore differed greatly from that customary in modern buildings.

A Greek theatre consisted of three parts—the auditorium, the orchestra, and the "stage-buildings". The heart of the whole is the orchestra or "dancing-ground" (ὀρχήστρα) upon which the chorus, throughout the action, were stationed—a circular area of beaten earth, later paved with marble. Beside the altar in this orchestra stood, in the earliest days of the theatre, the sacrificial table upon which the single actor mounted. This table in the fixed theatre is the descendant of the waggon from which the peripatetic actor of Thespis delivered his lines. In addition to the celebrants the passive worshippers were needed—the audience. Therefore the orchestra was placed at the bottom of a slope; and the spectators stood or sat on the higher ground. On the farther side rose the "stage-buildings," whatever from time to time they were. The general plan, then, of any Greek theatre was this :—

[1] Plato (*Symposium*, 175 E) makes Socrates congratulate Agathon on his success in the presence of "more than 30,000 Greeks". Modern archæologists, by statistics based on the seating-accommodation, would reduce this figure to 17,000.

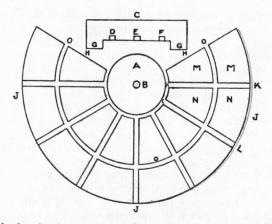

A is the circular orchestra, B the altar (θυμέλη) of Dionysus which invariably stood in the middle of it. C represents the "stage-buildings"; D, E, F, are the doors
which led from the building to the open air. The building usually projected into side-wings (G, G), called
παρασκήνια. H, H, are the passage-ways (πάροδοι), by
which the chorus generally entered the orchestra, and
by which the audience always made its way to the seats.
J, J, J, is the auditorium, a vast horseshoe-shaped space
rising up a hillside from the orchestra, and filled with
benches. This space was intersected by gangways,[1]
K, K, L, L, etc., called, perhaps, κλίμακες; the areas M,
M, N, N, etc., so formed, had the name "pegs" (κερκίδες).
In most theatres a longitudinal gallery O, O, O, was
made for further convenience in getting to the seats.
In the strictly Greek type the front line of "stage-buildings" never encroached on the circle of the orchestra.
But these theatres were used in Roman times also, and
altered to suit certain needs. The front of C was
thrown forward so that it cut into the orchestra and
obliterated the passages H, H. To replace these,

---

[1] There are fourteen of these at Athens.

entrances were tunnelled through the auditorium. Thus
at Athens the orchestra is now only little more than a
semicircle, though amid the ruins of the "stage-buildings" can still be seen a few feet of the kerbstone which
surrounded the original dancing floor—the only surviving
remnants of the Æschylean theatre; this masonry shows
that the diameter of the whole was about 90 feet.

The "stage-buildings," as we have called them for
convenience, require a longer discussion. Originally
there stood in that place only a tent, called *scēnē* (σκηνή),
which took no part in the theatrical illusion, but was used
by the one actor simply as a dressing-room. Soon, no
doubt, came the important advance of employing it as
"scenery"—the tent of Agamemnon before Troy, for example. Later a wooden booth was erected, and
Sophocles' invention of scene-painting—that is, of con-
cealing this booth with canvas to represent whatever
place or building was needed—added enormously to the
playwright's resources. This booth was afterwards built
of stone and became more and more elaborate; Roman
"stage-buildings" survive which are admirable pieces of
dignified architecture. The building of course contained
dressing-rooms and property-rooms. There were doors
at the narrow ends. The front of the building was
pierced by three, later by five, doors.

Upon what did these doors open? Was there a stage
in the Greek theatre? This problem has aroused more
discussion than any other in Greek scholarship save the
"Homeric Question". That all theatres possessed a
stage (λογεῖον) in Roman times is certain; the Athenian
building—which in its present condition dates from the
alterations made by Phædrus in the third century
after Christ—shows quite obviously the front wall of a
stage about 4½ feet high. But did the dramatists of
the fifth and fourth centuries before Christ write for a
theatre with a stage or not? There is a good deal of
prima-facie evidence for a stage, and a good deal to show
that the actors moved to and fro on that segment of the
orchestra nearest to the booth. That is, the question

lies between acting on top of the proscenium (or deco-
rated wall joining the faces of the *parascenia* G, G) and
acting in front of it.   A brief *résumé*[1] of the evidence is
all that can be attempted here.   It is confined to the
consideration of the fifth and fourth centuries B.C., to
which belongs practically all the extant work.   For the
period after 300 B.C. the use of a stage seems indisput-
able.

A. Arguments For a Stage

§ 1. *A High Stage.*—Vitruvius, the Roman architect,
who wrote at the end of the first century B.C., in his
directions for building a Greek theatre says : "Among
the Greeks the orchestra is wider, the back scene is
farther from the audience, and the stage is narrower.[2]
This latter they call *logeion* (speaking-place), because the
actors of tragedy and comedy perform there close to the
back scene, while the other artistes play in the ambit of
the orchestra, wherefore the two classes of performer are
called *scænici* and *thymelici* respectively."   [Literally,
"those connected with the booth" and "those connected
with the central altar".]   "This *logeion* should be not less
than 10, and not more than 12, feet in height."[3]   This,
says Dörpfeld, applies to the Greek theatre of Vitruvius'
own time, but has been extended by modern writers to
the fifth century.   Supposing, however, that Vitruvius
was thinking of the fifth century, then :—

(*a*) The stage is too narrow for performances, viz.
2·50 to 3 mètres, from which 1 mètre must be sub-
tracted for the background.   The remaining space is
not enough for actors and mutes, not to mention any
combined action of players and chorus.

(*b*) It is also too high.   Many passages in the plays

---

[1] This account is based on Dörpfeld (*Das griechische Theater*,
Abschnitt VII) who believes there was no stage, and on Haigh (*Attic
Theatre*[3], edited by Mr. Pickard-Cambridge, Chap. III) who believes
there was a stage.

[2] That is, shorter, viewed from left to right by the spectators.   The
depth of the Vitruvian stage was 10 feet.   [3] Vitruvius V, vii. 3-4.

show that chorus and actors are on the same level; in all these cases the chorus would have to mount steps, or the actors descend. This is absurdly awkward; nor is there evidence for steps. An attempt has been made [1] to meet the difficulties by the assumption of another platform about half the height of the stage, erected on the orchestra for the chorus. But the various objections to such a subsidiary platform are so strong that it is no longer believed in. With it, however disappears the only way by which plays with a chorus could be performed on the high stage of Vitruvius.

§ 2. *A Low Stage.*—Many scholars, abandoning Vitruvius as evidence for the fifth century, postulate a low stage. Their arguments are :—[2]

(*a*) Aristotle in the fourth century calls the songs of the actors τὰ ἀπὸ τῆς σκηνῆς, and says that the actor performed ἐπὶ τῆς σκηνῆς, phrases which seem to mean "from the stage" and "on the stage" respectively. And though Dörpfeld would take σκηνή as "background" (not "stage") translating Aristotle's phrases by "from the background" and "at the background," there remains the difficulty that Aristotle plainly thinks of actors and chorus as occupying quite distinct stations, which scarcely suggests that they move on contiguous portions of the same ground.

(*b*) The side-wings or *parascenia* must have been meant to enclose a stage. What else could have been their use?

(*c*) There are five phrases used by Aristophanes. Three times [3] an actor, on approaching other actors, is said to "come up"; twice [4] he is said to "go down". Nothing in the context implies raised ground as needed by the drama, so that we seem forced to refer these expressions to the visible stage itself. Dörpfeld and others would translate these two verbs by "come here"

---

[1] By Wieseler and others.
[2] Haigh [3], pp. 165-74.
[3] ἀναβαίνω : *Knights*, 148 ; *Acharnians*, 732 ; *Wasps*, 1342.
[4] καταβαίνω : *Eccles.* 1151 ; *Wasps*, 1514.

and "go away"; but there is no evidence for these meanings.

(*d*) The existing plays throw incidental light on the problem :—

(i) Certain characters[1] complain of the steepness of their path as they first come before the audience. Do they not refer to an actual ascent from orchestra to stage?

(ii) Ghosts sometimes appear. How can they have ascended out of "the ground" unless action took place on a raised area? This argument is, however, not strong. In later theatres such spectres did rise from below. But in the fifth century they may well have walked in.

(iii) A more striking[2] argument is that on several occasions the chorus, though it has excellent reason to enter the back scene, remains inert. In the *Agamemnon* the elders talk of rushing to the king's aid; a similar thing happens in the *Medea;* there are a number of such strange features. The inference is that there was a stage, to mount which would have appeared odd.

(iv) A stage was needed to make the actors visible, instead of being hidden by the chorus.[3] But, though there is no evidence that the chorus grouped themselves about the orchestra (as in the performances at Bradfield College), and they apparently stood in rows facing the actors, they could have been placed far forward enough to enable all to see the actors. Anyone who has visited a circus will appreciate this.

(v) Plato[4] remarks that Agathon and his actors

---

[1] Euripides, *Ion*, 727, *Electra*, 4 *sq.*, *Herc. Fur.* 119. As Haigh (3rd ed., p. 167) points out, "in the last passage it is the chorus which makes the complaint; so that in this case, if there was any visible ascent, it cannot have been the ascent to the stage".

[2] This is a strong and favourite argument for the stage; when Haigh (3rd ed., p. 168) denies this because "a sufficient reason is . . . the fact that, if they had gone into the palace, the scene of action would have been left empty for the time being," he forgets that such a departure of the chorus is quite possible. It occurs in *Eumenides, Ajax, Alcestis,* and *Helena,* not to mention Comedy.

[3] Haigh[3], p. 170 *sq.*   [4] *Symposium*, 194 B.

appeared on an ὀκρίβας, a "platform". But the word suggests a slight structure : Dörpfeld objects that this appearance was probably in the Odeum, or Music Hall, not the Theatre of Dionysus ; if it was in the theatre, the passage rather tells against a stage, for a temporary platform would not have been used if there was a stage.

(vi) Horace [1] says that " Æschylus gave his modest stage a floor of beams" or "gave the stage a floor of moderate-sized beams". Dörpfeld alleges (without evidence) that *pulpitum* (translated "stage" in the last sentence) may mean "booth," and suggests that the poet assumes a stage as matter of course : he is marking the advance made by Æschylus upon Thespis, who (according to Horace himself), performed his plays upon a waggon. But the proper answer is surely that Horace is regularly unreliable when he deals with questions of Greek scholarship, and that he is no doubt arbitrarily combining his knowledge of contemporary Greek theatres with his knowledge that Æschylus advanced in theatrical matters beyond Thespis.

Such are the main arguments in favour of a stage in the fifth and fourth centuries before Christ.

B. Arguments Against a Stage

(i) The evidence of the extant dramas. This, already adduced by many to prove that a stage was used, is taken by Dörpfeld [2] as "showing unmistakably that no separation existed between chorus and actors, that on the contrary both played on the same area ". He refers to action where people pass between house and orchestra with no apparent difficulty or hesitation. The chorus enter from the " palace " in the *Choephoræ*, the *Eumenides*, and Euripides' *Phaethon ;* the chorus of huntsmen enter it in the *Hippolytus*. There are other probable or possible instances. Particularly note-

---

[1] *Ars Poetica*, 278 : Æschylus et modicis instravit pulpita tignis,
[2] *Das Gr. Theater*, p. 350.

worthy is the fact that in *Helena* the chorus in the
midst of the play enter the building, and later reappear
from it.

(ii) The tradition in later writers. It is true, says
Dörpfeld, that we have no express assertion that there
was no stage—it never occurred to the older writers
to say so, for they knew of no such thing. The later
writers imply that there was none. Timæus,[1] com-
menting on ὀκρίβας, says : "for there was not yet a
thymele". *Thymele* there means "stage". Several
late writers tell us that the Roman *logeion* ("speaking-
place" or "stage") was once called "orchestra" : this
supports the view that the stage is part of the old
orchestra, higher than the other portion (see below).
The scholiast on *Prometheus Vinctus*, 128, remarks :
"They (the chorus) say this as they hover in the
air on the machine ; for it would be absurd for them
to converse from below [*i.e.* from the orchestra] to
one aloft". Now, the pro-stage theory makes all
choruses do this. The scholiast on Aristophanes'
Wasps, 1342, writes : "The old man stands on a certain
height (ἐπί τινος μετεώρου) as he summons the girl".
The word "certain" (τινός) implies that he knew
nothing of a regular stage. Finally, if there was a
definite and regular difference of position between
actors and chorus, is it not astonishing (*a*) that there
is in Greek literature no certain allusion to the fact,
(*b*) that the older literature contains no word for the
stage, the place where the acting was performed being
referred to merely by reference to the *booth* (ἐπὶ σκηνῆς
and ἀπὸ σκηνῆς)?

(iii) The architectural remains. Dörpfeld sums up
his celebrated architectural researches thus. No theatre
survives from the fifth century, but the theatre of
Lycurgus (fourth century) belongs to a period when
the plays of that century were still acted in the old
manner. Also we possess numerous buildings which
represent the rather later form of the theatre (the

[1] He wrote a lexicon to Plato in the third century after Christ.

building with fixed proscenium), and which belong to that period to which the remarks of Vitruvius apply. From the Lycurgean theatre we learn that there was no stage high or low. A platform for actor or orator is only necessary when the audience are all on a flat area. If they sit on a slope, a stage is more inconvenient than if the speaker stands on the ground.[1] And so, in the earliest times, when there was no sloping auditorium, Thespis, for example, performed upon a cart. In Italy the slope came into use only late, and the stage had been widely adopted before that time—for there was no chorus to provide for. When the Greek theatre was introduced into Italy, the Roman form was invented. They did not abandon their own stage, but divided the Greek orchestra into two parts of different height. The farther half, now superfluous (the chorus having vanished) could be used for spectators or gladiators. This portion was (in earlier theatres of the true Greek type) excavated and filled with fresh seats. The stage was, of course, not made higher than the lowest eyes.

The nature of the proscenium in Greek theatres was not suitable for the supporting wall of a stage. It would be absurd to see a temple in the air above a colonnade.[2] Again, it was impossible to act on top of the proscenium. The fear of falling, when the actor wore a mask and was forced to approach the edge in order to be well seen by the lowest spectators, would spoil his acting. Finally, why was the proscenium-front not a tangent of the orchestra circle? It should have been brought as far forward as possible if they acted on top of it.

To sum up. The orchestra in the earliest period was the place of the chorus and the actors. It kept

---

[1] Dörpfeld gives various optical diagrams to exhibit the effects.

[2] We incessantly see this effect in modern theatres. But in Greece the presence of the chorus performing below would force spectators to regard the building as suspended.

that function when the *scēnē* was erected beside it as a background. The chorus used the whole circle, the actors only part of it and the ground which lay in front of the *scēnē*. No change in this arrangement was made later. The actors in Roman times, of course, stood above the level of the excavated semicircle. But they remained throughout at the same distance from the spectators[1] and at the same level—that of the old orchestra.

How then are we to deal with Vitruvius' statement about the height of the stage? Dörpfeld suggested[2] that Vitruvius used plans and descriptions made by a Greek; Vitruvius, in absence of any warning, taking it (as a Roman) for granted there was a stage, saw it in the proscenium; or he may have misunderstood the the phrase ἐπὶ σκηνῆς in his Greek authority. But such a fundamental error made by a professional architect, who even if he had never been in Greece, must have known many persons familiar with Greek acting, is extremely hard to assume.[3] Yet the mistake is credible as regards the Greek theatre of the fourth and fifth centuries.

Amidst the mass of evidence and argument, only an outline of which is here presented, it is difficult to decide. The majority of inquirers will probably be swayed as regards the theatre of Sophocles and Astydamas by two considerations : the acting exigencies of the plays we now read or know of, and their own feeling as to how the performance would look with a stage and without. It seems, perhaps, most likely that Dörpfeld is right : that there was no stage, though when the façade represented a palace or temple a few steps might naturally appear.

[1] Save, of course, those on the new lowest seats, which went down to the new level of the excavated half. Dörpfeld has discovered evidence that the present lowest seats at Athens were added after the rest.

[2] *Das griechische Theater*, p. 364. After the publication of this view Dörpfeld altered his opinion, and suggested (*Bull. Corr. Hell.* 1896, p. 577 *sqq.* that V. means not the ordinary Greek Theatre, but the Graeco-Roman type found in Asia Minor. But this seems worse than his first thought. See Haigh[3], pp. 147 *sq.*

[3] *Ibid.* pp. 146 *sq.*

III. Supervision of Dramatic Displays

The authority superintending dramatic performances was the Athenian State, acting through the archon basileus for the Lenæa, the archon eponymus for the City Dionysia. The archon allotted the task of producing the three annual series of dramas to three persons for each series : the poet, the choregus, the protagonist. We will consider these persons in turn.

Playwrights submitted their work to the archon, who himself selected three : to each he was said to "give a chorus". The applications were many, and distinguished poets sometimes failed to "receive a chorus". The poet's business was not only to write the play and the music, (but in early times) to train actors and chorus. Near the end of the fifth century B.C. it became the practice to employ an expert trainer. Occasionally the poet caused some other person to "produce" the play. This was frequently done by Aristophanes, and we hear that Iophon competed with tragedies written by his father Sophocles.

The name "choregus" means "chorus-leader," but the choregus actually had quite other functions. He was a rich citizen who as a "liturgy" or public service bore all the special cost of the performance. To each choregus a flute-player was allotted, and it seems likely that the poet too was regarded as assigned to the choregus rather than the latter to the poet. ⁴The mounting of plays, which depended on the choregus, greatly influenced the audience, and their expressed opinion cannot but have had weight with the ten judges.[1] The wealthy Nicias, for example, obtained success for every tetralogy which he mounted.[2]

The third person with whom the archon concerned himself was the "protagonist" (the chief actor)—after the middle of the fifth century ; before then it appears that poets chose their protagonists. In the middle of

---

[1] In Plato's time this was notably so (*Laws*, 659 A-C, 700 C, 701 A).
[2] Plutarch, *Nicias*, 524 D.

the fifth century a protagonist was selected by the archon and one assigned to each tragic poet by lot. (The chief actor provided his subordinates himself.) This change came at about the time when three actors were regularly employed in each tragedy and when the contests in acting were instituted ; a prize for acting was awarded, and the successful actor had the right to perform the following year.   As the importance of the actor increased—Aristotle tells us that in his time the success of a play depended more upon the actor than upon the poet [1]—it was considered unfair that one poet should have the best performer for all his plays.   In the middle of the fourth century the arrangement was introduced that each protagonist should play in one tragedy only of each poet.

Each dramatist competed with a tetralogy [2] (that is, "four works") consisting of three tragedies and a satyric play, and the claims of these three tetralogies were decided by five [3] judges.   Some days before the competition began, the Council of the State and the choregi selected a number of names from each of the ten tribes. These names were sealed up in urns, which were produced at the opening of the festival.   The archon drew one name from each urn, and the ten citizens so selected were sworn as judges and given special seats.   After the conclusion of the performances each of the ten gave his verdict on a tablet, and five of these were drawn by the archon at random ; these five judgments gave the award.   In this method the principle of democratic equality and the necessity to rely on expert opinion were well combined.   When the votes had been collected, a herald proclaimed the name of the successful poet and of his choregus, who were crowned with ivy (a plant

---

[1] Aristotle, *Rhetoric*, III, i.

[2] This is the usual term employed.   See, however, Haigh [3], p. 13, note 3 : "the word τετραλογία was applied only to a group of four plays connected in subject," etc.

[3] This was certainly the number for comedy ; it is assumed for tragedy.

always associated with Dionysus). There is no evidence that a dramatic choregus was given any further reward: the prize of a tripod was only for dithyramb. The poet received, tradition said, a goat[1] in early times; after the State-supervision began, a sum of money from public funds was paid to each of the competitors. Records of the results were inscribed upon tablets and set up both by the victorious choregi and by the State. It is from these, directly or indirectly, that our knowledge of the facts is obtained; directly, because such inscriptions have been discovered in Athens, indirectly, because they were the basis of written works on the subject. Aristotle wrote a book called *Didascaliæ* (διδασκαλίαι), that is, " Dramatic Productions " ; though it is lost, later works were based upon it, and it is from these that the Greek " Arguments " to the existing plays are derived.

IV. THE MOUNTING OF A TRAGEDY

Scenery was painted on canvas or boards and attached to the front of the buildings. In satyric drama it appears to have varied little—a wild district with trees, rocks, and a cave. Tragedy generally employed a temple or palace-front, though even in the extant thirty-two there are exceptions—the rock of Prometheus, the tent of Ajax, the cave of Philoctetes, and so forth. In a façade there were three doors, corresponding to the three permanent doors in the buildings; when a cave or tent was depicted, its opening was in front of the central door. Statues were placed before the temple or palace—those of the deities, for instance, in the *Agamemnon* to whom the Herald utters his magnificent address. Individuality would be given to a temple by the statue of a particular god. Scene-painting was probably not very artistic or scrupulous of details. We never read any praise of splendid theatrical scenery

---

[1] τράγος. This was supposed to be the origin of the word "tragedy" (τραγῳδία " goat-song ").

such as is familiar to-day; and clever lighting effects were of course out of the question when all was performed in the daylight. Here and there the persons allude to the landscape, as in Sophocles' *Electra*, where the aged attendant of Orestes points out to the prince striking features of the Argolid plain. Such things were mostly left to the imagination of the audience, like the forest of Arden and the squares of Verona or Venice in Shakespeare. Undoubtedly, a Greek tragedy provided a beautiful spectacle, but this resulted from the costumes, poses, and grouping of actors and chorus.

Change of scene was rarely needed in tragedy; the peculiar arrangements of comedy do not concern us. Only two extant tragedies need it. In the *Eumenides* of Æschylus the change from the temple of Apollo at Delphi to Athena's temple in Athens is vital to the plot but need not have caused much trouble; probably convention was satisfied by changing the statue. In *Ajax* the scene shifts from that hero's tent to a deserted part of the sea-shore; no doubt the tent was simply removed. One reason against change of scene was the continuous presence of the chorus; when the playwright found he must shift his locality the chorus were compelled to retire and reappear. We read[1] of a permanent appliance by which scenery could be altered; there is, however, no evidence that it was known in the great age of Athenian drama. This consisted of the *periacti* (περίακτοι). At each end of the scene stood wooden triangular prisms standing on their ends and revolving in sockets, so arranged that one of the narrow oblong sides continued the picture. A different subject was painted on each side. A twist given to either marked a change of place; the alteration of one *periactus* meant a change of locality within the same region, while the alteration of both meant a complete change of district. Thus, had this contrivance been used in the fifth century, one *periactus* would have been moved in the *Ajax*, both in the *Eumenides*. Another and stranger use of this

---

[1] Vitruvius, V, vi., and Pollux, iv., 126.

contrivance is mentioned by Pollux: "it introduces sea-gods and everything which is too heavy for the machine". We shall return to this when we come to the "eccyclema" and the "machine". No curtain is known for the classical age.

Stage-properties were few and for the most part simple. Much the most important was the tomb of some great person; that of Darius in the *Persæ*, and of Agamemnon in the *Choephoræ*, are fundamental to the plot, and there are many other examples.[1] Statues have already been mentioned. The spaciousness of the orchestra made it easy to introduce chariots and horses, as in *Agamemnon*, Euripides' *Electra* and *Iphigenia at Aulis*.

Various contrivances were employed to permit the appearance of actors in circumstances where they could not simply enter the orchestra or *logeion*. We need not dwell upon certain quaint machinery which it is fairly certain was not used in the great age—"Charon's steps," by which ghosts ascended, the "anapiesma" which brought up river-gods and Furies, the "stropheion" which showed heroes in heaven and violent deaths, the "hemicyclion" by which the spectators were given a view of remote cities or of men swimming, the "bronteion," or thunder machine, consisting of a sheet of metal and sacks of stones to throw thereon, the "ceraunoscopeion" or lightning machine, a black plank with a flash painted upon it, which was shot across the stage. In the fifth century the theatrical contrivances amounted to four—the distegia, the theologeion, the "machine," and the eccyclema.

The distegia was employed when human beings showed themselves above the level of the "stage," for example on a roof or cliff. Such appearances are not common—the watchman (*Agamemnon*), Antigone and her nurse (*Phœnissæ*), Orestes and Pylades (*Orestes*),

---

[1] Professor Ridgeway makes much use of this custom in his theory that Greek drama originated in celebrations at the tombs of great persons. See his *Origin of Tragedy*, and pp. 2 *sq.* above.

Evadne (Euripidean *Supplices*), are all the occasions in existing tragedy; comedy supplies a few more. Probably it was "a projecting balcony or upper story, which might be introduced when required";[1] the word appears to mean "second story". The arrangement would then correspond closely to the gallery used at the back of the Elizabethan stage.

Similar to this was the "theologeion" ("speaking-place for gods"), on which gods or deified heroes appeared when they were not to be shown descending through the air. The arrangement seems to have been a platform in the upper part of the scenery. Whether it was fixed there and the actors entered through an opening to take their place, or whether it was used like the eccyclema (see below), is not clear.

We hear much more of the "machine" ($\mu\eta\chi\alpha\nu\dot{\eta}$) by which actors descended as from Heaven or ascended. It was a crane from which cords were attached to the actor's body; a stage-hand hauled the actor up or down by a winch. There are a good many instances of its use. The apparition of Thetis at the close of *Andromache* exemplifies the most customary happening. But sometimes the machine had to carry a greater burden; both the Dioscuri appear in Euripides' *Electra*, both Iris and Frenzy in *Hercules Furens*. Æschylus no doubt sent Oceanus on his four-legged bird by this route; possibly Medea, and the chariot containing her sons' bodies, were also suspended by it; and it has even been thought that the chorus of *Prometheus Vinctus* and their "winged chariot" enter in this way. But the last suggestion is very questionable. The weight would be excessive, and probably the car is supposed to be left outside, or may have been painted on a *periactus*. Aristophanes gets excellent fooling out of the machine. The celebrated basket in which Socrates "walks the air and contemplates the sun"[2] is attached to it; and in the *Peace* there is a delightful parody of Bellerophon's ascent to Heaven.

[1] Haigh³, p. 187.　　　[2] *Clouds*, 225.

Far more puzzling is the eccyclema. This celebrated device was employed to reveal to the spectators
events which had just taken place "within". After the
murders in the *Agamemnon* the palace doors are opened
and Clytæmnestra is shown standing axe in hand over
the corpses of Cassandra and the king. There are a
good many instances of precisely the same type: the
scene exhibited is a small *tableau*. But there are dissimilar examples which shall be discussed later. The
construction of this machine is usually described thus.
Inside the middle [1] door was a small oblong platform on
wheels, upon which the *tableau* was arranged; then the
platform was thrust out upon the stage and in a few
minutes drawn back again. Two quite different objections have been raised to this account.

First, it seems ridiculous to reveal what is supposed
to be inside a building—not to come out, be it observed,
but to stay inside—by thrusting forth one or two people
on a species of dray. But we must remember the
enormous and rightful influence of convention. If
Greek audiences wished to see such *tableaux* and were
convinced that by no other means could they be shown,
then it was their business to accept the eccyclema; that
in such circumstances they would accept and soon fail
even to notice it, is proved by the whole history of art.
We see nothing ludicrous in the spectacle of a man
telling his deepest secrets in a study one wall of which
is replaced by a vast assembly of eavesdroppers. The
Elizabethan theatre accepted precisely this contrivance
of the eccyclema. In our texts of *Henry VI* (Pt. II,
Act III, Sc. ii.) we read this stage-direction: "The
folding-doors of an inner chamber are thrown open, and
Gloucester is discovered dead in his bed: Warwick and
others standing by it". Instead of all this, the old
direction merely says: "Bed put forth". In another
early drama we find the amusing instruction: "Enter

---

[1] Pollux (iv. 128), who gives the most definite description, adds:
"one must understand it at each door, as it were in each house," but his
unsupported testimony on any subject is not trustworthy.

So-and-So in bed". The æsthetic objection to the eccyclema has no force whatever.

The other objection rests on the fact that a more elaborate *tableau* is sometimes indicated than could be accommodated on so narrow a platform. The most serious example is provided by the *Eumenides*, where we are to imagine upon the eccyclema an altar, Orestes kneeling by it, Apollo and Hermes standing beside him, and the whole chorus of Furies sleeping around them. In Aristophanes' *Clouds* the interior of Socrates' school is exhibited, with pupils at work amid lecture-room appliances. A brilliant scene of the same poet's *Acharnians* depicts Dicæopolis' interview with Euripides, who is too busy to come downstairs from his study-attic, but consents to be "wheeled out". Thus the eccyclema shows him outside and also aloft: how could this be represented on the dray? Perhaps by elevating poet and furniture upon posts? Even this is not inconceivable.[1] Nor is it impossible that the Furies of the *Eumenides* were arranged on two eccyclemata of their own, thrust out of the side doors, while Orestes and the gods were upon the central platform. For Pollux does say that there were three.

Other views of this machine have been offered, which explain the "wheeling" of which we read as the working of wheeled mechanism, such as a winch. Some would have it that the scenery opens, whether doors are flung wide, or the canvas is rolled back like curtains. In this way a considerable area behind the scenes could be revealed. This is, of course, infinitely more in accordance with modern ideas. But it will not fit all the available evidence, which talks of "wheeling in" and "wheeling out," "Roll this unhappy man within"[2] and the like. Moreover, in such a simple operation there would be nothing for Aristophanes to parody. A third

[1] In fact Pollux, who is fond of making a particular case into a general rule, may have had this instance in his head. He writes (iv. 128): "the eccyclema is a lofty stand raised upon timbers and carrying a chair" (ἐπὶ ξύλων ὑψηλὸν βάθρον ᾧ ἐπίκειται θρόνος).

[2] Ar. *Knights*, 1249.

explanation is that a considerable part of the back scene
was cut out and replaced so as to swing on a perpendicu-
lar axis. Projecting from this at the back was a small
platform, upon which the *tableau* was grouped; this
oblong portion was twisted round so that the platform
pointed towards the spectators. It resembled, in fact,
that contrivance in the modern Japanese theatre by
which one scene is prepared while the preceding action
takes place, and is swung into position when needed.
A grave objection to this is that some of the groups
—those in *Eumenides* and *Acharnians*—would be too
large for such a contrivance. The best view seems to
be the traditional, to which the evidence strongly points.
As for the large scenes so displayed, various tolerable
explanations may be found. Only one or two Furies
and Socratic novices may have appeared on the platform, and the others may have simply walked in through
the right and left doors, or even been shown on subsidiary
platforms at those entrances.

All other appurtenances of a performance were provided by the choregus—such things as chariots and
animals, and, far the most important, costumes of chorus
and actors. All dramatic performers, both actors and
chorus in tragedy, comedy, and satyric drama alike,
wore disguise throughout the whole history of the ancient
theatre. The reason in the first place was that masks
or some kind of facial disguise—in Thespis' time the
face was anointed with lees of wine—was a feature of
Dionysiac worship. The dressing of a tragic chorus
was generally a simple matter. It often represented a
company of people from the district with no special
characteristics. The dress was therefore the usual dress
of Greek men or women, with a special shoe, the *crēpis*
(κρηπίς), said to have been introduced by Sophocles.
There were also obvious indications of circumstances;
old men wore beards and carried staves; suppliants
bore olive-branches twined with wool. The occasional
choruses of peculiar character were of course equipped
specially. In Euripides' *Bacchæ* they were dressed in

fawn-skins and carried timbrels. When Æschylus brought out his *Eumenides* he designed the Furies' costume himself; their terrible masks and the snakes entwined in their hair are said to have terrified the spectators and produced most untoward effects on the more susceptible. The equipment of satyric choristers was very different. They were always dressed as satyrs or goat-men. A tight garment, representing the naked flesh, covered their bodies. Their masks were surmounted by horns, their feet were shod in hoof-shaped shoes, and round their middle they wore a woollen girdle like goatskin to which were attached the phallus and a tail, which, however, after about 400 B.C., resembled the tail of a horse, not a goat, the satyr-type being superseded by the Silenus-type. Satyric actors seem to have worn much the same costume as the tragic, save that the dress of Silenus represented the hides of animals.

The dress of tragic actors was mostly the invention of Æschylus and showed little change throughout ancient times. Everything was done to make the actor's appearance as stately as possible. His robes were heavy, sweeping, and of brilliant colours. His size was increased by various devices. The boot, the famous *cothurnus* (κόθορνος) or buskin, had an immensely thick sole; the limbs were padded and the height was further increased by an *oncus* (ὄγκος) or projection of the mask above the forehead. The mask itself was modelled and painted to correspond with the character: a tyrant's mask wore a frown, that of a suppliant a distorted look of misery, and so forth. Increased power was given to the voice by a large orifice at the mouth. Identity was indicated wherever possible by some obvious mark: Apollo was known by his bow, Heracles by his lion's skin and club, kings by crowns and sceptres. It was a joke against Euripides that his heroes so often entered in the rags of beggary.

Such a cumbersome equipment would be fatal to acting as we understand it. The mask at once destroys all chance of that facial play which we deem essential; the padded limbs, heavy garments, and gigantic boots made all life-like motion and *élan* impossible. This is no doubt one great reason why the playwrights rarely exhibit exciting physical action. Even so, the ludicrous sometimes occurred. Æschines when acting Œnomaus fell and had to be helped up by the chorus-trainer.[1] A natural supposition is that these impedimenta date not from Æschylus but from the period of vulgar elaboration. Certainly, it is not easy to imagine how such scenes as the delirium of Orestes, or the departure of Pentheus in the *Bacchæ*, could have been reasonably carried out—so to say—on stilts; indeed the whole spirit of such plays as *Orestes, Ion,* and *Iphigenia at Aulis* seems utterly alien to such equipment. But it is hard to set aside the voice of all the evidence. The best way would be to surmise that Euripides sometimes dispensed with buskins and the rest—though we should surely expect some allusion to so remarkable a change —for noble as is the work of his predecessors, it could be so performed without too absurd an effect. If Garrick's audience did not object to his playing Macbeth in a periwig and knee-breeches, it is likely enough that Athens was content with such a Clytæmnestra as Pollux would have us imagine.

V. The Performers and Their Work

A tragic performance was carried out by actors, extra performers, flute-player, and chorus. All these were men.

Extra performers, though they take up very little space in our text, were important to the spectacle. Mutes were often needed. Not only did these figure as attendants, crowds, and the like; they are sometimes important to the plot though they do not happen to speak. The jury of Areopagites in *Eumenides* is vital;

[1] This story occurs in the anonymous *Life* of Æschines.

children such as Eurysaces in *Ajax*, and the sons[1] of
Medea, are important. Other extra performers were
those who had very small speaking or singing parts,
such as Eumelus in *Alcestis*. This would seem to mean
a fourth actor, but, so slight was the part always[2] allotted,
that it is not an unreasonable statement that there were
never more than three actors. Thirdly, an extra chorus
was occasionally needed for a short scene, as the Pro-
pompi in *Eumenides* and the Huntsmen in *Hippolytus*.
Any such extra performer was called a *parachoregema*
(παραχορήγημα, " extra supply ") and was paid by the
choregus, as the name shows. (The regular chorus
was paid by the State.) At times a chorus sang behind
the scenes and was then called a " parascenion " ; this
function would, if possible, be performed by members of
the regular chorus.

Instrumental music was supplied by a single flute-
player, paid by the choregus. He was stationed in the
orchestra, very likely upon the step of the thymele, and
accompanied all songs. At times a harpist was added
to the flute-player ; Sophocles had great success with
that instrument in his own *Thamyris*. At the end of a
play the flute-player led the chorus out of the orchestra.
The music itself is a subject complicated and obscure.
Practically none of it has survived, and the details are
naturally difficult to determine ; but some main facts are
clear. Though there was much singing and dancing
the music composed by the tragedians was vastly more
simple than that of a modern opera. All choral singing
was in unison, and as a rule the words dominated the
music.[3] The result was that an audience followed the
language of an ode with ease, nor is it likely that such
lyrics as those of the *Agamemnon* or the Colonus-song,
not to mention many others, which are masterpieces of

---

[1] They are mutes, for the lines supposed to be uttered by one or both
behind the scenes were probably delivered by one of the actors not needed
" in front ".

[2] The *Œdipus Coloneus* is an exception. See Jebb's *Introduction*,
3rd ed., pp. 7, 8.

[3] Cp. the vigorous protest of Pratinas (p. 6).

literature, would have been written were they fated to
be drowned by elaborate music. Nevertheless a distinct change took place even in the fifth century, owing
chiefly to the eminent composer Timotheus, whose innovations were of course looked upon by conservative
taste as corrupt ; the comic playwright Pherecrates
grumbles about the way in which his notes scurry hither
and thither like ants in a nest,[1] a charge repeated almost
in the same words by Aristophanes against Agathon.
Euripides followed the new manner, and his novelties
are brilliantly caricatured in the *Frogs:* the elaborate
but thin *libretto* and the trills.[2] The increasing use
of monodies, or solos by an actor, which we find in
Euripides—the exotic but effective performance of the
Phrygian slave in *Orestes* is a conspicuous instance—
also points to the growing importance of musical virtu-
osity. Greek music was composed in certain modes
(νόμοι), the precise difference between which is not clear,
though the ethical distinctions are known. The Dorian
mode was austere and majestic, the Lydian and Mixo-
lydian plaintive, the Phrygian passionate.

We come now to the actors. These three performers were able to present more than three persons,
since they could change mask and costume behind
the scenes. One of them far outshone the others in
importance—the " protagonist " (πρωταγωνιστής, "first
competitor "). He alone was allotted to the poet by
the archon ; the " deuteragonist" and " tritagonist,"
he selected himself ; he alone could be a competitor
for the acting prize. The most important rôle was
of course performed by him. In many dramas this
was a vast responsibility ; Hamlet himself—the proverbial instance—is not more vital to his play than
Prometheus, Œdipus, or Medea to theirs. The other
two divided the minor parts among them ; it was the
custom to give a tritagonist the rôle of a king when
only spectacularly important—the Doge in *The Mer-*

---

[1] Pherecrates, *Cheiron*, frag. 1, cp. Arist. *Thesmoph.* 100.
[2] Ar. *Frogs*, 1314.

chant of Venice would have been just the part.   In
earlier dramas it is plain which rôle would be given
to the protagonist; there is no mistaking the pre-
eminence of Clytæmnestra in *Agamemnon* or of Philoctetes.   But in some later works it is not clear who is
the outstanding character.   In the *Bacchæ* Dionysus
and Pentheus, in the *Orestes* Electra and her brother,
have parts of fairly equal importance.   In such cases
the protagonist would take an important rôle and a
minor rôle.   Change of costume took little time, as
examination of structure sometimes shows.[1]

This restriction of the "company" to three actors
had important influence upon both plot and presentation.   As for plot, however many persons a dramatist
used, he clearly could not bring more than three of
them forward together.   But the power to do even
this was frugally used: there are but few instances
of a genuine three-cornered conversation; one of the
three in turn is generally silent.   In the Recognition-
scene of the *Tauric Iphigenia*, Orestes, Pylades, and
Iphigenia are all present, but though the *éclaircissement*
fills about two hundred lines, the only part of it in
which all three share is but twenty lines in length.
This frugality indicates that the simplicity of Greek
tragedy is a result not only of external conditions, but
of the poets' deliberate choice.   As for presentation,
the restriction to three actors would result in excellent
playing of minor parts: a thoroughly competent performer would discharge such short but important rôles
as that of the Butler in *Alcestis* and the Herald in
Agamemnon.   Anyone who has been depressed by
wooden Macduffs and Bassanios will realize the value
of this method.

A Greek actor combined the functions of a modern

---

[1] We hear from the scholiast on *Choephoræ*, 900, that the same actor
took the part of Pylades and of the servant who gives the alarm.   The
latter after arousing Clytæmnestra rushes within, and when the Queen has
uttered five lines Pylades appears accompanying Orestes.   This example
is given by Haigh[3], p. 232.

actor and of an operatic performer. Lyrics performed
by actor and chorus together were called "commi"
(κομμοί): the most elaborate instance is the great and
lengthy invocation of Agamemnon's shade in the
Choephoræ. A solo by an actor was known as a
"monody"; Euripides is particularly fond of these;
Ion's song is perhaps the most attractive. Finally, two
or three actors might sing alternately to each other without the chorus; no name for this has been preserved.
Certain other passages were neither sung nor spoken,
but delivered in recitative: in tragedy these were the
dialogue-trochaics and anapæsts. Iambics were spoken
(or "declaimed"). Obviously the voice is of great importance to an actor's proficiency, above all in a vast
open-air theatre, but Greek writers lay even more stress
upon it than we should have expected. Both volume
and subtlety were demanded. This is illustrated by a
famous story.[1] An actor named Hegelochus ruined the
sick-bed scene in *Orestes* by a slip in pronunciation.
Orestes, on recovering from delirium, says (v. 279):—

ἐκ κυμάτων γὰρ αὖθις αὖ γαλήν' ὁρῶ

"after the billows once more I see a calm". The un-
lucky player instead of saying γαλήν' said γαλῆν, "once
more do I see a weasel coming out of the waves". The
theatre burst into laughter, for correct pronunciation was
far more insisted upon than in the English theatre of
to-day.[2] The status of the acting profession rose steadily
as time went on. At first the poet acted as protagonist,
but this practice was dropped by Sophocles, owing to
the weakness of his voice. From that time acting was
free to develop as a separate profession. In the middle

---

[1] Told by the scholiast on Aristophanes, *Frogs*, 303.

[2] The slovenliness in this regard of many modern actors is mostly
due to "long runs". After saying the same thing hundreds of times, an
actor naturally tends to mechanical diction. The writer has heard a performer in an emotional crisis suddenly (as it appeared) call for cham-
pagne. Feeling sure that "Pommery" could not be right, he reflected,
and discovered that the mysterious syllables meant "Poor Mary!" Even
actors at the head of the profession are guilty of such things as "the lor
of Venice".

of the fifth century a prize for acting was instituted, and the actor's name began to be added in the official records of victories. In the fourth century the importance of the player increased still more. We have seen that he was so vital to the success of a playwright that for fairness' sake the three protagonists each acted in a single tragedy of each poet. We often hear of brilliant acting successes. In the fourth century an Actors' Guild was formed at Athens and continued in existence for centuries. Its object was to protect the remarkable privileges held by the "artists of Dionysus". They were looked upon as great servants of religion, and were not only in high social esteem but possessed definite privileges, especially the right of safe-conduct through hostile states and exemption from military service. About the beginning of the third century before Christ the Amphictyonic Council, at the instance of the Guild itself, renewed a decree, the terms of which have fortunately been preserved,[1] affirming the immunity of person and property granted to the Athenian actors.

The chorus, we have seen, was originally the only celebrant of the Dionysiac festival. As the importance of the actors increased it became less and less vital to the performance. Its numbers, its connexion with the plot, and the length and relevance of its songs, all steadily diminished.

Originally there were fifty choristers, but we learn that early in the fifth century there were only twelve, and it is suggested that this change was due to the introduction of tetralogies—the fifty choreutæ being divided as equally as possible between the four dramas. Sophocles, it is said, raised the number to fifteen. This account is doubtful. It is not in the nature of things likely that Æschylus (if it was he) caused or approved such an immense drop in numbers, from fifty to twelve : for the notion that the original chorus was split up into four is frivolous. Is it not obvious that a poet would

---

[1] See Haigh [3], p. 279 *sq.*, for some highly interesting extracts.

employ the same choristers for each play of his tetralogy?
Again, that Sophocles should chafe at Æschylus' twelve
singers and alter the number, and that by a mere trifle
of three, is quite unlikely. There is, moreover, strong
evidence that the elder poet used fifty choreutæ, at any
rate in his earlier time. The *Supplices* has for chorus
the daughters of Danaus, and their exact number, fifty,
was a familiar *datum* of the legend. The natural view
is that Æschylus began with fifty, that Sophocles
ended with fifteen, and that between these two points
the number gradually sank. Whether the choreutæ
after the fifth century became still fewer is not clearly
known; there is some evidence that at times they were
only seven.

Next, the dramatic value of the chorus steadily went
down. In our earliest tragedy, the Æschylean *Supplices*,
the chorus of Danaids is absolutely vital; they are the
chief, almost the sole, interest. In other works of the
same poet their importance is certainly less, but still very
great; everywhere they are deeply interested in the
fate of the chief persons—Xerxes, Eteocles, Prometheus,
Agamemnon, Orestes; the chorus of the *Eumenides* is
even more closely attached to the plot. In Sophocles a
certain change is to be felt. The connexion between
chorus and plot is of much the same quality as in the
five plays just mentioned, but the emotional tie and
(still more) the tie of self-interest are weaker. The
chorus of Greek seamen in *Philoctetes* are (in the ab-
stract) as deeply concerned in the issue as the Oceanids
in *Prometheus*, but most readers would probably agree
that they show it less; we can "think away" the chorus
more easily from the *Philoctetes*. In all the other six
Sophoclean dramas the interest of the chorus in the
action is about the same as in the *Philoctetes*—strong but
scarcely vital. Euripides' work shows more variety.
*Alcestis, Heracleidæ, Hecuba, Ion, Troades, Iphigenia in
Tauris, Helen*, and *Rhesus* all possess choruses which
are *prima-facie* Sophoclean in this regard, though their
language tends to show less personal concern. In other

dramas, *Medea, Hippolytus, Andromache, Electra, Phœnissæ, Orestes, Iphigenia at Aulis,* the chorus is simply a company of spectators. Thirdly, in two plays, *Supplices* and *Bacchæ,* the importance of the chorus is thoroughly Æschylean. In Euripides, then, there is found on the whole a weakening in the dramatic value of the chorus: in some instances the singers are little more than random visitors. In the fourth century Aristotle protests against this: "the chorus too should be regarded as one of the actors; it should be an integral part of the whole, and share in the action, in the manner not of Euripides but of Sophocles".[1]

A precisely similar change operated in the length of the ode. The lyrics of Æschylus' *Supplices* form more than half the work, those of *Orestes* only one-ninth. Even at the end of Æschylus' career we find in the *Agamemnon* odes magnificent, elaborate, and lengthy. Sophocles composed shorter songs which were still closely germane to the plot. But in Euripides there frequently occur lyrics whose connexion with the plot is slight, sometimes difficult to make out. Agathon carried this still further: his odes are mere interludes, quite outside the plot.[2]

The fifteen choristers usually entered through the *parodos,* marching like soldiers.[3] Drawn up in ranks upon the orchestra, they followed the action with their backs to the audience but faced about when they sang. Their work fell into two parts, the odes sung between the episodes, and participation in the episodes. The entrance-song was called the *parodos* or "entrance," and was written in anapæstic rhythm, suitable for marching. If so, it was chanted in recitative; lyrics were sung. Songs between episodes were called *stasima.* This means "stationary songs," not because the singers stood still but because they had taken up their station

---

[1] *Poetic,* 1456a (tr. Butcher). [2] *Ibid.*
[3] This was the normal mode of entry, but the plot sometimes demanded others. In the *Eumenides* the Chorus rush in pell-mell; so probably in the *Bacchæ;* in the Euripidean *Supplices* they are discovered grouped around the Queen.

in the orchestra. As they left at the end they sang an *exodos* or "exit" in anapæsts. Besides these, there were occasional *hyporchemes* (ὑπορχήματα, "dances"), short, lively songs expressing sudden joy. All lyrics were rendered by both song and dance. Singing was generally executed by all the choreutæ, but some passages were divided between them. The most frequent division was into two semi-choruses (ἡμιχόρια), but now and then individuals sang a few words. Incidental iambic lines were spoken by one person, and the short anapæstic system which at the end of the lyric often announces the approach of an actor was no doubt assigned to the *coryphæus*, or chorus-leader alone. Dancing was also an essential feature, but both Greeks and Romans meant more by dancing than do we, or than we did before the rise of "Salome" performances. It was in fact a mimetic display, giving by the rhythmic manipulation of all the limbs an imitation of the emotions expressed, or the events described, by the song. The whole company, moreover, went through certain evolutions over the surface of the orchestra. When they sang the *strophe*[1] they moved in one direction, back again for the *antistrophe*,[1] and perhaps stood still when there was an *epode*.[1] But nothing is known as to details here. The centre of all the dancing was the coryphæus (κορυφαῖος, "top man"), the leader of the chorus ; when two semi-choruses acted separately each had its leader. As was natural, choric dancing flourished mightily in the early days, and went down with lyrical performance in general. Thus Phrynichus congratulated himself on having devised "as many figures of the dance as are the billows on the sea under a dread night of storm". Æschylus too was a brilliant ballet-master. But Plato, the comic playwright, at the end of the same century grumbles[2] amusingly :—

---

[1] See pp. 344 *sq.*

[2] ὥστ᾽ εἴ τις ὀρχοῖτ᾽ εὖ, θέαμ᾽ ἦν · νῦν δὲ δρῶσιν οὐδέν,
ἀλλ᾽ ὥσπερ ἀπόπληκτοι βάδην ἑστῶτες ὠρύονται.

> There was something to watch when the dancing was good,
>   But now there's no acting to mention—
> Just a paralysed row of inflexible singers,
>   Who howl as they stand at attention.

During the best period of the chorus its mimetic dancing must have been a wonderful spectacle. We hear of highly-skilled performers who could reproduce action so that the audience followed every detail. They seem to have "accompanied" some portions of the episodes in this manner; and that fact may account for a rather curious feature in the *Ion*. The messenger gives a remarkably detailed description of the designs upon the embroideries wherewith Ion roofed his great banqueting-marquee — the constellations and " Dawn pursuing the stars" are all described. Possibly this was written for the sake of an unusually brilliant mimetic evolution by groups of choreutæ.

The chorus had other duties during the episodes. As a body they normally showed themselves interested spectators; thus the chorus of *Orestes* enter in order to inquire of Electra concerning her sick brother. Not infrequently they do more, taking an actual share in events. At the close of *Agamemnon* the Argive elders are at point to do battle with Ægisthus and his henchmen; in *Alcestis* they join the funeral procession; at other times they aid the persons of the play, not only by misleading enemies (*Choephoræ*) or directing friends (*Œdipus Tyrannus*) but by keeping watch (*Orestes*). Further, the coryphæus almost always delivers two or three lines at the end of every long speech, save when it ends a scene. These little interpolations are invariably obvious and feeble. After Hermione's tirade against women the coryphæus comments thus: "Too freely hast thou indulged thy tongue against thy sex. It is pardonable in thee, but still women should gloss over the weaknesses of women." Anyone who has listened to the delivery of some splendid passage in Shakespeare, an outburst of Lear or Mercutio's Queen Mab speech, will remember how the applause which follows it drowns the next speaker's opening lines. Some pause is needed. This is provided in Greek tragedy by the insertion of a line or two which will not be missed if inaudible.

The satyric chorus diverged little from the tragic in the points discussed under this section. It had, however, a special type of dance called the "Sikinnis". "One of the postures used . . . was called the owl, and is variously explained by the old grammarians as having consisted in shading the eyes with the hands, or in turning the head to and fro like an owl."[1]

VI. The Audience

The time of the Dionysiac festivals, especially the great Dionysia, was a holiday for all Athens, and the centre of enjoyment was the show of tragedies and comedies. At sunrise the theatre was filled with a huge throng prepared to sit packed together for hours facing the sun with no interval for a meal or for exercise. It is important to remember that in Athens that incalculable play-goer, "the average man," did really enjoy and appreciate first-class dramatic work.

There were a few rows of special seats for officials and persons otherwise honoured by the State. All the rest of the space, save for the separation of men and women, and the possibility that each *cercis* was allotted to a distinct tribe, was open to all without distinction of rank or means. The official seats were in the front rows, and the first row of all consisted of sixty-seven marble thrones, most of which are still preserved *in situ*. Of these sixty-seven, fifty belonged—as the inscriptions show—to ecclesiastics, and the famous middle throne— the best and most conspicuous[2] place in the theatre— was occupied by the priest of Dionysus of Eleutheræ.

---

[1] Haigh[3], p. 318. Both the gestures described sound like a curious anticipation of the gestures favoured by the performers of "coon-songs".

[2] This was not always an advantage when comedy held the scene. There is a delightfully impudent passage in the *Frogs* (v. 297) where Dionysus to escape a hobgoblin appeals to his own priest for protection.

Besides priests, the archons, the generals, and the ten judges had special places, also benefactors of the State or their descendants, and the sons of men who had fallen in battle. Ambassadors from abroad, too, received this compliment of προεδρία ("foremost seat").

Behind the dignified front circle of thrones rose tier after tier of stone benches, all alike and not marked off into separate seats, so that the audience must usually have been crowded. They were also cramped, for the height of each seat was but fifteen inches.[1] Spectators brought with them any cushions they needed. Admission to the theatre was allowed in the first instance to any Athenian citizen. In spite of the indecency which was a normal[2] feature of the Old Comedy, there is no doubt that women and boys were present at the shows both of tragedy and comedy. Slaves and foreigners also were admitted, obtaining admission, like the boys and women, through citizens. Foreigners, except the distinguished persons to whom *proedria* was granted, seem to have been confined to the extreme right and left *cercides*, next to the *parodoi*. All the seating which has been described dates from the time of the orator Lycurgus[3] in the fourth century ; during the fifth Athens was content with wooden benches, called *icria* (ἴκρια, "planks").

Admission was at first free, but the drama was so popular that the rush for seats caused much confusion ; it is said that the more sedulous would secure places the night before. In the fifth century the custom arose of charging for admission, and making every one book in advance, save those dignitaries whose places were reserved. The price for one day was two obols (about threepence in weight, but of much greater purchasing

---

[1] For a detailed description of the seating see Haigh[3], pp. 94-101.

[2] It is a fact familiar to students of comparative religion that obscenity is often a part of ritual. This is true of several Greek worships, including that of Dionysus. Hence even tragedy retained its satyric complement, though satyric drama regularly showed obscene features.

[3] Puchstein would date it earlier (end of the fifth century).

power).   At the end of that century this sum was paid
by the State to any citizen who claimed it.   The money
allotted for this purpose was called the "theoric" fund
(τὸ θεωρικόν, "money for the shows"), of which we
hear so much in the speeches of Demosthenes.   By
his time the system had grown to a serious danger.
Payments were made, not only for the original purpose,
but for all the numerous festivals, and a law was actually
passed that anyone who proposed to apply the fund in
any other way should be put to death.   Demosthenes
represents the theoric fund and the Athenian affection
for it as preventing Athens from supplying sufficient
forces to check the growing menace from Philip of
Macedonia.   On paying in his two obols the spectator
received a ticket of lead.   The sums taken were appro-
priated by the lessee or *architecton* who in consideration
thereof kept the theatre in repair.

As the auditorium was filled with many thousands of
lively Southerners, who had to sit crammed together
from sunrise till late in the day with no intermission,
the question of good order might seem to have been
a hopeless difficulty.   It was not so.   For, first, the
occasion was religious, and to use blows in the theatre
was a capital crime.   Next, stewards (ῥαβδοφόροι,
"rod-bearers") were at hand to keep order among the
choristers, who were numerous, seeing that each dithy-
rambic chorus consisted of fifty men.   Finally, a good
deal of exuberant behaviour was allowed.   Serious
disturbance occasionally happened : the high-spirited
Alcibiades once had a bout at fisticuffs with a rival
choregus, and the occasion of Demosthenes' speech
against Meidias was the blow which Meidias dealt the
orator when the latter was choregus.

Though an Athenian audience had no objection,
when comedy was played, to scenes which we should
have supposed likely to strike them as blasphemous,
they bitterly objected to any breach of orthodoxy in
tragic drama.   Æschylus once narrowly escaped death
because it was thought that a passage in his play con-

stituted a revelation of the mysteries. Euripides,[1] too, incurred great trouble owing to the opening lines of *Melanippe the Wise*. Approval and dislike were freely expressed. If the spectators admired a passage, shouts and clapping showed it : at times they would "encore" a speech or song with the exclamation αὖθις ("again"). Still more often do we hear of their proneness to "damn" a bad play. Hissing[2] was common, and there was a special custom at Athens of kicking with the heels upon the benches to express disapproval—a method which must have been effective in the time of wooden seats. Playwrights were known to take vigorous means to win favour. That distinguished writer of New Comedy, Philemon, is said to have defeated Menander himself by securing a large attendance of supporters to applaud his work, and it is certain that writers of the Old Comedy frequently directed their actors to throw nuts and similar offerings among the audience. In the *Peace* of Aristophanes barley was thus distributed. The spectators sometimes replied in kind. Bad performers were pelted with fruit, at any rate in the country, and even stones were used in extreme cases. The celebrated Æschines, during his career as a strolling tritagonist, was nearly stoned to death by his public.[3] But the fruit was generally used in the city itself for another purpose. Aristotle illustrates a detail of psychology by pointing to the fact that "in the theatre people who eat dessert do so with most abandon when the performers are bad".[4]

[1] Plutarch, *Liber Amatorius*, 756 B, C.
[2] ἐκσυρίττειν ("to hiss off").
[3] Demosthenes, *De Falsa Legatione*, §337.
[4] *Ethics*, X, 1175 B.

CHAPTER III

THE WORKS OF ÆSCHYLUS

THE place of Æschylus in dramatic history has been discussed in the first chapter. We have still to give some account of his seven extant plays and of the fragments.

The SUPPLICES [1] ('Ικετίδες, "Suppliant Women ") is no doubt the earliest of these. The scene is laid near the sea-coast, not far from Argos. The chorus, consisting of the fifty daughters of Danaus, enter, and in their opening song tell how they have fled from Egypt to escape marriage with their cousins, the fifty sons of Ægyptus. These suitors have pursued them overseas, but they call upon Zeus, who through Io is their ancestor, to defend them. Danaus, their father, urges them to take refuge upon the steps of the altar.[2] This they do, becoming suppliants of the State-deities and acquiring a claim upon the citizens. The King of Argos enters; to him the women make their appeal. He replies that he must consult the national assembly before facing the possibility of war with the Egyptians; meanwhile he sends Danaus into the city to engage the compassion of the Argives. After another song by the chorus, in which they relate the wanderings of Io and her final peace, Danaus returns with the news that the Argive assembly is unanimous in championing the

---

[1] *Date :* uncertain. Professor Tucker thinks the year 492-1 probable; Æschylus was then thirty-three years old. Historical considerations are here of doubtful value, but the technique of the play seems to prove beyond question that it is an early work.

Arrangement : protagonist, Danaus, Egyptian herald; deuteragonist, King of Argos.

[2] In the centre of the orchestra, as always.

Suppliants; the women burst forth into lyrical blessings upon the land. Danaus, who has been upon the watch, announces the approach of the hostile ships; he comforts his shrinking daughters, goes to fetch help, and does not return until the danger is over.[1] After a terrified lyric, the Egyptian herald appears, accompanied no doubt by warriors; he harshly bids them go to the ship and submit to their masters. They refuse. He is on the point of dragging them away when the King enters, rebukes the herald, and defies the power of Egypt. The intruder departs with threats of war. Danaus returns, and with his daughters is given lodging within the city-walls. The chorus end the drama with an ode voicing their fear of war and oppression.

Such a close evidently implies that the story was continued in another work, and it has been conjectured that the *Egyptians* and the *Danaides* ("Daughters of Danaus") formed the second and third parts of the trilogy. Scarcely anything of these two plays has been preserved, but there is good reason to suppose that the Egyptians were victorious, that the daughters of Danaus were compelled to marry their ferocious suitors, and that on the command of their father each slew her husband on the wedding-night. Hypermnestra alone spared her lover, by name Lynceus. It seems that she was put on her trial for this disobedience and was saved by the advocacy of Aphrodite, who thus foreshadows the Apollo of the *Eumenides*. The satyric play was perhaps the *Amymone;* this was the name of one of the Danaides, who was delivered from a satyr by Poseidon. Viewed not historically, but æsthetically, especially by a reader already familiar with the *Oresteia*, the play must be confessed bald and monotonous. Many of Æschylus' most splendid attributes, it is true, are to be discerned, but their fire too often sinks into smouldering grimness. The only really fine passages are those portions of the lyrics which bear the impress of

[1] Danaus is necessarily dismissed so that the actor who impersonates him may appear as the Egyptian herald.

the poet's masculine and profound theology.   Such
strictures, however, are merely one way of saying that
the *Supplices* is an early work.   It would be fairer
(were it only possible) to compare it with the drama of
Phrynichus rather than with the *Agamemnon*.   Here,
perhaps for the first time, we have a genuinely dramatic
situation—the collision between the king and the herald.
There is little characterization.   The chorus are simply
distressed damsels (save for their vivid and strong religious faith), the king is simply a magnanimous and
wary monarch, the herald simply a "myrmidon".
Danaus, however, shows some interesting traits.   He
is extremely sententious and rejoices in the fact : "In-
scribe this on your hearts beside the many other precepts
of your father written there".[1]   His exhortation[2] to
chaste behaviour, though long and (as his daughters
assure him) unnecessary, is, albeit corrupt textually,
one of the most striking passages in the play.   But one
feels that characterization is perhaps less needed in a
work which, literally from the first word, is filled with
the name of God, Zeus,[3] the ancestor of the Danaids,
the lord of the universe, the guardian of right.   "And
whensoever it is decreed by nod of Zeus that a thing
be brought to fullness, it falls not prostrate, but on its
feet.   Yea, through thicket and shadow stretch the
paths of his decrees, that no thoughts can spy them
out."[4]   Equally majestic is the language concerning
that other Zeus[5] who judges the sins of men in Hades.
Finally, though the thought and diction are in the main
stark if dignified, a change comes over the play before
the end : we get a little "atmosphere".   Danaus
already fears personal enemies (v. 1008), and the arrangements for lodging the suppliants show a tinge of
domesticity.

The PERSÆ[6] (Πέρσαι, "Men of Persia"), though

---

[1] vv. 991-2.   [2] vv. 994-1013.
[3] Ζεύς (or words derived therefrom) occurs about sixty times.
[4] vv. 91-5 (Professor Tucker's translation).   [5] vv. 230-1.
[6] *Date :* 472 B.C.   *Arrangement :* protagonist, Atossa and Xerxes ;
deuteragonist, Messenger and Darius.

perhaps twenty years later, comes next among the surviving plays. The action takes place before the palace of Xerxes. It opens with a song from the chorus, who represent aged councillors of the Persian Empire. They describe the departure of the host which is to conquer Greece, and their own anxiety for news. Atossa, widow of Darius and mother of Xerxes, enters, distressed by an ill-omened dream. The councillors discuss this portent and the prospects of victory. A messenger arrives who announces the complete overthrow of the "barbarians". The queen speedily rallies from her grief, learns that her son himself is safe, and hears the narrative of Salamis and the flight of the Persians back to Asia. She determines to offer supplications to Heaven and retires to fetch the materials of sacrifice; the chorus pour forth a lyric lament and deplore the loss of Darius the conqueror. Atossa· returns bearing the libation which she offers to the shade of Darius, while the chorus invoke the dead king, praying him to appear and give counsel. In answer, the ghost of Darius rises from his tomb. He learns the evil tidings, laments the impious folly of his son, and foretells the coming disaster of Platæa. After the shade has sunk back into the tomb, and Atossa has gone to meet Xerxes,[1] the elders sing of Persia's greatness under Darius. Finally, Xerxes appears, plunged in despair. Amid the antiphonal wailings of the king and his councillors the tragedy ends.

The scholiast says that " Æschylus won the prize in the archonship of Menon, with *Phineus, Persæ, Glaucus of Potniæ* and *Prometheus*".[2] This tetralogy seems (to judge from the titles and the fragments) to have been a collection of plays which had no relation of subject-matter. Interesting to the historian as the only extant tragedy dealing with a contemporary subject, the *Persæ* also wins the highest admiration as a piece of literature not unworthy of its theme. The muscular

---

[1] The actor who presents the queen has now to present the king.
[2] This was a satyric play, and must not be confused with the extant *Prometheus*.

and majestic diction of the speeches, the noble sweep
of the lyrics, the colossal dignity of the characters, the
picturesqueness and vigour which make the story of
Salamis one of the greatest passages even in Æschylus
—these are characteristics of the poet which the *Supplices* presents only in germ. But the noblest feature
of the whole is the manner in which Æschylus has faced
his chief obstacle. To dramatize the heroic spirit and
overwhelming success of Athens in the presence of
Athenians—was this an easy task? Nothing could be
more cloying at the moment, more thin and unsatisfying
to the after-reflection. Æschylus rises clear above all
this. First, he places the scene not in Athens, but before the gates of the palace at Susa; that dignity which
elsewhere in Greek tragedy is secured by remoteness in
time, is here obtained by remoteness in space.[1] The
whole incident is held at arm's length that it may be
viewed with soberness, and as a whole in perspective.
Next, it has often been observed that on the one hand
he chronicles a host of Asiatic nobles while on the other
not a single Greek—not even Themistocles—is named.
Both these facts spring from the same source. Æschylus,
it cannot be repeated too often, was a deeply religious
man. When he takes it in hand to dramatize an event
of recent history his instinct impels him, just as infallibly
as if he were writing of Heracles or Prometheus, to describe occurrences not in the language of politics or of
tactics, but of theology. Athens has been but the instrument of Heaven; Persia has fallen, not through the
brawn of oarsmen or the skill of captains, but through
the blasphemous infatuation of her prince and the wrath
of God following thereupon.

> O God, thy arm was here;
> And not to us, but to thy arm alone,
> Ascribe we all! When, without stratagem,
> But in plain shock and even play of battle,
> Was ever known so great and little loss
> On one part and on th' other? Take it, God,
> For it is none but thine![2]

[1] See Patin, *Eschyle*, p. 211.   [2] *Henry V*, IV, viii.

He is little concerned with that play of human psychology on the Greek side, which forms so brilliant a page of Herodotus.   Even when he narrates that trick by which the conflict was precipitated, the false message from Themistocles to Xerxes, nothing is said of the reasons for sending it.   Though the antecedent "facts" are known, yet he chooses to tell what he does indeed regard as the truth, that the whole error of the king came from "a fiend or evil spirit," and that he fell into the trap because "he perceived not the guile of the Greek nor *the spite of Heaven*".[1]   On the Greek side, then, "the creatures of a day" are lost in the vision of eternal righteousness.   But the poet has no such reason to obliterate the mighty names of Persia.   Almost the whole effect of them is for us lost ; but to an Athenian ear these barbaric polysyllables must have sounded with all the pomp of an ancient chivalry, the waves of the boundless and terrible Orient descending in deluge upon the tiny states of Hellas.   But the billows at their highest had been stayed and had sunk ; the appalling roll of warlike titles was changed into a proclamation of glory—but not the glory of Greece.   No Greek name is immortalized in this play, which resounds at every moment with the name of God.

The SEVEN AGAINST THEBES [2] (Οἱ Ἑπτὰ ἐπὶ Θήβας) was produced in 467 B.C. and deals with the fratricidal quarrel of the sons of Œdipus.   Eteocles, the elder, had become King of Thebes and expelled his brother Polynices.   The latter with six comrades-in-arms and an host led by Adrastus, King of Argos, attacked the city. The seven invading champions were met at the seven gates by as many Theban warriors.   The scene is laid in an open space in the town.   A messenger brings to Eteocles the news that the enemy are on the point of assaulting the walls.   The chorus, consisting of Theban maidens, enter, and in a vivid lyric express their frantic terror.

---

[1] vv. 361-2.
[2] *Arrangement :* protagonist : Eteocles and Antigone ; deuteragonist, messenger, and herald.   The part of Ismene was taken by a member of the chorus,

Eteocles attempts to calm them, urging that their out-cries will demoralize the citizens; but soon they burst forth again into wild forebodings. Then follows a long scene in which the messenger describes the seven heroes who are to attack at the seven gates. As each is de-scribed Eteocles allots one of his comrades for defence. The seventh enemy is Polynices, the king's own brother; Eteocles, spurred on by the curse of his house, declares that he will himself confront Polynices. He rushes away and the maidens lament the frightful story of Œdipus' curse. The messenger returns with the news that the invaders have been routed and that the brothers have fallen by each other's hand. After the chorus have lamented this crime, the corpses are brought forward, accompanied by Antigone and Ismene, sisters of the dead, who utter an antiphonal dirge. They are inter-rupted by a herald who proclaims the decree of the "people's councillors". Eteocles is to be honourably buried; his brother is to be left to the dogs and birds of prey. Antigone defies the decree and declares that she will bury Polynices. The chorus divide into two parties, one supporting Antigone, the other giving obedience to the State.

This tragedy won the prize. The trilogy consisted of *Laius*, *Œdipus*, the *Seven*, with the *Sphinx* as satyric play. Aristeas and Polyphradmon, the sons of Pratinas and Phrynichus respectively, were second and third. Very little is known about the companion plays. The *Laius* contained a reference to the exposure of the infant Œdipus; the *Œdipus* described the death of Laius.

The *Seven* is a magnificently vigorous and graphic presentment of war in one of its aspects. As such it is eulogized by Aristophanes, who puts into the mouth of Æschylus the boast that he "composed a drama full of the War-God—my *Seven against Thebes*".[1] The chief excellences are the first chorus and the celebrated Choos-ing of the Champions. This latter contained the best-

---

[1] *Frogs*, 1021.

known passage in the play, where the messenger says of
Amphiaraus:—[1]

σῆμα δ' οὐκ ἐπῆν κύκλῳ
οὐ γὰρ δοκεῖν ἄριστος, ἀλλ' εἶναι θέλει,
βαθεῖαν ἄλοκα διὰ φρενὸς καρπούμενος,
ἐξ ἧς τὰ κεδνὰ βλαστάνει βουλεύματα.

His buckler bore no blazon ; for he seeks
Not to seem great, but to be great indeed,
Reaping the deep-ploughed furrow of his soul
Wherefrom the harvest of good counsel springs.

As these lines were declaimed in the theatre, Plutarch[2]
tells us, every one turned and gazed at Aristides
the Just. The first half of the play is in strictness not
dramatic[3] at all—a merely static presentment of the
situation : a city in a state of siege, panic among the
women, resolution in the mind of the general. The
later portion gives us decisive action. The King rushes
to his fratricidal duel, spurred on by the invisible curse ;
but even here there is no dramatic conflict of personalities
like the altercation between the brothers in the *Phœnissæ* of Euripides. Such a collision is, however, provided at the very end, where Antigone defies the State.

As regards the PROMETHEUS VINCTUS (Προμηθεὺς
δεσμώτης, " Prometheus Bound ") we are in doubt as
to the date, the arrangement of the cast, and the other
parts of the trilogy.

Concerning the date, we know that the play was
written after 475 B.C., the year in which occurred that
eruption of Etna described by Prometheus (vv. 363-72).
Further, it is usually regarded as later than the *Seven*
owing to the increased preponderance of dialogue over
lyrics. Also, the supposition that three actors are required
has led some scholars to believe that the *Prometheus*
belongs to the period when Sophocles had introduced a

---

[1] vv. 591-4.   [2] *Life of Aristides*, III.
[3] Dr. Verrall, however, in his Introduction (pp. xiv, xv) sees technical
drama of the highest kind in the choosing of the champions. As the
Theban warriors are told off one by one, the chorus (and audience) see
with ever-increasing horror that Eteocles must be left as the opponent of
Polynices,

third actor, and so to place it in the last part of the poet's life.[1] The static nature of the drama might seem to forbid such a view, but possibly it formed the centre of the trilogy, the most likely place for an equilibrium of the tragic forces. And the theological basis of the whole series is so profound, that an approximation in date to the *Oresteia* is not unreasonable. On the whole, then, the *Prometheus* may be conjecturally assigned to about the year 465 B.C.

As for the division of the parts among the actors, we find in the opening scene three[2] persons engaged, Prometheus, Hephæstus, and Cratos (" Strength "). Prometheus, however, does not utter a word until his tormentors have retired, and it has been held that only two actors are needed here (as in the rest of the work). On this view, Prometheus would be represented by a lay-figure, either Hephæstus or Cratos would return unseen, delivering the later speeches of Prometheus from behind the figure, through a mouth-piece in the head. But as there was no curtain in the theatre, it would be necessary for the executioners to carry the lay-figure forth in view of the audience before the action began. The true objection to this is not its absurdity ; an audience will tolerate much awkwardness in stage-management, if only it is accustomed to such conventions. But it would scarcely have harmed the play if the poet had dispensed with Cratos ; the actor thus disengaged could have impersonated Prometheus from the beginning. That Æschylus saw this possibility cannot be doubted ; therefore he did not feel bound to use a lay-figure ; therefore he did not, and we must assume that he employed three actors.

Two other tragedies were associated with this, *Prometheus the Fire-bringer* (Προμηθεὺς πυρφόρος) and

---

[1] Müller-Heitz (*Griechische Litteraturgeschichte*, ii. p. 88) point out, also, that this play needs more elaborate machinery than any other extant drama. But it may well be doubted whether all the effects mentioned by the poet are realized.

[2] Bia (" Violence "), also present, is a mute.

Prometheus Unbound (Προμηθεὺς λυόμενος). That the latter followed the extant play is of course certain, but the position of the *Fire-bringer* is doubtful. One would naturally place it first in the trilogy : the offence, the punishment, the reconciliation. But, say some, in that case one can hardly imagine how Æschylus wrote the first tragedy without anticipating a great part of the second—the noble account which Prometheus gives of the victory of Zeus, his own offence, and the blessings it conferred upon men. Hence arises a theory that the *Fire-bringer* was the last play of the trilogy in which the Titan, reconciled to Zeus, became a local deity of Athens, the giver of fire. But this view has been discredited by evidence[1] that there is not enough matter, remaining for the *Fire-bringer* after the close of the *Prometheus Unbound.* These two difficulties about the position of the *Fire-bringer* have induced some to identify it with that *Prometheus* which we know as the satyric play appended to the *Persæ* trilogy, and to suppose that Æschylus told the story in two plays only, the present trilogy being completed by a tragedy unconnected with the subject. The best view is that the *Fire-bringer* was the first play ; the title suggests that it dealt with the transgression which led to the punishment portrayed in the extant drama; and the objection as to overlapping of the *Fire-bringer* and the *Prometheus Vinctus* is illusory.

The scene is a desolate gorge in Scythia. Hephæstus, the God of Fire, with Cratos and Bia, Strength and Violence, servants of Zeus, appear, dragging with them the Titan Prometheus. Hephæstus nails the prisoner to the rocks under the superintendence of Cratos; he has little liking for his task, but Cratos rebukes his tenderness for the malefactor who has braved Heaven in order to succour mankind. At length Prometheus is left to his lonely agony. Hitherto he has been silent, but now he voices his pain and indignation to the sea

[1] See H. Weil's masterly *Note sur le Prométhée d'Eschyle* (*Le drame antique*, pp. 86-92).

and sky and earth around him. His soliloquy breaks off as he catches the sound of wings, and the chorus enter—a band of sea-nymphs who have been startled from their cave by the clatter of iron. They strive to comfort him, and he tells how by his counsel Zeus was enabled to defeat the Titans. Then, consolidating his empire, the god determined to destroy mankind and create a new race. Prometheus, in love of men, saved them from destruction and bestowed upon them the gift of fire, which he stole from Heaven and which has been the beginning of civilization. At this point Oceanus enters, riding upon a four-legged bird; he is a Titan who stood aloof from the conflict with Zeus. An amiable but obsolete person, he wishes to release Prometheus (without running into danger himself) and urges submission. The prisoner listens with disdainful courtesy, refuses the advice, and hints to Oceanus that he had better not associate with a malefactor. His visitor soon bustles away, and the chorus sing how all the nations of the earth mourn over the torments of their deliverer. Prometheus then tells of the arts by which he has taught man to alleviate his misery. The Nymphs ask if he has no hope of release himself; he hints at the possible downfall of Zeus. Another lyrical passage hymns the power of that god and expresses surprise at the contumacy of the Titan. Then appears Io, the heifer-maiden, who at the request of the chorus describes her strange ill-fortune. Beloved of Zeus, she has incurred the wrath of his queen, Hera, who has changed her into a heifer and sent her roaming wildly over the earth pursued by a gadfly. Prometheus prophesies her future wanderings, which shall end in Egypt. He speaks more clearly of the fall of Zeus, who is preparing to wed one who shall bear a child greater than his father. Then he narrates the story of Io's course up to the present hour, ending with the prophecy that in Egypt she shall bear to Zeus a son named Epaphus. He speaks of the history of this man's line, particularly of one " courageous, famed for archery " who shall release Prometheus. Io, in a sudden paroxysm, rushes from the scene. The chorus sing of the dangers which lie in union with the Gods. Prometheus again foretells the overthrow of Zeus by his own son. Hermes, the messenger of Zeus, enters demanding that the prisoner reveal the fatal secret. Prometheus treats his message with defiance. Hermes warns him of still more fell tortures : the "winged hound of Zeus" will come each day to tear his liver ; a convulsion of the earth will hurl him into Hades. The nymphs again urge submission, but when the messenger declares that unless they leave Prometheus they will perchance suffer too, they haughtily refuse to listen. Amid an upheaval of the whole of Nature, the Titan, still defiant, sinks from sight.

The *Prometheus Vinctus* has impressed all generations of readers with wonder and delight ; in particular it has inspired poetry only less magnificent than itself. Shelley's *Prometheus Unbound* is a gorgeous amplification of its spiritual and material features. The sinister and terrific figure which dominates the early part of *Paradise Lost* is but Prometheus strayed at an untoward hour into Christian mythology. Again, this play is the noblest surviving example of the purely Æschylean manner. The *Oresteia* is greater, perhaps, certainly more interesting to us ; but there Æschylus has reacted to the spirit of Sophocles. Here, the stark hauteur of the *Supplices* has developed into a desolate magnificence. The lyrics which, since the *Seven*, have again dwindled in size, have yet grown in beauty, variety, and characterization. On the other side, there is a development of the dialogue which is amazing. Long speeches are still the rule, but line-by-line conversations are frequent. Characters in the *Supplices* and the *Seven* talk as if blank-verse dialogue were a strange and difficult art—as indeed it was till Æschylus forged it into shape. Throughout, whether in lengthy speeches or in conversation, the iambic metre has found a grace and suppleness which is too often ignored by those

who come to the *Prometheus* fresh from the *Medea* or
the *Œdipus Tyrannus*. Above all, the maturity of
Æschylus' poetic strength is to be seen in the terrific
perspectives which he brings before us—perspectives
of time, as the voice of the tortured prophet carries
us down a vista of centuries through the whole history
of Io's race to the man of destiny ; perspectives of
scenery, as the eye of the Ocean-Nymphs from the
summit of earth gazes down upon the tribes of men,
horde behind horde fading into the distance, all raising
lament for the sorrows of their saviour ; perspectives of
thought, as the exultant history of civilization leaps from
the lips of him who dies hourly through untold years to
found and uphold it, telling how that creeping victim of
his own helplessness and the disdain of Heaven goes
from weakness to strength and from strength to
triumph.

No less wonderful is the strictly dramatic economy
of the play. The action is slight. Prometheus works
no more ; it is his part to endure. All the secondary
characters act as a foil to bring the central figure into
massive relief. Each has some touch of Prometheus :
Hephæstus, pity without self-sacrifice ; Cratos, strength
without reflection ; the Nymphs, tenderness without
force ; Oceanus, common-sense without dignity ; Io,
sensibility to suffering without the vision which learns
the lesson of pain ; Hermes, the power to serve without
perception of the secret of sovereignty. Most essential
of all these is Io. The only human participant in the
action, she reminds us that the hand of Zeus has been
heavy upon innocent mortals as well as rebel gods, and
thus gives fresh justification to the wrath of Prometheus.
Still more, she is vital to the whole trilogy. As
Hephæstus links the *Fire-bringer* to the second play, so
does she join the second play to the *Prometheus Unbound*. It is her descendant Heracles who after thirteen
generations will free Prometheus and reconcile him to
Zeus ; the hero of the last drama is brought in a sense
upon the scene in the person of his ancestress. Prome-

theus himself suggests to us the thought of Christ; and yet (as has been said) the Satan of Milton is like him too. This double kinship is made possible by the conception of Zeus which here obtains. Under the sceptre of a god who hates mankind it is possible for the saviour of men to be a rebel and an outcast. Right or wrong, the Titan is godlike in his goodness, his wisdom, his courage. At one point only does his deity show a flaw; he endures his pangs not as a god, but as a man; he agonizes, he laments his pains, he utters exclamations of fear. Rightly, for if the actors in this world-drama are immortal, the spectators are not. To have portrayed Prometheus as facing his punishment without a quiver would have been perhaps sounder theology, but worse drama; the human audience must be made to understand something at least of these pangs, or the greatness of the sacrifice will elude them. A parallel on which we must not dilate cannot escape the reader. One strange outcome of his rebellion is generally overlooked. Zeus had wished to destroy mankind and create a new race. That is, he meant to treat men as he treated the Titans—or would have treated them had they been mortal. Prometheus thwarted this plan, so that we men are a survival of that pre-moral world which the new ruler supersedes. We are the younger brothers of the Titans and (so to put it) have all survived the Flood. Our pettiness and futility condemned us in the eyes of Zeus, who wished for progress; but Prometheus loved us in spite of our miserable failings, and so insisted on carrying us over into the new and nobler world at the cost of his own age-long agony.

The basic question must be briefly discussed—the relation of Prometheus to the new King of Heaven. Zeus is here described as a youthful tyrant, blind to all rights and interests save the security of his recent conquest. This cannot have been the picture presented by the whole trilogy. Not only is enough known of Æschylus' religious views to make such a theory impossible; though the *Prometheus Unbound* is lost we know the story in outline. Heracles in his wanderings came upon Prometheus, now released from Hades, but still chained to his rock and gnawed by the vulture. The hero slew the bird with an arrow, and procured the release of Prometheus by inducing the wounded Centaur Chiron to go down to death in his place, and by reconciling the Titan to Zeus, who promised to free him on hearing the secret of the fatal marriage.[1] Prometheus, to commemorate his captivity, assumed a ring of iron. The authority of the King of Gods was thus for ever established. It is only in a different atmosphere that any inconsistency can be felt. For Æschylus there was a progress in the history of Heaven as in the civilization of earth. Even Zeus in the early days of his dominion seeks to rule by might divorced from wisdom, a severance typified by his feud with Prometheus. He has his lesson to learn like all others; if he will not govern with the help of law, bowing to Fate, then the hope of the Universe is vain and the blind forces of unguided Nature, the half-quelled Titans, will bring chaos back. But youthful and harsh as he is, his will has a moral foundation, unlike theirs; and so perhaps it is that Prometheus cannot but exclaim "I sinned" in opposing that will. Upon the reconciliation between Zeus and his antagonist, Prometheus became a local Attic deity and no more. That eternal wisdom which he embodied is mysteriously assimilated into the soul of Zeus. This is the consummation; omnipotence and omniscience are at one.

We arrive finally at the trilogy which bears the name ORESTEIA and which obtained the prize in 458 B.C. This is the only instance in which the whole series has survived; the satyric play, *Proteus*,[2] has perished.

---

[1] Zeus had intended to wed Thetis. On hearing the secret, he married her to Peleus, who became the father of Achilles.

[2] It is fairly certain that it dealt with Menelaus' visit to Egypt on his way back from Troy. He was shipwrecked on an island and the prophetic Proteus gave him advice, sending him first to Egypt. See *Odyssey*, IV, 351-586.

The name *Oresteia* was applied to the whole tetralogy.

The background of the AGAMEMNON [1] is the palace of King Agamemnon at Argos. A sentinel is discovered upon the roof; he is watching for the beacon which shall signify that Troy has at length fallen. While waiting he broods, dropping hints that all is not well at home. Then the beacon flashes forth, and he shouts the news to the Queen Clytæmnestra within the house. On his departure the chorus enter, aged councillors of Argos, who have not yet heard the tidings. They sing of the quarrel between Greece and Troy and describe the sacrifice of Iphigenia, Agamemnon's daughter, who was offered up to Artemis in order to obtain a favourable wind for the fleet. All the altars are blazing with incense; Clytæmnestra enters, and they ask her the reason. Troy, she replies, was taken last night; a system of beacons has been arranged; the signal has spread over sea and land before dawn. She ponders over the state of the captured city and hopes that the victors have not sinned against the gods of Troy. The old men sing praise to Heaven and moralize on the downfall of human pride. A herald appears, announcing that Agamemnon has landed and will soon reach the city; he dilates on the miseries of the campaign, till the queen sends him away with her welcome to Agamemnon. The chorus call him back and ask news of Menelaus, the king's brother; Menelaus, he replies, is missing: as the Greeks were sailing home a tempest arose which scattered the fleet. Agamemnon's ship has returned alone. The elders, after he has gone, sing of Helen and the deadly power of her beauty. Agamemnon arrives, accompanied by the daughter of the Trojan King Priam, Cassandra the prophetess, who has become his unwilling concubine. Clytæmnestra greets him with effusiveness, to which he responds haughtily.

[1] *Arrangement:* protagonist, Clytæmnestra; deuteragonist, Herald, Cassandra; tritagonist, Sentinel, Agamemnon, Ægisthus.

She persuades him against his will to walk into the palace over rich carpets like an Oriental conqueror, and accompanies him within doors. The chorus express forebodings which they cannot understand. The queen comes forth and orders Cassandra within, to be present at the sacrifice of thanksgiving, but the captive pays no heed and Clytæmnestra in anger retires. The elders attempt to encourage the silent girl, who at last breaks forth into incoherent cries, not of fear but of horror, and utters vague but frightful prophecies of bloodshed and sin, punctuated by the bewildered questions of her hearers. She tells them that they will see the death of Agamemnon, bewails her own wretchedness, greets her death, and prophesies the coming of an avenger. She passes into the house. After a lyric on wicked prosperity, the voice of the king is heard crying within that he has been mortally wounded. Another shriek follows, and then silence. The chorus are in a tumult, when the doors are flung open and Clytæmnestra is seen standing over the corpses of Agamemnon and Cassandra. She has slain the king with an axe, entrapping him in the folds of a robe while in his bath. In reply to the furious accusations of the elders she glories in her act—she is the personification of the ancestral curse ; and she has avenged the murder of Iphigenia. The altercation has for the moment reached something like calm, when Ægisthus appears. He is the cousin of Agamemnon, but between the two families there is a murderous and adulterous feud ; Ægisthus himself is the lover of Clytæmnestra and has shared in the plot. The Argives turn on him in hatred and contempt, which he answers with tyrannical threats. They remind him that Orestes, the king's young son, is alive and safe abroad. Swords are drawn, but Clytæmnestra insists that the quarrel shall cease ; she and Ægisthus must rule with dignity.

A novel theory of the plot has been put forward by the late Dr. A. W. Verrall in his edition of the play.[1]

---

[1] See especially his *Introduction* (pp. xiii-xlvii of the 2nd edition).

He finds the following difficulties in the usual acceptation : (i) Agamemnon lands in Argos on the morning after the night in which Troy was captured, though as a matter of course and a matter of "history" several days (at the very least) must have elapsed before the Greek host so much as embarked ; and though a storm has befallen the fleet on its way. (ii) The story given by Clytæmnestra about the beacons is absurd. Why has the arrangement existed for only one year of the ten ? Why make an arrangement which would depend so entirely on the weather? How could the beacon on Mount Athos have been seen from Eubœa (a hundred miles away) when a tempest was raging on the intervening sea ? (iii) This mystery, that Agamemnon reaches home only two or three hours after his signal, is never cleared up : neither he nor the queen mentions it when they meet. (iv) Thus the whole affair of the beacons is gratuitous as well as incredible. (v) We are not told how Agamemnon was slain. That is, though the poet is precise enough about the details of the actual murder, we are not enlightened as to how a great and victorious prince could be killed with impunity by his wife and her lover, who thereupon, with no difficulty, usurp the government. (vi) What does Ægisthus mean by claiming to have contrived the whole plot ? On the face of it he has done nothing but skulk in the background. Dr. Verrall's explanation, set forth with splendid lucidity, skill, and brilliance, may be briefly summarized thus. For a year Clytæmnestra and Ægisthus have been joined in a treasonable and adulterous league. Ægisthus knows what is happening at Troy and has the first news of Agamemnon's landing (at night). He lights upon Mount Arachnæus a beacon which tells Clytæmnestra that all is ready. (Her story of the fire-chain is a lie to deceive the watchman and the elders.) Agamemnon thus naturally arrives only an hour or two after the news that Troy has fallen. The assassination-plot succeeds for various reasons. During the ten years' war many citizens of

Argos have been alienated from the king by the enormous loss of Greek lives. Hence the usurpers have
a strong body of potential adherents. In fact, several
passages which our texts attribute to the chorus
really belong to conspirators. Next, Agamemnon by
the accident of the storm has with him, not the great
host, but a single ship's company. Finally, though
he has heard much ill of his wife—this only can account
for the brutality wherewith he greets her—he does not
suspect her resourcefulness, wickedness, and courage.
Verrall's theory should probably be accepted.

This tragedy is beyond compare the greatest work
of Æschylus. The lyrics surpass those of any other
drama. To the majesty and scope familiar everywhere
in Æschylean choric writing, and to the tenderness which
diffuses a gentle gleam through the *Prometheus*, are
now added matchless pathos and the authentic thrill
of drama. The picture of Iphigenia (vv. 184-249) is
not merely lovely and tearful beyond words ; it is a
marvel that this gloomy colossus of the stage should
for a moment have excelled Euripides on Euripides'
strongest ground ; it is as if Michelangelo had painted
Raffaelle's " Madonna of the Grand Duke " amid the
prophets and sibyls of the Sistine Chapel. Even more
poignant, because more simple, are the brief lines (vv.
436-47) which tell how the War-God, the money-
changer of men's bodies, sends back from Troy a
handful of charred dust, the pitiful return for a man
who has departed into the market-place of Death.
Best known of all perhaps is the passage (vv. 402-26)
which portrays the numb anguish of a deserted husband.
Further, these lyrics are dramatic. The choric songs
do not suspend the action by their sublime elucidations ;
the comments enable us to understand the march of
events, giving us the keynote of the scene which follows
each lyric. For instance, when the first stasimon
dilates, not upon the glory of conquest, but upon the
fall of pride and the sorrows of war, we are prepared
for the herald and his tale in which triumph is over-

borne by the memory of hardship and tempest. The misgivings which brood over the third stasimon, in spite of the victorious entry of the king which has just been witnessed, is a fit prelude to the terrible outbreaks of Cassandra.

The characterization shows a marked advance on the *Prometheus* in variety and colour. This is not so much because three actors are needed as against two in the earlier play ; for though they are necessary, comparatively little use is made of the increased facilities. But, while Clytæmnestra is technically as great a creation as Prometheus, the secondary persons are much more interesting in themselves than in the earlier drama. They do of course form a series of admirable foils to the queen, but they are worthy of careful study for their own sakes, which cannot be said very heartily for the lesser personages of the *Prometheus*. The sentinel is excellent, sketched in a few lines with a sureness of touch which is a new thing in this poet's minor characters. The sense of impending trouble mixed with expected joy, the flavour of rich colloquialism about his speech, and the hearty dance upon the palace-roof wherewith he hails the beacon, make him live. Even more commonplace, theoretically, is the part given to the herald, but him again Æschylus has created a real man. The passionate joy with which he greets his native soil, and the lugubrious relish wherewith he details the hardships of the army before Troy, make him our friend at once, and present us with that sense of atmosphere which is often lacking in Greek tragedy. Agamemnon may seem a disappointing figure ; very naturally, for it is the poet's purpose to disappoint us. To depict a great and noble king would have spoiled the splendid effect of Clytæmnestra. Agamemnon's murder must be made for the moment as intelligible as may be, therefore the dramatist shows us a conceited, heavy-witted, pompous person who none the less reveals certain qualities which have made it possible for such a man to overthrow Troy.

Clytæmnestra is Æschylus' masterpiece—not indeed

a masterly picture of female character ; such work was left to others—but a superb presentment of a woman dowered with an imperial soul, pressed into sin by the memory of her murdered child, the blind ambition of her husband, and the consciousness of an accursed ancestry. Here, as elsewhere in these three tragedies, the architectural skill with which Æschylus plans his trilogy invite the closest study.   In this first part, all the justification which Clytæmnestra can claim is held steadily before the eyes.   The slaughter of Iphigenia, which killed her love for Agamemnon, is dwelt upon early in the play and recalled by her once and again during her horrible conversation with the chorus after the king's death. Another wrong to her is brought visibly upon the scene in the person of Cassandra.   The sordid side of her vengeance, her amour with Ægisthus, remains hardly hinted at until the very end, where it springs into overwhelming prominence—but at the very moment when we are preparing to pass over to the *Choephoræ*, the second great stage of the action, in which the mission of Orestes is to be exalted.   Clytæmnestra has been often compared to Lady Macbeth.   But Shakespeare's creation is more feminine than that of the Athenian.   She evinces inhuman heartlessness and cynicism till the task is accomplished ; before the play ends she is broken for ever.   Clytæmnestra never falters in her resolution, hardly a quiver reveals the strain of danger and excitement upon her nerves while success is still unsure.   When the deed is accomplished and the strain relaxed, then, instead of yielding to hysterical collapse, she is superbly collected.[1]   Years after, she re-appears in the *Choephoræ*, but time, security, and power have, to all seeming, left little mark upon this soul of iron.   At the last frightful moment when she realizes that vengeance is knocking at the gate, her courage blazes up more gloriously than ever : "Give me the axe, this instant, wherewith that

---

[1] This is noted by an admirable touch.   Almost always a tragedy ends with words of the chorus as the least impassioned parties.   In the *Agamemnon* the closing words are uttered by Clytæmnestra.

man was slain ".[1] It is a superb defiance ; for thrilling audacity this passage stands perhaps alone until we come to the splendid " Stand neuter, Gods, this once, I do invoke you," with which Vanbrugh [2] rises, for his moment, into the heights where Æschylus abode. Yet next moment the knowledge that her lover is dead brings her to her knees.

Cassandra and Ægisthus have not yet been considered, for they belong also to the next topic—the method in which the unity of the play is so handled that it does not interfere with, but helps to effect, the unity of the whole trilogy. The indescribable power and thrill of Cassandra's scene may easily blind us to the slightness of the character-drawing. Simply as a character, the princess is no more subtly or carefully studied than the herald ; the extraordinary interest which surrounds her arises not from what she is or does but from what happens to her. She is the analogue of Io in the *Prometheus*. The mere structure of both plays allots to Io and Cassandra precisely the same functions. Passive victims of misfortune, they are the symbol and articulation of the background in the particular drama ; further, they are vital to the economy of the whole series, in that they sum up in themselves the future happenings which the later portions of it are to expound. So far, they are the same ; but when we go beyond theoretical structure and look to the finished composition, Cassandra far outshines Io. The Argive maiden suffers, shrinks, and laments in utter perplexity. The Trojan suffers, but she does not quail ; her lamentations are hardly lamentations at all, so charged are they with lofty indignation, and the sense of pathos in human things. Io is broken by her calamity ; Cassandra is purified and schooled. The poet who in this very play sings that suffering is the path to wisdom has not made us wait long for an example. There is, too, a definite technical advance in this, that Io merely hears the prophecy of justification and the

----

[1] *Choephoræ*, 889.   [2] *The Relapse*, V, iv. 135

possibility of revenge, while Cassandra in her own person foretells the return of Orestes.

Ægisthus also, but less obviously, is important to the progress of the trilogy. His appearance and his speeches are no anti-climax to the splendid scene of Clytæmnestra's triumph. The queen and Cassandra have talked of the Pelopid curse ; Ægisthus is the curse personified. It is through ancient wickedness that he has passed a half-savage life of brooding exile ; the sins of his fathers have turned him into a man fit to better their instruction. Again, this last scene brings before us in full power that aspect of Clytæmnestra which has been almost ignored— her baser reason for the murder of her husband. This is done precisely at the right place. To dwell on the queen's intrigue earlier would have deprived her of that measure of sympathy which throughout this first play she needs. Not to have depicted it at all would have left that sympathy unimpaired, and we should have entered upon the *Choephoræ* fatally unable to side with Orestes in his horrible mission.

The story of the CHOEPHORŒ[1] (Χοηφόροι, " Libation-Bearers ") is as follows. The back-scene throughout probably represents the palace of Argos ; in the orchestra[2] is the tomb of Agamemnon. Something like ten years have elapsed since the usurpation of Ægisthus. Orestes, son of the murdered king, accompanied by his friend Pylades, enters and greets his father's grave, laying thereon a lock of his hair in sign of mourning ; they withdraw. The chorus (led by Electra) enter—attendants of Electra carrying libations, to be poured in prayer upon Agamemnon's tomb. Their song expresses their grief, hints at revenge, and explains that they have been sent by Clytæmnestra herself, who is terrified by a dream interpreted to signify the wrath of Agamemnon's spirit. Electra discusses the situation with her friends,

---

[1] *Arrangement :* protagonist, Orestes ; deuteragonist, Electra, Clytæmnestra ; tritagonist, Pylades, nurse, attendant, Ægisthus.

[2] This is of course a conventional *mise-en-scène ;* we are to imagine the tomb as distant from the palace.

and pours the libations over the mound in her own
name, not on behalf of her mother, calling upon the
gods and Agamemnon's spirit to bring Orestes home
and punish the murderess. Electra discovers the tress
of hair left by Orestes. That it has come from him she
knows, as it resembles her own;[1] he must have sent it.
In the midst of her excitement, she perceives footprints;
these, too, she recognizes as like her own. Suddenly
Orestes appears and reveals himself. She still doubts,
but he exhibits a piece of embroidery which she herself
worked long ago. Electra falls into his arms; Orestes
explains to his friends that Apollo has sent him home
as an avenger. In a long lyrical scene (κομμός), the
chorus, Electra, and Orestes invoke Agamemnon to
assume life and activity in aid of his avenger.[2] The
chorus leader tells Orestes of Clytæmnestra's vision.
She dreamed that she gave birth to a snake, which
drew blood from her breast. He expounds this as fore-
telling the death of the queen at his hands. Explaining
that he and his followers will gain admission to the
palace as travellers, he departs. The maidens raise a
song of astonishment at the crimes of which mortals are
capable, dwelling especially upon the treachery of an
evil woman. Orestes comes back accompanied by his
followers, and tells the porter that he brings news for
the head of the house. Clytæmnestra appears, and receives the feigned message that Orestes is dead. The
queen is apparently overwhelmed, but bids the visitors
become her guests. While the chorus utter a brief
prayer for success, the aged nurse of Orestes comes
forth, in grief for the loss of her foster-son. She tells
the chorus she has been despatched by Clytæmnestra
to summon Ægisthus and his bodyguard, that he may
question the strangers. They persuade her to alter the

---

[1] On this and the other "tokens" see below, p. 258.
[2] The dead man is undoubtedly supposed to send aid in a mysterious
way, but no ghost appears, as in the *Persæ*. This discrepancy points to
a change in religious feeling. Clytæmnestra's shade "appears" in the
Eumenides, but as a dream (see v. 116).

message ; let Ægisthus come unattended. When she
has gone, they raise another lyric in passionate encour-
agement of Orestes. Ægisthus enters and goes into
the guest-wing of the house; in a moment his scream
is heard ; the chorus retire.[1] A servant of Ægisthus
bursts forth, proclaiming the death of his master. He
flings himself upon the main door, desperately shouting
for Clytæmnestra, who in a moment appears. His
message, "The dead are slaying them that live," is
clear to her : doom is at hand, but she calls for her
murderous axe. Orestes rushes out upon her with
drawn sword. His first words announce the death of
Ægisthus, and she beseeches him piteously for mercy.
Orestes, unnerved, asks the counsel of Pylades, who for
the first and last time speaks, reminding the prince of
his oath and the command of Heaven. Clytæmnestra
is driven within to be slain beside her lover. After a
song of triumph from the chorus, the two corpses are
displayed to the people ; beside them stands Orestes
who brings forth the blood-stained robe wherein
Agamemnon was entangled. The sight of it brings
upon the speaker a perturbation strange even in such
circumstances. It is the coming of madness. He sees
in fancy the Furies sent by his mother's spirit, and
rushes away to seek at Delphi the protection which
Apollo has promised. The play ends with a few lines
from the chorus lamenting the sinful history of the
house.

The *Choephoræ* is less popular with modern readers
than either of its companions. This is owing partly to
the difficulty of perusal, for the text of the lyrics is often
corrupt ; it is still more due to no accident, but to
technique. The second play of a trilogy was usually
more statuesque than the other two. There is, of course,
a progress of events, not merely a Phrynichean treatment of a static theme ; but the poet carefully retards
his speed. Thus the *Choephoræ* should be compared

---

[1] vv. 870-4. It seems most natural to suppose that they altogether
quit the orchestra, returning before v. 930.

rather with the *Prometheus* than with the *Agamemnon*. We then observe an improvement—if we wish to call it so—in construction. The great Commos keeps the play almost[1] at a standstill; but the rest of the work is full of dramatic vigour.

It is true that none of the characters has the arresting quality of those in the *Agamemnon*. The nurse is a worthy companion to the watchman—her quaint and explicit references to the trouble caused her by Orestes when a baby are the most remarkable among the few comic touches found in our poet; and the part of the slave who gives the alarm, minute indeed, is yet the finest of its kind in Greek tragedy. But the persons of greater import—Electra, Ægisthus, and Pylades—would not have taxed the skill of a moderate playwright. Clytæmnestra is magnificent, but less through her present part than through the superb continuation of her rôle in the *Agamemnon;* her scenes are brief, like the glimpse of a fierce sunset after a lowering day. She is the only person characterized, except, indeed, Orestes, and even he through most of the drama is not a character, but a purpose and a few emotions speaking appropriate sentences. This is true even of the scene where he condemns his mother. The only touch of genuine drama is the instant where he quails before her entreaty; but though this is real enough, it is not great. The undoubted power of the scene is due not to dramatic skill, but to the intrinsic horror of the situation. Æschylus has given us almost as little as we could expect. But turn the page and study Orestes' address to the Argive state—the increase in dramatic force is appalling. He begins by stately, vigorous, and impassioned eloquence equal to almost anything in the *Agamemnon*. The blood-stained robe is displayed, and the hideous sight seems to eat into his brain. His

---

[1] Not quite, however. The poet is to depict a man, with whom we are to sympathize, almost in the act of slaying his mother. Not only Orestes, but the spectator also, needs as much spiritual fortification as can be provided.

grip on what he means to say slips; he struggles to re-
capture it; one can see his failing mind stagger from
the mother of whom he strives to speak to the garment
of death before him.   A word rises to the surface of his
thoughts, he snatches at it, but it brings up with it the
wrong phrase.   The horror passes into us; this half-
madness is not lunatic incoherence but the morbidly
subtle coherence of a masterful mind struggling against
insanity.   The deadly net entangles his brain as it entangled his father's body.   By a final effort he collects
himself and declares that he goes to Delphi to claim
the protection and countenance of Heaven.   Then his
doom settles upon him; the Furies arise before him and
he flees distraught.

That such immense force should be manifested only
at the end of the play, that until and during the crisis
Æschylus exerts only sufficient dramatic energy to present his situations intelligibly, is the most significant
fact in the *Choephoræ*.   This is deliberate in an artist
who has composed the *Agamemnon* and the *Eumenides*.
In the opening stage it is human sin and courage which
provide the rising interest; in the third the righteousness and wisdom of the Most High unloose the knot and
save mankind; at both periods personality is the basis
of action.   But in the middle stage the master is not
personality, but the impersonal Fury demanding blood
in vengeance for blood, a law of life and of the universe,
named by a name but possessing no attributes.   This
law may be called by a feminine title Erinys; it is called
also by a phrase : " Do and Suffer ";[1] it is the shade of
Agamemnon, thirsting—is it for blood as a bodily drink
or for death as expiation?—and sending the dark pro-
geny of his soul up from Hades.   This fact, then, and
no person, it is which dominates the play, and that is
why the persons concerned are for the time no magnificent figures of will or valour or wisdom, but the panting
driven thralls of something unseen which directs their
movements and decides their immediate destiny.

---

[1] vv. 313 : δράσαντι παθεῖν.

The plot of the third play, the EUMENIDES [1] (Εὐμενί-
δες, "the Kindly Ones," an euphemistic name of the
Furies) is as follows.   Outside the shrine at Delphi, the
Pythian priestess utters a prayer to all the deities connected with the spot, after which she enters the sanctuary.
Almost instantly she returns in horror, and tells how she
has seen a blood-stained man seated upon the *Omphalos*
and round him a band of sleeping females, loathly to the
sight.   She departs.   From the temple the god appears [2]
with his suppliant Orestes, whom he encourages and
sends forth (led by the god Hermes) on his wanderings,
which are to end in peace at Athens.   When the two
have disappeared, the ghost of Clytæmnestra rises and
awakens the sleeping Furies.   They burst forth from
the temple in frenzy at the escape of their victim.   In
the midst of the clamour Apollo, with words of contemptuous hatred, bids them begone.   The scene now changes
to Athens, where Orestes throws himself upon the protection of the goddess Athena, whose statue he clasps.
In a moment the chorus of Furies enter in pursuit ; they
discover Orestes and describe the horrible doom which
he must suffer.   He defies them and calls upon the
absent Athena.   But they circle about him chanting
their fearful "binding-song"—the proclamation of their
office and rights as the implacable avengers of bloodshed
and every other sin.   As their strains die away Athena
enters.   She hears the dispute in outline, the Furies insisting that for matricide there can be no pardon, Orestes
declaring that he has been purified ritually by Apollo
who urged him to his deed.   The goddess determines
that the suit shall be tried by a court of her own citizens.
Meanwhile the Furies sing of the danger to righteousness which must result if their prerogatives are withdrawn : "terror *has* a rightful place and must sit for ever

[1] *Arrangement.*—Croiset gives : protagonist, Orestes ; deuteragonist,
Apollo ; tritagonist, Athena, priestess, ghost of Clytæmnestra. This *grouping* is certainly right, but it is not easy to suppose that the part of Athena
was given to the tritagonist.   It seems better to give Athena, etc., to the
protagonist, Apollo to the second, and Orestes to the third actor.
[2] Probably the *eccyclema* was used.   See pp. 66-8.

watching over the soul ".[1]   The court of justice is now
assembled on the Areopagus.   Athena presides ; with
her are the jurymen (generally supposed to number
twelve) ; before her are the Furies and Orestes ; behind
is a great crowd of Athenian citizens.   A trumpet blast
announces the opening of the session, and Apollo enters
to aid Orestes.   The trial begins with a cross-examination of Orestes by the Furies, in which he is by no
means triumphant.   Apollo takes his place and gives
justification for the matricide, under three heads : (i) it
was the command of Zeus ; (ii) Agamemnon was a
great king ; (iii) the real parent of a child is the father,
the mother being only the nurse.   To prove this last
point Apollo instances the president herself, Athena,
born of no mother but from the head of Zeus.   He ends
by promising that Orestes, if acquitted, will be a firm
and useful ally to Athens.   The goddess now declares
the pleading at an end, but before the vote is taken she
delivers a speech to the jury, proclaiming that she now
and hereby founds the Areopagite Court which shall for
ever keep watch over the welfare of Athens by the re-
pression of crime.   The judges advance one by one and
vote secretly ; but before the votes are counted Athena
gives her ruling that if an equal number are cast on
either side Orestes shall be acquitted, for she gives her
casting vote in his favour.[2]   The votes are counted and
found equal, and the goddess proclaims that Orestes is
free.   Apollo departs, and Orestes breaks forth into
thanksgiving and promises that Argos shall ever be the
friend of Athens.   He leaves Athena and her citizens
confronted by the Furies, who raise cries of frantic in-

---

[1] vv. 517-9 :—

> ἔσθ' ὅπου τὸ δεινὸν εὖ
> καὶ φρενῶν ἐπίσκοπον
> δεῖ μένειν καθήμενον.

[2] The actual rule of the Areopagite Court was that if the votes were
even the defendant was acquitted.   This rule was explained as derived
from the "Vote of Athena" in the trial of Orestes.   It seems then that
Athena's vote here makes inequality, not equality.   Therefore her pebble
is not put into either urn, but laid between them.

dignation, turning their rage upon Athens and threatening to blight the soil, the flocks, and the people. Athena seeks to placate them by offering a habitation and worship in Attica. For a time they refuse to listen, but after their fourth song of vengeance they relent. Athena promises that they are to become kindly earth-deities [1] domiciled in Attica, blessing the increase of crops, of herds, and of the family. The citizens, with torches in their hands, form a procession led by Athena, and conduct the new divinities to their dwelling in a cave beneath the Acropolis.

It remains to deal with the literary and religious aspects of the play. The poet sketches Orestes in but a rudimentary style. There is, indeed, hardly any character-drawing in him ; he is simply any brave, sensitive, religious man. The " human interest " is almost confined to the gods, without our forgetting that they are surrounded by human auditors. Athena and the Furies are made to live by a few noble sweeping strokes ; Athena, the majestic presentment of Olympian wisdom and the visible head of her favoured city ; the Furies majestic in their rage, unanswerable in their claim that punishment of crime cannot be done away if the world is to endure. Apollo is a curious study, less sublime than we expected. His manner under cross-examination by the Furies is a little too human ; indeed he loses his temper. The fact is that, though Æschylus has no desire to treat Apollo irreverently, he is by no means concerned to depict a perfect being ; and for two reasons. Firstly, he insists on reminding us that Apollo is but the minister of Zeus ; it is Zeus only whom he is bent on exalting. Secondly, he knows well that his audience, as between the Furies and Apollo, have a strong bias in favour of the latter. The poet does acquit Orestes, but it is of the deepest importance in his eyes that we

---

[1] It is implied by the title of the drama that they assume the title Eumenides or "Gracious Ones," but this title is not used in the play itself. Their most usual name was Σεμναί, "Awful Ones".

should not complacently regard the Furies as mere malicious fiends, routed by a gloriously contemptuous Olympian; the Furies may be wrong, perhaps, but *prima facie* they have a terribly strong case. Therefore in the scene of the pleadings they at least hold their own. Apollo may be more right than they; he is emphatically not their superior, his personal fiat is not a spiritual sanction profounder than theirs. Neither party has got to the root of things. The Furies say: "This man shed the blood of a kinswoman; he must be for ever damned". Apollo says: "He has not sinned, for Zeus bade him act thus". The acquittal of Orestes is not the solution of this disagreement, it is but the beginning; we can hardly understand the dispute as yet.

We thus come to the religious aspect of the *Eumenides*. Æschylus is of course too sincere to be satisfied, or to allow us to be satisfied, with the fact that Orestes actually escapes. His pursuers attack not the Argive prince only; much of their language is an indictment of Apollo, and ultimately of Zeus. It is very well for Apollo to revile them as "beasts detested by the gods,"[1] but the gods are themselves arraigned. The earth-powers stand for the principle that sin, especially bloodshed, must be punished; this demand is recognized as just by Athena,[2] and is not repudiated by Apollo. Yet Zeus, the Sovereign of all things, extends his hand over the man who has fallen under their sway by his act. How shall these claims be reconciled?

The solution of Æschylus is not unlike that which (it appears) he offered at the end of the Prometheus-trilogy. We are to imagine that we witness the events of a time when Zeus himself has not attained to full stature. His face is set towards the perfection of righteousness, but development awaits even him. In the instance of Orestes, the jar between Furies and

---

[1] v. 644.

[2] In her great speech to the court she plainly adopts the language of the Furies. See below.

Apollo, or more ultimately between the earth-powers
and Zeus, shows that neither party is perfectly right.
None the less, it is essential that there should be but
one master of the universe, and the Furies are compelled to submit. But Æschylus does not lay down
his pen at this point; nothing does he avoid more
carefully than an ending which might appear as de-
sirable as obvious to a vulgar playwright, some showy
tableau of grovelling fiends and triumphant goddess.
The Furies themselves look for nothing less than
moral annihilation [1] as the result of defeat. But something of which they have never dreamed—of which,
probably, no Greek in the theatre has dreamed—is in
store for them; neither victory nor defeat, but recognition by the power to which they have been
forced to bow, assimilation to that religion from which
they have kept themselves so jealously sundered.
They are still to be mighty powers of earth, yet
their function is to be cursing no more, but blessing
only.

But is this a solution at all? Is it enough to hint
at the thunderbolt, to offer a bribe of power and
worship that the Furies may forget their rage against
Attica? [2] What is to become of their function as
inflexible champions of righteousness, which has been
the moral safeguard of men? This duty the goddesses
leave as a legacy to the newly-formed court of chosen
Athenians :—[3]

[1] v. 747 : ἡμῖν γὰρ ἔρρειν, ἢ πρόσω τιμὰς νέμειν.
[2] Dr. Verrall (*Introduction* to his edition, pp. xxxii, xxxiii) explains the
reconciliation of the Furies as the result of a mystic revelation conveyed
not in words but through a kind of spiritual magnetism exercised by
Athena when she draws near to them at v. 886 (he notes the break in
syntax at this point) ; such an influence could not be shown forth in words—
it is too sacred and mysterious.   But if a poet does undertake to dramatize
the truths of religion, he must do so in dramatic form ; he ought not suddenly to throw up his task. Several places in Æschylus can be found
where he does put such ideas into words.
[3] This appears to me certain from Athena's language to the court,
but the reader should not suppose that the Furies say so definitely ; they
acquiesce.

τὸ μήτ' ἄναρχον μήτε δεσποτούμενον
ἀστοῖς περιστέλλουσι βουλεύω σέβειν
καὶ μὴ τὸ δεινὸν πᾶν πόλεως ἔξω βαλεῖν.[1]

" Loyalty and worship do I urge upon my citizens for
a polity neither anarchic nor tyrannical ; fear must not
be banished utterly from the State." These are the
words of Athena ; they are also the words of Æschylus
—a solemn warning to his fellow-citizens ; finally, they
are the words of the Furies themselves—the very
phrases which they have used are here borrowed—and
go far to explain why they consent to relinquish their
prerogative. First they have regarded the Areopagus
with misgiving as a possibly hostile tribunal ; then
with hatred as an enemy ; at the last they look upon
it with benevolence as their heir to those stern duties
which must not be suffered, under whatever ruler of
the world, to fall into oblivion. It is true at the same
time that the poet wished, for reasons of contemporary
politics, to impress upon his countrymen the sacredness
of this ancient court, then threatened with curtailment
of its powers and prestige at the hands of the popular
party led by Pericles and Ephialtes ; and the manner
in which he weaves this consideration of temporal
interests into the fabric of a vast religious poem is magnificently conceived. What in a smaller man would
have been merely a vulgar dexterity is sanctified by
religious genius. It is not the degradation of religion,
but the apotheosis of politics. The close of the
Eumenides is anything but an anti-climax. It is closely
knit to the body of the whole trilogy, showing the
manner in which the playwright supposes the necessary
reconciliation between Zeus and the Furies to be made
possible and acceptable. The King of Heaven is
mystically identified now and for ever with Fate.[2] The
joyful procession of προπομποί is the sign not only
that the moral government of the world has been set

[1] vv. 696-8.
[2] This vital point is admirably demonstrated by Dr. Verrall on
v. 1046.

at last upon a sure basis, but also that this government is already in operation and sanctifying human institutions.

These seven plays are all that survive complete of the eighty [1] tragedies and satyric dramas written by Æschylus. Our knowledge of the lost works rests upon some hundreds of fragments and scattered mention or comment in ancient writers.

Most interesting and important are those plays which were associated with the extant dramas ; these have been already discussed. Next in attractiveness is the *Lycurgea* (Λυκουργεία, or trilogy of Lycurgus), to which the *Bacchæ* of Euripides had close affinity in subject. Lycurgus was a king of the Edoni, a Thracian people, who opposed the religion of Dionysus when it entered his realm, and was punished with death. The first play, the *Edoni* ('Ηδωνοί), depicted the collision between Dionysus and his enemy. There was an interview in which Lycurgus taunted the god with his effeminate looks,[2] and which apparently closed with the overthrow of his palace by the might of the god.[3] The longest fragment gives an interesting account of the instruments of music used in the bacchic orgies. The name of the second play is not certain ; it was either *Bassarides* (Βασσαρίδες) or *Bassaræ* (Βασσάραι) —the *Women of the Fawn-Skin*. Here the anger of Dionysus fell upon Orpheus the musician, who neglected the new deity and devoted himself to Apollo. He was torn to pieces by the Bacchantes and the Muses gathered his remains, to which they gave sepulture in Lesbos. The *Youths* (Νεανίσκοι) formed the last piece of the trilogy ; practically nothing is known of it. It was the chorus which gave its name to the play in all three cases. The satyric drama was called *Lycurgus ;* if we may judge from one of the three fragments the tragic

---

[1] This number is not certain. It is probably an under-statement.
[2] ποδαπὸς ὁ γύννις ;   [3] ἐνθουσιᾷ δὴ δῶμα, βακχεύει στέγη.

treatment of wine was transformed into a comic discussion of beer.[1]

Another celebrated trilogy had for its theme the tale of Troy. The *Myrmidons* (Μυρμιδόνες), named from the followers of Achilles who formed the chorus, dealt with the death of Patroclus. Achilles, withdrawn from battle because of his quarrel with Agamemnon, is adjured by the chorus to pity the defeat of the Greeks. He allows Patroclus, his friend, to go forth against the Trojans. After doing valiantly, Patroclus is slain by Hector. The news is brought by Antilochus to Achilles, who gives himself up to passionate lament. This play was a favourite of Aristophanes, who quotes from it repeatedly. In this drama occurred the celebrated simile of the eagle struck to death with an arrow winged by his own feathers, which was cited throughout antiquity and which Byron paraphrased in one of his most majestic passages.[2] The story was apparently continued in the *Nereides* (Νηρηίδες). Achilles determined to revenge Patroclus. The magic armour made for him by Hephæstus was brought by his mother Thetis, accompanied by her sisters, the sea-nymphs, daughters of Nereus, who formed the chorus. The last play was the *Phrygians* (Φρύγες) or *Ransom of Hector* (Ἕκτορος Λύτρα) in which Priam prevailed upon Achilles to give up the corpse of Hector for burial. It appears likely that in the two preceding plays Æschylus followed Homer somewhat closely. But in the *Ransom* he did not. Besides the detail to which Aristophanes[3] makes allusion, that Achilles sat for a long time in complete silence, no doubt while the chorus and Priam offered piteous and lengthy appeals, there are differences of conception. In Homer, one of the most moving features of the story is that Priam goes to the Trojan camp

---

[1] βρῦτον.
[2] *On the death of Kirk-White:* "'Twas thine own genius gave the fatal blow," etc. The fiery verse, ὅπλων ὅπλων δεῖ· μὴ πύθῃ τὸ δεύτερον, recalls the famous line : "A horse, a horse ! My kingdom for a horse ! "
[3] *Frogs*, 911-3.

practically alone. He is met by the God Hermes who conducts him to the tent of Achilles. Then, solitary among his foes, he throws himself upon the mercy of his son's destroyer. No such effect was to be found in Æschylus. The chorus of Phrygians accompanied their king, and we find in a fragment of Aristophanes [1] a hint of much posturing and stage-managed supplication.

The *Women of Etna* (Αἰτναῖαι) was produced in Sicily at the foundation of Hiero's new city. In the *Men of Eleusis* ('Ελευσίνιοι) Æschylus dealt with the earliest struggle of Athens—the war with Eleusis, his own birth-place. More ambitious in its topic was the *Daughters of the Sun* ('Ηλιάδες) which dealt with the fall of Phaethon. A pretty fragment alludes to that "bowl of the Sun" so brilliantly described by Mimnermus, in which the god travels back by night from West to East. It seems that the geographical enumerations prominent in the Prometheus-trilogy were found here also, tinged less with grimness and more with romance. In the *Thracian Women* (Θρῆσσαι) Æschylus treated the same theme as Sophocles in the *Ajax*. It is significant that the death of the hero was announced by a messenger. Possibly, then, it was a desire for novelty which caused the younger playwright to diverge so strikingly from custom as to depict the actual suicide. The *Cabiri* (Κάβειροι) was the first tragedy to portray men intoxicated. In the *Niobe* (Νιόβη) occurred splendid lines quoted with approbation by Plato :—

> Close kin of heavenly powers,
> Men near to Zeus, who upon Ida's peak
> Beneath the sky their Father's altar serve,
> Their veins yet quickened with the blood of gods.[2]

The *Philoctetes* is the subject of an interesting essay by

---

[1] Meineke, II, p. 1177.

[2] οἱ θεῶν ἀγχίσποροι
οἱ Ζηνὸς ἐγγύς, ὧν κατ᾿ Ἰδαῖον πάγον
Διὸς πατρῴου βωμός ἐστ᾿ ἐν αἰθέρι,
κοὔπω σφιν ἐξίτηλον αἷμα δαιμόνων.

Cp. Plato, *Republic*, 391 E.

Dio Chrysostom.[1] All the three great tragedians wrote plays[2] of this name, and Dio offers a comparison. Naturally, but for us unfortunately, he assumes a knowledge of these works in his readers; still, certain facts emerge about the Æschylean work. Men of Lemnos —the island on which Philoctetes had been marooned— constituted the chorus. To them the hero narrated the story of his desertion by the Greeks, and his wretched life afterwards. Odysseus persuaded him to come and help the Greeks at Troy by a long recital of Hector's victory and false reports of the death of Agamemnon and Odysseus. Neither Neoptolemus nor Heracles (important characters in Sophocles) seems to have been introduced by Æschylus. Dio comments on the style and characterization. The primitive grandeur of Æschylus, he remarks, the austerity of his thought and diction, appear appropriate to the spirit of tragedy and to the manners of the heroic age. Odysseus is indeed clever and crafty, but "far removed from present-day rascality"; in fact he seems "absolutely patriarchal when compared with the modern school". That the play is named after one of the persons and not the chorus, leads one to attribute it to a comparatively late period in the poet's life. Finally, the *Weighing of the Souls* (Ψυχοστασία) is remarkable for the scene in Heaven, modelled upon a passage in the *Iliad*, where Zeus, with Thetis, mother of Achilles, on one hand, and Eos, mother of Memnon, on the other, weighed in a balance the souls or lives of the two heroes about to engage in fight before Troy.

In attempting a general appreciation of this poet one should avoid making the error of judging him practically by the *Agamemnon* alone. Otherwise we cannot hope to understand the feeling of fifth century Athens towards him. Most of his work has vanished, but the collection we possess seems fairly representative

---

[1] *Oration* 52.　　　　[2] Only one has survived, that of Sophocles.

of his development; if we give weight to his comparatively inferior plays we may understand the feeling of
two such different men as Aristophanes and Euripides.
Incredible as it may seem, by the end of that century
Æschylus was looked on as half-obsolete. Euripides
thought of him much as Mr. Bernard Shaw now thinks
of Shakespeare; Aristophanes, lover of the old order
as he was, seems to have felt for the man who wrote the
Agamemnon a breezy half-patronizing affection; while
putting him forward in the *Frogs* to discomfit Euripides,
he handles the older poet only less severely than he
handles the younger. He and his contemporaries
viewed Æschylus as a whole, not fixing their eyes
exclusively on his final trilogy.

Let us consider him first as a purely literary artist,
a master of language, leaving his strictly dramatic
qualities on one side. We find that his three great
notes are grandeur, simplicity, and picturesqueness. To
describe the grandeur of Æschylus is a hopeless task;
some notion of it may be drawn from the account of his
individual works just given, but the only true method is
of course direct study of his writings. The lyrics, from
the *Supplices* to the *Eumenides*, touch the very height
of solemn inspiration and moral dignity; as it has been
often said, his only peers are the prophets of Israel.
The non-lyrical portions of his work, stiff with gorgeous
embroidery, are less like the conversations of men and
women than the august communings of gods; that
majestic poem which has for auditors the Sun himself,
the rivers, the mountains, and the sea, and for background the whole race of man, is not merely written
about Prometheus: it might have been written by
Prometheus. But such magnificence has its perils.
The mere bombast for which Kyd and even Marlowe
are celebrated, and which has given us such things as

> The golden sun salutes the morn
> And, having gilt the ocean with his beams,
> Gallops the zodiac in his glistering coach,[1]

[1] *Titus Andronicus*, II, i. 5-7.

was not unknown to.Æschylus, as his wayward sup-
porter Aristophanes with much relish demonstrates.   It
seems that such extravagances, "the beefy words, all
frowns and crests, the frightful bogey-language," [1]
occurred entirely in the lost plays.   But in those which
survive we have much bombast of phrase, if not of
words ; the "thirsty dust, sister and neighbour of
mud," [2] Zeus, "chairman of the immortals," [3]

> Typhos, who belcheth from fire-reeking mouth
> Black fume, the eddying sister of the flame, [4]

" drill these words through thine ears with the quiet
pace of thy mind," [5] "breathe upon him the gale of
blood and wither him with the reeking fire of thine
entrails ". [6]   Æschylus, indeed, like all poets, understood
the majesty of sounding words, apart from their meaning.   As Milton gloried in the use of magnificent proper
names, so does the Athenian delight in thunderous
elaboration.   Therefore, not possessing the chastity of
Sophocles, he is occasionally barbarous and noisy ;
Aristophanes [7] jests at his lyrics for their frequent exhibition of sound without sense.

Oddly combined with this occasional savagery of
phrase is the second quality of simplicity.   Æschylus,
so far as we know, was the creator of tragic diction.
However greatly his successors improved upon him in
flexibility, grace, and subtlety, it was he who first worked
the mine of spoken language, strove to purify the ore,
and forged the metal into an instrument of terror and
delight.   But even the creator needed practice in its
use.   He has a giant's strength, and at times uses it
like a giant, not like a gymnast.   In his earlier work
he seems muscle-bound, clumsy in the use of his new-
found powers.   He wields the pen as one more familiar
with the spear ; the warrior of Marathon does fierce

---

[1] *Frogs*, 924-5.
[2] *Ag.* 494-5.   In spite of Dr. Verrall's ingenious remarks, it seems
best to take this phrase in the traditional way, as a mere extravagance.
[3] *P.V.* 170.   [4] *Septem*, 493-4.   [5] *Choeph.* 451-2.
[6] *Eum.* 137-8.   [7] *Frogs*, 1261-95.

battle with particles and phrases; he strains ideas to his breast and wrestles with elusive perfection; we seem to hear his panting when at last he erects as trophy some noble speech or miraculous lyric. This stiffness of execution persists faintly even in the *Oresteia*. The earlier tragedies, both in the characters and in the language, are rough-hewn, for all their glory. In the *Supplices* this stark simplicity is actually the chief note. Here, more than elsewhere, the poet has a strange way of writing Greek at times as if it were some other language. The opening words of the Egyptian herald —σοῦσθε σοῦσθ' ἐπὶ βᾶριν ὅπως ποδῶν [1]—can only be described as barbaric mouthing. Throughout this play the complete absence of lightness and speed, the crude beginnings of greatness, a certain bleak amplitude, are all typical of a new art-form not yet completely evolved. The poet, himself the beginner of a new epoch, fills us with an uncanny impression of persons standing on the threshold of history with little behind them but the Deluge. In the *Persæ* and the *Septem* there is the same instinct for spaciousness, but the canvas shows more colour and less of the bare sky, for we are now more conscious of background, the overthrow of Persia and the operations of human sin.

The third characteristic, picturesqueness, is the most obvious of all. The few instances of bombastic diction noted above are but the necessary failures of a supreme craftsman. Homer does not stay to embroider his language with metaphor, which belongs to a more reflective age; Pindar's tropes are splendid and elaborate, a calculated jog to the attention. For Æschylus, metaphor seems the natural speech, unmetaphorical language a subtlety which requires practice. Danaus in his perplexity ponders "at the chess-board";[2] when the assembly votes, "heaven bristles with right hands";[3] an anxious heart "wears a black tunic";[4] heaven "loads the scales"[5]

---

[1] *Suppl.* 836-7. I see no reason for supposing that the Greek is defective.

[2] *Ibid.* 12. [3] *Ibid.* 608. [4] *Persæ*, 115. [5] *Ibid.* 346.

to the detriment of Persia; the trumpet "blazes";[1] misfortune "wells forth";[2] Amphiaraus "reaps the deep furrow of his soul";[3] "the sea laughs in ripples without number";[4] the snow descends "with snowy wings";[5] for an intrepid woman "hope treads not the halls of fear";[6] "Fate the maker of swords is sharpening her weapon";[7] Anarchy in the State is the "mixing of mud with water".[8]   The best example of all is the celebrated beacon-speech in the *Agamemnon*: "The flame is conceived as some mighty spirit. . . . It 'vaults over the back of the sea with joy'; it 'hands its message' to the heights of Macistus; it 'leaps across' the plain of Asopus, and 'urges on' the watchmen; its 'mighty beard of fire' streams across the Saronic gulf, as it rushes along from peak to peak, until finally it 'swoops down' upon the palace of the Atreidæ."[9]

Allied to this picturesqueness of phrase is a picturesqueness of characterization: Æschylus loves to give life and colour even to his subordinate persons.   Attic literature is so frugal of ornament that the richness of this writer gains a double effect.   The watchman of the *Agamemnon* has the effect of a Teniers peasant; Orestes' nurse in the *Choephorœ* is a promise of the nurse of Juliet; the Egyptian herald conveys with amazing skill the harem-atmosphere—one seems to see that he is a negro; Hermes in the *Prometheus* is the father of all stage courtiers.   Again, direct appeals to the eye were made by various quaint devices—the winged car of the Ocean Nymphs, their father's four-legged bird, and the "tawny horse-cock" (whatever it was) which so puzzled Dionysus.[10]   Such curiosities were meant merely as a feast for the idle gaze, at first; but the serious mind of the poet turned even these to deeper issues.   The red carpets of the *Agamemnon*, and the king treading upon them in triumph, provided a handsome spectacle to the

---

[1] *Persæ* 395. [2] *Ibid.* 815. [3] *Septem*, 593.
[4] *P.V.* 89-90. [5] *Ibid.* 993. [6] *Ag.* 1434.
[7] *Choeph.* 647. [8] *Eum.* 694.
[9] Haigh, *Tragic Drama*, pp. 82 *sq.* [10] *Frogs*, 932.

eye ; but the mind at the same instant fell into grimmer bodements as the doomed man seemed to walk in blood. So, too, the word-pictures which please the ear are raised by genius to an infinitely higher power, as in that same scene, when Agamemnon complains of the waste of purple stuffs, and the queen seems but to say that there is dye enough left in the sea : " There is a sea, and who shall drain it dry ? "   The meaning of the words is as inexhaustible as the ocean they tell of, revealing abysses of hatred and love hellishly intertwined, courage to bear any strain, an hereditary curse whose thirst for blood is never sated, a bottomless well of life.

If we now consider Æschylus on his purely dramatic side, as a builder of plays, we find again the three distinctive notes, grandeur, simplicity, and picturesqueness. The grandeur of his architecture is an authentic sign of his massive genius—it by no means depends on his selection of divine or terrific figures ; the *Persæ* and the *Septem* are witnesses.   It is the outcome of his conception of life as the will of God impinging upon human character.   Æschylus knows nothing about "puppets of fate".   Around and above men is a divine government about which many things may be obscure, but of which we surely know that it is righteous and the guardian of righteousness.   Man by sin enters into collision with the law.   The drama of Æschylus is his study of the will and moral consciousness of man in its efforts to understand, to justify to itself, and to obey that law. Supreme justice working itself out in terms of human will—such is his theme.   Another source of grandeur lies in the perspectives which his works reveal.   This, perhaps most evident in the *Prometheus*, runs through the other plays ; and a technical result of this power is the skill with which the whole trilogies are wrought. To compose trilogies rather than simple tragedies shows indeed the instinct for perspective working at the very heart of his method.   Again, if this instinct likens his work to painting, still more are we led by historical considerations to make a comparison with sculpture.   It has

been said [1] that the earliest play is "like one of those
archaic statues which stand with limbs stiff and countenance smiling and stony". This brilliant simile is full
of enlightenment. Just as those early Greek statues
which seem to the casual observer merely distressing are
to be contrasted, not with the achievement of Praxiteles
but with non-Hellenic art, the winged bulls of Assyria
and the graven hummocks which present the kings of
Egypt, whereupon we perceive the stirrings of life and
beauty; so should the *Supplices*, were it only in our
power, be compared to the rigid declamations from which,
to all seeming, tragedy was born. In the *Supplices*
tragedy came alive like the marble Galatea. Dædalus
was reputed to have made figures that walked and ran;
it is no fable of Æschylus, but the history of his art.

Simplicity, the second note of Æschylus, needs little
demonstration after the detailed account of his plots.
The four earlier works contain each the very minimum
of action. The characterization is noble, but far from
subtle. All the persons are simply drawn, deriving
their effect from one informing concept and from the
circumstances to which they react. Euripides in the
Frogs [2] fastens upon this, remarking, "You took over
from Phrynichus an audience who were mere fools".
A later generation demanded smartness and subtlety;
Æschylus was anything but artful, and so the same
critic accuses him of obscurity in his prologues. [3] The
Oresteia exhibits a marked advance in construction.
Leaving on one side the vexed question of the plot in
the *Agamemnon*, [4] we observe in the *Choephoræ* what we
may call intrigue. Orestes has a device for securing
admission to the palace; the libations by which Clytæmnestra intends to secure herself are turned into a weapon
against her; the chorus intercept the nurse and alter
her message so as to aid the conspiracy. This ingenuity
is perhaps due to the influence of Sophocles.

---

[1] Professor Gilbert Murray, *Literature of Ancient Greece*, p. 217.
[2] vv. 908 *sqq.*   [3] *Frogs*, 1119 *sqq.*
[4] Dr. Verrall's theory is still, I believe, accepted only by a minority.

Thirdly, what may be termed picturesqueness in structure is a matter of vital import for Æschylus. To write dramatically is to portray life by exhibiting persons, the vehicles of principles, in contact and collision. For an artist of the right bent, it is not difficult to select a scene of history or an imagined piece of contemporary life which under manipulation and polishing will show the hues of drama. But the earliest of dramatists turns aside in the main from such topics. His favourite themes are the deepest issues, not of individual life, but the life of the race, or the structure of the universe. What is the relation between Justice and Mercy? Why is the omnipotent omniscient? May a man of free will and noble instincts escape a hereditary curse sanctioned by heaven? Such musings demand surely a quiet un-hurried philosophic poem, not the decisive shock of drama. Æschylus devoted himself, nevertheless, not to literature in the fashion of Wordsworth, but to tragedy. How was he to write a play about Justice and Mercy, to discuss a compromise between the rigidity of safe government and the flexibility of wise government? Justice and Mercy are both essential to the moral universe, says the theologian—but they are incom-patible. Friendship and strife are both essential to the physical universe, says Empedocles—but how can they be wedded? This impossibility is everywhere, and every-where by miracle it is achieved. This union of opposites pervades the world, from the primitive protoplasm which must be rigid to resist external shock but flexible to grow and reproduce itself, to the august constitution of the eternal kingdom in which " righteousness and peace have kissed each other ". Where, then, is the playwright to find foothold? His innumerable instances merge into one another. Æschylus, with noble audacity, lifts us out of the current of time and imagines a special instance, an instance which presents the problem in dual form—for example the human tangle of the Atridean house and the superhuman conflict between Zeus and the powers of earth. It is assumed that there has been no earlier,

less decisive, jar.   In the future, there will be no more.
The great question is raised once for all in its completest,
most difficult form.   The gradual processes of time are
abolished.   Thus Atlas[1] is punished by condemnation
to the task of upholding heaven for ever; how it was
sustained before his offence is a question we must not
raise.   Hypermnestra[2] is put on trial for disobeying her
father that her husband may live.   She is saved by
Aphrodite; and the innumerable cases of conflicts of
duty which have broken hearts in days past are summed
up (rather than disregarded) by this ultimate example.
In the *Oresteia* a man is hunted well-nigh to death by
fiends because he has obeyed the will of God.   Why?
It can only be said that until the judgment in the
Eumenides all is nebulous, the world is being governed
desperately as by some committee of public safety;
morals, justice, and equity are still upon the anvil.
After this one case no man will ever again be tortured
like Orestes; nor indeed, we may conjecture, will the
oracles of Zeus issue behests so merciless as that which
he received.

Finally, something should be said about Æschylus'
views on religion.   Other subjects had an interest for
him, geography, history, and politics,[3] but his never-
failing and profound interest in religion overshadows
these.   Not only was he interested in the local cults of
Athens, as were his great successors; he is at home in
the deepest regions of theology.   Even more than this,
he brings back strange messages from the eternal world,
he seeks to purify the beliefs of his fellows by his deep
sense of spiritual fact; he writes the chronicles of Heaven
and bears witness to the conquests of the Most High.
Among Greek writers he is the most religious, and, with
Plato and Euripides, most alive to the importance of belief to the national health.   He is not ashamed of the

---

[1] *P.V.* vv. 350-2.   [2] *Danaides.*
[3] Cp. *Septem*, 592-4 (Aristides), *P.V.* 1068 (Themistocles), and the
references to the Areopagus (vv. 681-710) and to the Athenian Empire
(vv. 398-401) in the *Eumenides*.

traditional gospel when he thinks it true : "the act comes back upon him that did it ; so runs the thrice-old saw ".[1] Still less is he ashamed to denounce false maxims : "From of old hath this hoary tale been spread abroad among men, that when prosperity hath grown to its full stature it brings forth offspring and dies not childless ; yea, that from good hap a man's posterity shall reap unendingly a harvest of woe. But I stand apart from others, nor is my mind like theirs."[2] This originality and sincere mood is shown everywhere. Already we have noted how earnestly just he is towards the claims of the Furies. The case was no foregone conclusion for him. To realize how terrible the quarrel was in his eyes we have only to imagine our feelings had Apollo been defeated. And defeated he nearly is ; the human judges vote equally.

The poet's clear thinking and ethical soundness are shown in his treatment of the hereditary Curse or Até (ἄτη). Some great sin brings this curse into being, and it oppresses the sinner's family with an abnormal tendency to further crime. But the descendants are not forced to sin. The action of the curse, according to Æschylus, is upon their imagination. When some temptation to wrong-doing occurs to them, as to all men, they may suddenly remember the curse and exclaim in effect : "Why struggle against this temptation? our house is ridden by an Até which drives us to sin ". Thus they rush upon evil with a desperate gusto and abandon. So Eteocles[3] cries :—

> Since Heav'n thus strongly urges on th' event,
> Let Laius' race, by Phœbus loathed, all, all
> Before the wind sweep down the stream of Hell !

But the curse can be resisted. The house of Atreus fed its curse from generation to generation by criminal bloodshed. But Orestes shed blood only at the behest of

---

[1] *Choeph.* 313 *sq.* : δράσαντι παθεῖν, τριγέρων μῦθος τάδε φωνεῖ.
[2] *Ag.* 750-7.   [3] *Septem*, 689-91.

Heaven, and so combined necessary vengeance with innocence.   Thus the curse was laid to rest.[1]

The revision to which he subjected the myths of
popular religion is therefore characteristic.   There were
four leading phenomena which it was necessary somehow to co-ordinate if a consistent faith was to be possible.
First, there was the Olympian hierarchy, the object of
the State-religion at Athens as elsewhere.   Secondly,
there was Chthonian religion or the worship of earth-
powers.   Thirdly, there was the vague, less personal,
power called Fate.   And lastly, there was conscience,
the feeling that sin polluted the soul, not merely the
hands of the wrong-doer.[2]   None of these four conceptions was by itself adequate in the eyes of Æschylus.
The Olympians, though the rulers of men and on the
whole their friends, were according to universal report
stained with all the crimes of humanity.   The earth-
deities ruled only by fear ; they punished but they did not
inspire ; nor was it clear that their power was not somehow subordinate to that of Heaven.   Fate was impersonal and had no moral aspect on which men could base
their understanding of its law.   The conception of personal righteousness had no visible basis in the scheme of
things ; there was no power outside man who guaranteed
the authenticity of his thirst for holiness.   When once
Æschylus set out on his self-appointed path, he brooked
no obstacle.   First, as to the Olympian gods, he explains away the difficulties.   Most of them are frankly
ignored,[3] edifying accounts being substituted for them ;
some few are accepted with a shrug.[4]   Zeus is no longer
the head of a turbulent confederacy ; he has become the
father and lord of powers who obey him implicitly and

[1] *Choeph.* 1076.

[2] Æschylus never worked himself entirely free from this savage conception of sin as a material defilement.   Orestes, among the proofs that
he has expiated his offence, mentions the use of swine's blood as a
cleansing power (*Eum.* v. 283).

[3] See Dr. Verrall's discussion of the prologue to the *Eumenides,*
Euripides the Rationalist, pp. 220-4.

[4] *Eum.* vv. 640-51.

derive their prerogatives from his will. The earth-deities, as has been shown, surrender their moral functions and become mere spirits of fertility, localized, in the case of the Furies, upon Attic soil. Nothing, even in this writer, is more audacious than the monotheistic fervour which transforms these terrific beings into a species of fairy. Fate, again, is mysteriously assimilated to Zeus; the unvarying laws of the universe are invested with a moral tendency and a personal will. And lastly, the conception of human holiness finds its sanction in that will. Zeus bids us be righteous, and our faith affirms that he will punish the guilty and reward the good.

CHAPTER IV

THE WORKS OF SOPHOCLES

OF more than a hundred plays written by Sophocles, only seven survive entire. These shall now be discussed in what is probably the chronological order.

The Ajax[1] (Αἴας, sometimes called Αἴας μαστιγοφόρος, from his scourging of the cattle) cannot be dated. It is generally agreed that this work and the *Antigone* are the two earliest extant plays; which of the two was produced first it is difficult to say.[2] Perhaps an important feature of technique settles this—both tragedies need three actors, but the *Ajax* in this respect is more tentative than the *Antigone*.

The scene is laid before the tent of Ajax on the plain of Troy. Enraged by the action of the Greeks in awarding to Odysseus instead of to himself the arms of the dead Achilles, Ajax sought to slay Agamemnon, Menelaus, and others in their sleep. The goddess Athena sent madness upon him so that he slaughtered cattle in their stead. Coming to himself he realizes his shame, and eluding his friends—the chorus of Salaminian sailors and the Trojan captive, Tecmessa (who has borne him a son),—he retires to a lonely spot by the sea and falls upon his sword. His brother Teucer returns too late to save him, but in time to confront and defy Agamemnon and Menelaus, who

[1] *Arrangement:* protagonist, Ajax, Teucer (Ajax, when dead, is represented by a lay figure); deuteragonist, Odysseus, Tecmessa; tritagonist, Athena, messenger, Menelaus, Agamemnon.

[2] For the arguments see Jebb's *Introduction* (pp. li-liv) to the *Ajax*. He thinks *Antigone* the earlier.

have decreed that Ajax' body shall be left unburied.
At length Agamemnon is induced by Odysseus to forgo
his purpose.

No Greek play gains so much by re-reading as
the *Ajax*. The character of the hero steadily grows
on us; it is not that we admire him more, but that
we feel a deeper sympathy. As he gains in clearness,
he lifts the other characters into the light. Ajax is a
man dowered with nobility, sensitiveness, and self-reliance, but ruined by the excess of those qualities. His
nobility has become ambition, his sensitiveness morbidity,
his self-reliance pride. He offends Heaven by his
haughtiness, and is humbled; then, rather than accept
his lesson, he shuns disgrace by suicide. This resolution
is strong enough to overbear the appeals of Tecmessa
and the silent sway of his little son; he faces death
calmly and even thoughtfully. Grouped round the
central figure are first Tecmessa and Teucer, and on
a lower plane Odysseus, Menelaus, Agamemnon, and
the chorus. Athena stands apart.

Tecmessa is one of the loveliest creations of Sophocles; there clings about her a silvery charm
which is strangely refreshing amid the turbid grandeur
of the play. Tenderness, patience, courage—these are
commonplace enough upon the stage; yet Sophocles
has made of them something frail but indestructible,
and touched her with his own greatest charm—an
unearthly eloquence of which we shall speak later :—

> ἀλλ' ἴσχε κἀμοῦ μνῆστιν· ἀνδρί τοι χρεὼν
> μνήμην προσεῖναι, τερπνὸν εἴ τί που πάθοι.[1]

When Ajax is dead, it is she, not Teucer (as Ajax
had hoped) who finds the body, and this marvel of
quiet tenderness gleams forth again. She hardly
laments at all; the chorus who accompany her are
more moved. So accustomed is she to sorrow and
self-repression that grief is her natural element; she

---

[1] vv. 520-1 : "Nay, have thought even of me. A man should sure be
mindful of any joy that hath been his." But of course the quality spoken
of evaporates in such a " translation ",

utters a few quiet words of noble pity, and when the sailors press forward to view the dead she gently says "ye must not look on him," and covers the body with a robe. Her self-command is so absolute that it can bend; she will even say "Alas! What shall I do?" when confronted with a mere perplexity about the removal of the corpse.

Teucer is Ajax himself without the madness and the illumination; he stands in the same relation to his half-brother as Mark Antony in Shakespeare to Julius Cæsar; he is an ideal presenter of Ajax' claims if they are to be presented at all to people like Menelaus and Agamemnon. Menelaus is more active in debate, more brilliantly vulgar, than his brother, who wisely takes his stand upon general principles, and hardly mentions at all the decision not to bury Ajax. Agamemnon is conscious of his weak position; finally, he succeeds in retiring without complete loss of dignity. Odysseus is apparently intended as the antithesis to Ajax—discreet, forgiving, and impressed by the power of Heaven. Though but a sketch, he is a striking figure; after all the anguish and outcry, it is the normal man who emerges as the pivot of events and saves the situation.

The Salaminian sailors offering no special features, there remains only Athena, who dominates the "prologue". In contrast with the fully-developed beings whom we have studied in the *Oresteia* she is amazingly crude. The fact is that we ought not to consider her "character" at all. She is simply divine punishment roughly (but not casually) personified and given the name Athena. She gloats over the madman whom even the mortal standing beside her pities, and the only lesson she draws for him is that men must shun pride. It is natural, but useless, to call her a fiend; she serves merely as the visible and audible symbol that Heaven punishes haughty independence of spirit. That instead of mere evolutions of puppets we have a striking drama is due simply to the fact that Sophocles is interested far more in Ajax than in the goddess.

Two real or apparent defects must be noted. Firstly, we are shocked, or we should be shocked, by the actions (if not the character) of Ajax—a point often disregarded, probably through an idea that his bloodshed was caused by madness. But the goddess, by so deluding him, turned his rage from man to beast. He makes a deliberate attempt to murder the Atridæ in their sleep, together with an indefinitely large number of their followers, and this in the course of a campaign. It can hardly be doubted that the doom pronounced by the general, that such a man (to ignore his personality for the moment) shall not be buried, would have met with faint reprobation, either at the time supposed or among the contemporaries of the poet. Again, the indifference with which Ajax treats Tecmessa amounts to sheer brutality. Many readers have supposed that the prince cherishes affection for her, but conceals it under a show of roughness to avoid "breaking down". This is a mere fancy. Nothing in Ajax' conduct, and practically[1] nothing in his words, betrays any interest whatsoever in Tecmessa. The man is absorbed almost entirely by his sense of wounded dignity. He bids an affectionate farewell to his child, he speaks lovingly of his own parents and of Teucer; but nothing can prevent him from escaping disgrace by self-destruction. When about to fall upon his sword he mingles with his farewells a fierce behest to the Furies to destroy the whole Greek host which has slighted him. So far as the first part of this tragedy is concerned, Ajax is a magnificent brute; he is better dead.

The second difficulty is that Ajax dies at v. 865, but the play continues for five or six hundred lines more. This great space is occupied by a long dispute about his burial, which modern readers find tedious. But the difficulty arises from a mischievous idea that the culmination of every tragedy is the hero's death. Often it is only

[1] In the address to his child he throws a half-line to the mother (v. 559) and at the beginning of his disguised farewell to the chorus he expresses pity for Tecmessa (vv. 650-3), but there is nothing to show that this is not feigned, like his implied renunciation of suicide.

a step towards the real crisis.   In *Ajax* the theme is not
his death, but his rehabilitation : the disgrace, the suicide,
the veto on his burial, Teucer's defiance, the persuasions
of Odysseus, are all absolutely necessary.   The culminating point is the dispute about his burial, especially
since Ajax was one of the Attic "heroes," and the
centre of a hero's cult was his tomb.[1]   This explanation
enables us to regard the whole play as an organic unity.
It helps, moreover, to meet the first difficulty—the character of Ajax.   It must be remembered that a man became a "hero" not necessarily through any nobility or
holiness of his life.   It was rather the fact that he had
passed through strange, unnatural experiences, had even
committed morbid crimes, so long as those offences were
purged by strange sufferings and death, violent, superhuman, or pitiable.   Such was Œdipus, and such is
Ajax.   Greek feeling would have made a "hero" of
Lear, of Hamlet, perhaps of Othello.   Ajax is a man of
essentially noble mould—this the speeches of Teucer express admirably—who sins deeply and suffers strangely.
That he happens to evoke less admiration from us than
the other tragic figures just mentioned matters little.
Lack of tenderness towards women was the rule at
Athens ; and hatred of enemies, which Ajax carried to
such insane length, was commoner still.   But what of
the lowered tone which marks the end of the tragedy ?
Teucer's speech on the warlike achievements of his
brother is, indeed, beyond praise ; but much of his other
remarks, and of the language held by the Atridæ, is
mere brawling.   But these quarrels bring into relief the
proud nobility of the man who lies between the disput-
ants, dead because he would not stay to rehabilitate himself by such bickering.

The ANTIGONE[2] (Ἀντιγόνη) was produced about 441

[1] See Jebb's *Introduction* to the play (pp. xxviii-xxxii).
[2] The *arrangement* is uncertain.   Jebb gives, protagonist : Antigone, Tiresias, Eurydice ; deuteragonist : Ismene, guard, Hæmon, the
messengers ; tritagonist : Creon.   Croiset gives, protagonist : Antigone,
Hæmon ; deuteragonist : Ismene, guard, Tiresias, messengers ; tritagonist : Creon, Eurydice.

B.C. ⸏The scene is laid before the palace at Thebes, on the morning after the repulse of the Argives who had come to restore Polynices. Creon, King of Thebes, publishes an edict that no one shall give burial to the corpse of Polynices on pain of death. Antigone, sister of the dead man, despite the advice of her sister Ismene, performs the rite and is haled before Creon. She insists that his edict cannot annul the unwritten primeval laws of Heaven. The king, disregarding the admonitions of his son Hæmon, betrothed to Antigone, sends her to the cave of death. The prophet Tiresias warns him that the gods are angered by the pollution which comes from the unburied corpse. Urged by the chorus, Creon relents, and hastens first to bury Polynices, then to release Antigone, who has, however, already hanged herself. Hæmon stabs himself by her body. On hearing of his death his mother Eurydice, wife of Creon, commits suicide. The play ends with Creon's helpless grief.

This play is perhaps the most admired of Sophocles' works. But the admiration often rests on a misunderstanding. It is customary to regard Antigone as a noble martyr and Creon as a stupidly cruel tyrant, because of an assumption that she must be what a similar figure would be, and often has been, in a modern play. Memories of Cordelia confronting Lear, of Dorothea in *The Virgin Martyr* of Massinger and Dekker, beguile us so that we read that character into the play. The principle upheld by Antigone, and that upheld by Creon, are *prima facie* of equal validity. The poet may, possibly, agree with Antigone rather than with the king, but the current belief, that the princess is splendidly right and her oppressor ignobly wrong, stultifies the play; it would become not tragedy but crude melodrama. In judging Attic literature there is nothing which it is more vital to remember than the immense importance attached by Athenians to the State and its claims. We are alive to the sanctity of human life, but think far less of the sanctity of national life. An English reader, therefore, regards Creon with all the reprobation which his treatment of Antigone can possibly deserve; but whatever justification is inherent in the case he almost ignores.

The truth is that Creon commits a terrible act owing to a terrible provocation. His act is the insult to Polynices' body, which he maintains at the cost of Antigone's life; his justification is the fact that the dead man, though a Theban, was attacking Thebes and would have destroyed the State. Antigone stands for respect to private affection, Creon for respect to the community. It is impossible to say at the outset which is the more important, and the problem may well be insoluble. But it is precisely because of this that the *Antigone* is a tragedy. To accept the customary view, and yet insist that Sophocles is a great dramatist, is mere superstition; the work becomes the record of an insane murder. On *a priori* grounds, then, we may believe that Sophocles by no means condemns Creon offhand. It is not satisfactory to argue that Thebes should have been satisfied with the death of the invader. Since he was a Theban his attack was looked on as the foulest treachery, which merited extreme penalty, both by way of revenge and as a warning to others. (Just the same view is held by the authorities in the *Ajax.*) The play presents a problem both for the king and for his kinswoman: "I am right to punish this traitor's corpse; am I justified in killing others who thwart the punishment?" "I am right to show love and pity for my dead brother; am I justified in flouting the State?" Antigone is only Creon over again with a different equipment of sympathies. That one loves his country with a cold concentration which finds enemies and treachery everywhere, while the other passionately loves her dead brother, should not blind us to the truth that Antigone has all Creon's hardness and narrowness, and especially all his obstinacy. That tenderness and womanly affection which we attribute to the princess are amiable inventions of our own, except the love which she bears Polynices. This love is not to be in any sense belittled, but it is simply an instinct, like that of Creon in matters of State, an instinct to which she will, like him, sacrifice all else. If Creon sacrifices Antigone for his ideal, she sacrifices Hæmon for hers. He shows brutality to his son, she to her sister. That a compromise between the demands of the State and private conscience is, however unwelcome, necessary, never occurs to either party, and those who, like Hæmon and Ismene, urge such a thought upon them are insulted. This blindness to the psychology of Antigone has led to actual meddling with Sophocles' text. In her last long speech occurs a celebrated "difficulty," namely, her statement [1] that if the dead man had been a child or husband of hers, she would not thus have given her life; but the case of Polynices is different, since (her father and mother being dead) she can never have another brother. These lines are generally bracketed as spurious because unworthy of Antigone's character and inconsistent with the reason for her act which she has already [2] given, namely, the "unwritten and unshaken laws of Heaven". Any idea that the passage was inserted in "later times" is rendered impossible by the fact that Aristotle [3] quotes it (about 340 B.C.) and the presumption is that the words are the poet's own. Indeed, the "difficulty" exists only in the minds of those who attribute inconsistency in a character to incompetence in the playwright. But while illogical people exist it is hard to see why a dramatist should not depict them. Antigone's "reason" is stupid, no doubt, but what could be more dramatic? It is no novelty that a person capable of courageous action cannot argue well about it; there is a logic of the heart that has little to do with the logic of the brain. Antigone *has* no reasons; she has only an instinct. Here, and here only, Sophocles has pressed this point home, and the popular view has no resource but to reject the passage.

[1] vv. 904-12. See Jebb's discussion in his *Appendix*.
[2] vv. 450-70.   [3] *Rhetoric*, III, xvi. 9.

Whom does Sophocles himself approve, the king or his opponent? Neither. Attention to the plot will make this clear. The *peripeteia* or "recoil" is the revelation that the gods are angered by the pollution arising from the body, and that owing to their anger grave peril threatens Creon's family. It is this news which causes his change of purpose. Polynices is therefore buried by the king himself despite his edict. These facts show that ultimately both Antigone and Creon are wrong. Heaven is against Creon, as he is forced at last to see— Antigone's appeal to the everlasting unwritten laws is in this sense justified. But Antigone is wrong also. She should have left the gods to vindicate their own law. Such a statement may seem ignobly oblivious of religion, human nature, and the courage which she shows. But it is not denied that Antigone is noble and valiant: she may be both, yet mistaken and wrong-headed. One is bound to consider the facts of the plot. Why is she at first undetected yet compelled by circumstances to perform the "burial"-rites twice? Simply to remind us that, if Creon is resolved, she *cannot* "bury" Polynices. The king has posted guards, who remove the pious dust which she has scattered; and this gruesome contest could continue indefinitely. She throws away her life, *and with no possible confidence that her brother will in the end be buried*. It is precisely this blindness of hers which makes the tragedy—her union of noble courage and unswerving affection with inability to see the crude facts of a hateful situation. Her obstinacy brings about the punishment of Creon's obstinacy, for Eurydice's death is caused by Hæmon's, and Hæmon's by Antigone's. Had she not intervened all these lives would have been saved. The whole action might have dwindled to a mere revolting incident: the king's barbarity, the anger of the gods, and the king's submission. The tragedy would have disappeared: it is Antigone's splendid though perverse valour which creates the drama.

A difficulty of structure has been found[1] in the fact that Creon, despite his haste to free Antigone, tarries for the obsequies of Polynices. Why does he not save the living first? This "problem" arises merely from our insistence on the overwhelming importance of Antigone and our disregard of the real perspective. The explanation is simply that Creon has just been warned of the grave danger to the whole State and his family from the anger with which the gods view his treatment of Polynices—an offence which Tiresias emphasizes far more than that against Antigone; and the community, nay, even the several persons of Creon's family, are more important than one woman.

The lyrics of this play are among the finest in existence. The first ode expressing the relief of Thebes at the destruction of the ravening monster of war, the third which describes the persistence of sorrow from generation to generation of the Theban princes, the brief song which celebrates the all-compelling influence of love, with its exquisite reminiscence of Phrynichus,[2] the last lyric, a graceful invocation to the God Dionysus, and above all, the famous ode upon man and his quenchless enterprise, all these are truly Attic in their serene, somewhat frigid, loveliness.

The ELECTRA[3] ('Ηλέκτρα) has by most[4] critics been regarded as next in time to the *Antigone*. The scene shows the palace of Agamemnon now inhabited by his murderers, Clytæmnestra and her lover Ægisthus. Orestes, son of Agamemnon, returns to avenge him by slaying his own mother Clytæmnestra; he is accompanied by Pylades, his friend, and by an old slave. Chrysothemis, daughter of Agamemnon and sister of Electra, is sent by Clytæmnestra to appease the ghost of Agamemnon, but is persuaded by Electra to pray his

---

[1] Jebb's *Introduction*, pp. xvii-xx.   [2] See pp. 8, 15.
[3] *Arrangement* probably: protagonist, Electra; deuteragonist, Orestes and Clytæmnestra; tritagonist, Pædagogus, Chrysothemis, Ægisthus.
[4] Jebb, however, gives substantial reasons for putting it later. See his *Introduction*, pp. lvi-lviii.

help for Orestes. The slave of Orestes brings false news to the palace that Orestes has been killed in a chariot-race at Delphi, so that the queen is relieved from fear of vengeance. Chrysothemis returns, joyfully announcing Orestes' arrival—she has seen a lock of his hair on the tomb ; but her sister replies that he is dead. While Electra mourns for her brother he himself brings in an urn, pretending to be a messenger who has conveyed home the ashes of Orestes. Electra's lamentation over it reveals who she is, and Orestes makes himself known. Then the men go inside to slay Clytæmnestra, while Electra remains watching for Ægisthus. After the slaughter he arrives and triumphantly orders the body to be carried forth, but when he uncovers it he finds the corpse of Clytæmnestra. He is then driven within to death.

The *Choephoræ*, the *Electra* of Sophocles, and the *Electra* of Euripides supply the only surviving instance in which the three tragedians handled the same story ; at present it is enough to note the differences between the method of Sophocles and that of the *Choephoræ*. For Æschylus the slaying of Clytæmnestra is a question of religion and ethics, for Sophocles it is a matter of psychology, the emotional history of Electra. He is content to take the religious facts for granted, and then to proceed with no misgivings to a purely human drama. The play begins amid the bright, cheerful surroundings of dawn and ends with happiness. When Orestes comes forth, his sword wet with his mother's blood, he is entirely satisfied and untouched by any misgivings, simply because the question of matricide has been settled for him by Heaven. He is a personified theory of Olympian religion. His words to Electra after the queen is dead: "In the house all is well, if Apollo's oracle spoke well," [1] are the summary of Sophocles' religious point of view. Carefully and confidently referring the question of this matricide to a higher judge than Man, he proceeds to his actual business. Equally marked is

[1] vv. 1424-5.

the difference between the closing sentence of the *Choephoræ*, "Where then will end the fatal fury, when pass into closing calm?"[1] and that of the later work: "O house of Atreus, through how many sufferings hast thou come forth at last in freedom, crowned with good by this day's enterprise!"[2] For Sophocles the deed is done and behind us; for Æschylus it lives to beget new sorrows.

Electra dominates the action, scarcely leaving the scene after her first entry. Though not a great character-study, she impresses us by the pathos of her situation and by the splendid expression of her emotions; her lament over the funeral urn is perfect in the rhetoric of sorrow. Almost motionless throughout the long and varied action; the mark for successive onslaughts of insult, misery, surprise, grief, hatred, and joy, she is thrown into relief by all who approach her, especially Chrysothemis, whose princely robes add emphasis to the heroic meaning of the sordid dress worn by her royal sister. She is a simple character and needs little ornament; her devotion, patience, and courage are plain to behold. But we should note the masterly, yet unobtrusive way in which her feelings towards Clytæmnestra are portrayed. Hating her steadily as the slayer of Agamemnon, she cannot quite forget (as does Euripides' heroine) that Clytæmnestra is her mother. After her outburst of reproach against the queen she has enough flexibility of mind to own[3] that she is in a way ashamed of it—a simple touch which shows Sophocles a master, not a slave, of his own conceptions. A more subtle indication of her spirit is shown in Electra's speech to Chrysothemis urging her to aid in the deed of vengeance. All she proposes is that they should slay Ægisthus. But there is an undercurrent of emphasis which shows[4] that she intends the death of Clytæmnestra also.

---

[1] *Choeph.* 1075-6 (Verrall's translation).
[2] vv. 1508 *sqq.* (Jebb's translation).   [3] vv. 616-21.
[4] This seems a fair deduction, not only from the whole situation, but from the pause after Αἴγισθον in v. 957; also perhaps from the emphatic

The other personages are mostly well-drawn. Orestes is commonplace, but the other four are distinctly imagined. The tiny part of Ægisthus admirably reveals the malicious upstart ; Chrysothemis is another Ismene, with more energy and lightness. The Pædagogus reminds one of the guard in the *Antigone* by his quaint witticisms—" if I had not been watching at the door from the first, your plans would have entered the house before your bodies ".[1] Clytæmnestra, too, is admirable. More closely akin to an Euripidean than to an Æschylean character, she defends herself elaborately and gives way to fits of ill-temper and petty rancour ; but she has some maternal feeling left—witness the confusion of emotions with which she greets the news of Orestes' death.

The sorrows and character of Electra form one of the two great features of this tragedy. The other is the stage-craft. First there is a distinct element of intrigue, that is, of plot as contrived not by the poet but by the characters. Not only do the avengers gain access to the house by a false story ; this much is to be found already in the *Choephoræ*. There are two distinct visitors to the house : the Pædagogus with his tale of the fatal race, and Orestes bringing the funeral urn. It is to this duplication—for otherwise Clytæmnestra would have been present when the urn was brought—that we owe the splendid scene of the Recognition, with its introductory lament by Electra. Again, as in Æschylus the nurse sent by Clytæmnestra is induced to change her message to Ægisthus in a way vital to the conspirators, so here Chrysothemis is caused by her sister to invoke the aid of Agamemnon against the queen instead of seeking to assuage his wrath. Further, whereas Ægisthus might have entered the house and been slain without more ado, Electra, by telling him that the messengers have brought the

ἐμοί of v. 974. Cp. also 582 *sqq.* and especially the comment of the chorus in v. 1080 (διδύμαν ἑλοῦσ' Ἐρινύν).

[1] vv. 1331-3.

very body of Orestes home, induces the king to summon them forth with the corpse ; thus the end of the play is rendered vigorous (indeed melodramatic) by his triumphant unveiling of the body which proves to be that of the queen.

Besides these admirable strokes of a rather sophisticated " sense of the theatre " there are powerful effects which arise naturally from the circumstances. Clytæmnestra offers a prayer to the very god who has sent the avenger. Electra's wonderful address to the ashes of her brother gains greatly by the fact that he stands living beside her. A splendidly dramatic effect is obtained by the return of Chrysothemis—the most "modern" point of the whole work. She has been sent away for a certain purpose, but in the stress of later happenings we forget her. Suddenly she reappears with news—the result of her mission—news startling in itself, but ten times more so because of the events which (without her knowledge) have just occurred. Again, it is quite natural that Electra should come forth while Clytæmnestra is being slain, since some one must be on the alert for Ægisthus. This gives opportunity for the terrible little passage where the queen's agonized appeals inside the house are answered by the tense answers or comments of this tragic figure rigid before the gate.

The ŒDIPUS TYRANNUS[1] (Οἰδίπους Τύραννος), often called *Œdipus Rex* or *Œdipus the king*, is a play of uncertain date, but it seems later than *Electra* and earlier than *Philoctetes*.

The plot is rather intricate and must be given at greater length. The scene shows the palace of Œdipus at Thebes. The people are smitten by a pestilence ; and all look to the king, who has already sent his wife's brother, Creon, to ask advice from the Delphic oracle. Creon enters, bringing tidings that Thebes will be freed if the city is purged of those who killed Laius, the former

---

[1] *Arrangement:* protagonist, Œdipus ; deuteragonist, Priest, Jocasta, servant of Laius ; tritagonist, Creon, Tiresias, the two messengers.

king. Œdipus asks for particulars, and learns that
Laius was killed by some robbers. Only one man escaped. The king calls upon the slayer to declare himself, promising no worse treatment than exile; he asks
also any man who knows the guilty one to speak. If
no one confesses, he denounces civil and religious ex-
communication against the unknown. The chorus-
leader suggests that the prophet Tiresias should be consulted; Œdipus replies that he has been already
summoned. The coryphæus remarks casually that some
say Laius was slain by certain wayfarers. Tiresias enters,
but shows a repugnance even to discuss the problem, till
Œdipus in a rage accuses Tiresias of complicity in the
murder. An altercation follows in which the prophet
accuses Œdipus of having killed Laius. The other,
filled with wrath, proclaims that Tiresias and Creon are
plotting to make Creon king in his stead. Tiresias
threatens the king with mysterious horrors and downfall. Œdipus bids him begone, and rates him for a fool.
" Foolish, perhaps, in your eyes," says the old man, "but
thought wise by the parents that begat thee." Œdipus
is startled. "Parents? Stay! What man begat me?"
The answer is: "This day shall show thy birth and thy
destruction". The king again bids him go. As he
turns away, Tiresias utters his farewell speech. The
murderer of Laius is here, supposed an alien, but in
reality Theban-born. Bereft of his sight and his riches he
shall go forth into a strange land, and shall be found
brother and father of his children, son and husband of
his wife, murderer and supplanter of his father. Creon
enters, dismayed by the charges of Œdipus, when the
king appears, heaps reproaches upon the supposed traitor,
and insists that Creon shall die. The noise of their dispute brings from the palace Jocasta, sister of Creon and
wife of Œdipus; she brings about a half-reconciliation
between the two princes, and asks the cause of the
quarrel. Œdipus tells of the accusation pointed at
himself by Tiresias. Jocasta seeks to console him by
a proof that soothsaying is not trustworthy. "An oracle

once came to Laius that he should be slain by a son of his and mine. None the less, he was slain by foreign robbers at a place where three roads meet ; and the child, not three days old, was cast out upon a mountain, his ankles yoked together." This speech, so far from comforting the king, fills him with alarm. The phrase " a place where three roads meet " has struck him. He anxiously asks for a description of Laius and the number of his followers. The replies disturb him still more, and he asks that the single survivor, now a herdsman far from the city, should be sent for. Jocasta asks the reason. He tells the story of his early manhood : he is the son of Polybus, King of Corinth, but one day a man insulted him by saying he was no son of Polybus. The youth asked the Delphic oracle of his birth, but the god, instead of answering directly, announced that he was fated to marry his mother and kill his father. Œdipus cheated the oracle by never seeing his parents again. On his way from Delphi he met a body of men such as Jocasta has described, and after a quarrel slew them all. It seems that he is himself the slayer of Laius and is subject to the curses which he has himself uttered. His only hope lies in the survivor who, it is understood, always spoke of robbers, not of a single assailant. If this is accurate, Œdipus is not meant by the recent oracle. A messenger from Corinth enters, bringing news that the people of that city intend to make Œdipus their king ; Polybus is dead. Jocasta exclaims that Polybus was the man whom Œdipus feared he must slay. She mocks at the oracle and summons Œdipus, who shares her relief, but reminds her that his mother still lives. The messenger asks what woman they are discussing. " I can free you from that fear," he exclaims ; " Œdipus is not the son of Polybus and Merope." Further questioning from Œdipus brings forth the explanation. The present messenger gave Œdipus, when a babe, to Polybus. He was found in the glens of Cithæron, where the man was tending flocks, his ankles fastened by an iron thrust through them. Who did this the Corinthian cannot say, but the man who gave him to the Corinthian should know——another herdsman brought him, one of the household of Laius. Œdipus asks if this man can be found. The chorus answer that probably he is the person already summoned, and that perhaps the queen can tell. Œdipus turns to Jocasta, who flings him a few words of agony and sorrow and rushes into the house. Œdipus turns away in contempt, for he believes that Jocasta's distress springs from a fear that he will be found of ignoble birth. The aged servant of Laius now approaches, and is recognized by the Corinthian as the man who gave him the child. A conversation of intensest thrill follows between the two herdsmen, in which the Corinthian is eager, while the Theban is utterly reluctant, only answering under the direst threats from the king. At length it becomes plain that the babe Œdipus is the son of Laius and Jocasta. The king with a cry of horror rushes into the palace. A slave enters and tells how Jocasta has hanged herself, and how Œdipus has destroyed his own sight. After an interval Œdipus staggers forth, a sight of ghastliness and woe. Creon now appears as ruler of the city and bids Œdipus be hidden in the house. The wretched man asks that he be cast forth to dwell upon Cithæron ; Creon replies that the oracle must first be consulted. Œdipus bids a heart-broken farewell to his little daughters, and Creon takes them all into the palace.

The *Œdipus Tyrannus* has been universally admired as a masterpiece, ever since the time of Aristotle, who in his *Poetic* takes this play as a model of tragedy. The lyrics are simple, beautiful, and even passionately vigorous ; the dialogue in language and rhythm is beyond praise ; and the tragic irony, for which this poet is famous, is here at its height. But the chief splendour of the work is its construction, its strictly dramatic strength and sincerity. The events grow out of one another with the ease of actual life yet with the accuracy and the power of art. We should note the two great stages : first, the king fears that he has slain Laius ;

second, that he has slain *his father Laius*. This distinction, so vital to the growing horror, is kept admirably clear and is especially pointed by the part of the aged Theban. When he is summoned, it is to settle whether Laius was slain by one man or by a company; by the time he arrives, this is forgotten, and all wait to know from whom he received the outcast infant. Equally wonderful is the skill with which almost every stage in the discovery is made to rise from the temperament of Œdipus. He is the best-drawn character in Sophocles. Not specially virtuous, not specially wise—though full of love and pity for his people and vigorous in his measures for their safety, he is too imperious, suspicious, and choleric. His exaggerated self-confidence, dangerous in a citizen, is almost a crime in a prince. The only notable virtue in his character is the splendid moral courage with which he faces facts, nay, more, with which he insists on unearthing facts which he might have left untouched. And the core of the tragedy is that this virtue of Œdipus, his insistence on knowing the truth, is the source of his downfall. Had he not sent for Tiresias, Tiresias would not have come forward. Had he not urged the prophet to reply, Tiresias would not have uttered his accusations. By these apparently mad charges, Œdipus is stung into accusing Tiresias of plotting with Creon. This in turn brings Creon to the palace. The anger with which he reviles Creon causes a dispute which draws Jocasta from the house. Then, to calm Œdipus, she gives him the dreadful " consolation "—that oracles have no weight—which first makes the king fear he may have done the deed which is plaguing Thebes. And so to the end. One exception to this sequence should be noticed. The arrival of the Corinthian messenger at this moment is purely accidental. Without it, the witness of the old retainer would have fastened upon Œdipus the slaying of Laius (not known to be the king's father); and he would have gone forth from the city, but not as a parricide; moreover, the relation between him and the queen would

have remained unknown.   Judged by the standard of
the whole play, this fact constitutes a flaw in construction.
Why did not the poet contrive that the news of Polybus' death should arrive, and arrive now, as the direct
result of something said or done by Œdipus, just as the
arrival of the old Theban, with his crushing testimony,
is due to the king's own summons?   No doubt this
occurrence is meant to mirror the facts of life, which
include accidents as well as events plainly traceable to
character.

At this point should be mentioned other possible
faults, whether inherent in the drama or antecedent to it.
Some of the preliminary facts are to a high degree unlikely.   These points are three.   First, Œdipus and
Jocasta, though each separately has received oracular
warning about a marriage, make no kind of inquiry at
the time of their own wedding.   Secondly, Œdipus all
these years has never heard or inquired into the circumstances in which Laius was killed.   Third, Jocasta has
never yet been told of the incident at Corinth which
sent Œdipus to Delphi ; indeed she has apparently not
even heard that he is the son of the king and queen of
Corinth.[1]   Within the play itself is the strange feature
that when Tiresias accuses Œdipus of slaying Laius and
hints darkly at greater horrors—hints which in spite of
their obscurity might surely (one would think) have
united themselves in the mind of Œdipus with the
oracle of long ago—Œdipus is merely moved to fury,
not to misgiving.[2]   Now of the first three difficulties it
must be owned that despite the palliatives suggested,
they are irritating.   These things are "impossible," or,
if not, they are oddly irrational, which is the same thing
so far as the enjoyment of dramatic art is concerned.
They are, however, to be explained thus.   The unques-
tioning marriage of Œdipus and Jocasta is a *datum* of

---

[1] vv. 774 *sqq.*

[2] It is true that when the prophet mentions the parents of Œdipus
quite definitely (v. 436) the king is startled.   But this is one point only.
All the other remarks of Tiresias are ignored,

the legend with which the poet could not tamper. All that the dramatist could do he did—he placed the unlikely fact "outside the plot"[1] and dwelt on it as little as possible. Indeed, he hints at some sort of excuse—the confusion in Thebes owing to the oppression of the Sphinx.[2] Next, the postponement of explanations about the death of Laius and the exile of Œdipus from Corinth is a direct result of dramatic treatment. Just as Æschylus,[3] in order to handle dramatically a religious question, the bearings of which fill the whole of time, insists on contracting the issue to a single great instance, so Sophocles forces into the compass of one day's happenings the life of years. In actuality, this tragedy would have been spread over a great lapse of time. The climax and the horror would have been much the same essentially, but the poet presents the whole in a closely-knit nexus of occurrence, so as to make the spectator feel the full impact undissipated by graduations.

The difficulty concerning Tiresias is of another sort. Œdipus' apparent madness is not so great as it seems. Not only is he by his rank and superb self-confidence shielded from misgivings, not only is he already suspicious that the murderer must be some treacherous Theban,[4] but he has now lost his temper, and has just been furious enough to accuse Tiresias himself of complicity in the deed. It is therefore easy for him to assume that the prophet in his turn is only uttering his accusations as a wild insult.

It might also be asked, why is not the scene with Jocasta, in which she fortifies the king against soothsayers and oracles, not placed at the end of the Tiresias-episode? This question leads one to suppose that there is great importance in the quarrel with Creon which intervenes between the departure of Tiresias and the queen's appearance. Its importance clearly is, partly to depict Œdipus more plainly, by contrast with his equable

---

[1] See Aristotle, *Poetic*, 1454*b*.
[2] vv. 130-1.   [3] See pp. 127-8.   [4] vv. 124-5.

kinsman, but most of all to give force and impressiveness to the end of the play, in which Creon appears
as king. After the appalling climax of the play, and
the frightful return of the blind Œdipus, there is danger
that Creon's entry will fall flat.[1] But with faultless
skill Sophocles has prepared the ground so well that
when the agony is at its worst our interest is not indeed
increased, but refreshed and relieved by the appearance of this man whom we have forgotten, but whom
we recognize in a flash as being now the pivot of
events. This admirable stroke reminds one of the
return of Chrysothemis in the *Electra*, but it is far
more powerful.

Another feat of dramatic power must be noted,
marvellous even where all is masterly : the re-appearance
of Œdipus after the climax. Nothing in Greek tragedy
is more common than for a person after learning frightful news to rush within the doors in despair. But he
does not return ; a messenger tells the news of his
fate. In this play news is indeed brought of the bloody
deeds that have befallen. Then comes a sight almost
too appalling for art : the doors open and the man of
doom staggers into the light of day once more. Spiritually he is dead, but he may not destroy himself since
he cannot go down to Hades where his father and
mother dwell. He must live, surviving himself, as
it were a corpse walking the upper earth. The waters
of doom have closed over his head, but he re-appears.

Jocasta is more slightly drawn than Œdipus, yet
what we have suffices. Two features are stressed by
the poet—her tenderness for Œdipus and her flippant
contempt in regard to the oracles. This last is clearly
a dramatic lever of great power ; through it the king
is first brought to suspect that he is the guilty man.
It has a strong and pathetic excuse. Because of the
oracle, she was robbed of her child and yet all in vain—

---

[1] The entry of Fortinbras at the end of *Hamlet* is closely similar.
Perhaps it is fear of anti-climax which causes producers nowadays to omit
this finale.

the infant not yet three days old was cast away, but
none the less Laius was killed. It is precisely her
rage against the oracle for cheating her which brings
to Œdipus the knowledge that it has been fulfilled.
Further than this Sophocles has not characterized the
queen ; he places an ordinary woman in a situation
of extraordinary horror and pathos, leaving us to feel
her emotions, without any elaboration of his own.
To read the conversation between Œdipus and the
Corinthian, with the short colloquy of Œdipus and
Jocasta which follows, is to experience as perhaps
nowhere else can be experienced that "purgation of
pity and terror" which is the function of tragedy. It
all centres for the moment in Jocasta, yet she says
very little. We are required to imagine it for ourselves
—the intertwined amazement, joy, loathing, despair,
which fill the woman's heart during the few minutes
for which she listens in silence to the king and the
messenger. To have lost her child at birth, then
after mourning his death for many years at length to
find that he lives, that he stands before her, mature,
strong, and kingly, but her own husband ; then to
realize that not now but long ago did she recover
him, yet did not know him but loved him otherwise—
this even Sophocles has not put into speech. Only
one hint of it comes to us in the queen's last words :—

> ἰού, ἰού, δύστηνε · τοῦτο γάρ σ' ἔχω
> μόνον προσειπεῖν, ἄλλο δ' οὔποθ' ὕστερον.

First she screams at his ignorance and would tell all
in one word "Son!" But she cannot say it, nor dare
she use again the name "husband". All dear titles
have been forfeited by being all merited together ; and
with the cry "Unhappy one!" she goes to death.

The two herdsmen are perfect in their degree.
Instead of mere machines for giving evidence we
have a pair of real men, subtly differentiated and delightful. The Corinthian, as befits a man coming
from a great centre of civilization to the quieter town

of dull Bœotians, is polite, rhetorical,[1] ready of tongue, and conscious of his address ; eager and inquisitive, he increases his importance by telling the tale piecemeal, and will even tell it wrongly[2] for that purpose. The Theban herdsman is an excellent foil to his brisk acquaintance ; quiet and slow, with the breeding and dignity often found in the lowly members of a backward community, he does his best to recall the memories on which a king and a nation are hanging in suspense, until he begins to see whither the questions tend ; then, only the fiercest threats can drag the truth from his stubborn loyalty. Sophocles loved this character ; long before he appears we have a charming little description of him from hints of Jocasta[3] and the chorus ;[4] the poet has even given him one[5] of those magical lines to which we shall come again later :—

λέγεις ἀληθῆ, καίπερ ἐκ μακροῦ χρόνου.

THE WOMEN OF TRACHIS[6] (*Trachiniæ*, Τραχινίαι) is, perhaps, the next play in chronological order. The scene is before a house in the state of Trachis not far from Eubœa. Deianira, the wife of Heracles, is troubled by his absence because of an oracle which says that in this last enterprise he shall either die or win untroubled happiness. Hyllus, her son, goes off to help him in his attack on the city of Eurytus in Eubœa. The messenger Lichas brings news of Heracles' triumph ; with him are certain captive girls, one of whom, Iole, daughter of Eurytus, is beloved by Heracles. Deianira learns this fact after a pathetic appeal to Lichas ; then she sends him back with a gift to Heracles—a robe which she has anointed with the blood of the Centaur Nessus as a charm to win back her husband's love. After Lichas has gone she finds by an accident that the robe is

---

[1] Note his preciosity, vv. 942, 959, 1028.
[2] He first (v. 1026) says that he found the infant Œdipus ; only later (1038) does he admit that another man has been concerned.
[3] vv. 758-64.   [4] vv. 1117-8.   [5] v. 1141.
[6] *Arrangement:* protagonist, Deianira, Heracles ; deuteragonist, Hyllus, Lichas ; tritagonist, nurse, messenger, old man,

poisoned. Then Hyllus returns with news that his father is dying in torments, and reproaches his mother. She goes into the house and stabs herself. Hyllus learns the truth, and when the dying hero is carried in, cursing his false wife, he explains her error. Heracles gives orders that his body is to be burnt on Mount Œta and that Hyllus must marry Iole.

It is customary to regard the *Trachiniæ* as the weakest extant play of Sophocles. The picture of Heracles' physical agony near the close seems wearisomely elaborate ; and in the second place we are utterly dissatisfied with him. He does not seem worthy of the trepidation, awe, and grief which he has excited throughout the play. All that follows the suicide of Deianira appears empty or offensive. This objection may be put[1] thus, that there are two tragedies, that of Deianira and that of the hero. Now though it is quite true that one can point to a thought which unifies the play—the passion of Heracles for Iole, or more fundamentally, the destructive power of love, this does not meet the difficulty, which will then simply be restated thus, that the poet has not maintained a due perspective ; the story of Deianira's emotions and of her plan bulks too largely and impedes what should have been the climax. But it is a fundamental law in the criticism of Greek Tragedy, and especially in the study of Sophocles, that we must ponder it until we find some central thought which accounts for the whole action and for the perspective in which the details are placed. Such a central thought is, after all, not lacking in the *Trachiniæ*. It is the character of Deianira, her instincts, and her actions. This play is in structure very similar to the *Ajax*. In the earlier work Ajax' death occurs far from the end, but the latter portion is no anti-climax. So here : the topic is not especially the death of Deianira or the end of Heracles ; it is the heroine's love for her husband and the attempt she makes to win him back. The poet's

---

[1] See Jebb's *Introduction*, pp. xxxviii *sq.*

interest in her does not vanish at the moment of her silent withdrawal. Her act, her love, survive her. What is the result of her pathetic secret wooing of Heracles? She has longed for two things, his return and a renewal of his affection. To both these purposes is granted a dim painful phantom of success. Instead of tarrying in Eubœa Heracles hastens home, though every movement of his litter is torment; Deianira's passion has brought him back, though not as she meant. As for her plan to regain his love, it is true that when he learns her innocence not a word of pity or affection falls from him; he never mentions her again. It may be that he is merely stupid and callous; it may be that he is ashamed to recant his bitter words; it may be that he is at once engrossed in the sudden light which is thrown upon his own fortunes. However this may be, the promise of Nessus on which she relied is fulfilled: "This shall be to thee a charm for the soul of Heracles, so that he shall never look upon any woman to love her more than thee!"[1] —the hero's passion for Iole is quenched. This conception gives a wonderful beauty to what is otherwise a mere brutality of the dying man. In forcing his son to marry Iole he outrages our feelings as well as the heart of Hyllus—unless we have understood. But this is his reparation to Deianira. The charm of Nessus has been potent indeed; the maiden is nothing to him: he "loves no woman more" than Deianira. But this act is more than cold reparation; it is a beautiful stroke of silent eloquence. Heracles not only relinquishes Iole, he gives her to his son, to one many years his junior. This is an unconscious reply to the touching complaint[2] made by the wronged wife:—

> The flower of her age is in its spring,
> But mine in autumn. And the eyes of men
> Still pluck the blossom, shunning withered charms.

For him his wife was the true mate; let Iole wed a

---

[1] vv. 575-7 (Jebb's translation).   [2] vv. 547-9.

man of her own years.[1] Thus the hope of Deianira is
in a terrible way half-fulfilled. Just as Heracles was
mistaken in his reading of the oracle which promised
him "rest" at the end of his toils, so was she mistaken
in the meaning she put upon the Centaur's promise. The
oracles of heaven, by their own power and still more by
the terrible misinterpretation of man, help to mould the
play, as they mould the *Œdipus Tyrannus*. Thus the
Trachiniæ becomes a real unity. Deianira's fate is now
no over-developed episode, for in a spiritual sense it
fills the tragedy. The doom of Heracles is no anti-climax
or tedious addendum ; it is the exposition before our
eye of the havoc which can be wrought by sincere love
misled. A great structural danger lies herein, that the
picture of Heracles' torment may eclipse the tragedy of
his wife. But the poet has surmounted this by making the
agony-scene not too long, and above all by reminding us
of Deianira through the repeated allusion to her made
by Heracles and through the explanation of Hyllus.

Certain peculiarities of detail in the plot strongly support the view that Deianira is the subject of the whole
drama. First is the conduct of Lichas. This part is
carefully constructed so as to lead up to the great appeal
in which the heroine describes the might of Love. If
Lichas had really kept his secret instead of tattling to
the townsfolk, Deianira would not have known it and so
appealed to Lichas. If, on the other hand, Lichas had
not tried to deceive his mistress, she would not have
needed to offer any appeal. His conduct has been devised solely to portray her character by means of this
marvellous speech. A second point is the way in which
Hyllus learns his mother's innocence. After his speech
of denunciation she goes without a word into the house.
The Trachinian maidens know the truth and have heard
from Deianira [2] herself that she will not survive her

---

[1] These remarks are not vitiated by the fact (see Jebb on v. 1224)
that legend wedded Iole to Hyllus. If the command of Heracles is as
objectionable as Jebb appears to think, why did Sophocles go out of his way
to cause the hero himself, instead of some other, to enjoin the marriage?

[2] vv. 719 *sq.*

husband, but they say nothing to Hyllus. Yet the playwright who is here so strangely reticent allows the prince
to learn the facts in a few minutes "from the people
in the house" as he casually phrases it. The reason is
that if Hyllus were informed at once he would prevent
his mother's suicide. This would have destroyed
the dramatic treatment without altering events. For
Deianira is not concerned in being proved innocent;
she wishes to die now that Heracles is destroyed.
Hyllus' intervention would only mean procrastination of
death.[1] In the interests of drama, it must happen now.
Further he must learn the truth as soon as she is dead,
for some one must confront Heracles with a defence of
the dead woman, if her fate and her love are, as we said,
dominant throughout the play. Here, too, there is a
resemblance between the *Trachiniæ* and the *Ajax*;
Hyllus, in this last scene, resembles Teucer championing
the fame of Ajax.

The character-drawing is here as admirable as elsewhere. Lichas, well-meaning but foolish and shifty, is
contrasted with the messenger who is perfectly honest
though spiteful. Hyllus is a character of a type which
we have often discussed already—he has no personality,
and we are interested in him not because of what he is
but because of what happens to him. The women of
the chorus are simply a band of sympathetic friends.
Heracles, on the customary reading of the tragedy, is the
most callously brutal figure in literature. One need not
labour the proof; his treatment of Deianira, of Iole, of
Hyllus, of Lichas, of every one whom he meets,[2] is
enough. The poet has taken the only possible course
to make us witness the hero's pangs at the close with a
certain satisfaction. But the other possible theory does
away with this sham "tragedy". Heracles as a coarse
stupid "man of action" who is yet capable of reflection

[1] This accounts also for the absurd behaviour of the nurse (vv. 927 *sq.*)
who instead of interfering hastens away to Hyllus, entirely unlike other
such women in tragedy.

[2] See the speech of Lichas (vv. 248-86).

and a touch of "the melting mood" shown by his giving Iole to Hyllus when the secret of his wife's heart is at last irresistibly pressed upon him, is dramatic indeed.

But the glory of this work is Deianira. A comparison of the *Trachiniæ* with the *Ajax* illustrates the development of ideas in the poet's mind. Tecmessa's character and position have been analysed, and we find, instead of one woman, two—Iole and Deianira. Iole is mute ; it is not her conduct, but her involuntary influence, which contributes to the tragedy. In Deianira, however, we meet the Trojan princess once more, older and with more initiative—tenderer she could not be. It is this union of gentleness with force of mind, of love and sad knowledge of the world, which makes her character so appealing and gracious. A smaller poet would have made her haughty or abject, revengeful or contemptible ; Sophocles has portrayed a noble lady, who will bend, but not kneel. Her interview with Iole and the later conversations in which first she excuses her husband and then on reflection finds that she cannot share his home with the newcomer—these scenes, painted with quiet mastery, are the greatest work of Sophocles in the portraiture of women.

There can be no doubt that the *Trachiniæ* is the work of Sophocles ; considerations of style, hard to describe but overwhelming, settle the case beyond dispute. None the less we cannot ignore the influence of another school of drama—the Euripidean. The features more or less certainly due to this influence are : (i) The subject itself. Sophocles has studied a woman's love and its possibilities of unintended mischief in a way which recalls many plots [1] of Euripides. (ii) The "prologue," especially the explanatory speech of Deianira, is not in the usual manner of the playwright, but quite in that of Euripides. (iii) The last lines, with their reproach against the hardness of the gods who neglect

---

[1] Deianira's plan, moreover, reads like a sort of dilution of Medea's, and her last moments (vv. 900-22) recall the description in the *Alcestis* (vv. 158-84).

their children, and the total silence about the deifica-
tion of Heracles, which was the most familiar fact of
this story, a silence emphatic throughout, are in spirit
Euripidean.   (iv) The chorus is almost negligible as
a dramatic factor, and one of its songs — the first
stasimon—is literally "commonplace"; it would fit
any kind of joyous occasion. (v) The turns of expression occasionally recall those of the younger poet.   The
colloquial ποίαν δόκησιν [1] cannot be paralleled in tragedy
except in his work. One line [2] seems borrowed almost
without change. Deianira's homely, almost coarse,
words, "and now we two await his embrace beneath
one rug," are not what one expects from the stately
Sophocles. The prosaic φαρμακεύς [3] and the allusion [4]
to Heracles' unheroic side (ἡνίκ' ἦν ὠνωμένος, "when he
was deep in wine") are on the same level.   But most
Euripidean of all is the description [5] Deianira gives of
her dreadful suitor.   There is nothing unlike Sophocles
in this acceptance of the legend that Deianira was
wooed by a river-god.   But the studied nonchalance of
the first line " my suitor was a river, Acheloüs that is,"
and the absurdity of the second, in which the divine
wooer is represented as applying (with a punctilio
strange to river-gods of legend) to the lady's father for
her hand, and "calling" (φοιτῶν) on different occasions
as a different animal—all this mixture of horror and
comedy is absolute Euripides.   The fact appears to be
that Sophocles deliberately took up the attitude of
Euripides, for two reasons—firstly, for the sheer delight
of a strange and difficult feat of artistry ; secondly, in
order to show how Euripides, even from his own standpoint, ought to have written. [6]

---

[1] v. 427. Cp. Eur. *Helena*, 567 : ποίας δάμαρτος;
[2] Jebb points out that *Trach.* 416 and *Supplices* 567 are practically
identical.
[3] v. 1140.   [4] 268.   [5] vv. 9-14.
[6] That even the equable Sophocles did on occasion embody criticism
of other playwrights in his works is shown by such passages as *Electra*
1288 *sqq.*, *Œd Col.* 1148-9.

PHILOCTETES [1] (Φιλοκτήτης) was produced in the
spring of 409 B.C., when the poet was eighty-seven years
old, and won the first prize. The hero Philoctetes was
one of the chieftains who sailed for Troy. When the fleet
touched at Chryse, he was stung in the foot by a snake.
The wound was incurable and its noxious odour, together with the cries of the sufferer, were so troublesome
to the Greeks that they deserted him when asleep upon
the island of Lemnos, leaving with him a little food and
clothing, and his bow and arrows, the last a legacy from
Heracles. In the tenth year of the war the Greeks
learned that Troy could only be taken by help of
Philoctetes and the weapons of Heracles. Two men
were sent to Lemnos with the purpose of bringing the
maimed warrior to Troy—Odysseus because of his craft,
Neoptolemus because he was unknown to Philoctetes.

The scene is a desolate spot on the island, in front
of the cliff-face in which is the cave inhabited by
Philoctetes. Neoptolemus wins the confidence of the
sufferer while Odysseus keeps in the background, though
by a subtle device of a false message he aids the plot
greatly. But when the fated weapons are secured and
Philoctetes (who supposes he is to be conveyed back to
Greece) is ready to accompany Neoptolemus, the latter
tells him the truth. Philoctetes' misery, rage, and reproaches induce the youth to restore the weapons despite Odysseus' opposition, and to promise Philoctetes
a passage home. But at the last moment Heracles
appears in glory above their heads and commands
Philoctetes to proceed Troywards. He willingly consents, and bids farewell to the scene of his long sorrow.

In structure this play is perhaps the most interesting
extant work of Sophocles. As elsewhere, we find a
great simple character of vast will-power exposed to a
strong temptation—Philoctetes confronted by the chance
of healing, happiness, and glory, if only he will meet in
friendship men whom he is determined to hate. But

---

[1] *Arrangement :* protagonist, Philoctetes ; deuteragonist, Neoptolemus ; tritagonist, Odysseus, merchant, Heracles.

for once there is a secondary interest which is not purely secondary. Many will even find the development of Neoptolemus more impressive than the situation of Philoctetes. While the latter shows the heroic character as it appears after the experience of life, strong, reflective, sad, a little fierce if not soured, the other is the hero before such experience, eager and noble but too responsive to suggestion. Neoptolemus has just begun life, and his first task is to betray—for the public good, no doubt, but still to betray—a noble stranger who merits not only respect but instant pity and tendance. "Oh! that never had I left Scyros!" he exclaims. Life after all is not a blaze of glorious war as his father Achilles found it, but a sordid affair of necessary compromises. One of the most charming things in the drama is the clearness with which Philoctetes, in the midst of his rage, sees the tragedy of his youthful captor.[1] Confronted by the kindness of the youth, he reveals himself not as a mere savage, living only on thoughts of revenge; he becomes more flexible, open-hearted, almost sociable. So revealed, he is the direct cause of the change in Neoptolemus' purpose.

Beside these stands Odysseus, only less striking and equally indispensable. For a chief note of this drama is the skill with which the poet avails himself of the three actors, whose possibilities are here for perhaps the first time fully employed. It is easy, but mistaken, to label Odysseus as "the villain". In reality he is the State personified. There is no modern reader who does not hate and contemn him, but it remains true that whereas Philoctetes whom we pity and Neoptolemus whom we love both take a strictly personal view, Odysseus at the risk of his life insists on pressing the claim of the community. It is necessary to Greece that Troy should fall. She can only fall through the arrows of Heracles. The man who owns them will assuredly not consent. It follows that he must be compelled to help, by force or

[1] vv. 1007-15.

guile. A conquering nation must have its Philip as well
as its Alexander ; Odysseus stands for facts which
twenty years of the Peloponnesian war had driven home
into Athenian minds.   Neoptolemus is the type of many
a young warrior who has learned with aching disgust
that the knightly exploits which tales of Marathon had
fired him to perform must be thwarted unceasingly by
the politic meanderings of Nicias, by considerations of
corn-supply, or the " representations " of some remote
satrap.

And in the end Odysseus gets his way. As the two
friends start for home, leaving the Greeks at Troy to
defeat and the oracles of Heaven to non-fulfilment, a
god appears to command from the sky that self-sacrifice
shall be revoked and hate forgotten. What are we to
think of this intervention of Heracles ? Is he not an
extreme instance of the *deus ex machina* ? Is not mere
compulsion employed to change a settled resolve ?
This is the most striking and the most difficult feature
of the construction : rather it seems the negation of
structure. Why is it employed? Some[1] have been
content to suggest Euripidean influence—of course no
answer at all. Some[2] have thought that Heracles is
personified conscience, rising to remind Philoctetes of
his duty to Greece ; a suggestion ruled out by the fact
that his duty has been urged clearly by Neoptolemus.
A more attractive idea[3] is that the genuine *peripeteia* of
the play consists in Neoptolemus' change of front ; in
this way an inner dramatic unity is secured, while the
external change induced by Heracles is a mere conces-
sion to the data of legend. This in its turn is vitiated
by the fact that for the dramatist Philoctetes, and not
Neoptolemus, is the central figure : this is proved by
the work as a whole and by the title which the poet

---

[1] *E.g.* Mahaffy (*History of Gk. Lit., Poets*, pp. 309-12).

[2] Christ (*Geschichte der Gr. Lit.* p. 210) who compares Heracles
here to the δαιμόνιον σημεῖον of Socrates.

[3] K. O. Müller (*Gr. Lit.*, ii. p. 124) who is opposed by Bernhardy
(II, ii. p. 370).

himself gave it.   If the *deus ex machina* is not to be
condemned utterly, it follows from the basic law of Attic
art that the play up to the moment of Heracles' appearance, however complete it seemed to us a moment ago,
is not complete—that some coping-stone is still needed.
And if we consider the action up to that point we cannot really be content.   To disregard the oracles which
tradition said were fulfilled, the action, as Sophocles
depicts it, is unsatisfactory.   Philoctetes is to get the
revenge which seems rightly his, and we approve his
young companion who aids him at such cost.   But by
this time we feel a little dubious about the sufferer.
There has been perhaps too much detail in his outcries
and his account of his sufferings.   Hatred which will
refuse both health and fame, without any loss but that
of aged intentions, has begun to seem a moral falsetto.
But who can say, without misgiving, that (on pagan
principles) he is wrong?   One person only in Heaven
and earth—Heracles.   Every ordinary consideration
of public and personal interest has been put before
Philoctetes in vain.   But there is another thought which
neither the victim himself nor Odysseus nor Neoptolemus
has strength enough to suggest, or even to remember.
One character alone in Greek story rises above the conception of personal injury or personal benefit as a motive
to action ; Heracles is the great reminder, not so much
that wrongs to oneself should be forgiven, as that life
is too short and precious to be wasted on revenge.
Heracles would return a blow with vigour, but a vendetta, in the light of his career, seems a childish folly.
One does not forget that some pictures of his character
(that, for instance, in the *Trachiniæ*) belie this conception ; but Sophocles here sees fit to choose a different,
and the more usual, view.   Suddenly the husk of selfish
spite falls away from the sufferer's soul.   He who has
just promised[1] to use the weapons of Heracles in a
private quarrel and has already attempted[2] so to use

---

[1] vv. 1404 *sqq.*
[2] When he threatens to shoot Odysseus (vv. 1299 *sqq.*).

them, at last remembers that they are the rightful instrument of well-doing, and that it was for such a reason[1] that he received them from the hero at his passing into glory. Heracles then is introduced as the only person who can press upon Philoctetes an argument which the cunning of Odysseus and the candour of Neoptolemus have alike ignored. That he appears as a *deus ex machina* is in part accident—he is not selected by the poet for that reason. But it is a happy accident, for the glory which envelops him is the visible warrant of his inspiring behests—anything rather than the sign of overwhelming might summoned to break a reasonable human resolve. Thus the close of this play is a real ending, not a breakdown; it is the pagan analogue of the *Quo Vadis* legend.

The whole play is an example of intrigue. The episode of the pseudo-merchant[2] is the most brilliant feat of Sophocles in this department. It reveals to Philoctetes that he is being pursued by the Greeks, without arousing his suspicion of Neoptolemus, and so gives occasion for the transfer of the bow when the sufferer's fit seizes him; it conveys a strong reminder of urgency to Neoptolemus; and it enables Odysseus to learn how his plot progresses. Odysseus merely by telling of his promise to capture Philoctetes is in a fair way to fulfil it, as it throws his prey into the arms of Neoptolemus. One apparent fault of construction is of a type which we have already noted. It is vital that Philoctetes, before his first consent to leave the island, should know his friend's real purpose of taking him to Troy. But why is he told of it? The merest beginner in duplicity would surely postpone such a revelation until the victim was at sea. But Sophocles chooses to tighten his plot up in order to give the situation in one picture.

Dio Chrysostom in one of his most valuable essays[3]

---

[1] v. 670: εὐεργετῶν γὰρ καὐτὸς αὔτ' ἐκτησάμην.
[2] See Jebb's 2nd edition (p. xxvii with footnote).
[3] *Or.* 52.

sets up a comparison between the plays on Philoctetes composed by the three tragedians. The work of Sophocles is the latest, and two peculiarities help us to see how far his originality went. Firstly, as a companion to Odysseus he introduces, not Diomedes as Euripides had done, but a figure new to the Trojan war, an ingenuous lad whose sympathy brings out what gentleness remains in the sufferer's heart. Secondly, the chorus consists of Greek sailors, not of Lemnian natives as in the two other playwrights. Sophocles will have no Lemnian visitors because for him it is a cardinal fact that Philoctetes all these years has been alone save for a chance ship. Thus we gain for a moment a glance into the actual thoughts of Sophocles : he has made up his mind that his Philoctetes must be quite solitary. So essential is this that he falsifies known facts. Lemnos, he says in the second line of his play, is "untrodden, uninhabited by men," whereas, both in the times supposed and in the poet's own day, it was a populous place. This, then, gives an invaluable indication of the extent to which Sophocles felt himself free to re-model his subject-matter. On the play itself it throws light. The question is to be studied not from the point of view of the Greek army, but from that of their potential helper, soured as he is by a more extreme suffering than Æschylus and Euripides had imagined.

The picture thus conceived is painted with splendid power. Romantic desolation makes itself felt in the opening words of Odysseus, and this sense of the frowning grandeur of nature to which Philoctetes in his despair appeals [1] is everywhere associated with the pathos of lonely suffering. "While the mountain nymph, babbling Echo, appearing afar, makes answer to his bitter cries." [2] All that he says, from his first exclamation of joy at hearing again the Greek language to the noble speech in which he bids farewell to the

[1] vv. 936 *sqq.*, 987 *sq.*, etc.
[2] vv. 187-90 (Jebb's reading and translation).

bitter home which use has made something like a friend, is instinct with this mingling of romance and pathos. Deserted by all men he has yet found companions whom in his misery he addresses ; his hands, his poisoned foot, his eyes, his bow, and the familiar landscape, vocal with the "bass roar of the sea upon the headland ".[1]   Closer even than these is his eternal unseen companion, Pain, whom he found at his side on first awakening after the departure of the Greek host : "When my scrutiny had traversed all the land, no inhabitant could I find therein save Sorrow ; and that, my son, could be met at every turn ".[2]

It has been suspected that the play contains allusions to contemporary politics, that the poet is thinking of Alcibiades' return from exile.   In 410—the year before this play was produced—he had gained credit from the naval victory of Cyzicus.   Some, moreover, have seen in Odysseus the cynical politician of the day.   Other passages read like criticism of the public "atmosphere" at Athens in the closing years of the great war.   The dramatist is making deliberate comments on contemporary Athenian politics, but he assuredly did not choose the whole theme of Philoctetes merely because of Alcibiades' restoration.[3]

The ŒDIPUS COLONEUS [4] (Οἰδίπους ἐπὶ Κολωνῷ) or Œdipus at Colonus was according to the customary view produced in 401 B.C., three years after the poet's death, by his namesake and grandson.   The background

[1] v. 1455.

[2] vv. 282-4.   Notice also the phrase ξὺν ᾗ (v. 268) used of his malady.

[3] Jebb (Introd. pp. xl, xli, 2nd ed.) seems unwilling to allow any direct allusions.   But see vv. 385 sqq., 456 sqq., and particularly 1035 sqq. ; all three passages show a peculiar emphasis ; vv. 1047-51 are quite in the tone of Thucydides' "Melian dialogue".

[4] The arrangement of the parts is not certain.   But the important fact seems clear that a fourth actor was here used not tentatively (as in other cases) but in a very remarkable degree.   Jebb gives : protagonist, Œdipus; deuteragonist, Antigone ; tritagonist, Ismene and Creon ; fourth actor, "Stranger," Theseus, Polynices, messenger.   Croiset : protagonist, Œdipus ; deuteragonist, Antigone ; fourth actor, Theseus ; all the other parts to the tritagonist.

represents the grove of the Furies at Colonus, a village
near Athens. Œdipus, exiled from Thebes, an aged
blind wanderer, enters led by his daughter Antigone.
They obtain the favour of King Theseus and the citizens,
Œdipus promising that after his death his spirit shall
defend Athens. Ismene, his daughter, brings news that
an oracle has said that in the struggle between Thebes
and the Seven led by Polynices, son of Œdipus, that
side shall win which has possession of Œdipus. Both
parties are now eager for his support, but he curses both
his sons. Creon, King of Thebes, enters, and failing to
gain aught but reproaches, carries off the two girls, and
is about to seize the father also when he is checked by
the arrival of Theseus, who rescues the maidens. Polynices next comes to beg his father's aid, but is sent to his
doom with curses. Then a peal of thunder announces to
Œdipus that the moment of his passing is at hand. He
bids farewell to his daughters, and, watched only by
Theseus, descends to the underworld; the place of his
burial is to be known to none save Theseus and his successors. Ismene and Antigone in vain beg to be shown
the spot, and finally Antigone resolves to seek Thebes
that she may reconcile her brothers.

This play is simple in structure, superbly rich in
execution. Œdipus dominates all the scenes, which
reveal with piercing intensity his physical helplessness
and the spiritual might which, marked at the opening, is
overwhelming at the close. The poet's task is not
merely to portray the last hours of a much-tried man,
but the novitiate of a superhuman Power. Œdipus at
last reaches peace and a welcome from the infernal gods
—he becomes a δαίμων. The terrific feature is that even
in the flesh he anticipates his dæmonic qualities. In the
interview between him and Polynices, the implacable
hatred, the strength, the prophetic sight of the father,
and the hopeless prayers, the wretchedness, the despair
and moral collapse of the doomed son, are nothing but
the presentation in human life of the actual dæmon's
power as prophesied for future generations. Before the

close we feel that the aged exile's sufferings, sombre wisdom, and simple burning emotions have already made him a being of unearthly powers, sundered from normal humanity; his strange passing is but the ratification of a spiritual fact already accomplished. But this weird climax is preceded by an equally wonderful study of the human Œdipus. The king who appears in the *Œdipus Tyrannus* can here still be recognized. Passionate anger still directs much of his conduct, as friend and foe alike remind[1] him. But even his faults are mellowed by years and contemplation; his very anger shows some gleam of a profounder patience. Throughout, the temper of Œdipus is like that of the heavens above him—gloom cleft by flashes of insight, indignation, and love. Unlike other aged sufferers, he does not dwell in the past; unlike the saint and martyr whom a Christian dramatist might have portrayed, he does not lean upon a future of glory or happiness. Nor again has he sunk into a senile acquiescence in the present; he is far from being absorbed by the loving tendance of his daughters. The centre of his life has shifted, but not to any period of time—rather to another plane of being. Still in the flesh, his human emotions as essential as ever, his life is growing assimilated to the non-human existence of the whole earth. And so it is that Œdipus meets "death" with cheerfulness; he is departing to his own place. At the last moment the blind man leads those who see to the place of his departure. What to them is dreadful and secret is to him the centre of his longing; the terrific figures who inhabit his new home are welcome friends—at the beginning of the play he addresses the Furies themselves as "*sweet* daughters of primeval Night".[2] The whole drama at the end is full of this sense. In the farewell song of the chorus which commends the wanderer to the powers of Earth, there is an eerie precision and picturesqueness in the description of the lower world; the "infernal moor"[3] and the guardian

---

[1] Creon, vv. 854 *sq.*; Antigone, v. 1195.   [2] v. 106.

[3] vv. 1563 *sq.* The same word recurs in Antigone's lament (v. 1682): ἄσκοποι δὲ πλάκες ἔμαρψαν.

hound gleam forth for an instant into strange familiarity.

The other characters are carved, though in lower relief, yet with richness and vigour. Theseus is the ideal Athenian gentleman,[1] suddenly called to show pity to a pair of helpless wanderers, then unexpectedly involved in battle with a neighbour state, and finally confronted with the most awful mysteries of divine government, without ever losing his courage or his discretion. Creon and Polynices, such is the immense understanding of the aged poet, share too in this nobility of mind. They can face facts ; and whether villains or not, they are men of breeding. The "stranger" who first accosts Œdipus is a charming embodiment of that local patriotism to which we shall return in a moment. The two sisters are beautifully distinguished by the divergent experiences of years. Antigone's wandering and hardship have made her the more intense and passionate ; Ismene's life in Thebes have given her comprehension of more immediate issues. It is through Antigone, moreover, who declares that she will seek Thebes and attempt to save her brothers, that the poet obtains one of his noblest effects. Overwhelming as is the story of Œdipus, his end does not close all ; life goes on to further mysteries of pain and affection.

On the purely literary side the *Œdipus Coloneus* is certainly the greatest and the most typical work of Sophocles. The most celebrated lyric in Greek is the splendid ode in praise of Colonus—" our white Colonus ; where the nightingale, a constant guest, trills her clear note in the covert of green glades, dwelling amid the wine-dark ivy and the god's inviolate bowers, rich in berries and fruit, unvisited by sun, unvexed by wind of any storm ; where the reveller Dionysus ever walks the ground, companion of the nymphs that nursed him," [2]—and of the whole land with its peculiar glories,

---

[1] Note specially the word τοὐπιεικές (v. 1127) though the idea is of course expressed by the whole play.

[2] vv. 670-80 (Jebb's version).

the olive of peace and the steed of war. To this should be added that address of Œdipus to Theseus concerning the fickleness of all things earthly which is less the speech of one man than the voice of Life itself.[1] Noblest of all is the account of Œdipus' last moments, a passage which in breathless loveliness, pathos, and religious profundity is beyond telling flawless and without peer. It is curious that Sophocles in this work which, more than any other, reveals his own poetic mastery should have definitely drawn attention to the power of language. At various crises in the play he speaks of the "little word"[2] and its potency. Œdipus reflects how his two sons for lack of a "little word" in his defence have suffered him to be thrust forth into exile; the nobility of Theseus, the sudden hostility of Thebes in days to come, the appearance of Polynices, are all matters of the "little word" which means so much. And in his marvellous farewell to his daughters, Œdipus speaks of the "one word" which has made all his sorrows vanish—"love".

Every master-work of literature has a prophetic quality, and sending its roots down near to the deepest wells of life is instinct with unconscious kinships. The *Œdipus Coloneus* is rich in this final glory of art. The whole conception of the sufferer, aged and blind but gifted with spiritual sight, recalls the blind Milton's sublime address to the Light which "shines inward"; and the thought adds charm to Sophocles' description of the nightingale[3] which

> Sings darkling, and in shadiest covert hid
> Tunes her nocturnal note.

Again, just as the whole scheme suggests *King Lear*, so does the simple vigour of Theseus' words,[4] when he

---

[1] See below, p. 185.

[2] σμικρὸς λόγος four times (vv. 569, 620, 1116, 1152), σμικρὸν ἔπος once (v. 443), and ἐν μόνον ἔπος once (v. 1615 *sqq.*). Dr. Mackail (*Lectures on Greek Poetry*, p. 150) has indicated this point. See also *Electra*, 415.

[3] vv. 670 *sqq.* : The parallel I owe to Jebb's note.

[4] vv. 1503 *sq.*

enters at the terrific close amid the bellowing of the unnatural tempest :—

$$\pi\acute{a}\nu\tau a \ \gamma\grave{a}\rho \ \theta\epsilon o\hat{v}$$
$$\tau o\iota a\hat{v}\tau a \ \chi\epsilon\iota\mu\acute{a}\zeta o\nu\tau o\varsigma \ \epsilon\grave{i}\kappa\acute{a}\sigma a\iota \ \pi\acute{a}\rho a,$$

recall the "pelting of this pitiless storm".[1] So too the
divine summons[2] which comes "many times, and manifold" to Œdipus brings to mind the call "Samuel!
Samuel!" The mystery of Œdipus' tomb suggests the
passing of another august soul : "No man knoweth of
his sepulchre unto this day,"[3] and of Joseph, named
among the faithful, who "when he died, made mention
of the departing of the children of Israel ; and gave
commandment concerning his bones ".[4]

This play is deeply religious in the very details of
its theme as well as in its tone. Besides the usual
orthodox background there is the lovely presentation of
a minor local worship—the cult of the Eumenides
at Colonus, Sophocles' native village. The aged poet
in his last years seems to have returned with special
affection to the simple observances which he had learnt
as a boy, and which evoke one of his most characteristic
phrases :—[5]

$$\tau o\iota a\hat{v}\tau\acute{a} \ \sigma o\iota \ \tau a\hat{v}\tau' \ \acute{e}\sigma\tau\acute{\iota}\nu, \ \hat{\omega} \ \xi\acute{e}\nu', \ o\grave{v} \ \lambda\acute{o}\gamma o\iota\varsigma$$
$$\tau\iota\mu\acute{\omega}\mu\epsilon\nu', \ \acute{a}\lambda\lambda\grave{a} \ \tau\hat{\eta} \ \xi\upsilon\nu o\upsilon\sigma\acute{\iota}a \ \pi\lambda\acute{e}o\nu,$$

the piercing simplicity of which, as well as the theme,
suggests Wordsworth. The lustral bowls, he is careful
to tell us, are "the work of a skilled craftsman" ;[6] he is
almost on the point of telling us his name—one can
imagine the boy of eighty years ago gazing on these cups,
and his first sense of beauty in workmanship. Those
who would offer sacrifice will find dwelling on the spot
a sacristan to instruct and aid them.[7] Everything on this
ground is both familiar and hallowed ; the mysterious
"brazen threshold," the statues of local deities and

---

[1] *King Lear*, III, iv.   [2] vv. 1627 *sq.* Cp. 1 Sam. iii. 10.
[3] Deut. xxxiv. 6.   [4] Heb. xi. 22.
[5] vv. 62 *sq.*: "Such . . . are these haunts, not honoured in story,
but rather in the life that loves them" (Jebb).
[6] v. 472.   [7] v. 506.

heroes, the hollow pear-tree, and the other local sanctities are carefully particularized, so that the calm beauty of the country-side and the terrors of religion are strangely and beautifully interwoven. As for religion in the broader, profounder sense, we have as elsewhere a reference of human suffering merely to an inscrutable, divine purpose.[1] But the dramatist indicates carefully the contribution of human nature to the fulfilment of the oracles ; Polynices [2] becomes subject to his father's curse because his own sense of honour forbids him to relinquish his foredoomed enterprise. Œdipus himself has attained to a wiser conception of sin [3] than that which rules him at the close of the *Tyrannus*. He has acted wrongly, therefore his suffering is just ; but he is morally innocent, and his past actions afflict him as sorrows, not as crimes.[4]

The fragments of the lost plays are on the whole disappointing ; a large proportion are single rare words quoted by ancient lexicographers, and most of the rest are short sentences or phrases. There remain the few longer fragments, to which in recent years important additions have been made.

It seems that the *Triptolemus* was his first play, produced in 468 B.C. when the poet was twenty-eight. It would then be one of the works with which he won his victory [5] over Æschylus, and it bore marks of the older writer's influence. The theme is the mission of Triptolemus, who traversed the earth distributing to men corn, the gift of Demeter, and founded the mysteries at Eleusis. This topic gave room for a long geographical passage which recalls those of the *Prometheus*. Other early dramas were the *Thamyras* in which the dramatist himself took the name-part and played the cithara, and

---

[1] vv. 964 *sq.*   [2] vv. 1422-5.
[3] See Jebb, *Introduction*, pp. xxi *sq.*
[4] See his splendid exculpatory speeches to the chorus (vv. 258-91) and to Creon (vv. 960-1013).
[5] See pp. 10, 12 *sq.*

the *Nausicaa* or *Women Washing* wherein Sophocles acted the part of that princess and gained applause by his skill in a game of ball. The satyric drama *Amphiaraus* contained a curious scene wherein an illiterate man conveyed some name or other word to his hearers by a dance in which his contortions represented successive letters. Another satyric play *The Mustering of the Greeks* ('Αχαιῶν Σύλλογος) or the *Dinner-Party* (Σύνδειπνοι) earned the reprobation of Cicero [1] apparently for its coarseness, which can still be noted in the fragments. In *The Lovers of Achilles* ('Αχιλλέως ἐρασταί) there was a passage describing the perplexity of passion, which in its mannered felicity recalls Swinburne or the Sonnets of Shakespeare :—

> Love is a sweet perplexity of soul,
> Most like the sport of younglings, when the sky
> In winter-clearness scatters frost abroad :
> They seize a glittering icicle, filled a while
> With joy and wonder ; but ere long the toy
> Melts, and they know not how to grasp it still,
> Tho' loth to cast it from them. So with lovers :
> Their yearning passion holds them hour by hour
> Poised betwixt boldness and reluctant awe.

The *Laocoon*, which dealt with a famous episode in the capture of Troy, supplies a fragment describing Æneas' escape from the city with his father upon his shoulders ; one or two other passages [2] besides this recall Vergil's treatment. Another tragedy from the same cycle of stories, the *Polyxena*, is praised by "Longinus" [3] in the same terms of eulogy as the culmination of the *Œdipus Coloneus* itself. The *Tereus*, [4] to judge from the number of fragments, was very popular ; it dealt with the frightful fable of the Thracian King Tereus, his wife Procne, and her sister Philomela, all of whom were at last changed into birds. Aristophanes [5] has an obscure

---

[1] *Ad Quintum Fratrem*, II, xv. 3.

[2] Fr. 344 : πόνου μεταλλαχθέντος οἱ πόνοι γλυκεῖς, and fr. 345 : μόχθου γὰρ οὐδεὶς τοῦ παρελθόντος λόγος ; recall *Æneid*, I, 203 : *forsan et haec olim meminisse iuuabit*.

[3] *De Subl.* XV, 7 : ἄκρως πεφάντασται.

[4] For the Recognition-scene of this play, cp. Aristotle, *Poetic*, 1454*b*.

[5] *Birds*, vv. 100 *sqq.*

series of jests about this play and the beak-mask with which Sophocles "outraged" the Thracian monarch. A solitary relic of the *Orithyia* tells how the maiden was carried off by the wind-god Boreas

> Unto Earth's verge, beyond the farthest sea,
> Vistas of Heaven, and well-springs of the dark,
> To the Sun's ancient garden.

In 1907 there came to light at Oxyrhynchus in Egypt considerable fragments[1] of two Sophoclean dramas.

Most of these once formed part of the *Ichneutæ* ('Ιχνευταί) or *Detectives*. Formerly we had only two brief and obscure fragments, and one word quoted by Athenæus; it was known that the play was satyric. The theme was quite uncertain; and conjecture[2] is now shown to have gone quite astray. Sophocles, we find, has dramatized the myth so admirably treated in the Homeric *Hymn to Hermes*. A considerable portion of the work can now be read. The god Apollo announces that his cattle have been stolen and that he cannot trace them; he offers a reward to anyone who catches the thief. Silenus and the chorus of satyrs undertake the quest; they are the "trackers" from whom the play is named. After a time they spy the footprints of oxen and exclaim that "some god is leading the colony". A noise[3] which they cannot understand is heard behind the scenes. The numerous tracks now give them trouble; they point backwards here and there—"an odd confusion must have possessed the herdsman!" Next the satyrs fall on their faces, to the amazement of Silenus who likens this "trick of hunting on your stomach" to the position of "a hedgehog in a bush". They bid him listen; he importantly replies that they are not helping "my investigation," loses his temper, and roundly reviles

---

[1] These have been published and annotated by Dr. A. S. Hunt (who, with Dr. B. P. Grenfell, discovered these and so many other precious remains) in Vol. IX of the *Oxyrhynchus Papyri*.

[2] Welcker thought that the wanderings of Europa formed the subject.

[3] The word ῥοῖβδος is inserted as a stage-direction (παρεπιγραφή). It no doubt means that the babe Hermes is playing his lyre "within".

their cowardice. They recover themselves and soon
arrive at a cave. Silenus kicks at the door until the
nymph Cyllene comes forth. She protests against their
boisterous behaviour, but is appeased by their apologies.
When they ask the meaning of the strange sound,
Cyllene reports the birth of the god Hermes whom she
is tending within, and his amazingly rapid growth. The
noise is produced by the babe from "a vessel filled with
pleasure made from a dead beast". The "detectives"
are still perplexed ; what is this creature? The goddess
describes the creature in riddling language. They make
laughably divergent guesses : a cat, a panther, a lizard,
a crab, a big-horned beetle ; and at last they are told that
the beast is a tortoise. She describes the delight[1] which
the child draws from his playing. The satyrs inform
Cyllene that her nursling is the thief; she indignantly
denies that a son of Zeus can have so acted, and takes
the accusation as a joke. They vigorously repeat their
charge, and begin to quarrel with Cyllene. From this
point onwards practically nothing can be made of the
papyrus-scraps, except that Apollo re-appears, and
seems to be giving the "detectives" their reward.

The papyrus which contained the other play, the
Eurypylus,[2] is in tiny fragments, but some of these,
combined with our independent knowledge of the story,
enable us to give an outline of the plot. Astyoche,
mother of Eurypylus, was induced by Priam to allow her
son to help the Trojans against the Greeks. He met
Neoptolemus, son of Achilles, in battle and was slain.
A messenger related the encounter to (it seems) his
mother Astyoche. The body was received by Priam
with lamentation as if for a son of his own. This fragment is much the most striking of the collection.

---

[1] The passage is amusing : χαίρει ἀλύων, "he is in a rapture of joy," is
an excellent phrase for this earliest of *maestri;* but, as Dr. Hunt
remarks, his audience of one (Cyllene) seems not to share his ecstasy :
παραψυκτήριον κείνῳ μόνον.
[2] The name is not certain. All that can be asserted is that the tragedy
dealt with Eurypylus' death, in defence of Troy, at the hands of Neoptolemus.

Sophocles' position in literary history has already been indicated.[1] We shall here discuss his mind and his art in general outline. Of his political opinions little is known. Though his work abounds in saws of state-craft, these are of quite general application ;[2] and it would be dangerous to declare which side, if any, he took in the political crises which were so numerous and so grave in fifth-century Athens ; there is perhaps one hint[3] that he did not approve the ascendancy of Pericles. As for religion, he seems to have accepted both the orthodox cults of his country and the current beliefs of the ordinary Athenian with little reserve or none. This brings us at once to a fact which must not be ignored— the feeling among readers of our own day, that Sophocles for all his merits is a little too complacent, too urbane, lacking somehow in profundity and real grip upon the soul. The answer is that we come to Sophocles pre-occupied by the religious questionings which fill our own time and which, moreover, interest both Æschylus and Euripides ; but there is no reason why Sophocles should share our disquiet or that of his fellow-craftsmen. That which for Æschylus is the foreground of his work, forms for Sophocles only the background. He is not especially interested in religion itself, but in humanity. For Æschylus religion is an affair of the intellect ; for Euripides it is an affair of morals ; for Sophocles it be-longs to the sphere of emotion. And the two great instruments with which he constructs his plays are human emotions and human will. For all the plays which we possess the same genesis exists: the chief character experiences some mighty appeal to the emo-tions—the feeling of self-respect in Ajax and Œdipus at Athens, of family love in Antigone and Electra, of re-vengefulness in Philoctetes, of wifely dignity and affection

---

[1] See pp. 15-17.
[2] See *e.g.* the remarks in Creon's opening speech (*Ant.* vv. 175-90).
[3] *O.T.* 587-8 :

> ἐγὼ μὲν οὖν οὔτ' αὐτὸς ἱμείρων ἔφυν
> τύραννος εἶναι μᾶλλον ἢ τύραννα δρᾶν.

in Deianira, of pity in Œdipus at Thebes, and then
creates drama by the magnificent pathetic staunchness
wherewith the will, taking its direction from the emotion
so aroused, presses on ruthlessly in its attempt to satisfy
this impulse. Nothing seems so dear to him as a purpose which flaunts cold reason, the purpose of any others,
and indeed every other emotion save that which has
started the action upon its course. He sets before us a
person determined on some striking act, and subjects him
to all conceivable assaults of reason and preachments
on expediency, showing him unbroken throughout. The
onslaughts upon Ajax, Antigone, Philoctetes, Œdipus,
are not mere stage-rhetoric ; they are " sound common-
sense," "appeals to one's better self"; and no logical
denial can be opposed to them. Only one power in man
is able to withstand them—the will, taking its stand once
for all upon some instinct for clear, simple action. If
we never listen to reason we are lost ; but if we always
listen we are lost equally. That these heroes of the
will so often come to misery or death matters little ; they
have saved their souls alive instead of sinking themselves
in a sordid acceptance of a second-hand morality. Over
against these figures, to emphasize their defiant grandeur,
the poet loves to set persons admirable indeed, but more
commonplace, who emerge in the dread hour when the
haughty will has brought ruin, and approve themselves
as the pivot of the situation. The hero is great and
strikes the imagination, but it is on the shoulders of men
like Creon in the *Œdipus Tyrannus*, Odysseus, Hyllus,
Theseus in the *Œdipus Coloneus*, that the real burden of
the world's work may be safely cast. None the less he
loves Antigone better than he loves Ismene, Œdipus
rather than Theseus. In one place at least, in his dislike for the "reasonable" spirit of compromise, he suffers
himself a malicious little *reductio ad absurdum*. When
Chrysothemis finds Electra uttering her resentment at
the palace gate she says :—[1]

---

[1] *Electra*, vv. 328 *sqq.*

> Sister! Again? Why standest at the door
> Holding this language? Will no span of years
> Teach thee at length to grudge thy foolish spleen
> Such empty comfort? Yet mine own heart too
> Knows how it sorrows for our present state. . .
>   I avow
> That in thy spirit dwelleth righteousness
> Not in my words. *Yet, if I would be free*
> *I must in all things bend to those in power.*

As for the plots themselves, their main feature is that deliberate complexity which we have called intrigue and which was made possible by the poet's use of a third actor. After the great achievements of Æschylus it became necessary to add some fresh kind of interest; this Euripides found in a readjustment of sympathies, Sophocles in an increase of dramatic thrill. It is an exciting moment in the *Trachiniæ* when, just as Deianira is about to re-enter the palace, the messenger mysteriously draws her apart and reveals the truth about the captive Iole. The magnificent death-scene of Ajax is the outcome of the cunning wherewith he has thrown his friends off the scent. The *Electra* is full of this method; the mission of Chrysothemis is turned into a weapon against the murderess who sent her, and the episode of Orestes' funeral-urn is a magnificent piece of dramatic artistry. In the *Œdipus Tyrannus* the king brings about his own fatal illumination by sending for the herdsman. The *Philoctetes*, above all, is filled with the deliberate plotting of Odysseus. The marked increase in complexity which Sophocles' work thus shows as compared with that of Æschylus is undoubtedly the chief (perhaps the only) reason for his desertion of the trilogy form.[1] Side by side with this attention to mechanism is that curious indifference to the fringes of the plot which we have had occasion to notice in several places.

Another characteristic of Sophocles is that famous "tragic irony" by which again he imparts new power to old themes. It turns to magnificent profit a circumstance which might seem to vitiate dramatic interest

[1] See p. 16.

—the fact that the spectator knows the myth and therefore cannot be taken by surprise. Between an audience which foresees the event, and the stage-personages who cannot, the playwright sets up a thrilling interest of suspense. ↘ He causes his characters to discuss the future they expect in language which is fearfully and exquisitely suitable to the future which actually awaits them. Ajax, while his madness still afflicts him, stands amid the slaughtered cattle and proclaims his triumph over the Greek chieftains, just before he awakes to the truth that by his "triumph" he has ruined himself. More elaborate is the scene in which Deianira explains her stratagem of the robe which is to bring back the love of Heracles. But the *Œdipus Tyrannus* provides by far the finest instance. As the king in scene after scene accumulates horror upon his own unconscious head, the spectator receives, always at the right moment and in full measure, the impact of increasing disaster. Yet since his perception is a discovery which he himself has made, horror is tempered by an intellectual glow, a spiritual exaltation.

In the art of iambic verse Sophocles stands beyond all other Greeks unrivalled. Beside him Æschylus sounds almost clumsy, Euripides glib, Aristophanes vulgar. Only Shakespeare has that complete mastery over every shade of emphasis, every possibility of grandeur and simple ease alike. The iambic line in Sophocles' hands can at will display a haunting romantic loveliness, the profoundest dignity, the sharpest edges of emotion, or the quiet prose of every day. Consider the following lines,[1] which begin near the end of Electra's long speech of complaint to the chorus :—

HΛ. ἐγὼ δ' Ὀρέστην τῶνδε προσμένουσ' ἀεὶ
παυστῆρ' ἐφήξειν ἡ τάλαιν' ἀπόλλυμαι.
μέλλων γὰρ ἀεὶ δρᾶν τι τὰς οὔσας τέ μου
καὶ τὰς ἀπούσας ἐλπίδας διέφθορεν.
ἐν οὖν τοιούτοις οὔτε σωφρονεῖν, φίλαι,
οὔτ' εὐσεβεῖν πάρεστιν · ἀλλ' ἐν τοι κακοῖς
πολλή 'στ' ἀνάγκη κἀπιτηδεύειν κακά.

[1] *Electra*, 303-16.

ΧΟ. φέρ' εἰπέ, πότερον ὄντος Αἰγίσθου πέλας
λέγεις τάδ' ἡμῖν, ἢ βεβῶτος ἐκ δόμων;
ΗΛ. ἦ κάρτα μὴ δόκει μ' ἄν, εἴπερ ἦν πέλας,
θυραῖον οἰχνεῖν· νῦν δ' ἀγροῖσι τυγχάνει.
ΧΟ. ἦ κἂν ἐγὼ θαρσοῦσα μᾶλλον ἐς λόγους
τοὺς σοὺς ἱκοίμην, εἴπερ ὧδε ταῦτ' ἔχει;
ΗΛ. ὡς νῦν ἀπόντος ἱστόρει τί σοι φίλον.

Electra's speech is solemn poetry. The large number
of spondees [1] (there are three in the last line), the slow
elaboration of the ideas—an elaboration admirably
pointed by τοι, which brings the rhythm almost to a
standstill—make a strong contrast with the following
conversation. There the relaxation of the rhythm is
unmistakable ; φέρ' εἰπέ is almost casual in its lightness,
and it is at once followed by a tribrach. The rather
odd use of the bare dative ἀγροῖσι is a delightfully neat
tinge of colloquialism, supported by τυγχάνει. The
Philoctetes will repay special study from this point of
view. There is a remarkable tendency to divide [2] lines
between speakers in order to express excitement ; this
device is elsewhere very uncommon. From this play
we may select one example [3] of amazing skill in rhythm.
Philoctetes is explaining how he contrives to crawl to
and fro in quest of food and the like :—

γαστρὶ μὲν τὰ σύμφορα
τόξον τόδ' ἐξηύρισκε, τὰς ὑποπτέρους
βάλλον πελείας· πρὸς δὲ τοῦθ', ὅ μοι βάλοι
νευροσπαδὴς ἄτρακτος, αὐτὸς ἂν τάλας
εἱλυόμην δύστηνος ἐξέλκων πόδα
πρὸς τοῦτ' ἄν.

The dull repetition of πρὸς τοῦτο and of ἄν ; the extremely slow movement of the penultimate line with
its three spondees and the word-ending at the close
of the second foot ; above all, the manner in which the
whole dragging sentence leads up to the monosyllable
ἄν, so rare at the end of a sentence, and there stops
dead, is a marvellous suggestion of the lame man's
painful progress and of the way in which at the end of

---

[1] For this and other metrical terms which follow see Chapter VI.
[2] There are no less than thirty iambic lines thus divided. The name
for such division is ἀντιλαβή.
[3] *Phil.* vv. 287-92.

his endurance he falls prone and spent upon the object of his endeavour.

Specially striking phrases are not common. Sophocles obtains his effect not by brilliant strokes of diction, but by the cumulative effect of a sustained manner. There are such dexterities of course, like Antigone's πόθος τοι καὶ κακῶν ἄρ' ἦν τις,[1] and the cry of Electra to her brother's ashes :—[2]

> τοίγαρ σὺ δέξαι μ' ἐς τὸ σὸν τόδε στέγος
> τὴν μηδὲν εἰς τὸ μηδέν.

A poet who can, by that infinitesimal change from τὸν μηδέν to τὸ μηδέν, indicate the very soul of grief, may claim to be one of the immortal masters of language.

Modern readers find one great fault in this poet—colourlessness, coldness, an absence of hearty verve ; he seems a little too polished and restrained. The truth is that in Sophocles the Attic spirit finds its literary culmination. Æschylus lives in the pre-Periclean world ; Euripides is too restless and cosmopolitan to reflect the spirit of one nation only ; Plato and Demosthenes belong to the age of disillusionment which came after Ægospotami ; and Thucydides, though he shows many Attic qualities, is without limpidity. Anyone, then, who would understand the Athenian genius as embodied in letters must read Sophocles. He will find the most useful commentary in the Parthenon and its friezes, and in the remains of Greek statuary. One of the most marvellous and precious experiences in life is to gaze upon works like the so-called Fates in the British Museum, the Venus of Melos, or the Ludovisi Hera. Many a casual visitor has glanced for the first time at these works and known strong disappointment. A mere piece of marble accurately worked into a female face or figure ; majestic to be sure—but is this all ? If he will look again he at last perceives that the stone has put on, not merely humanity, but immortality. An

---

[1] *O.C.* 1697, translated by Jebb : " Ah, so care past can seem lost joy ! "

[2] *Electra*, 1165 *sq.*

invisible glow radiates from it like the odour from a flower. We have never found any name for it but Beauty. It is indeed the quintessence of loveliness, delicate as gossamer yet indestructible as granite. So with the tragedies of Sophocles: it is possible to read the *Œdipus Tyrannus* in certain moods and find it mere frigid elegance. But, as with the beauties of Nature, so with the glories of art, it is the second glance, the lingering of the eye beyond the careless moment, that surprises something of the ultimate secret.

For reticence is one of the notes of Athenian art. No writer ever effected so much with so scanty materials as Sophocles; he carries the art of masterly omission to its extreme. Shakespeare attempts to express everything; the mere exuberance of his phraseology is as wonderful as anything else in his work. But even *King Lear* or *Hamlet*, being written by a man, share the weakness of humanity and leave the foundation of life undisclosed. Such a disability may daunt the scientist; it is the salvation of the artist; for the effect of all art rests on co-operation between the maker and the spectator of the work. In literature, then, the author knows that he must omit, and the reader or hearer must supply for himself the contributions of his own heart and experience. How much then is he to omit? On the varying answers to that question rest the different forms of literature and the divergent schools of each form. Sophocles has left more to his hearer than any other writer in the world. Another note of Athenian art is simplicity. It is not crudeness, nor *naïveté*, nor baldness of style. In a thousand passages of Sophocles, Thucydides, and Plato, the line between savourless banality and the words they have written is fine indeed, but that little means a whole world of art. Many a fine author—Marlowe is a conspicuous example—writes nobly because he writes violently, or with a conscious effort to soar. But let him once trip, and he sprawls in bombast or nerveless garrulity. Simplicity without baldness is the most difficult of all literary excellences, and is yet achieved everywhere by Sophocles except when he rises to a different level, of which we shall speak later.

Such then is the cause of Sophoclean frigidity and lack of colour. He is led to write so by his Attic frugality and economy of effect, by his knowledge that his audience can follow him into his rarefied atmosphere, and by another cause. In our own time men have looked to art for a "message" from more exciting or more lovely spheres. We talk of "the literature of escape"; for us art must be an expanding influence. The Athenian sought in it a concentrating influence. Each citizen who witnessed the *Antigone* was a member of a sovereign assembly; he understood foreign policy at first hand; war or peace depended upon his voice. Many came to watch the *Ajax* who had but a while ago fought at Oenophyta or in Egypt. Such men did not need "local colour" and exciting technicalities. Their own lives were full of great events. What they asked of art was serenity, profundity, to blend their own scattered experiences into one noble picture of life itself, life made beautiful because so wonderfully comprehended. This was the function of Sophocles and his brother-craftsmen.

Beyond the normal lucid beauty of lyrics and dialogue, and beyond the frequent outpourings of splendid eloquence in long speeches, there is a still higher level of poetry which should be noted. Now and again his pages are filled with an unearthly splendour. Reference has been made before to certain isolated lines which combine utter simplicity with bewildering charm.[1] But here and there the poet has given us whole speeches in this divine manner. They are always a comment on the matter in hand, but they are conceived in the spirit of one who "contemplates all time and all existence,"

[1] Dr. J. W. Mackail (*Lectures on Greek Poetry*, p. 150 *sq.*) has described these lines with brilliant aptness. "The language is so simple, so apparently unconscious and artless, that its overwhelming effect makes one gasp: it is like hearing human language uttered, and raised to a new and incredible power, by the lips of some one more than human,"

who stands apart from man and sees him in his place amid the workings of the universe. One of these ethereal utterances is the speech [1] of Œdipus to Theseus who has expressed his doubt whether Thebes will ever desert the friendship of Athens ; it begins :—

> Fair Aigeus' son, only to gods in heaven
> Comes no old age nor death of anything ;
> All else is turmoiled by our master Time.
> The earth's strength fades and manhood's glory fades,
> Faith dies, and unfaith blossoms like a flower.
> And who shall find in the open streets of men
> Or secret places of his own heart's love
> One wind blow true for ever ?

More personal, but instinct with the same glow of imaginative beauty is the soliloquy [2] of Ajax when at the point of death. It is in passages like these that one realizes the value of the restraint which obtains elsewhere ; when the author gives his voice full scope the effect is heartshaking. Ajax' appeal to the sun-god to " check his gold-embossèd rein " fills with splendour at a word the heavens which were lowering with horror. It recalls Marlowe's lines of the same type and effect though in different application, which suffuse the agony of Faust with bitter glory :—

> Stand still, you ever-moving spheres of Heaven
> That time may cease, and midnight never come !

The greatest achievement of Sophocles was, however, reserved till the close of his life. The messenger's speech, [3] narrating the last moments of Œdipus, is the culmination in Greek of whatever miracles human language can compass in exciting awe and delight. The poet has bent all his mastery of tense idiom, of varied and haunting rhythm, all his instinct for the pathos of life and the mystery of fate, to produce one mighty uplifting of the hearer into the region where emotion and intellect are no longer opposed but mingle into something for which we have no name but " Life ".

---

[1] *O.C.* 607 *sqq.* The wonderful version of these first few lines is by Professor Gilbert Murray.

[2] *Ajax*, 815 *sqq.*   [3] *O.C.* 1586 *sqq.*

CHAPTER V

THE WORKS OF EURIPIDES

OF nearly one hundred dramas composed by Euripides nineteen[1] have survived. These are now discussed in the approximate chronological order ; the precise date of production is, however, known in but few cases.

The ALCESTIS[2] (Ἄλκηστις), acted in 438 B.C., when the poet was already forty-two years old, is the earliest. It formed the fourth play of a tetralogy which contained the lost works *Women of Crete*, *Alcmæon at Psophis*, and *Telephus*. Euripides obtained the second prize, being vanquished by Sophocles—with what play is not known. The scene is laid at Pheræ and presents the palace of Admetus, King of Thessaly. The god Apollo relates how he has induced the Fates to allow Admetus to escape death on his destined day, if he can find some one to die in his stead. All refused save his wife, Alcestis, whose death therefore is to happen this very day. Thanatos (Death) enters and Apollo in vain asks him to spare the queen ; a quarrel follows, and Apollo departs with threats. The chorus of Pheræan elders enter and hear, from a servant, of Alcestis' courageous leave-takings. Next the queen is borne forth and dies amid

---

[1] This figure includes the *Rhesus*, the authenticity of which is not certain.

[2] It is almost certain that only two actors were employed, Alcestis being mute in the last scene (*i.e.* the character was apparently borne by a supernumerary, not the actor who had delivered her earlier speeches), and the few lines of the child Eumelos being sung by a chorister. Croiset suggests : protagonist, Apollo, Alcestis, Heracles, Pheres ; deuteragonist, Thanatos, maidservant, Admetus, attendant.

the lamentations of her husband and little son. All save the chorus retire to prepare for the funeral, when Heracles enters. Admetus comes forth and insists on making the hero his guest, pretending that it is a stranger who has died. Heracles is taken to the guest-chamber and the elders reproach Admetus for his unseasonable hospitality. The funeral procession is moving forward when Pheres, father of Admetus, enters to pay his respects to the dead. His son with cold fury repels him : why did he, an aged man, not consent to die, and so save Alcestis? A vigorous and coarse altercation follows. When all have gone the butler enters, complaining of Heracles' drunken feasting ; the latter soon follows, and is quickly sobered by learning the truth. He proclaims his intention of rescuing Alcestis from Thanatos, and hurries away. Admetus returns followed by the chorus, expressing his utter grief and desolation. Heracles arrives with a veiled woman, whom he says he has won as a prize at some athletic contest ; he must now depart to fulfil his next " labour " —the capture of Diomedes' man-eating steeds—and requests Admetus to take care of the woman till his return. The king reluctantly consents, and Heracles unveils her, whereupon Admetus recognizes his wife. She does not speak, being (as Heracles explains) for three days yet subject to the infernal deities.[1] The play ends with the joy of Admetus, a dry remark of Heracles on true hospitality, and a few lines[2] from the chorus expressing wonder at the mysterious ways of Heaven.

The Greek introductions to this play contain interesting criticisms : "the close of the drama is somewhat

---

[1] The true explanation, as Dr. Hayley points out, is that the two actors are already engaged (as A. and H.) so that the queen is presented by a mute. I cannot, however, agree that this is " a clumsy device ". Admetus deserved some modification of his delight ; we may, moreover, feel that Alcestis would not wish to show precipitation in greeting the husband who had interred her with such strange promptitude.

[2] The celebrated "tag" beginning πολλαὶ μορφαὶ τῶν δαιμονίων (vv. 1159-63), which is found also at the close of *Medea* (practically), *Helena*, *Andromache*, and *Bacchæ*.

comic"; "the drama is more or less satyric, because it ends in joy and pleasure". These remarks, coupled with the fact that the *Alcestis* (as the last play of the tetralogy) occupied the place of the customary satyric drama, have caused much discussion. It is enough to say here : first, that the *Alcestis* is in no sense a satyric play;[1] second, that it undoubtedly presents comic features; third, that none the less the work belongs to the sphere of tragedy. It is sometimes difficult, and often undesirable, to label dramatic poems too definitely ; but we must certainly avoid the impression that this play is a comedy. It deals poignantly with the most solemn interests of humanity; the comic scenes merely show, what is almost as obvious elsewhere, that Euripides imitates actual life more closely than his two great rivals. Nothing is gained, however, by ignoring the comic element. The altercation between Apollo and Thanatos contains much that surprises us—the wit[2] and the eager, wrangling, bargaining tone of the dispute. Again the quarrel between Pheres and his son, admirable in its skilful revelation of character, jars terribly when enacted over the body of Alcestis. Heracles half-tipsy lecture to the slave shocks us in a demigod about to wrestle with Death himself. But the whole situation as between Alcestis and Admetus, Admetus and Heracles, is handled with dignity and extraordinary pathos. The death scene, especially Admetus' despairing address to his wife ; the even finer passage when the king returns but shrinks from the cold aspect of his widowed house; the magnificent and lovely odes, above all the song which describes the wild beasts of Othrys' side sporting to the music of Apollo—these are thoroughly suited to tragedy.

The plot is apparently[3] quite simple, but one fact

---

[1] There are no satyrs and no indecency of language.

[2] *E.g.* v. 58 : πῶς εἶπας; ἀλλ' ἦ καὶ σοφὸς λέληθας ὤν; "What ! *you* among the philosophers !"

[3] The late Dr. A. W. Verrall's brilliant theory of this play it will be better to discuss later (see pp. 190 *sq.*).

should be mentioned. The rescue of Alcestis is due directly to the drunkenness of Heracles. He is prevented from learning the facts in an ordinary way by Admetus; had he behaved normally, he would have left Pheræ still unenlightened, since Admetus has forbidden[1] his slave to speak. It is his intoxication alone which goads the butler to explain.

The character-drawing is skilful, often subtle. Heracles, good-hearted but somewhat dense, sensual and coarse-fibred, is half-way between the demigod of the *Heracles Furens* and the boisterous glutton of comedy. Capable of splendid impulses, he is yet a masterpiece of breezy tactlessness, as when with hideous slyness he suggests to Admetus (in the presence of the restored wife) that the king may console himself by a new marriage. Pheres and Admetus are an admirable pair. Both are selfish, Admetus with pathetic unconsciousness, his father with cynical candour. Pheres is quite willing to give elaborate honour to the dead woman so long as it costs little; Admetus—is it true of him that he is ready to utter splendid heroic speeches so long as the sacrifice is made to save him? Not so; he feels terribly. But the comparison between father and son reminds us how easily sentiment can become aged into etiquette. At present, however, he is a man of generous instincts—"spoiled". He needs a salutary upheaval of his home: from afar he prophesies of Thorvald Helmer in *A Doll's House*. Alcestis herself is a curious study. Innumerable readers have extolled her as one of the noblest figures in Euripides' great gallery of heroines; this in spite of the fact that she is frigid and unimaginative, ungenerous and basely narrow, in her spiritual and social outlook. One great and noble deed stands to her credit—she is voluntarily dying to preserve Admetus' life. Our profound respect Alcestis can certainly claim, but the love and pity of which so much is said are scarcely due to her. They are extorted, if at all, by the elaborate

[1] vv. 763 *sq.*

exertions of the other characters, who vie with one another in painting a picture of the tenderness which has illumined the Pheræan palace like quiet sunshine. But a dramatist cannot build up a great character by a series of testimonies from friends. He has undoubtedly portrayed an interesting personality, as he always does, but to put her beside creations like Medea and Phædra is merely absurd. From the beginning of her first intolerable speech[1] we know her for that frightful figure, the thoroughly good woman with no imagination, no humour, no insight. One hears much of the failures of Euripides; this is perhaps a real failure. For we are not to suppose that the rigidity and coldness of Alcestis are a dexterous stroke of art; it is not his intention to give a novel, true, and unflattering portrait of a traditional stage favourite, as he so often delighted to do. Everything indicates that he wished to make Alcestis sublime and lovable. But there is a fatal difference between her and the later women. Euripides has realized her from the outside. He has given us in the mouths of the other characters warm descriptions of her charm, but he has not succeeded in drawing a charming woman. She has not "come alive" in his hands.

The plot of the *Alcestis* has been studied by the late Dr. Verrall in an essay[2] of extraordinary skill and interest. He lays special emphasis on certain peculiar features in the treatment. First, Heracles is represented as in no way the sublime demigod who ought to have been depicted, in view of the amazing exploit which awaits him; the only heroic language put into his mouth is uttered when he is intoxicated, and the account—if it can be called such—which he gives later of Alcestis' deliverance shows a studied lack of impressiveness. Second, Alcestis is interred with unheard-of speed; Admetus, seeing her expire, instantly makes ready to convey her body to the tomb. From these facts in chief and from many details Dr.

---

[1] vv. 280-325.　　[2] *Euripides the Rationalist*, pp. 1-128.

Verrall deduces his theory that Alcestis never dies at all. Her expectation of death (tound d on the story about Apollo's bargain) and the atmosphere of mourning which hangs over Admetus' house and capital on the fatal day, have so wrought upon the queen that she finally swoons. Later Heracles visits the tomb, finds Alcestis recovering, and restores her to the king. His annoyance with Admetus, which leads him to allow his host to "think what he pleases," coupled with his own rodomontade at the palace gate, gave rise to the legend that Heracles fought with Death for a woman who had actually quitted life. Finally, the quasi-theological prologue, in which Apollo and Thanatos appear and give warrant to the orthodox rendering of the story, is a mere figment, revealed as such to the discreet by its utterly ungodlike tone, and only tacked on to a quite human drama in order to save the poet from legal indictment as an enemy of current theology.

This superb essay has met with wide-spread admiration, some adhesion, much opposition, but no refutation. If we are to judge of the existing plays as one mass, the examination of outstanding specimens of rationalism such as the *Ion* will convince us that the *Alcestis* is what Dr. Verrall thought it. But this play does stand apart from the rest, as do the *Rhesus* and the *Cyclops*. However close it may lie to the *Medea* in date, it is very early in manner; a capital instance of this, the character of Alcestis, has already been mentioned. The best view is, perhaps, that curious features which in other works might appear so bad as to be evidently intended for some other than the ostensible purpose, are in this case due to inexpertness.[1] For example, the extraordinary fact that Alcestis' rescue

---

[1] The hurried obsequies probably do not fall into this category. We are almost certainly to assume that as Alcestis' sacrifice is to be made on a certain day, that day must see her not only expire, but actually delivered up to the power of death. See Dr. H. W. Hayley's *Introduction* to the play (pp. xxxi *sq.*) and my *Riddle of the Bacchæ*, pp. 143 *sq.*

is due to nothing but the drunkenness of Heracles, is perhaps a mere oversight on the poet's part. Similarly the poorness of the last scene may be no cunning device, but comparative poverty of inspiration. It is a tenable view that Euripides intended to write a quite orthodox treatment of the story, but has only partially succeeded in reaching the sureness and brilliance of his later compositions.[1]

The MEDEA (Μήδεια) was produced in 431 B.C. as the first play of a tetralogy containing also *Philoctetes*, *Dictys*, and the satyric play *The Harvesters* (Θερισταί). Euripides obtained only the third prize, and even Sophocles was second to Euphorion, son of Æschylus. The scene represents the house of Medea at Corinth. She has come there with her two young sons, and her husband Jason, whom she helped to gain the Golden Fleece in Colchis. Jason has become estranged from Medea, owing to his projected marriage with Glauce, the daughter of King Creon. At this point the play opens. The aged nurse of Medea comes forth and, in one of the most celebrated speeches in Euripides, laments her mistress' flight from Colchis and her subsequent troubles; she fears that Medea will seek revenge. The two boys return from play, attended by their old "pædagogus," who informs his fellow-servant that King Creon intends to banish Medea and her children. The nurse sends them within. The chorus of Corinthian women enter and inquire after Medea, who comes from the house in the deepest distress. She speaks with deep feeling about the sorrows and restraints which society puts upon women,[2]

[1] I cannot write with decision about the *Alcestis*, because on the one hand universal testimony and opinion date it as only seven years anterior to the *Medea*, while my own instinct would put it quite twenty years earlier than that play. To me it reads essentially like the work of a young but highly-gifted playwright who has recently lost his wife.

[2] These celebrated lines (vv. 230-51) are not in character. They form a splendid and moving criticism of the attitude adopted by the poet's own Athenian contemporaries towards women, but have only a very partial application to herself.

and after a pathetic description of her own forlorn
state, begs her visitors to aid by silence if she finds
any means of revenge. They have just consented,
when Creon appears and orders her to leave the land
on the instant, with her children. When she ex-
postulates, he explains that he fears her : she is well
known as a magician ; moreover, she has uttered
threats against himself, his daughter, and Jason. Medea
in vain seeks to escape her reputation for "wisdom" ;
in spite of her offer to live quietly in Corinth, Creon
repeats his behest. By urgent pleading, she obtains
from him one day's grace. When the king has departed, Medea addresses the chorus with fierce triumph :
she now has opportunity for revenge. After considering
possible methods, she decides on poison. But first,
what refuge is she to find when her plot has succeeded?
she will wait a little, and if no chance of safe retirement
shows itself, she will attack her foes sword in hand.
The chorus, impressed by her spirit, declare that after
all the centuries during which poets have covered
women with infamy, now at last honour is coming to
their sex. They lament the decay of truth and honour,
as shown in Jason's desertion. Jason enters, re-
proaching Medea for her folly in alienating the king,
but offering help to lighten her banishment. Medea
falls upon him in a terrible speech, relating all the
benefits she has conferred and the crime she has committed in his cause. Jason replies that it was the
Love-God which constrained her to help him, nor is
he ungrateful. But she has her reward—a reputation
among the Greeks for wisdom. He is contracting
this new marriage to provide for his children ; Medea's
complaints are due to short-sighted jealousy. After
a bitter debate, in which Medea scornfully refuses his
aid, he retires. The chorus sing the dread power
of Love, and lament the wreck which it has made
of Medea's life. A stranger enters—Ægeus, King
of Athens, who has been to Delphi for an oracle
which shall remove his childlessness. Medea begs

him to give her shelter in Athens whenever she comes thither from Corinth; in return for this, she will by her art remove his childlessness. He consents, and withdraws. Sure of her future, Medea now triumphantly expounds her plan. She will make a pretended reconciliation with Jason and beg that her children be allowed to remain. They are to seek Jason's bride, bearing presents in order to win this favour. These gifts will be poisoned; the princess and all who touch her will perish. Then she will slay her children to complete the misery of Jason. The chorus in vain protest; she turns from them and despatches a slave to summon Jason. The choric ode which follows extols, in lines of amazing loveliness, the glory of Attica —its atmosphere of wisdom, poetry, and love. But how shall such a land harbour a murderess? Jason returns, and is greeted by Medea with a speech of contrition by which he is entirely deceived. She calls her children forth, and there is a pathetic scene which affects her, for all her guilty purpose, with genuine emotion. She puts her pretended plan before Jason, and watches the father depart with the two boys and their pædagogus carrying the presents. The ode which follows laments the fatal step that has now been taken. The pædagogus brings the boys back with news that their sentence of exile has been remitted, and that the princess has accepted the gifts. Medea addresses herself to the next task. Now that her plot against Glauce is in train, the children must die. The famous soliloquy which follows exhibits the sway alternately exerted over her by maternal love and the thirst for revenge; after a dreadful struggle she determines to obey her " passion " and embrace vengeance. The children are sent within. The next ode is a most painfully real and intimate revelation of a parent's anxiety and sorrows. A messenger hurries up, crying to Medea that she must flee; Creon and his daughter are both dead. Medea greets his news with cool delight, braces herself for her last deed, and enters the house. The chorus utter a desperate prayer to the Sun-god to save his descendants; but at once the children's cries are heard. Scarcely have they died away when Jason furiously enters, followed by henchmen. His chief thought is to save his children from the vengeance of Creon's kinsmen. The chorus at once tell him they are dead, and how. In frenzy he flings himself upon the door. But he suddenly recoils as the voice of Medea, clear and contemptuous, descends from the air. She is seen on high, driving a magic chariot given to her by the Sun-god. There breaks out a frightful wounding altercation, Jason begging wildly to be allowed to see and to bury his children's bodies, Medea sternly refusing; she will herself bury them beyond the borders of Corinth. She departs through the air, leaving Jason utterly broken.

The literary history of this play is extremely interesting, though obscure. First, is it later, or earlier, than the *Trachiniæ?* One general idea is common to the two tragedies; but the treatment is utterly dissimilar, and one may not unreasonably believe that Sophocles has sought to reprove Euripides, to paint his own conception of a noble wronged wife, and to show how a woman so placed should demean herself. Secondly, there is some reason [1] to believe that two editions of the *Medea* were for a time in existence. Euripides almost certainly himself remodelled the work, presumably for a second "production," but to what extent it is hard to say. Thirdly, and above all, there is the question of his originality. The longer Greek "argument" asserts that he appears to have borrowed the drama from Neophron and to have

[1] (i) In vv. 1231-5, there is a very clear dittography. That is, either 1231-2, or 1233-5 would serve excellently as a speech of the chorus-leader; but it is unlikely that the poet meant both to be used; (ii) vv. 1236-50 read like another and far shorter version of the great soliloquy 1021-80; (iii) it seems odd that Medea, after finally gaining courage to slay her children, should before doing so, be seen again and join in conversations; (iv) vv. 1375-7 give the impression (as Dr. Verrall has pointed out) that the play is to end, not as it does, but with some kind of arrangement between Medea and Jason; (v) one or two ancient quotations purporting to come from this play are not to be found in our texts.

introduced alterations. This interesting problem has been discussed elsewhere.[1] Neophron's play, if one is to judge by the style and versification of his brief fragments, should be regarded as written early in the second half of the fifth century.

The dramatic structure of the *Medea* calls for the closest attention. In Sophocles we have observed how that collision of wills and emotions, which is always the soul of drama, arises from the confrontation of two persons. In the present drama that collision takes place in the bosom of a single person. Sophocles would probably have given us a Jason whose claim upon our sympathy was hardly less than that of Medea. Complication, with him, is to be found in his plots, not in his characters. But here we have a subject which has since proved so rich a mine of tragic and romantic interest—the study of a soul divided against itself. Medea's wrongs, her passionate resentment, and her plans of revenge do not merely dominate the play, they *are* the play from the first line to the close. Certain real or alleged structural defects should be noted. First, we observe the incredible part taken by the chorus; they raise not a finger to stay the designs of Medea upon the king and his daughter; and we are given no reason to suppose that they are unfriendly to the royal house. The episode of Ægeus, moreover, is puzzling. Though quite necessary in view of Medea's helpless condition and prepared for by her remarks as to a " tower of refuge,"[2] it is quite unneeded by one who can command a magic flying chariot. Moreover, this chariot itself has been often censured, notably by Aristotle,[3] who regards it as to all intents and purposes a *deus ex machina*, and on this ground very properly objects to it.

Dr. Verrall's[4] theory meets all these difficulties. He supposes that several of Euripides' plays were originally written for private performance. The *Medea*, so acted, had no obtrusive chorus, and no miraculous

---

[1] See pp. 21 *sq.*　　　[2] v. 389 *sqq.*　　　[3] *Poetic*, 1454*b.*
[4] *Four Plays of Euripides*, pp. 125-30.

escape of the murderess. To the episode of Ægeus corresponded a *finale* in which Medea, by allowing her husband to bury the bodies of his children, and by instituting the religious rites referred to in our present text,[1] induced both Jason and the Corinthians to allow her safe passage to Athens. This view, or a view essentially resembling it, must be accepted, not so much because of the absurdity involved (as it appears to us) by the presence of the chorus, as the utter futility of the Ægeus-scene in the present state of the text.

The characterization shows Euripides at his best. In the heroine he gives us the first and possibly the finest of his marvellous studies in feminine human nature. Alcestis he viewed and described from without ; Medea he has imagined from within. Her passionate love, which is so easily perverted by brutality into murderous hate, her pride, will-power, ferocity, and daemonic energy, are all depicted with flawless mastery and sympathy. Desperate and cruel as this woman shows herself, she is no cold-blooded plotter. Creon has heard of her unguarded threats, and his knowledge wellnigh ruins her project. Her first words to Jason, " thou utter villain," followed by a complete and appalling indictment of his cynicism[2] and ingratitude, are not calculated to lull suspicion. But however passionate, she owns a splendid intellect. She faces facts[3] and understands her weaknesses. When seeking an advantage, she can hold herself magnificently in hand. The pretended reconciliation with Jason is a scene of weird thrill for the spectators. Her archness in discussing his influence over the young princess is almost hideous ; and while she weeps in his arms we remember with sick horror her scornful words after practising successfully the same arts on the king. Above all, there is here no petulant railing at " unjust gods," or " blind fate ". Her undoing in the past has come from " trust in the words of a man that is a Greek " ;[4] her present

---

[1] vv. 1381-3.   [2] v. 472 : ἀναίδεια.
[3] v. 364 : κακῶς πέπρακται πανταχῇ· τίς ἀντερεῖ;   [4] vv. 801 sq.

murderous rage springs from no *Até* but from her own passion (θυμός). The dramatist has set himself to express human life in terms of humanity.

Jason is a superb study—a compound of brilliant manner, stupidity, and cynicism. If only his own desires, interests, and comforts are safe, he is prepared to confer all kinds of benefits. The kindly, breezy words which he addresses to his little sons must have made hundreds of excellent fathers in the audience feel for a moment a touch of personal baseness—"am I not something like this?" That is the moral of Jason and countless personages of Euripides: they are so detestable and yet so like ourselves. Jason indeed dupes himself as well as others. He really thinks he is kind and gentle, when he is only surrendering to an emotional atmosphere. His great weakness is the mere perfection of his own egotism; he has no power at all to realize another's point of view. Throughout the play he simply refuses to believe that Medea feels his desertion as she asserts. For him her complaints are "empty words".[1] To the very end his self-centred stupidity is almost pathetic: "didst thou *in truth* determine on their death for the sake of wifely honour?"[2] One of the most deadly things in the play hangs on this blindness. Medea has just asked him, with whatever smile she can summon up, to induce "your wife" to procure pardon for the children. Jason, instead of destroying himself on the spot in self-contempt, replies courteously: "By all means; and I imagine that I shall persuade her, *if she is like the rest of women*".[3] Considering all the circumstances, this is perhaps unsurpassed for shameless brutality. Medea, however, with a gleam in her eye which one may imagine, answers with equal urbanity, even with quiet raillery. She has perhaps no reason to complain; it is precisely this portentous insensibility which will secure her success.

---

[1] v. 450.   [2] v. 1367.
[3] vv. 944 *sq.* Two MSS., however (followed by Murray), give the second line to Medea.

The minor characters are, in their degree, excellently drawn—Creon above all. His short scene is unforgettable ; it is that familiar sight—a weak man encouraging himself to firmness by exaggerating his own severity. His delicious little grumble, " my chivalrous instincts have got me into trouble more often than I like to think of," [1] stamps him as the peer of Dogberry and Justice Shallow.

As a piece of Greek, the *Medea* is perhaps the finest work of Euripides. The iambics have a simple brilliance and flexible ease which had been unknown hitherto, and which indeed were never rivalled afterwards. Such things as

σὺ γὰρ τί μ᾽ ἠδίκηκας ; ἐξέδου κόρην
ὅτῳ σε θυμὸς ἦγεν,[2]

in Medea's appeal to Creon, or Jason's rebuke to her :

πᾶν κέρδος ἡγοῦ ζημιουμένη φυγῇ,[3]

or the expression of her " melting mood " :

ἔτικτον αὐτούς· ζῆν δ᾽ ὅτ᾽ ἐξήχου τέκνα,
εἰσῆλθέ μ᾽ οἶκτος εἰ γενήσεται τάδε,[4]

are in their unobtrusive way masterpieces of language. But it is in vain to quote specimens ; the whole work is as novel and as great in linguistic skill as in dramatic art. In particular the speeches of the nurse at the opening, of Medea when rebuking and again when conciliating Jason—above all, her fearful soliloquy and address to her children, touch the summit of dramatic eloquence. The lyric passages are on the whole less remarkable, but the mystic loveliness of the ode [5] celebrating the glories of Attica, and the anapaests [6] which give so haunting an expression to a parent's yearning over his children, are among the most precious things this tender as well as terrible poet has bequeathed to us.

---

[1] v. 349 : αἰδούμενος δὲ πολλὰ δὴ διέφθορα.
[2] vv. 309 *sq.*   [3] v. 454.   [4] vv. 930 *sq.*
[5] vv. 824-45.   [6] vv. 1081-1115.

The HERACLEIDÆ[1] ('Ηρακλεῖδαι) or *Children of Heracles*, is a short[2] play of uncertain date, usually referred to the early years of the Peloponnesian War (431-404) and by some to the date 422 B.C. Nothing is known as to the companion plays, or the success obtained by the tetralogy.

The scene is laid before the temple of Zeus at Marathon in Attica. The young sons of Heracles are discovered with the aged Iolaus, their father's comrade, who explains how, after Heracles departed to Heaven, Eurystheus of Argos has hunted the hero's family through Greece. They have taken refuge in Attica ; Alcmena, mother of Heracles, and the daughters are now within the temple ; Hyllus, the eldest son, has gone to seek another refuge in case Athens fails them. Copreus,[3] a herald from Argos, enters and is dragging the suppliants away when the chorus of aged Athenians enter. Copreus disregards their remonstrances, but is confronted by the king, Demophon, and his brother Acamas. He insists that the Heracleidæ are Argive subjects : let not Demophon risk war with Argos. Iolaus appeals for protection, and is granted it ; Copreus retires with threats of instant war. After an ode of defiance by the chorus, Demophon returns with news that a noble virgin must be sacrificed to Persephone, and he will not slay an Athenian girl. Iolaus is in despair, when Macaria, one of Heracles' daughters, comes forth and offers herself. After a proud but melancholy farewell she goes. A serf of Hyllus arrives, bringing, he says, good news. At this Iolaus joyfully summons Alcmena, who imagines that another herald is assaulting him ; but he announces that Hyllus has returned with a large host of allies. Iolaus, despite the serf's rueful gibes, insists on going to the fray

[1] *Arrangement :* protagonist, Iolaus, Eurystheus ; deuteragonist, Demophon, Alcmena ; tritagonist, Copreus, Macaria, attendant, messenger. There were a great number of mutes : Acamas, the sons of Heracles, and probably some Athenian soldiers.

[2] It has only 1055 lines, but there are probably gaps in our text.

[3] This name is not mentioned by Euripides. The scholiasts have taken it from *Iliad*, XV, 639.

and, dressed in ancient arms from the temple, totters off.
The chorus proclaim the justice of their cause, invoking
Zeus and Athena. The attendant returns with news of
complete victory. Iolaus was taken into Hyllus' chariot
and being (by favour of Heracles and Hebe) miraculously restored for a while to his youthful vigour, captured
Eurystheus. The chorus celebrate the glory of Athens and
acclaim Heracles, who is now proved (despite report) to be
dwelling in Heaven. Eurystheus is led in and Alcmena
gloats over him, promising him death. The messenger
intervenes: Athenians do not kill prisoners. She insists. Then Eurystheus breaks silence: it was Hera
who forced him to these persecutions, and if he is now
slain in cold blood, a curse will fall on the slayer. The
chorus at length accept Alcmena's evasion that he
be killed and his corpse be given to his friends. Eurystheus presents Athens with an oracle which declares that
his spirit shall be hostile to the Heracleidæ, when, forgetting this kindness, they invade Attica.[1] Alcmena bids
her attendants convey Eurystheus within and destroy
him. The chorus[2] briefly express satisfaction at being
free from this guilt, and the play ends.

The *Heracleidæ* is one of the least popular[3] among
Euripides' works. It has indeed unmistakable beauties.
The heroic daughter of Heracles and her proud insistence on no rivalry in her sacrifice have always moved
admiration. The Greek style, moreover, though not
equal to that of the *Medea*, has all the Euripidean limpidity and ease. Such lines as

$$\text{τίς δ' εἶ σύ; ποῦ σοι συντυχὼν ἀμνημονῶ;}\ [4]$$

in Iolaus' conversations with Hyllus' thrall, and the
lyric phrase

$$\text{ἁ δ' ἀρετὰ βαίνει διὰ μόχθων}\ [5]$$

[1] In the Peloponnesian war. The Spartans were believed the descendants of Hyllus and his brothers.
[2] Professor Murray, however, supposes another lacuna here, and
thinks there were two semi-choruses, one party supporting Alcmena, the
other disagreeing.
[3] Even in ancient times it seems to have enjoyed little attention.
[4] v. 638.   [5] v. 625.

haunt the ear. Moreover, the chivalry with which
Demophon and his citizens champion the helpless must
have stirred Athenian hearts. But our pleasure is
repeatedly checked by incidents grotesque, horrible, or
inexplicable. To the first category belongs the absurd
scene in which Iolaus totters away amid badinage to do
battle with Argos. There is a comic note, again, in the
scene where Alcmena for the first time appears and supposes that Hyllus' messenger is another hostile herald
from Argos. As we know who he is, her attack on
him shows that painful mixture of the pathetic and
the ludicrous which so often marks Euripides' work ;
here the comic prevails over the touching. Secondly,
the interview in which Eurystheus is presented to
Alcmena, who gloats at her ease over him, is horrible,
however natural. And finally the inexplicable or at
least puzzling features are perhaps the most striking
of all.

The first difficulty concerns the personality which
forms the background of the whole ; the apotheosis
of Heracles is treated in equivocal fashion throughout.
Iolaus[1] alone seems entirely convinced. Alcmena,
after news of the victory to which her son has given
miraculous aid, utters the candid words :—[2]

> After long years, O Zeus, my woes have touched thee,
> Yet take my thanks for all that hath been wrought.
> My son—though erstwhile I refused belief—
> I know in truth doth dwell amid the gods.

And her faith is echoed in less prosaic language [3] by the
chorus, who proclaim the falsehood of the story that
Heracles after his passing by fire went down to the
abode of Hades ; in truth he dwells in Heaven and in the
golden court lives as the spouse of Hebe. But these
confessions are due to the marvels on the battle-field,
marvels upon which the narrator himself takes pains to
throw grave doubt.[4] Macaria, though she has every

---

[1] vv. 9 sq., 540.   [2] vv. 869 sqq.   [3] vv. 910 sqq.
[4] Down to v. 847 his story contains nothing superhuman. Then "up
to this point I saw with mine own eyes ; the rest of my tale depends

reason[1] to dilate on the glories of her father, speaks of him but briefly and with only the normal filial respect.[2] Of the others, Copreus ignores him; from the man's character we expect sneers and refutations of the miraculous stories such as are put by our poet in the mouth of Lycus.[3] Eurystheus speaks of him generously, but in terms which imply that he has never heard, much less accepted, the marvellous accounts of his enemy: "I knew thy son was no mere cypher, but in good sooth a man; for even though he was mine enemy, yet will I speak well of him, that man of worth".[4] Demophon himself, the champion of Heracles' children, even when he has been reminded (by Iolaus) how the hero rescued Theseus, father of Demophon, from Hades itself, in his reply treats this overwhelming claim ambiguously and with nothing more than politeness.[5] All this seems to show the dramatist's belief that Heracles was simply a "noble man"—an ἐσθλὸς ἀνήρ—whose divine traits are the offspring of minds like those of Iolaus and Alcmena, whose sagacity throughout the drama is painfully low.

Macaria's fate, also, at first sight causes perplexity. After she leaves the scene, nothing[6] more is heard of her. When and where she dies we are not told; the promise[7] of Iolaus that she shall be honoured by him in death, as in life, above all women, produces no effect

on hearsay," τἀπὸ τοῦδ' ἤδη κλύων λέγοιμ' ἂν ἄλλων, δεῦρο δ' αὐτὸς\εἰσιδών· And when he mentions the identification of the miraculous lights with Hebe and Heracles, he attributes the theory to οἱ σοφώτεροι, "cleverer heads than mine," as we may translate it.

[1] The oracle has demanded the daughter of "a well-born father," and she of course mentions her own qualification in this respect, without proceeding to dilate (as one would think inevitable in Euripides—or any-one else) on the quite unrivalled "nobility" of her father.

[2] vv. 513, 563.   [3] *Hercules Furens*, vv. 151-64.

[4] vv. 997-9 ; v. 990, referring to the hostility of Hera, is too vague to stand as a warrant for the divine birth of Heracles.

[5] vv. 240 *sq.*

[6] It has been thought that vv. 819-22 indicate the sacrifice of the maiden. They describe the soothsayers' offering just before the battle: ἀφίεσαν λαιμῶν βροτείων εὐθὺς οὔριον φόνον. If βροτείων is right (though βορείων, "of sheep," is a tempting alteration) the reference to the girl's heroism is brutally curt.

[7] vv. 597 *sqq.*

—for we are told nothing about her burial; whether
the advent of Hyllus' reinforcements should or does
make any difference to the necessity for the sacrifice is
not discussed.   But there is good reason to suppose
that a whole episode, on Macaria's death, has been lost.

The army of Hyllus is the most astonishing feature
in the play.   All the action and all the pathos depend
upon the helplessness which involves the Heracleidæ.
Every other city has rejected them; if Athens fails all
is lost—so we are told repeatedly.[1]   Yet at the last
moment Hyllus returns with a positive army.   Whence
has it come?   How can Iolaus have been ignorant that
such aid was possible?   We are told nothing.   The
Athenian leaders apparently, Iolaus and Alcmena[2]
certainly, receive these incredible tidings with no
feeling save placid satisfaction.

Finally, if this drama is composed in order to extol
the nobility of Athens in espousing the cause of the
weak, it is extraordinary that so dubious an example
should be selected.   The suppliants are ancestors of
those very Spartans who, when the drama was produced,
were the bitter and dangerous enemies of Athens.   Was
not her ancient kindness in saving the first generation of
these foes a piece of folly?   Eurystheus points this moral
at the close.[3]   Alcmena herself, in her cold ferocity[4]
and her quibbling[5] over the dues of piety, is a clear
prophecy of what fifth-century Athenians most detested
in the Spartan character.   Moreover, the plea of Copreus
is perfectly just: Argos has a right to punish her own
people if condemned; whether they were wrongly so
condemned is no concern of Athens.

The upshot seems to be that Eurystheus has a bitter
quarrel with a powerful noble, so bitter that when his
enemy dies the king dares not leave his children at

---

[1] There is, however, in vv. 45-7 an isolated statement which vaguely
contradicts this.

[2] Her remark on hearing the news (v. 665): τοῦδ' οὐκέθ' ἡμῖν τοῦ λόγου
μέτεστι δή, sets the seal upon her utter feebleness of mind.

[3] vv. 1035-7.   [4] vv. 1049-52 and elsewhere in the last scene.

[5] vv. 1020-5.

arge. Through the sentimental weakness of her ruler
Athens is drawn into the dispute, and history shows that
she made a frightful mistake.

The HIPPOLYTUS ¹ ('Ἱππόλυτος Στεφανίας ² or Στεφανη-
λόρος) was produced in 428 B.C. and obtained the first
prize. The scene is laid in Trœzen before a house
belonging to Theseus, King of Athens. Aphrodite, the
goddess of love, speaks the prologue, explaining how
Hippolytus, son of Theseus, scorns her and consorts
always with Artemis, the virgin huntress-deity. Aphrodite therefore has caused Phædra, the wife of Theseus,
to fall in love with her stepson. The king in his wrath
shall bring about the death of his son. The prince
enters followed by his huntsmen, and turning to the
statue of Artemis with a beautiful prayer places garlands
upon it, but disregards the image of Aphrodite. After
the hunters have entered the palace, the chorus of
Trœzenian women come to inquire after the ailing
Phædra. She is borne forth, attended by her nurse, who
seeks to calm the feverishness of her mistress and her
passionate longing for the wild regions of the chase.
She gradually learns that the queen is consumed by
passion for Hippolytus. Phædra, now quite calm,
describes her fight with temptation; when she saw that
victory was impossible she chose death, and for this
reason has refused food. The nurse offers very different
counsel. Why should Phædra strive against her instincts? Even the gods have erred through love; she
will cure her mistress. The remedy, she soon hints, is
nothing but surrender. At this Phædra is so indignant
that the other again takes refuge in ambiguity; she
retires to fetch certain charms. The ode which follows
proclaims the irresistible sway of love. The queen, in
the meantime, has been standing near the palace-door

¹ *Arrangement* (according to Croiset): protagonist, Hippolytus ;
deuteragonist, Aphrodite, Phædra, Theseus (the body of Phædra being
represented by a lay-figure) ; tritagonist, Artemis, servant (who announces
the suicide), nurse, messenger.

² This additional name (*The Crowned H.*) was given to distinguish
the play from the earlier 'Ἱππόλυτος Καλυπτόμενος (now lost), or *Hippolytus
Veiled*.

and now recoils in horror—she has heard Hippolytus
reviling the nurse ; nothing, she cries, is now left to her
but speedy death.   Hippolytus enters in fury, followed
by the nurse.   After an altercation in which he threatens
to break his oath of secrecy, he breaks forth into a
lengthy and bitter tirade against women, but finally
promises to keep his oath.   When the prince has retired
Phædra proclaims her resolve to avoid shame for her
family and herself by death, obtaining from the chorus
a promise not to divulge what has occurred ; at the
same time she obscurely threatens Hippolytus.   After
she has gone, the chorus voice their yearning to be free
from this world of sin and woe; surely this trouble is
a curse brought by Phædra from her house in Crete, a
curse which is even now forcing her neck into the noose.
A messenger rushes forth crying out that the queen has
hanged herself.   Theseus returns home and is speedily
apprised of his loss.   Suddenly he sees a letter clutched
in his dead wife's hand ; on reading it he announces
in fury that Hippolytus has violated his connubial
rights.   He appeals to his father Poseidon, god of the
sea, who has promised to grant him any three prayers
to destroy Hippolytus.   The prince returns, and Theseus,
after a stinging attack on his son's pretensions, banishes
him.   Hippolytus is prevented by his oath from defending himself effectually, and sorrowfully turns away.
The chorus ponder upon the mysterious ways of Heaven
and lament the downfall of the brilliant prince.   One of
Hippolytus' attendants returns and informs Theseus
that his son is on the point of death.   A gigantic bull,
sent by Poseidon out of the sea, terrified Hippolytus'
horses, which bolted and mangled their master.   Theseus
receives these tidings with grim satisfaction, but the
goddess Artemis appears and reveals all the facts.
Theseus is utterly prostrated.   Hippolytus is carried
in, lamenting his agony and unmerited fate.   Artemis
converses with him affectionately and there follows
between the two men a few words lamenting the curse
fulfilled by Poseidon.   Artemis consoles her favourite and

disappears. Hippolytus gives his father full forgiveness, and dies in his embrace.

The main impression left by a repeated study of this magnificent drama is a sense of the loveliness and delight which the transfusing genius of a poet can throw around the ruin worked by blind instinct and hate, even around a whole world tortured by belief in gods whose supreme intelligence, will, and power, are quick to punish, but never pardon. No poem in the world conveys more pungently the aroma of life's inextinguishable beauty and preciousness. Life does not become ugly because full of sin or pain. It can only become ugly by growing unintelligible. So long as it can be understood, it remains to man, whose joys are all founded upon perception, a thing that can be loved; this is the one and sufficient reason why tragic drama is beautiful.

For the writer of the *Hippolytus*, then, life is something profoundly sorrowful yet profoundly dear. Hippolytus' address to Artemis on his return from the chase is compact of that mystic loveliness which fills remote glades with a visible presentment of the beauty of holiness :—

> For thee, my Queen, this garland have I twined
> Of blossoms from that meadow virginal,
> Where neither shepherd dares to graze his flock,
> Nor hath the scythe made entry : yet the bee
> Doth haunt the mead, that voyager of spring,
> 'Mid Nature's shyest charm of stream and verdure.
> There may no base man enter ; only he,
> Who, taught by instinct, uninstructed else,
> Hath taken Virtue for his star of life,
> May pluck the flow'rets of that pleasance pure.
> Come, Queen belovèd, for thy shining hair
> Accept this wreath from hands of innocence !
> To me alone of all mankind is given
> Converse to hold and company with thee,
> Hearing thy voice, although thy face be hid.
> To the end of life, as now, may I be thine ! [1]

This passion for natural beauty as the background of emotional life recurs throughout. The Trœzenian women as they enter tell of their informant—not " some

[1] vv. 73-87.

one talking near the place where men play draughts,"
as in the *Medea*, but a woman in a picture :—

> Where waters leap,
> Waters that flow (men say) from the far-off western sea,
> Down the rock-face,
> And gush from the steep
> To a deep place
> Where pitchers may dip far down—thence hath come a message to me.[1]

Phædra in her delirium sees visions of unfettered life
"beneath the poplars, amid the deep grass," she fancies
herself cheering on the hunting hounds through the
pine-glades, and yearns to feel in her grasp "the iron-
pointed shaft"—words to which we come back with
deeper pain when in almost the same language Hippolytus, now himself delirious, longs to let out his
tortured life with a "two-edged spear".[2] When she
enters the house to seek death, the chorus pour forth
their yearning for escape from the sin and sorrow of
this life to romantic regions where all is grace and un-
stained peace :—[3]

> In yon precipice-face might I hide me from sorrow,
> And God, in his love, of the air make me free !
> Ah, to speed with the sea-gulls—alight on the morrow
> Where Eridanus mingles his waves with the sea !
> There for ever the sisters of Phaethon languish,
> For grief of his fate bowing hush'd o'er the stream ;
> Like eyes in the gloaming, the tears of their anguish
> Up through the dark water as amber-drops gleam.
> Or far let me wing to the fäery beaches
> Where the Maids of the Sunset 'neath apple-boughs dance,
> And the Lord of the Waters his last purple reaches
> Hath closed to the mariner's restless advance ;
> Where from Atlas the sky arches down to the streaming
> Of the sea, and the spring of Eternity flows
> Where the mansion of Zeus on earth's bosom is dreaming
> 'Mid life like a lily and bliss like a rose.

Theseus himself expresses this sense of the fragile
beauty of life in lines [4] which recall the unearthly charm
of Sophocles :—

> ὄρνις γὰρ ὥς τις ἐκ χερῶν ἄφαντος εἶ,
> πήδημ᾽ ἐς Ἅιδου κραιπνὸν ὁρμήσασά μοι.

[1] vv. 121-5.   [2] vv. 208-31.   Cp. vv. 219-21 with vv. 1375 *sq.*
[3] vv. 732-51.   [4] vv. 828-9.

Even Artemis the unloving can tell of life's charm surviving death itself in some wise, an immortality of
beautiful remembrance.[1]   Throughout, the poet has
used all his power to invest the theme with loveliness of
phrasing.   Elsewhere, skilful as his writing is, he often
gives us what is practically prose ; the *Hippolytus* is his
nearest approach to the manner of Sophocles.

Nor is the likeness confined to verbal expression.
The theology is, or claims to be, the theology of
Sophocles.   The traditional Olympians are accepted as
persons, with the powers and purposes which current
belief attributed to them.   This is the view which
Sophocles accepts and expounds.   Euripides who certainly did not accept it, here expounds it—in his own
way and with deadly results.   Many times Euripides
questions the very existence of these deities, but now he
sees fit to accept them for a moment, and depicts life as
lived under such rulers.   Men and women can feel and
recreate the beauty of this world, but these gods time and
again dash all into pitiful fragments.   " The world is ruled
by stupid fiends, who spend eternity thwarting one another.   Do we dwell in a universe or a grinning chaos ? "

Is this all?   Very far from it.   Almost all the
action of the tragedy could be accounted for—had we
not this disconcerting divine explanation—on purely
" human " lines, though what " human " means is, as
the poet plainly perceives, no less difficult a question
than that of theology.   But at least the sorrows of
Trœzen scarcely need the baneful *persons* of Olympus.
For the three sufferers are, after all, not blameless.
They share that casual sinfulness—for we cannot avoid
the use of question-begging words—which is the lot
of man.   Hippolytus errs (in Greek eyes) by his complete aversion from sexual passion ; he errs in all eyes
by the arrogance with which he proclaims it.   His
famous speech[2] is too long for a spontaneous burst of

---

[1] vv. 1423-30.
[2] vv. 616-68.   He seems to begin listening to the sound of his own
voice at v. 654.

resentment; it becomes a frigid piece of self-glorifica-
tion. It is precisely this arrogance which stings Phædra
to the thought of revenge.[1] Theseus, in spite of the
pathetic blindness with which he imputes[2] his misery to
some ancestor's sin, is the original cause of it. Hippolytus is the offspring of his youthful incontinence.[3]
Then, when he has "settled down," it is precisely his
respectable marriage which brings the consequence of
his early amour to fruition; his son and his young wife
are of nearly the same age. As for Phædra herself, the
passion which she feels need not be attributed to a personal goddess. Lawlessness is in her veins; her mother
and sister have both sinned:[4] Crete, "the Isle of Awful
Love,"[5] brands its name upon line after line of the play.
For this predisposition to unchastity many of Euripides'
contemporaries, as of our own, would have blamed her
heartily. The poet himself does not, as his splendidly
sympathetic treatment of her shows; but neither does
he feel any need to lay the blame upon Aphrodite.
Phædra's offence, her contribution to disaster, lies in
her early toying with her passion, when she founded
a shrine of the love-goddess in Hippolytus' name;[6]
in her accompanying Theseus (apparently without a
struggle) to Trœzen and the society of the prince; in
her determination to punish Hippolytus for his bitter
pride.

To banish "the gods" and attribute sin to "heredity," is that not merely to substitute one word for
another? Yes, but the poet herein has his eye fixed on
formal theology. Well aware that the glib invocation
of "heredity" or "environment" is no more conclusive
than "the will of the gods," he yet insists that sin is a
matter of psychology. We must study human nature if
we mean to understand and conquer sin. If we regard

[1] vv. 728-31.   [2] vv. 831-3. Hippolytus agrees, vv. 1379-83.
[3] vv. 967-9, where note the emphatic ἐγώ. And the word νόθος is
frequent in the play; see especially Hippolytus' exclamation in vv. 1082-3,
which, by a finely dramatic stroke, immediately turns Theseus' anger to
hot fury.
[4] vv. 337-41.   [5] Professor Murray.   [6] vv. 29-33

Aphrodite or Artemis as *persons* external to ourselves and of superhuman power we lose all hope of moral improvement in our own hearts. But if we accept these devastating powers as forces in human nature, we may hope by study and self-discipline in some degree to control them.

Thus the drama is full of subtly wise psychology : it is an interesting comment on much that has been written about " realist" play-writing that the *Hippolytus*, which contains some of the most romantic poetry in Greek literature, is also as sincere and profound in characterization as the work of Ibsen himself. Theseus and his son we have already considered ; Phædra and her nurse require deeper study. The latter is a masterpiece among the " minor" characters of Euripides. Her tenderness for the young queen and passionate desire at all costs to win her peace ; the dignity which life and its contemplation can give even to coarse-fibred [1] natures ; her feeling for the deepest pathos of life—these things constitute a great dramatic figure. It is to her that the poet gives his most poignant expression of that mingled pain and beauty which we discussed a moment ago :—

> But if any far-off state there be,
> Dearer than life to mortality ;
> The hand of the Dark hath hold thereof,
> And mist is under and mist above,
> And so we are sick for life and cling
> On earth to this nameless and shining thing.
> For other life is a fountain sealed,
> And the deeps below us are unrevealed,
> And we drift on legends for ever ! [2]

She, too, it is who in words [3] of almost equal beauty urges Phædra to yield to her passion :—

> Thy love—why marvel thereat ? 'Tis the tale
> Of many. Wouldst thou lose thy life for love ?
> Good sooth ! A guerdon strange, if lovers now
> And evermore must meet such penalty !
> Who shall withstand the Cyprian's rising flood ?

[1] Cp. vv. 490 *sq.*
[2] vv. 191-7 (Professor Murray's translation). [3] vv. 439-61.

> Yield to her spell : she comes in gentleness ;
> Make high thy pride and stand on niceties,
> She flings thee pell-mell into ignominy.
> Amid the sky she walks, amid the surge
> Of the sea-billows. All things live from her.
> The seed is hers and hers the yearning throe
> Whence spring we all that tread the ways of earth
> Ask them that con the half-forgotten seers
> Of elder time, and serve the Muse themselves.
> They knew how Zeus once pined for Semele,
> How for love's sake the Goddess of the Dawn
> Stooped from her radiant sphere to Cephalus
> And stole him to the sky. Yet these abide
> In Heaven, nor shun the converse of the gods,
> Bowing, belike, to conquering circumstance.
> And wilt not *thou?* Nay, if this law thou spurnest,
> Thy sire, when he begat thee, should have writ
> Some compact countersigned by gods unknown !

The nurse makes moral weakness into a very religion,[1] and Phædra's heart, one would suppose, is finally broken when, to this appeal that the gods themselves are against her, is added proof that man is utterly unable to understand. " If thy life had not been in such danger," says the nurse, "and thou hadst *happened to be a chaste woman,* I should not thus lead thee on,"[2] and again : " *Thy duty, to be sure, forbids sin ; but, as things are,* be advised by me ".[3] This hideous purring is perhaps Phædra's bitterest shame. No one can understand, except the prince who seems so utterly remote. Hippolytus, after her death, can say[4]

> Unchaste in passion, chaste in soul was she ;
> Me hath my passionless purity dishonoured.

What does Phædra herself say ? Is there any reply to the dreadful eloquence of her old attendant? There is only one reply conceivable, and she offers it : " Whatever gods may do, or men think, I must so act as to be able to respect myself ".[5] Euripides insists that the centre

---

[1] Cp. vv. 474 *sq.* :—

> ληξον δ᾽ ὑβρίζουσ᾽ · οὐ γὰρ ἄλλο πλὴν ὕβρις
> τάδ᾽ ἐστί, κρείσσω δαιμόνων εἶναι θέλειν.

[2] vv. 493-6.   [3] vv. 507 *sq.*   [4] vv. 1034 *sq.*
[5] vv. 415 *sqq.* Compare her whole attitude. Indeed the poet suggests, as at any rate a collateral reason for her destruction of Hippolytus, a fear that he will reveal her secret (vv. 689-92).

of ethics lies in man himself. For Phædra there is no soul on which she can rely but her own ; the conflict must be fought out within herself. The great speech [1] in which she tells her spiritual history to the chorus without any reserve or faltering, is the kernel of the tragedy. We realize how empty of all comfort life can be for those who resolutely reject outworn creeds and turn to seek for a better. Here is no thought, no hint, of a saviour ; the puny soul must struggle alone with an uncomprehended universe. Æschylus had found a saviour in Zeus ; [2] Euripides can see no comfort in gods who are less virtuous than men. In this speech, too, we note for the first time a portrayal of moral temptation and a clear conception of conscience. Sophocles understands well how duty can brace the soul to heroic life or death, but for him the sanction of duty lies in the will of external deities. For Euripides conscience is sufficient as a rule of conduct.

Phædra is a masterpiece of characterization. Whatever we are to guess of the earlier [3] picture, she is here a noble and spirited woman, who cannot help her instincts but who can and will dispute their power over her life. She is, of course, not perfect—if she were she would be no fit subject for drama—and the manner in which Euripides has caused the action to hinge precisely upon her weaknesses, without lessening our respect and affection, is one of the most improving studies provided by dramatic art. The little crevices of circumstance by which wrong-doing—the destruction of Hippolytus— creeps into her soul are beautifully indicated. She is wasted by fasting,[4] a state conducive to keener perception and weaker will. She has been brought—without any attempt on her part, so surely she may indulge in the disastrous joy [5]—from Athens to the little town where the prince lives. Her husband, as it chances,[6] is from

---

[1] vv. 373-430.　　[2] *Agamemnon*, vv. 160-83.
[3] In the first edition of the play, to which it seems that most of the ancient strictures apply.
[4] vv. 135-40.　　[5] v. 384 : τερπνὸν κακόν.
[6] v. 281 : ἔκδημος ὢν γὰρ τῆσδε τυγχάνει χθονός.

home and her life is left empty for "long, long thoughts".[1] When she dwells upon her passion the recollection of her mother's and her sister's fate half attracts while it half repels.[2] Her passionate nature insists on revealing some part of her distress to the keen eyes of the nurse, who forthwith joins the claims of old affection[3] to this new secret pain. So it is that she is half-conquered by what she will not do :—

> Nay, in God's name, forbear ! Thy words are vile
> But wise withal. Love in my soul too well
> Hath mined his way. Urge sin thus winningly
> And passion sweeps my fears into the gulf.[4]

But the nurse will not forbear, and the comforting promise of a charm which shall "still this disease,"[5] as Phædra perhaps half-suspects,[6] is an undertaking to win Hippolytus. The dread strain of illness, passion, and shame have turned the woman for a moment into a nervous child.[7] Thus it comes about that without disgrace, without forfeiture of her conscience, Phædra moves towards the dread moment[8] at which she hears the outcry of Hippolytus. Then after all the anguish, she listens to his intolerable endless speech ! Such is the situation in which murder is conceived. In this way Hippolytus' σωφροσύνη has certainly been his undoing.[9]

We are told[10] that this play is a second version of the theme, and that it was called *The Crowned Hippolytus* (from the lovely address to Artemis) to distinguish it from the first, called *The Veiled Hippolytus*. This version (now lost) is said to have contained "im-

---

[1] v. 384 : μακραί τε λέσχαι καὶ σχολή, τερπνὸν κακόν.
[2] vv. 337 *sqq.* [3] v. 328, etc. [4] vv. 503-6. [5] v. 512.
[6] See Professor Murray's admirable remarks (p. 81 of his translation).
[7] In the trivial question, v. 516 : πότερα δὲ χριστὸν ἢ ποτὸν τὸ φάρμακον ; she is dangerously toying with the proposal. The nurse's reply is a half-quaint, half-heartbreaking quotation from childish days when the little Phædra was querulous with her "medicine" as now : ὄνασθαι, μὴ μαθεῖν, βούλει, τέκνον.
[8] We notice incidentally the amazing dexterity shown by the line (565) in which she announces her discovery : σιγήσατ', ὦ γυναῖκες, ἐξειργάσμεθα. It is a perfectly clear piece of Greek ; it is also a series of gasps.
[9] v. 1035. [10] See the Greek *Argument*.

proprieties" which the poet afterwards removed. This refers to the attitude of Phædra, who showed less reserve in her passion than in the later play. She invoked the moon-goddess, perhaps to aid her in winning Hippolytus, and boldly pointed to the infidelities of Theseus as an excuse for her own passion.[1] The reproaches[2] which Aristophanes lays upon Phædra refer perhaps only to this earlier version, but his most famous gibe[3] is upon a line[4] of our text,

ἡ γλῶσσ' ὀμώμοχ', ἡ δὲ φρὴν ἀνώμοτος,

"My tongue hath sworn; my soul abides unsworn." This seems to give us the measure of the comic poet's criticism; he blames Euripides for this sentiment, and yet Hippolytus even in his most desperate trouble will not clear himself by breaking his oath. One cannot, however, refrain from pointing out that even if he had broken it, Theseus would not have believed him,[5] and that Hippolytus realizes this.[6]

The HECUBA (Ἑκάβη) is the next play in order of date; it was performed about 425 B.C.[7] This tragedy was enormously popular throughout antiquity, as the great volume of the scholia proves. It was one of the three plays—the others were *Phœnissæ* and *Orestes*—used as an Euripidean reading-book in the Byzantine schools.

The scene is laid in Thrace, where the Greeks are encamped after the fall of Troy; the background is a tent wherein captive Trojan women are quartered. The ghost of Polydorus, Priam's youngest son, tells how he has been murdered by the Thracian king, Polymestor; he has appeared in a dream to his mother Hecuba. On his departure, Hecuba enters, and soon learns that her

---

[1] In our play the poet leaves his heroine silent on this topic, but hints it himself for us. See vv. 151-54, 967-70.

[2] *Frogs*, 1041; *Thesm*. 497, 547.

[3] *Frogs*, 101, 1467; *Thesm*. 275-6.   [4] *Hipp*. 612.

[5] vv. 960 *sq*., 1076 *sq*.   [6] vv. 1060-3.

[7] Aristophanes in the *Clouds* (v. 1165 *sq*.) parodies vv. 174 *sq*. The *Clouds* was produced in 423 B.C. In *Hecuba*, v. 462, reference seems to be made to the re-establishment of the Delian festival in 426 B.C.

daughter Polyxena is to be sacrificed at the tomb of
Achilles. Odysseus comes to fetch the maiden, who
welcomes death as a relief from slavery. Soon Talthybius enters, summoning Hecuba to bury Polyxena, whose
noble death has filled the Greeks with admiration.
Hecuba sends a woman to fetch sea-water for the
obsequies, and this messenger returns with the body
of Polydorus. Hecuba exclaims that the murderer is
Polymestor: her dream has told her. Agamemnon
enters, and she induces him to connive at her taking
vengeance upon the Thracian, his ally. Next she sends
for Polymestor and his children, and (after a beautiful
ode on the last hours of Troy), they arrive. Polymestor
is induced to go with his little sons within the tent,
where they are slaughtered and he himself blinded. His
cries bring back Agamemnon, who rejects the pleas of
Polymestor. The Thracian, in his despair, prophesies the
strange end both of Agamemnon and of Hecuba. He
is dragged away, and the drama ends with preparations
for the voyage to Greece.

This tragedy, let it be said plainly, is on the whole
poor and uninteresting.[1] It has been frequently noted,
for example, that the plot is "episodic," that it falls into
two divisions, the story of Polyxena and the vengeance
upon Polymestor, which are really two small dramas

---

[1] Its popularity in Byzantine times is no bar to this statement. Probably all the three plays, *Hecuba*, *Phœnissæ*, and *Orestes*, were chosen
because the Greek was comparatively easy. Euripides was already sufficiently ancient to make this an important consideration.

Miss L. E. Matthaei's essay should, however, be read (*Studies in
Greek Tragedy*, pp. 118-57). With admirable insight and skill this
scholar seeks to show that the *Hecuba* is a study, first, of "conventional"
justice, the claim of the community, shown in the sacrifice of Polyxena;
and, secondly, of "natural" justice, seen in Hecuba's revenge. Miss
Matthaei's treatment, however subjective, is trenchant and illuminating,
especially as regards the psychology of Hecuba and Odysseus, the value
of Polyxena's surrender, and the *finale*. But concerning the vital point,
lack of dramatic unity, she has little to say, apparently only the suggestion (p. 140) that "the cumulative effect of finding the body of Polydorus
after having seen Polyxena taken away is the deciding factor; otherwise
the end of the play would have been simply unbelievable". The strength
of this argument is very doubtful,

with no genuine connexion.   To this it has been replied
that the spiritual history of Hecuba supplies unity to the
whole ; that these episodes bring out her development
from a victim into a fiend.[1]   But this is scarcely satisfactory.   For the two parts are developed so completely
along their several lines, they have so little dependence
upon one another, that they could stand apart ; and that
is the real test.   Further, the poet himself is uneasy.
He is anxious to make some sort of connexion, but it is
curiously adventitious.   His device, that the corpse of
Polydorus is discovered by the woman sent for water
wherewith to bathe the body of Polyxena, has won too
high praise.   An attempt to strengthen it, or rather to
draw attention to its neatness, is supplied in the conversation between Hecuba and Agamemnon :[2] " How
did he die ? "   " By the hands of his Thracian host." . . .
" Who brought his body hither ? " . . . " This woman.
She found it upon the sea-shore."   " *Was she looking for
it, or busied with some other task ?* " The last question is
absurd ; Agamemnon has no reason to ask it.   Other
little hooks,[3] less obtrusive than this, are provided here
and there to connect the two parts.   If the play were an
unity they would not be needed.

Again, the favourite charge against Euripides, that
he delights in quasi-judicial disputes, is brought in here
also.   The accusation is generally unfair.   Critics have
been so eager to condemn this poet that they forget the
trial scene of the *Eumenides*, the altercation between
Œdipus and Creon in the *Œdipus at Colonus* and
various other passages in the earlier tragedians.   If
a dispute occurs at all, it is in accordance with the
genius of Greek tragedy to set it out in formally opposed
speeches.   One might as well complain of Hamlet's solilo-
quies.   But in the *Hecuba* there is more than this.   The
queen has a gusto not merely for eloquent appeals or
invective, but for self-conscious rhetoric, " Filled with

---

[1] See Mr. Hadley's admirable *Introduction* to the play (pp. ix-xii).
[2] vv. 779 *sq.*   [3] vv. 428-30, 671, 894-7, 1287 *sq.*

lament, not destitute of tears," [1] is abominable. One is not surprised to learn that the queen is interested in professional teachers of rhetoric,[2] and one remembers that Gorgias, the greatest of them, paid his first visit to Athens a year or two [3] before this play was produced.

The whole piece in its tone and method is far below the best of Euripides' work. Certain things are undoubtedly excellent—the famous chorus [4] already mentioned, and above all the speech [5] of Polyxena and the narrative of her death.[6] The whole work has not enough calibre. The pathos has no subtlety; the characterization is machine-made; the style, though clear and even elegant—one must allow that the first speech [7] of Polymestor, as a piece of conversational Greek, is unobtrusively perfect—has remarkably few of those feats [8] of idiom which delight us elsewhere.

Polyxena is charming, but a slight sketch only compared with the Medea and the Phædra who have preceded her. Agamemnon the cautious prince, Odysseus the opportunist, Polymestor the brutally wicked barbarian, are characters whom dozens of Euripides' contemporaries could have produced with ease. Talthybius the herald, still more shadowy, claims remembrance by his naïve conceit.[9] Hecuba herself is hardly better. True, the poet has shown admirably how she progresses from weakness to frightful strength under the pressure of injustice, but without any very sympathetic psychology we fall short of genuine tragedy and touch only melodrama. And she is more than a little grotesque. Her strange passion for rhetorical studies we have already noted.

---

[1] v. 230. [2] vv. 814-9, 1187-94. [3] In 427 B.C.
[4] vv. 905 *sqq.* [5] vv. 342-78. [6] vv. 518-82.
[7] vv. 953-67.
[8] vv. 796 *sq.* provide an example :—

> ἔκτεινε, τύμβου δ᾽, εἰ κτανεῖν ἐβούλετο,
> οὐκ ἠξίωσεν, ἀλλ᾽ ἀφῆκε πόντιον.

[9] Note his absurd insistence (vv. 531-3) on his own trivial part in the sacrifice-scene.

She has, moreover, a taste for inopportune theorizing,[1] even concerning theology.[2] Her griefs themselves command our respect, and she can in one or two flashes of inspiration speak of them in language[3] not unworthy of Shakespeare himself; but there is too much repetition of merely melancholy adjectives, and though there should be only one emotion in us towards a woman who has lost all her children, we can hardly retain it when she reminds us that they were fifty in number.[4]

The apparition of the murdered Polydorus is an interesting element in the action. First, we view the early part of the drama with greater sympathy for the queen, knowing as we do the new horror which awaits her. Secondly, it is necessary that Hecuba should know how Polydorus died. Though but vaguely affected by the vision at first,[5] when parts of it are fulfilled, she remembers and believes definitely in the rest, and knows that Polymestor is the murderer.[6]

The ANDROMACHE (Ἀνδρομάχη) is perhaps the next[7] extant play in the order of time. It was not originally brought out at Athens.[8]

The action takes place before the house of Neoptolemus, prince of Phthia in Thessaly ; at one side of the orchestra is the shrine of Thetis. Andromache delivers the prologue. After the fall of Troy she became the prize of Neoptolemus to whom she has borne a son, Molottus. Later the prince married Hermione, daughter of the Spartan king Menelaus. Andromache has hidden the child and herself taken sanctuary in the shrine of Thetis ; the boy's father is from home, having gone to

---

[1] vv. 592-603 (the last line being an apology for the digression), 864-7.

[2] vv. 799 sqq.   [3] vv. 585 sqq., 806-8.

[4] v. 421 : ἡμεῖς δὲ πεντήκοντά γ᾽ ἄμμοροι τέκνων. Comment seems obvious : "Actually enough children to row a galley ! " (πεντηκόντορος ναῦς).

[5] vv. 68 sqq.   [6] vv. 702 sqq.

[7] Probably it was composed during the early years of the Peloponnesian war, as the scholiast suggests in a note on v. 445.

[8] Schol. on v. 445.

Delphi to ask Apollo's pardon for demanding reparation
for Achilles' death. Andromache now sends a fellow-slave
to ask the aid of Peleus, king of Phthia and her master's
grandfather. Soon she is joined by the chorus, a company of Phthian women who sympathize but urge submission. Hermione enters, and after a spiteful altercation,
in which she tries in vain to make the captive leave her
sanctuary, departs with threats. Menelaus enters, leading Molottus; he offers Andromache her choice: will
she submit to death, or see the boy slain? Andromache
gives herself up, whereupon Menelaus announces that,
while she must die, Molottus lies at the mercy of Hermione. By this treachery Andromache is goaded into
the most bitter invective to be found in Euripides. The
chorus dwell upon the folly of domestic irregularities
such as those of Neoptolemus. Next Menelaus leads
forth Andromache and Molottus for death, when Peleus
hurries in and releases them. After a violent quarrel
Menelaus throws up his daughter's cause and departs.
Peleus leads the captives away while the chorus sing his
youthful exploits. From the palace comes Hermione's
nurse: deserted by her father and dreading her husband's
vengeance the princess is seeking to destroy herself.
Next moment Hermione rushes out in distraction and
the nurse is attempting to calm her when Orestes enters,
explaining that he has called to inquire after his cousin
Hermione. She begs him to take her away to Menelaus
before her husband returns. Orestes agrees, reminding
her that she has in the past been betrothed to him; now
Neoptolemus shall pay for his insults by death at Delphi.
After their departure the chorus sing of the gods who
built but abandoned Troy, and of Orestes' vengeance
upon Clytæmnestra. Peleus returns, having heard of
Hermione's flight. In a moment arrives a messenger
who tells how Neoptolemus has been murdered by
Delphians at the instigation of Orestes. The body is
borne in, and Peleus laments over it until interrupted by
the goddess Thetis, his bride of long ago. She comforts
him with a promise of immortality. Andromache is to

marry Helenus, king of Molossia,[1] and her son is to be
ancestor of a dynasty in that land.

Certain remarkable difficulties in the plot must
be faced.

First is the breakdown of Menelaus in the presence
of Peleus. The first half of the play has exhibited
his unswerving resolve to destroy Andromache and
her child. Every conceivable argument save one has
been addressed to him in vain. That one argument
is physical compulsion, and Peleus certainly does not
offer it.[2] After a storm of mutual abuse the Spartan
withdraws from the whole situation, muttering an excuse
which is scarcely meant to be taken seriously: he is
in a hurry to chastise an unfriendly state.[3] He goes
just far enough to embitter his enemies to the utmost and
not far enough to redeem his threats; and he retires
without a word to his daughter after committing her to a
deeply dangerous project. Menelaus has faults, but crass
stupidity is not one of them; on the contrary he is
reviled as the type of base cunning. Why, then, does
he act with such utter futility at a crisis which anyone
could have foreseen?

In the second place, when was Neoptolemus
murdered? Orestes declares that the prince will be
slain at Delphi, and at once departs with Hermione.
After a choric song Peleus comes back, and almost at
once receives the news of his grandson's death. When
Orestes utters his prophecy the messenger from Delphi
can hardly be more than a mile from the house. Has
he already committed the murder as a prelude to an
innocent and irrelevant pilgrimage to Dodona? And,
if so, why does he reveal, or rather not reveal, the

---

[1] Her son, who is not given a name in the play, no doubt obtains it
from this prophecy.

[2] Mention of such a conflict naturally occurs (vv. 588 *sq.*) in the heat
of their quarrel, but it comes to nothing. That the old king has no
military following seems certain from the silence of both parties. See
particularly vv. 752 *sqq.*

[3] vv. 732 *sqq.* Note the stammering repetition of τις—he cannot even
suggest a name.

fact? And why has he risked himself in Phthia when
the news of his crime may at any moment be revealed?[1]

Thirdly, there is a grave difficulty in the structure,
independent of Menelaus' conduct and the dating of
Orestes' crime. The play seems to fall into two halves
with but a slight connexion—the plight of Andromache
and the woes of Neoptolemus' house.

The late Dr. Verrall's theory[2] of the play explains
all these things together. Menelaus has come to see
that it is to his interest that his daughter should be the
wife of the Argive rather than of the Phthiote prince.
He and Orestes therefore concoct a plan to this end.
Two things must be achieved: Neoptolemus must be
removed, and Hermione, passionately as she loves
her lord, must be induced to accept his assassin. The
cunning of Menelaus fastens upon the failings of his
son-in-law as the path to success. First, he has offended
the Delphians, and thus Orestes finds it easy to compass
his death. Second, he has caused bitterness in his
own house by his connexion with Andromache. Menelaus, while Orestes is at Delphi, urges Hermione into
action which her jealousy approves but which her
intellect (when it is allowed to speak) must and does
condemn. The Spartan has no intention of killing
the captives, but he sees to it that Hermione is, in
the eyes of Peleus and his subjects, irretrievably committed to such an intention, which will beyond doubt
incense Neoptolemus most bitterly—or would, were
he still alive as Hermione supposes. Then, when
she has committed herself, he calmly bows to the outburst of Peleus and leaves her ready to snatch at any

---

[1] It may be answered that here, as elsewhere, the time consumed by
the choric ode is conventionally supposed long enough to allow for the
alleged synchronous action. But how much time is required? Orestes
is to place Hermione in Menelaus' care, journey to Delphi, and arrange
his plot; then the slaves are to carry the body home. This certainly
means three days; one would expect a week. Thus Peleus only hears
of Hermione's departure three days (perhaps a week) after it has occurred.
Is this credible? See also the conversation between him and the chorus
which implies that the news has reached him within an hour or two.

[2] *Four Plays of Euripides*, pp. 1-42.

hope in her hysterical despair. At this moment, carefully awaited by the plotters, Orestes appears. He has already murdered Neoptolemus, and is now ready to take Hermione away. But this is not enough. She must appear to come by her own suggestion, and it must appear that she has known at the moment of her elopement what has happened at Delphi. As she hurries from the scene he utters, apparently in consolation of her (though really she is out of hearing), so that it may lodge in the minds of the chorus, a prophecy of Neoptolemus' fate. Later, she is to be reminded by her father and her new suitor how completely she is involved in suspicion of complicity. Thus she will be thrown into the arms of Orestes, and whatever blame there is will be laid upon Delphi.[1]

This view should in its essentials be adopted. Every dramatist commits faults; but these apparent faults in the *Andromache* prove too much. They tend to show not that Euripides is here inferior in construction and psychology to Sophocles, but that he is insane. Few readers could compose a speech like that of Andromache beginning ὦ πᾶσιν ἀνθρώποισιν ἔχθιστοι βροτῶν, or like the messenger's narrative. But we could all manage the exit of Menelaus better. There is one great general objection to Verrall's theory. Is it not much too subtle? If readers have always missed the point, would not spectators do so even more certainly? Verrall, in answer, points to a passage in the Greek *Argument*: τὸ δὲ δρᾶμα τῶν δευτέρων, which he takes to mean "this play is one of the sequels".[2] He believes that the audience had a sufficient knowledge of the earlier part of the story to follow the *Andromache* with no perplexity. Whether this knowledge was given by an earlier play of Euripides is not of course certain, but may be regarded as likely.

We next note a feature of equal importance—the atmosphere. Every reader observes strange anachron-

---

[1] vv. 1239 *sqq*. (Δελφοῖς ὄνειδος).
[2] It is usually supposed to mean " one of the second-rate plays ".

isms of sentiment and allusion—Hermione's outburst [1]
against women who destroy the confidence between
husband and wife, Peleus' comments on Lacedæmonian
society,[2] and the like, which have no relevance to the
"Homeric age" of the Trojan war. But the whole
tone of the play is unheroic; even if these special
features were removed it would remain quite unlike
a Sophoclean drama. Euripides has, in fact, written
a play about his own generation with a definite purpose.
He takes stories from myths as the foundation of his
plays, but his interest is in his own time. In spite of
"thy mother Helen" and "the hapless town of the
Phrygians," his work concerns essentially fifth-century
Athenians. Hence the almost complete absence of
poetic colour, which is only found in the conventional
lyrics and the goddess of the epilogue, who is no more
in tune with the rest of the piece than a fairy-queen
would be at the close of *A Doll's House*. His chief
concern is the danger to family life involved in the
practice of slave-holding. Neoptolemus loses his life,
and Hermione consents to the wreck of her own
happiness, simply because of Andromache's position in
the home. She is the fulcrum which the astute villains
employ; without her Hermione would never have
been manageable.

In harmony with this realistic spirit is the character-
drawing. None of the personages is of heroic stature,
but all are amazingly real, however disagreeable. The
two conspirators, Menelaus and Orestes, of course, do not
reveal their natures plainly. The latter, as far as this
incident alone is concerned, might strike one as almost
featureless; but there cling to him significant little
fragments from the earlier history of Hermione. A
sinister faithfulness actuates him. In spite of his repulse
he has not forgotten his affection for Hermione, not even
her last words of renunciation.[3] Nor has he ceased to

---

[1] vv. 929-53.   [2] vv. 595-601.

[3] v. 964: ἦλθον δὲ σὰς μὲν οὐ σέβων ἐπιστολάς, κτέ. There can be
hardly a doubt that these words refer to their parting before her marriage,
when she forbade him to see her again.

brood on the insults of Neoptolemus—perhaps nothing
in the play is more effective than the gloomy triumph
with which he flings back the hated word : "and the
matricide shall teach thee". . . . . Menelaus, as a
study in successful villainy combined with the domestic
virtues, is quite perfect in his kind ; *ces pères de famille
sont capables de tout*. But it is upon the three victims,
Hermione, Andromache, and Peleus, that the poet has
lavished his skill most notably. Each has precisely the
virtues and the failings which are fit to make them
answer with the precision of machinery to each string
pulled by the Spartan diplomatist. Peleus may be
relied upon to provide Menelaus with an excuse for
retiring when he wishes, and to utter wild language
which can be used to prove that he is responsible for
Hermione's flight.[1] Andromache, earning and receiving
our pity for her past woes and her present anguish, yet
alienates us by her arrogance and a certain metallic
brutality in repartee and invective which again are
invaluable to the men whose puppet she is. That she
should not cower before Hermione or her father is natural,
but that is not the point ; her trampling tactlessness[2] is
a positive disease. She is indeed (except in her love
for Molottus) as callous as Menelaus. This is a point
of absolutely fundamental import. That interview
early in the play, which might have been priceless to
both women, ends only in the hopeless embitterment
of Hermione. The latter is the best-drawn character
of all. Swayed by strong primitive impulses, jealousy
and fear, without any balance of mind or emotion,
curiously liable to accept the domination of a stronger
personality, she is fatally suited to the machinations of
her father. When she first appears, it is fairly plain
that she has come to suggest a compromise to Andromache.[3] What she wishes is not blood, but servility.
Spiteful and vulgar, she cannot forgive the captive for
the effortless dignity which she has inherited from Trojan

[1] vv. 639, 708 *sqq.* Cp. Verrall, p. 38.
[2] *Eg.* vv. 229 *sq.*   [3] Cp. Verrall, pp. 29 *sq.*

kings.   Hers is no vision of a murdered rival: how petty
yet how horribly natural it is—she wishes to see Andromache scrubbing the floor!¹   But vulgar and spiteful
as she is, the princess can be wrought upon, as the later
part of the action shows, and if only to self-respect
Andromache had added tact and sympathy Hermione
would have been her passionate friend before thirty
lines had been spoken.   The pathos of the scene lies
above all in the misunderstanding which pits the two
women against one another, where they should have
combined against the callous craft which was using them
both for the ends of politics.

The deities whom we find in this play need detain
us only a moment.   Thetis is no more than sweetening
for the popular taste.   Soothing and beautiful as are
her consolations to the aged sufferer, such a personage
has no real concern with a drama so utterly secular.
As for Apollo, it is here plainer than usual that his name
is nothing but a convenient short term for the great
priestly organization at Delphi.   That there is a genuine
divine person who has aided Orestes and punished
Neoptolemus we cannot believe.   The only touch of
religious awe to be found lies in the messenger's report.
When the assassins are fleeing before their courageous
victim, "from the midst of the shrine some one raised
an awful voice whereat the hair stood up, and rallied
the host again to fight".²   It is this same speaker,
however, who thus sums up his account of the whole
event : "And thus hath he that gives oracles to others,
he who for all mankind is the judge of righteousness,
thus hath he entreated the son of Achilles who offered
him amends.   Like a man that is base hath he remembered an ancient grudge.   How, then, can he be wise ?"
To the simple Thessalian confronted for the first time

¹ v. 166.   This is the type of drama at which Sophocles shook his
head and which Aristophanes reviled.   But it must have made many a
slave-holding citizen in the theatre suddenly raise his brows and fall
to thinking of words let drop an hour ago at home.

² vv. 1147 *sqq.* : The some one of course might be anyone.   The
speaker elects to assume that the god is actually present.

with doubts of Olympian justice, such phrasing is natural.
For Euripides the conclusion is that Apollo does not
exist at all. "Apollo" does not take vengeance upon
the blasphemer at the time of his offence, but waits
unaccountably till his second visit, when he comes to
make amends and when by an accident, fortunate for
the god, a conspiracy of villainous men happens to make
his enemy their victim.[1]

In keeping with all this is the literary tone of the
work. The lyrics are of little interest to a reader,
though one[2] of them markedly sums up the situation
and forces home the moral. For the rest, the dialogue
is utterly unheroic and unpoetical but splendidly vigorous,
terse, and idiomatic; in this respect the *Andromache*
is equal to the best work of Euripides. Could anything of its kind be more perfect than the first speech
of Hermione[3]—this mixture of pathetic heart-hunger,
of childish snobbery and petulance, this terribly familiar
instinct to cast in the teeth of the unfortunate precisely
those things for which one formerly envied them, these
scraps of ludicrously inaccurate slander against "barbarians" picked up from the tattle of gossiping slaves,
and the heavy preachments about "the marriage-
question" which cry aloud their origin from the lips of
Menelaus? In

> δεῖ σ' ἀντὶ τῶν πρὶν ὀλβίων φρονημάτων
> πτῆξαι ταπεινήν, προσπεσεῖν τ' ἐμὸν γόνυ,
> σαίρειν τε δῶμα τοὐμόν, ἐκ χρυσηλάτων
> τεύχεων χερὶ σπείρουσαν Ἀχελῴου δρόσον,
> γνῶναι θ' ἵν' εἶ γῆς,[4]

the last phrase is marvellous. The very sound and
fall of the words, with the two long monosyllables, can
only be described as a verbal box on the ears. Observe
too the great speech[5] of Andromache. In the lines

> νῦν δ' ἐς γυναῖκα γοργὸς ὁπλίτης φανεὶς
> κτείνεις μ'· ἀπόκτειν', ὡς ἀθώπευτόν γέ σε
> γλώσσης ἀφήσω τῆς ἐμῆς καὶ παῖδα σήν,

---

[1] vv. 1002 *sqq.*, especially 1004.   [2] vv. 464-94.
[3] vv. 147-80.   [4] vv. 164 *sqq.*   [5] vv. 445-63.

one can hear the words gurgling in her throat before they issue in speech ; at the end she is positively hissing. Peleus, too, ineffectual as he may be in argument, is a master of pungent rhetoric.[1]

For readers who admire exclusively the Sophoclean type of play, the *Andromache* is a painful experience to be forgotten as soon as possible. For any who find interest in the behaviour of ordinary beings at a great testing moment, this work is an endless delight.

The HERCULES FURENS[2] or *Mad Heracles* ('Ηρακλῆς Μαινόμενος) is perhaps the next play in order of time. Most critics place it about the year 420 B.C. or a little earlier ; the chief reason for this is the celebrated chorus about old age—it is natural supposition that the poet had recently passed beyond the military age, and so would now be just over sixty.

The scene is laid before the house of Heracles at Thebes. Amphitryon, reputed father of the hero, explains the situation. Heracles, leaving his wife Megara and his three sons with Amphitryon, has departed to Hades in quest of Cerberus. In his absence one Lycus has seized the throne and intends to murder Heracles' family. Megara would submit, but Amphitryon still hopes for Heracles' return. Certain aged Thebans, who form the chorus, arrive, followed by Lycus who, after sneers at Heracles, orders his henchmen to burn his victims in their house. Megara begs of Lycus that they be given time to array themselves for death. He consents, and the sufferers retire. Lycus departs, and soon the sad procession returns. Suddenly Heracles himself enters. He tells that he has brought back Cerberus and released Theseus, King of Athens, from the lower world ; he promises to destroy Lycus and goes within. A splendid ode laments

---

[1] *Eg.* vv. 632 *sqq.*

[2] *Arrangement* (according to Croiset): protagonist, Amphitryon, Madness ; deuteragonist, Megara, Iris, Theseus ; tritagonist, Lycus, Heracles, messenger. Of course the dead bodies are lay figures. Other arrangements are possible.

the weakness of old age but glorifies the Muses. Lycus returns, enters the house, and is slain ; the chorus greet his yells with delight and hail Heracles as now proved the son of Zeus. Suddenly Iris and Frenzy sweep down from the sky, sent by Hera to drive Heracles mad. Frenzy herself is reluctant, but enters the house, and the chorus raise cries of horror, amid which the house totters in ruin. A messenger relates how Heracles, after slaying Lycus, has been seized with madness and destroyed his wife and children. The eccyclema shows the hero sunk in stupor. He awakes and, realizing his situation, meditates suicide, but Theseus arrives and wins him back to courage ; after terrible outbursts against Heaven he departs to live with Theseus in Athens.

After a cursory reading of this play one's impressions are doubtful. Many features excite warm admiration, such as the superb lyric [1] on old age, the speeches [2] of Megara about her fatherless boys, Heracles' replies [3] to Theseus ; even the wrangle between Lycus and Amphitryon is full of idiomatic vigour. [4] But to be blunt, what is the play about? It works up to a climax in the deliverance of Amphitryon and his kin, and then begins again. Long before the close we have forgotten Lycus. We feel that the play is structureless, or (which is worse) that it falls so clearly into two dramas that we cannot view it as a single piece of art. But if we seriously seek for unity, we naturally look for it in the fortunes of Heracles himself. This granted, we shall expect to find that the incident which in a bare summary seems to disjoint the whole is specially treated. Looking then at the incursion of Lycus, we find that at every moment the events are considered from the point of view of Heracles, in terms of his actions, and the sentiments which cling to his personality. We are only prevented from seeing this at first by the modern supposition that the culmination of a tragedy is the death of

---

[1] vv. 637-700.
[2] vv. 70-9, 460-89.
[3] vv. 1255-1310, 1340-93.
[4] vv. 140-235.

a leading person, not a spiritual crisis. The discussion between Amphitryon and Megara about instant submission is dominated by despair of the hero's return in the latter's mind and by hope of it in the former's. As soon as Lycus arrives, he asks : " What hope, what defence find ye against death? Believe ye that the father of these lads, he who lies in Hades, will return?" Whereupon he proceeds to a long tirade in abuse of the hero, and Amphitryon's even more garrulous response deals almost solely with his son's achievements and the gratitude which he merits from Thebes and Greece. As the doomed party go indoors the old man reminds Heaven itself of the help it owes to Heracles, and the following lyrics are an elaborate chronicle of his marvellous exploits. Finally, when at point to die, Megara in a beautifully natural manner turns her farewell to her sons into a painful memory of the plans which their father used to make for them. In this way the danger of his family is considered as a test of Heracles' powers and greatness. Will he make good the promise of his past glories? Will he return and free them from Lycus?

Dr. Verrall [1] follows this line of thought, giving to it far greater precision and colour. He believes that the subject of this play is the miraculous tone investing the traditional stories about Heracles. According to popular belief in the poet's day, Heracles was a son of Zeus ; he performed many exploits which were definitely superhuman, culminating in a descent to Hades and return therefrom. These stories are untrue. The play indicates this simply and directly, giving, however, most attention to the method by which they won credence. In a primitive civilization, when men had not yet attained to clear thinking, remarkable but human feats like those of Heracles were extolled as miraculous by the uncritical. Such are Amphitryon and the chorus, who when challenged by Lycus are capable only of violent reiteration of their belief, but offer, and can offer, no

[1] *Four Plays of Euripides*, pp. 134-98.

proof that the miracles happened. It is a curious symptom of the former's vague credulity that while loving and defending Heracles as his own son, he yet claims [1] the help of Zeus on the ground that the god is himself Heracles' father. The Theban elders join [2] in this irrational belief—as soon as it appears that the divine parentage is established by the return from Hades, which even if true would of course have nothing to do with the question. It is in such minds as this that belief in the miraculous life of Heracles first sprang up. But this belief rests largely upon the accounts of his adventures given by Heracles himself; thus we come to the heart of the tragedy, the mental condition of the hero.

Near the end he exclaims against the consolations of Theseus: " Alas! such words as thine are too trivial for my sorrows. I think not that the gods love unlawful unions, and that they put chains upon one another is a belief I never held nor will I ever. God, if he be God, in truth needs naught. These are but poets' wretched tales." [3] Plainly, the sober and reasonable speech which begins thus repudiates the highly-coloured but pernicious stories of tradition to which Theseus has just appealed. Heracles believes in one God utterly above human weaknesses. Then what of Zeus' love of Alcmena, the jealousy of Hera, the whole basis of his suffering as conceived by the orthodox? And what of his own semi-divine nature, the foundation again of his superhuman deeds? They are delusions. Heracles is no demi-god; his exploits, however great and valuable, are in no sense miraculous. This view, moreover, is precisely that which we ought to gain from the early part of the drama. Lycus is no doubt an insolent bully, but would certainly not brave annihilation (whether at the hands of Zeus or of his son) by slaughtering a demi-god's family. That he acts so proves that he does not believe in the divine parentage of Heracles; and the support so

---

[1] vv. 339 *sqq.*, etc.   [2] vv. 798 *sqq.*   [3] vv. 1340-6.

readily given by Thebes to his policy shows as plainly that to the mass of citizens no real proofs of superhuman nature have been offered. In brief, the actions and language of every one in the play except Heracles himself, Amphitryon, and the chorus—of every one, including Theseus and even Megara, imply that in this play Heracles is indeed a person of note, but an "eminent man" of no very startling eminence.

But the hero himself long before this repudiation of "poets' wretched tales" has himself given them authority. He tells his father that in truth he has visited Hades, dragged Cerberus thence, and rescued Theseus. At many places [1] in the drama he refers without misgiving or query to legendary monsters which he has quelled, and to his safe return from Hades. This inconsistency, according to Dr. Verrall, is the root of the drama. Heracles suffers from a growing tendency to madness; in his sane moods he knows that all his story is human, all the nobler for its humanity, but in his dark hours he accepts the vulgar splendours which rumour throws round his adventures, at such times lending nascent myth the support of his own false witness. The tragedy of his life has been this mental distemper, which has finally caused him to destroy his wife and children. It appears in dreadful paroxysms throughout the first speech which he addresses to Theseus—first an attempt to account for his murderous outbreak by an account of purely human events; then inconsistently a reference to Zeus' fatherhood and the attempt of Hera upon his infant life, followed by a splendidly vigorous catalogue of legendary deeds, Typhos, the giants, and the rest, culminating with despairing comments on his hopeless guilt and on the complete victory of Hera; then he suddenly rends the goddess with his scorn: "to such a deity who would pray?—for a jealous quarrel she has destroyed the guiltless benefactor of Greece".

Two important details should be noted in connexion

---

[1] Especially vv. 1269 *sqq.*

with this theory. First the apparition [1] of Iris and
Frenzy seems to overthrow it utterly by a demonstration in presence of the audience that Heracles' afflictions
are caused by Hera. But the past scene, before ever
Frenzy arrives, has shown the hero, if not mad, yet not
in full possession of his senses. [2] Moreover, she is not
seen by him at the moment when he goes mad, yet, if
the chorus see her, *a fortiori* she should be visible when
attacking her victim himself ; again the scene in which
the fiend herself shows kind-hearted scruples, is ludicrous. These personages (Verrall suggests) are a dream
beheld by a member of the chorus who has been
impressed by what he has already seen of Heracles'
malady. This is proved by an absence of allusion to the
event afterwards when the fatal incident is discussed,
and when silence is incredible. The aged man (or men)
will gradually remember the dream afterwards ; this is
another way in which stories like that of Hera's vengeance obtain currency.

The second point arises from the conversation between Theseus and his friend when clearly sane. Does
he confirm the story of the visit to Hades ? Now,
Heracles and he several times refer to his rescue " from
below," but never do they use language which necessarily
refers to Hades. " Thou didst bring me back safe to
the light from the dead (or corpses) " [3]—such is the style
of allusion. Undoubtedly the language can be applied
to Hades ; undoubtedly also it could fit some natural
event like a disaster in a cave or mine which may
actually have been suggested [4] by rationalists of the day
as an explanation of the myth—a suggestion which the

---

[1] The appearance of Pallas (vv. 1002-6) is regarded by Verrall as " a
chance blow received by the madman from the falling ruins of the
chamber ".

[2] In vv. 562-82 he raves, however eloquently. One man cannot capture
a whole fortress and punish a hostile population as Amphitryon (vv. 585-
94) feels, though his caution and prosaic advice are painfully ludicrous
considering the vast claims he has made for his son an hour ago.

[3] v. 1222.

[4] Compare the similar explanation of a wonderful feat actually offered
by Lycus (vv. 153 *sq.*).

poet is inclined to adopt and for which therefore he leaves room in his phraseology.

Theseus, amiable as he is, yet presents little of interest; it is his function to voice the opinions of the normal unimaginative man. Megara, however, of whom little has been said, deserves sympathetic study. She does not share Amphitryon's extraordinary beliefs about his son,[1] but loves and admires him with an affection beautifully expressed throughout the too brief portion of the drama in which she appears; it is she who long before the other realizes his mental state.[2] In her, too, poetical imagination shines forth with a radiance which surpasses the charm of the lyrics and Heracles' impetuous eloquence. It is she who utters the Sophoclean description[3] of sovereignty :—

> ἔχων τυραννίδ᾽, ἧς μακραὶ λόγχαι πέρι
> πηδῶσ᾽ ἔρωτι σώματ᾽ εἰς εὐδαίμονα,

and that expression[4] of her yearning grief which in its strange felicity of pathos suggests Shakespeare's Constance :—

> πῶς ἂν ὡς ξουθόπτερος
> μέλισσα συνενέγκαιμ᾽ ἂν ἐκ πάντων γόους,
> εἰς ἓν δ᾽ ἐνεγκοῦσ᾽ ἀθρόον ἀποδοίην δάκρυ;

The SUPPLICES[5] (Ἱκετίδες), or *Suppliant Women*, is generally supposed on internal evidence[6] to have been produced about 420 B.C.

The Suppliants, who form the chorus, are the mothers of the Seven who attacked Thebes and their attendants. They surround Æthra, mother of Theseus, the Athenian king, and beg her to win his aid for them, since the Thebans have refused burial to the slain. Theseus at first refuses, but Æthra persuades him. A Theban herald enters to forbid Theseus, in the name of

---

[1] Cp. Verrall, pp. 147 *sq.*   [2] *Ibid.* pp. 156, 162.
[3] vv. 65-6.   [4] vv. 485-9.
[5] *Probable Arrangement :* protagonist, Theseus, messenger ; deuteragonist, Adrastus, Evadne ; tritagonist, Æthra, herald, Iphis, Athena.
[6] The plot strongly recalls the incident after the battle of Delium (424 B.C.), when the victorious Bœotians at first refused to surrender the Athenian dead, and the alliance between Athens and Argos (420 B.C.).

the Theban king Creon, to aid the Suppliants. Theseus
rejects this behest and prepares for war. After an ode,
news comes of the Athenian victory. The remains of
five heroes are brought in (of the other two, Amphiaraus
was swallowed up by the earth and Polynices is supposed
still at Thebes). Adrastus delivers funeral speeches over
them. The obsequies now take place. The body of
Capaneus is burned separately, and Evadne his wife
throws herself upon his pyre despite the entreaties of her
father Iphis. The young sons of the chieftains bear in
the funeral urns, and Adrastus promises that Argos will
cherish undying gratitude towards Athens. The goddess Athena appears and bids Theseus exact an oath
to this effect; she comforts the fatherless boys with a
promise of vengeance.

This drama is perhaps the least popular and the least
studied of all Greek plays, which is not surprising when
one considers that, in spite of the praise merited by
certain parts, the whole work considered by really
dramatic standards is astonishingly bad. There is no
character-drawing worth the name, and though it may
be said that the real heroine of the drama is Athens,[1] it
is still strange to find Euripides contented with such
colourless persons as Theseus, Æthra, and indeed all
the characters. Still more striking are the irrelevancies.
Theseus' address[2] to Adrastus and the assembly at large
concerning the blessings conferred by Heaven upon man,
have hardly a semblance of connexion with the urgent
and painful subject of debate. Even more otiose, and
far longer, is the dispute[3] between Theseus and the
herald on the claims of monarchy and democracy.
The scene of Evadne's *suttee*, however striking, is
dramatically unjustifiable; it is an episode in the bad
sense meant by Aristotle—no integral part of the action.
The last scene is spoiled by the intervention of Athena,
who merely causes the Argives to give an oath instead

[1] The Hypothesis says: τὸ δὲ δρᾶμα ἐγκώμιον Ἀθηναίων (altered by
Dindorf with general approval to Ἀθηνῶν).
[2] vv. 195-218.   [3] vv. 403-56.

of a simple promise that they will ever be loyal friends
of Athens. That this intervention corresponds to very
definite historical fact (the league between the two states
in 420 B.C. brought about by Alcibiades) makes no difference to the æsthetic fact. None the less one notes in
the *Supplices* certain excellent features. The appeal[1] of
Æthra to her son, and the lyric dirge of Evadne over
her husband's pyre, are admirably composed. Several
parts of the work are magnificent as spectacle—the
opening in which the sorrowing mothers, Adrastus, and
the fatherless boys are grouped about the aged queen,
the return of Theseus and his troops with the dead
bodies, the episode of Evadne as it struck the eye,[2] and
the procession of boys carrying the funeral urns.

The ION[3] (Ἴων) is a play of uncertain date, but was
probably produced late in Euripides' life; some would
place it as low as 413 B.C.

The scene is laid before the temple at Delphi.
Hermes tells how the Athenian princess Creusa, owing
to the violence of Apollo, bore a child, which Hermes
brought to Delphi, where the boy grew up as a temple-
attendant. Later Creusa married Xuthus, and to-day
they will come to ask the oracle some remedy for their
childlessness. Apollo will give Ion to Xuthus as the
latter's son; later he is to be made known to Creusa
as her own. Ion enters, and in a beautiful song expresses his joy in the service of Apollo. The chorus
(attendants of Creusa) draw near; they converse with
Ion and admire the temple façade. Creusa arrives; she
and Ion are mutually attracted, and she tells how "a
friend," having borne a child to Apollo and exposed it,
wishes to know whether it still lives. Ion rejects the
story, and urges her not to put such a question to the

---

[1] vv. 297-331.

[2] She has arrayed herself, not in black but in festal robes (vv. 1054-6)
—an interesting parallel with the fine ending of the second act of Mr.
Shaw's *Doctor's Dilemma*.

[3] *Probable Arrangement:* protagonist, Ion, Pædagogus; deuteragonist, Hermes, Creusa; tritagonist, Xuthus, servant, prophetess,
Athena.

oracle.   Xuthus now appears, and goes within to
consult the god ; Creusa retires, while Ion muses on
the immorality of gods.   After a choric ode Xuthus
returns and greets Ion as his son : the oracle has
declared that the first man to meet him will be his
offspring.   Ion asks who is his mother ; they agree that
she must be some Delphian Bacchante.   The youth is
dismayed at the prospect of quitting Delphi for Athens,
but Xuthus genially bids him prepare a farewell banquet
for his friends, and departs to offer sacrifice upon
Parnassus.   The Athenian women express their con-
sternation : Athens is to have an alien ruler and Creusa
must remain childless.   When she returns they tell
her the news, and in bitter disappointment she breaks
into an agonized recital of her old sorrow.   An aged
male attendant undertakes to murder Ion by poison at
the banquet.   Creusa consents.   After an ode praying
for vengeance, a messenger brings news that the plot
has failed and Creusa has been condemned to death.
The queen hurries in, pursued by Ion and a mob ; she
takes refuge on the altar.   Bitter reproaches pass
between the two till the Pythian prophetess appears ;
giving Ion the basket in which he was discovered as a
babe, and which still contains the articles then found
with him, she bids him seek his mother.   Creusa greets
him as her son and names the three objects.   They
embrace with joy, but Ion, learning that not Xuthus but
Apollo is his father, determines to ask the oracle which
account is true.   Athena, however, appears and explains
that Apollo has been compelled to change his plans ;
Xuthus must continue to believe Ion his own son.

This drama suggests a rich tasselled robe of gorgeous
embroidery ; were it not that the basis of the story is
so painfully sexual, the *Ion* would be perhaps the most
popular of Greek plays.   The sudden changes of situation, the emotional crises, the sheer thrill of many
passages, the lovely study of the Greek Samuel at his
holy tasks—all these things make a glorious play.   But
our delight is blurred by a recurrent perplexity.

Theology is obtruded throughout, and such a theology as never was.

Apollo ravishes Creusa and by help of Hermes brings her child to Delphi, where he lives happily up to manhood, but Creusa is allowed to suppose her child destroyed by wild beasts. The god, however, intends to secure Ion his rights as prince of Athens. Xuthus is to accept the lad as his son, while Creusa and Ion are to be made secretly known to each other. But this plan is disturbed by the Athenian women, and the god, revising his intention, sends the doves to save Ion, and the prophetess to save Creusa. All would now be well, since both Xuthus and the queen accept Ion as a son. But Ion wishes to know whether the oracle speaks truth or lies.[1] Apollo therefore sends Athena to prevent him from taxing the oracle with inconsistency. She explains the various activities of Apollo, prophesies concerning the Athenian race, and bids Creusa keep Xuthus in ignorance.

Apollo is as much fool[2] as knave.[3] Athena may say that " Apollo hath done all things well," [4] but mortals will not endorse her sisterly admiration. Even the revised plan cannot succeed. How long will Xuthus remain ignorant of facts which are being proclaimed, not only to Creusa and her son, but also to the crowd of Delphians and the Athenian women? Even if this could be secured, things are no better: Apollo has said both that he himself, and that Xuthus, is the father of Ion. Which of these statements is true matters comparatively little. One of them must be a lie. The god who gives oracles to Greece is a trickster, and no celestial consolations or Athenian throne can compensate the youth for the loss of what filled his heart only this morning.

The *Ion* is the one play in which Euripides attacks the Olympian theology beyond all conceivable doubt.

---

[1] vv. 1537 *sq.*
[2] ἀμαθής (v. 916, used by Creusa).
[3] ὁ κακός (v. 952, used by the Pædagogus).   [4] v. 1595.

It is certain (i) that he does not believe in the existence of Apollo and Hermes; (ii) that the Delphic oracle is a human institution making impossible pretensions; and (iii) that his method of attack is by innuendo and implication. Verrall's theory of the poet's method is here on absolutely unassailable ground. The story is purely human, and the theological story is a mere addendum designed to suit the religious occasion and many of the spectators. What, then, is this human story? Verrall explains that Creusa was wronged by some man unknown, and that her child perished. The Pythian priestess bore[1] a child which she reared with a natural tenderness.[2] This child was Ion, whom the managers of the shrine determined to place in a station which could assist their influence. Then occurs the deadly scene in which the youth is about to kill Creusa. To save the Delphians from the responsibility of murdering a foreign queen in the open street, and the boy from conduct which would make his admission to Athens impossible, a plot is hastily concocted. It will prevent war with Athens, it will destroy Creusa's hatred for Ion, and secure his future throne. The priests have already heard, even if Apollo has not, the story shrieked[3] out at him by Creusa. By an impudent master-stroke they determine that Ion shall be the queen's long-lost child. To this end the history of the two persons supplies most of the means; all that is needed is something tangible to tie the knot. Hurriedly the clues are provided. The necklace exposed long ago upon the babe is an easy matter; its fellow was found upon the person of the Pædagogus.[4] The ever-blooming olive of the Acropolis can be equalled in freshness by sprays plucked to-day in Delphi; and for the embroidery, it is fairly certain that some such covering must have been wrapped round the

---

[1] vv. 550 *sqq.* are probably significant (and Ion actually the son of Xuthus).
[2] Cp. v. 1324 and the rest of the short conversation between her and Ion, which is of course charming on any view of the play.
[3] vv. 859 *sqq.*   [4] vv. 1029 *sqq.*

child, and its pattern is sufficiently vague.[1]   The queen
in her heart-hunger and peril snatches at these clues,
and in a moment the two fall into one another's arms.
Finally, the clear-headed persistence of Ion is met by
what may in truth be called a *dea ex machina*.[2]   Over
the temple façade is protruded the gigantic head[3] of a
figure, through which some one offers such fumbling
"explanations" as are possible.   All this is enough for
Creusa—she has a son.   As for Ion, whose life has
been in his faith, he commits himself to nothing ; in one
day he has grown to the full stature of a man, but one
hardly supposes that he visited Delphi again.   Thus
may Verrall's theory be summarized.   It has never been
answered, nor does it seem possible to make any answer,
except that the alleged real story is "far-fetched"—of
course ; for any rationalistic explanation of a supposed
miracle must be strange, otherwise no one would have
hitherto believed the miracle in order to account for the
facts.

The "theological background" then being merely
theatrical gauze and canvas, what of the human action ?
Though it forms an extraordinarily brilliant, powerful,
fascinating spectacle, is it a tragedy ?—the story ends
with the appearance at any rate of joy and contentment.
Yet tragedy is found not only in the death of the body
but in the death of ideals ; and the destruction of Ion's
faith in his all-knowing unerring father is a fate from
which, when we remember his happy carolling upon the
dawn-lit temple-steps, we could wish to see him saved
even by the Gorgon's venom.   Any out-cry wherewith
he might have challenged Creusa's is checked by the cold
disgust which fills him at the sound of Athena's bland
periods ; but one knows the kind of man Athens will
receive to-morrow—one who will agree with Xuthus

---

[1] Cp. v. 1419 : οὐ τέλεον, οἷον δ' ἐκδίδαγμα κερκίδος, and Ion's ac-
knowledgment (v. 1424) : ἰδού· τόδ ἐσθ' ὕφασμα, θέσφαθ' ὡς εὑρίσκομεν.
This latter surely means that Ion is as satisfied as one can expect to be in
tracing the fulfilment of oracles.

[2] Cp. v. 1565 : μηχαναῖς ἐρρύσατο.   [3] v. 1550 : πρόσωπον.

that "these things don't happen,"[1] who will be an admirable connoisseur of party politics,[2] but who has lost his vision. This, then, is spiritually, though not technically, a tragedy. Further, it is technically a melodrama. That is, the external form and texture is calculated to produce not as in tragedy simple, profound, and enduring exaltation, but more superficial, violent, and transitory emotion. The Pædagogus is pure melodrama, witness his change from senile helplessness[3] to ruthless vigour,[4] the wildness of his suggestions—"burn down the temple" . . . "murder your husband"; the utter absence of remorse and secondary interests, characteristic of villainous subordinates in melodrama; his complete breakdown when it is demanded by the plot.[5] Such also is the confrontation of Ion and Creusa with the terrified women and scowling Delphians as a background. But the finest thrill, and the touch least justified by any standards save those of melodrama, occurs in the speech of Ion as he stands with the fateful basket in his arms and determines not to open it but to dedicate it to Apollo. The next moment he reflects that he must carry out the god's will and discover his origin. The genuine plot halts so as to cause theatrical sensation.

It is natural in such a play that the characterization should be simple. Xuthus, the Pædagogus, and the Prophetess, are scarcely more than foils to the two chief persons. Creusa attracts us rather because the poet has so well portrayed woman than because he has created a particular woman. More than this can be said of Ion. He is marked out from all the other persons of this play by sheer intelligence, by the power of facing facts, and of constantly readjusting his perspective.[6] He is a figure of somewhat quaint pathos.

---

[1] οὐ πέδον τίκτει τέκνα says the elder man (v. 542), casually turning his back on the glory of his wife's family (cp. vv. 265-8).

[2] vv. 585 sqq. [3] vv. 738-46.

[4] v. 768 sqq. [5] vv. 1215 sqq.

[6] His very religion, when put to the test, is mostly intellectual. Apollo's moral shortcomings only cause him to shake his head gravely; but when the god's truthfulness is exploded, the whole fabric of his belief collapses.

The happy child who sings to the birds on the temple-
steps and thinks of nothing but his tranquil existence
of pious routine, turns in a moment to the discreet
adviser who can imagine incredible things : " There
is no man who will transmit to thee response to such
a question. For were he in his own house proved
a villain, Phœbus would justly wreak mishap upon
him that gave thee such reply." [1] As he moves to
and fro, filling the holy-water stoups, we can hear him
murmuring to himself serene blasphemies. " But I must
blame Phœbus. Such conduct! Use violence upon
maidens, and betray them? Beget children in secret
and leave them to die? Come, come! Since you
have the power, remember its responsibility. You
punish mankind for wrong-doing " . . . [2] and so forth,
including the suggestion that if Zeus, Poseidon, and
Apollo were compelled to pay damages for their
lustful offences, their temples would become bank-
rupt. In politics, as in religion, Ion observes and
deduces for himself. Athenian public life he well
understands before entering it ; [3] he has views about
the influence of perverted religious feelings upon
public opinion and the execution of the law. [4] All this
prepares us for the splendid moment [5] when forgetting
his own rule [6] he insists on bearding the oracle, and
for the reception he gives to the patching-up of Apollo's
infallibility.

For the rest, the work is a study of emotions deeply
conceived and wonderfully expressed. Creusa is induced to tell her story, though disguised, to Ion largely
by her sudden feeling for the youth himself. [7] The
revelation which she makes to the Pædagogus and

---

[1] vv. 369-72.
[2] vv. 436-51. The above paraphrase is probably not too colloquial
(cp. especially v. 437 : τί πάσχεις ; and v. 439 : μὴ σύ γε). In fact, as the
speech is so very explicit and unadorned, and as Ion is probably uttering it
while he performs his tasks (see 434-6, after which these reflections begin
in the middle of a line), we perhaps overhear thoughts rather than words.
[3] vv. 589 sqq.   [4] vv. 1312 sqq.   [5] vv. 1546 sqq.
[6] vv. 369 sqq.   [7] vv. 308, etc.

the chorus is wrung from her after all these years by
the sudden loneliness which the gift of a son to her
husband brings upon her heart. And the gloriously
successful climax[1] where she suddenly addresses her
executioner as her son is purely emotional also. Even
the intellectual revolt of Ion is introduced by a sudden
turn of the feelings in the recognition-scene : " Mother,
let my father, too, share in our joy ".[2]

The TROADES[3] (Τρῳάδες), or *Trojan Women*, was
produced in 415 B.C. together with *Alexander, Pala-
medes*, and *Sisyphus* as satyric play. This group
obtained the second prize, being defeated by the work
of Xenocles " whoever he is ".[4]

The action takes place outside Troy after its capture ; in the background is a tent wherein are captive
Trojan women. Before the tent lies Hecuba in a
stupor of grief. The deities Poseidon and Athena
explain in a dialogue that they are quitting Troy with
reluctance ; Poseidon will destroy the Greek fleet
on its way home. When they have departed, Hecuba
stirs and laments ; soon she is joined by the chorus
of Trojan women. Talthybius tells her that Cassandra
is to become the concubine of Agamemnon ; concerning
Polyxena he speaks evasively ; Andromache is given
to Neoptolemus, Hecuba herself to Odysseus, whom
she detests above all Greeks. Cassandra rushes
forward uttering in frenzy a horrible parody of a
marriage-song in her own honour ; she prophesies the
woes of Agamemnon and Odysseus. Hecuba ponders
her former greatness and present misery ; the chorus
sing the fatal day when Troy welcomed the Wooden
Horse. Andromache and her infant Astyanax are
brought in, and from her Hecuba hears Polyxena's
death. Though prostrated by grief she urges Andromache to please her new lord, that perchance his son

[1] vv. 1397 *sqq.*   [2] vv. 1468 *sq.*
[3] *Arrangement* (probable) : protagonist, Hecuba ; deuteragonist,
Athena, Cassandra, Andromache, Helen ; tritagonist, Poseidon, Talthybius, Menelaus.
[4] Ælian, *Var. Hist.* ii. 8.

may revive something of Troy's greatness. Talthybius returns with tidings that Astyanax is to be hurled from the battlements. After an ode on the first siege of Troy, Menelaus enters rejoicing in his long-deferred opportunity of slaying Helen. Hecuba bursts into rapturous thanks to the Power which rules mankind, and when Helen pleads innocence refutes her bitterly. Talthybius brings in the mangled body of Astyanax over which Hecuba utters a speech of reproachful lament. The play ends with the burning of Troy.

In structure archaic, this play is in spirit something quite new to the Attic stage. On the one hand there is little unfolding of a plot; we are reminded strongly of the *Prometheus* by the portrayal of a situation which changes with extreme slowness. It is the manner of this portrayal which is new and terrible. The *Troades* was performed after the sack of Melos and before the departure of the Sicilian expedition; it is a statement, by a member of the nation which annihilated Melos, of the horrors wherewith the vanquished are overwhelmed. The glory won by the Greeks who overthrew Troy was the best-known and most cherished gift of tradition. Now a Greek writer reveals the other side of conquest. After the crime of Melos, Euripides never felt as he had felt towards Athens or Greece. His intellect and his heart were appalled by the cold ferocity of which his fellows showed themselves every year more capable. Hitherto he has attacked the evils of human nature; now he impeaches one definite nation, and that his own. No spectator could doubt that "Troy" is Melos, "the Greeks" Athens. Such uncompromising hostility must have produced deep effects on so impressionable an assembly. For it is not merely a denunciation; it is a threat. The poet takes the whole picture of misery and stupid tyranny, and puts it into sinister perspective in his prologue. All the cruelties of the play are committed by the Greeks under shadow of the calamity denounced against them by the deities of the prologue, whereof we are again and again reminded by the sentences casually dropped by Talthybius and others, that the host is eager to embark. And this when the great Athenian armament was itself thronging the Peiræus in preparation for the voyage to Sicily.[1]

Of characterization, therefore, little is to be found. Cassandra, though her pathos is less deep and wide than that of her namesake in the *Agamemnon*, is yet valuable, as aiding in that perspective which is given mainly by the prologue. Talthybius and Andromache are ably sketched, but Menelaus and Helen are introduced merely for the sake of the elaborate dispute between Hecuba and Helen. It is upon Hecuba that the whole poem hangs—not upon her action or even her character, but upon her capacity for suffering. With the progress of the play she changes from the Queen of Troy to a figure summing up in herself all the sorrows of humanity. As each woe is faced, lamented, and at last assimilated into an ennobling experience, another disaster flings her back into the primitive outcry to begin once more the task of resignation. She is a pagan *mater dolorosa*. As each billow of grief descends upon her, leaving her still sentient, nay, filled with eager sympathy for others, the Greeks who oppress her become strangely puny and unreal like the legionaries in some mediæval picture of martyrdom. Even when she confesses to complete despair she yet the next moment begins to fashion within the abyss a tiny abode for hope : Astyanax may grow to manhood, " so that—if chance is kind—sons of thy blood may dwell again in Ilium, and there might yet be a city ".[2] Next moment the child is torn away to be flung from the battlements. Even so, Hecuba recovers her balance in the end and can deliver, as she stands over the little body, the stinging reproach[3] of a "barbarian" revolted by the crimes of "civilization".[4]

---

[1] There are reminders of the western lands in vv. 220 *sqq.*
[2] vv. 703 *sqq.*   [3] vv. 1158 *sqq.*
[4] v. 764 : ὦ βάρβαρ' ἐξευρόντες Ἕλληνες κακά (Andromache's phrase).

It is to this endless capacity for facing sorrow and trans-
muting it into rich experience that we owe one of the
most beautiful and definite philosophic *dicta* to be found
in Euripides :—

> ὦ γῆς ὄχημα, κἀπὶ γῆς ἔχων ἕδραν
> ὅστις ποτ' εἶ σύ, δυστόπαστος εἰδέναι,
> Ζεύς, εἴτ' ἀνάγκη φύσεος, εἴτε νοῦς βροτῶν,
> προσηυξάμην σε · πάντα γὰρ δι' ἀψόφου
> βαίνων κελεύθου κατὰ δίκην τὰ θνήτ' ἄγεις.[1]

" O Throne of earth, by earth upheld, whosoe'er Thou
art, beyond conjecture of our knowledge—Zeus, or the
law of Nature, or the mind of Man, to Thee do I
address my prayer ; for moving along Thy soundless
path Thou dost guide all mortal life with justice." As
for the Olympian gods, they are scarcely attacked ;
there is little more than a jaded recognition that belief
in them is no help or inspiration.[2] To this plaintive
agnosticism there is here no alternative but fierce
pessimism, as when in the frightful eloquence of Hecuba
we are told that Fate is "a capering idiot".[3]

Most mournful of all Greek tragedies, this is yet
beautiful, and full of splendid spectacular effects: Cassandra bounding wildly forth with her bridal torches ; the
entry of Andromache seated in the waggon among the
spoils of Troy ; Hecuba bending over Astyanax' body
within the great buckler of his father; the little procession
which carries the shield to burial, princely robes hanging
therefrom ; and the aged queen addressing her farewell
to the blazing city.

[1] vv. 884 *sqq.* (The first line refers to air.) If we possess any evidence as to the theological belief of the poet himself it is probably contained in these lines.
[2] vv. 469 *sqq.*, 841 *sqq.*, 1060 *sqq.* (especially the poignant μέλει μέλει
μοι), 1240 *sqq.*
[3] vv. 1204 *sqq.* :—

> τοῖς τρόποις γὰρ αἱ τύχαι,
> ἔμπληκτος ὡς ἄνθρωπος, ἄλλοτ' ἄλλοσε
> πηδῶσι.

The phrasing points back effectively to Poseidon's description of Athena's
fickleness (vv. 67 *sq.* ; τί δ' ὧδε πηδᾷς ἄλλοτ' εἰς ἄλλους τρόπους ;).

IPHIGENIA IN TAURIS [1] (Ἰφιγένεια ἡ ἐν Ταύροις) or
Iphigenia among the Taurians, is a work of uncertain
date.[2] Nothing is known of its success when produced,
and the absence of scholia suggests that it was not
popular in later times.

Iphigenia, before the temple of Artemis among the
Taurians (in South Russia), relates that she was not
slain at Aulis, but brought by Artemis to serve as her
priestess here, close to the city of King Thoas, where
she is compelled to sacrifice all strangers. A dream has
suggested to her that her brother Orestes is dead ; she
goes within to prepare offerings to his shade. Orestes
and Pylades enter ; they have been sent by the Delphian
oracle to steal the image of Artemis ; in this way
Orestes will be freed from the Furies. They postpone
their attempt till nightfall, and retire. The chorus of
Greek captive maidens enter in attendance upon
Iphigenia, and a cowherd brings news that two Greeks
have been captured and are being brought for sacrifice.
After a choric ode, the rustics enter with their prisoners.
A conversation follows, in which neither Iphigenia's
name nor that of Orestes is revealed, and she offers to
spare his life if he will take a letter to Argos. He insists
that Pylades shall go, and the latter asks that the
message be read. It proves to be an appeal to Orestes,
and, exclaiming that he will at once perform his task,
Pylades hands it to his friend. Brother and sister thus
become known to one another, and all three agree to
escape, taking the image with them. They enter the
temple, after Iphigenia has enjoined secrecy upon the
chorus, who sing their yearning for home. King Thoas
enters and is tricked by Iphigenia into aiding the escape.
The chorus sing Apollo's conquest of Delphi. A messenger rushes in, seeking Thoas ; the chorus misdirect him,
but in vain. Thoas learns how his people have been

---

[1] The *arrangement* is uncertain. Perhaps : protagonist, Iphigenia ;
deuteragonist, Orestes, messenger, Athena ; tritagonist, herdsman,
Pylades, Thoas.

[2] Murray and others place it about 414-2, Wilamowitz, 411-9.

beguiled into allowing the Greeks to embark. However, a contrary wind is even now driving them back. Thoas is preparing to hunt the fugitives down when Athena appears and stops him; he is, moreover, commanded to send the Greek maidens home. He consents, and the play ends with the joy of the chorus.

This drama is one of the finest among Euripides' works. It provides a marked contrast with the *Troades*; there is bitterness here indeed, but it is the bitterness of Voltaire rather than that of Swift. And whereas in the former play plot is almost non-existent, here it is vital. Perhaps the most brilliant piece of construction in Euripides is the celebrated Recognition-scene of this drama. Indeed the whole tragedy is the story of a plot, skilful and breathless. Iphigenia's method —to deceive by telling the truth (about Orestes' matricide)—was particularly dear to Greeks, connoisseurs of falsehood both in life and in literature; so beautifully does she succeed that (partly for her own amusement) she tells the king further the news she has just heard concerning her brother's welfare. But the poet is no more the slave of his wit than of his sympathies, and we are brought to realization of the facts—namely, that the three Greeks are thieves and Iphigenia a traitress— by her own self-mockery: "Falsehood, thy name is Hellas," [1] and by the simple generosity with which the prince accepts her suggestions.

The second feature of importance is the atmosphere of adventure. A strange grim glamour lies upon this story of breathless dangers in a region which is itself a mystery and a menace. We must forget modern notions about South Russia, lines of steamboats, and Odessa as civilized as Hull. This kingdom of Thoas is as remote from Athens as Thibet or the Upper Congo from us; indeed at many points we recall the African stories of Sir Rider Haggard. Amid these ghastly altars, the secret fire and the cleft of death, [2] deserted seas and

---

[1] v. 1205 : πιστὸν Ἑλλὰς οἶδεν οὐδέν.

[2] v. 626 : πῦρ ἱερὸν ἔνδον, χάσμα δ' εὐρωπὸν πέτρας—a marvellous line,

bloodthirsty savages, there is an infinite painful sweetness in Orestes' reminder of a dusty heirloom in his
sister's bedchamber at home.[1] The poem is filled with
suggestions of remoteness, the heaving of strange
billows, legendary landing-places. Flowing from this
is the home-sickness which breaks out again and again,
in Pylades' recollection, during his worst agony, of the
winding Phocian glens,[2] and in the lyric songs where
the Greek captives long to fly homeward with the
halcyon to the hallowed places of Greece.[3]

But not only does religion as a radiant emotion
setting a glow around "the hill of Cynthus" and the
"circling mere" mark the play. Euripides here, as
so often, treats religion intellectually as well as emotionally. By the lips of Orestes he passes judgment upon
Olympian religion as a guide of conduct. Taking the
story of Æschylus, he acts not as a lesser unbeliever would
have acted ; he does not dub the reconciliation of the
Eumenides a delusion. With a studiously bungling air
he explains that one section of the Furies was appeased,
and the other not.[4] If the manner of this revision is
delightfully impudent, the intention is deadly. Orestes
has been sent away by the Delphian priests to *do* something, to seek and undergo, if possible, a physiological
effect simply through the excitement of a far journey.
We are very near to the "long holiday and change of
air". The Furies exist nowhere but in his own brain.
On the Athenian Areopagus he went through a climax
of hallucination. Surrounded by stray animals,[5] he saw
in imagination all the tremendous events imagined by
Æschylus as objective reality. His mind only partly
cleared by this paroxysm, he fled back to Delphi for
complete healing. The "oracle" sent him to the re-
motest region known to Greeks, to a land, moreover,

[1] vv. 823-6.
[2] v. 677 : Φωκέων τ' ἐν πολυπτύχῳ χθονί.
[3] See especially the lovely song, vv. 1089 *sqq.*
[4] vv. 968 *sqq.*
[5] One can hardly doubt that this is the intention of the scene on the
Taurian beach (vv. 281-94).

where the natives are wont to murder all strangers.
Phœbus is ashamed of his "former responses" and seeks
to be rid of his too obedient, too persistent devotee.[1]
Such is the opinion of Orestes himself when at last in
the "toils,"[2] and the whole work (with an exception
presently to be noticed) is pervaded by this unflinching
rationalism. The pious herdsmen who see marine
deities in the Greek visitors are laughed to scorn by a
companion who, though dubbed "a fool reckless and
irreverent,"[3] is entirely justified. Iphigenia's reflections[4]
on the human sacrifices of the Tauri lead her to acquit
the goddess of "such folly" and to attribute this practice to ferocious savages who make gods in their own
image. At one point indeed simple faith is justified.
Orestes when faced by death is comforted by his friend :
"The god's oracle hath not yet destroyed thee, close as
thou dost stand to slaughter".[5] In a moment Orestes
is free from peril at the priestess' hands. But no one,
least of all Euripides, expects even the "gods" to
blunder always. Finally, the ode on Apollo's conquest
of Delphi is a delicate but pungent satire : the "oracle"
is a magnificent trade connexion.[6]

This cynical clearness is a guide in studying the
exceptional passage above mentioned : in the last scene
orthodox piety is upheld by the apparition of Athena.
Does then the *Iphigenia* in the end refute the rationalism
impressed on it almost everywhere? We can take our
choice, accepting Athena, Apollo's divinity, and all the
other traditional garnishments, but stultifying many passages, and the tone of nine-tenths of the play ; or we
can accept the latter as a thrilling and pathetic study in
human superstition and intrepidity, but reject Athena as
a conventional phantom. In this latter case we shall,
with Dr. Verrall, consider that the play, for all artistic

[1] vv. 711 *sqq.* The feelings of the Delphian hierarchy, when Orestes
after all actually returned, bringing with him the image—about which they
cared not a farthing—may be imagined by the irreverent.

[2] v. 77. [3] v. 275. [4] vv. 380 *sqq.* [5] vv. 719 *sq.*

[6] See Verrall, *Eur. the Rationalist*, pp. 217-30 (*Euripides in a
Hymn*).

and intelligible purposes, ends at v. 1434, leaving
Thoas to capture and destroy the Greeks. Many will
find such a choice difficult. The *Iphigenia* is certainly
not as clear a case as the *Orestes*, to say nothing of the
Ion. But it is difficult to believe that here he has composed a magnificent play to bolster up theology which
elsewhere he strenuously attacks. Nevertheless, the
speech of Athena is not in itself contradictory or
ludicrous.

The mental pathology—it can hardly be called the
character—of Orestes, deserves close study. He provides an admirable instance of that skill in portraying
madness for which Euripides was famed.[1] A man of
strong simple instincts, he is shaken terribly by the murderous events of his childhood. His brain is over-
thrown by the sway of the hierarchy and by the deeds
to which he was impelled. From this overthrow he
never quite recovered, as the dramatist himself carefully
indicates.[2] Throughout the *Iphigenia* we discern, drawn
with extraordinary skill and tact, the struggle between
the old obsession and an intellect originally clear and
acute. The prologue, when he explores the ground
with Pylades, shows him (in spite of a ghastly brilliance
of thought fit only for frenzy or the nightmare[3]) possessed
of shrewdness which, if consistently applied, would have
saved him from the expedition altogether. Later he is
seen hurled by the excitement of his quest into complete,
though temporary, insanity[4]—a fit which throws back
strange light upon his "trial" at Athens and provides a
comment upon the later scene,[5] where, though at the
moment sane, he yet believes in the delusive experience. Everywhere we find this superstructure of sanity
on an insane foundation. Though he can see through
the "oracle" as clearly as any man with regard to its

---

[1] Longinus, *de Subl.* xv. 3.   [2] vv. 970 *sqq.*
[3] v. 73: ἐξ αἱμάτων γοῦν ξάνθ᾽ ἔχει τριχώματα, a grotesque thought
which we have just heard (as Murray points out in his *apparatus*) from
Iphigenia as part of her dream.
[4] vv. 281 *sqq.*   [5] vv. 961 *sqq.*

past deceptions, he is pathetically enthusiastic for the latest nostrum.[1]   The long account[2] of his sorrows which he gives his sister is full of such sinister meaning. He essays to describe the origin of the court which tried him: " There is a holy . . . *vote*,[3] which long ago Zeus founded for Ares owing to some blood-guiltiness, whatever it was. . . ."   He has forgotten half the facts, and bungles the rest.   This speech, full of obscurity, irrelevancy, and disconnected thought, is practically ignored by his sister, who realizes his condition both from the report of the herdsman and from the occasional lunacy he manifests in conversation.[4]   Orestes, too, knows[5] how it is with him, and the complete absence of lament on his part when faced with death is one of the grimmest things in the drama.

The ELECTRA[6] ('Ηλέκτρα) was probably acted in 413 B.C.[7]   The scene is laid before the cottage of a peasant, who explains that he is the husband of Electra, but in name only; she comes forth and they depart to their several tasks.   Orestes and Pylades arrive; Orestes has come at Apollo's bidding to avenge his father, at whose tomb he has offered sacrifice.   Seeing Electra they retire.   She is invited to a festival by the chorus of Argive women, but refuses, urging her sorrow and poverty.   The two strangers approach, Orestes pretending that he has been sent by her brother for tidings of her; she gives him a passionate message begging Orestes to exact vengeance.   The peasant returns and

---

[1] θεᾶς βρέτας is now the prescription, as we may call it.   Cp. vv. 980, 985-6, and 1038-40.

[2] vv. 939 *sqq.*

[3] ψῆφος (v. 945).   He means "assembly (which votes)," but he has ψῆφος on the brain, as well he might have (vv. 965 *sq.*).

[4] vv. 739 *sq.* and 1046: Πυλάδης δ' ὅδ' ἡμῖν ποῦ τετάξεται φόνου— if this is a task set by Apollo there must be murder in it.

[5] v. 933.

[6] *Arrangement*: protagonist, Electra; deuteragonist, Orestes, Clytæmnestra; tritagonist, farmer, old man, messenger, Castor.   Pylades and Polydeuces were represented by a mute actor.

[7] From vv. 1347-56 it is clear that the Sicilian expedition had already sailed, but that news of the disaster had not yet reached Athens.

sends the strangers within as his guests ; the chorus sing the expedition to Troy.   An aged shepherd enters with the provisions for which Electra sent, and tells her that he has seen upon Agamemnon's tomb a sacrifice and a votive lock of hair.   He in vain seeks to convince Electra that her brother must be in Argos, but later recognizes Orestes by a scar.   Brother and sister embrace with joy ; after passionate prayers to Agamemnon's shade he departs to seek Ægisthus.   The chorus sing the crime of Thyestes which caused sun and stars to change their course.   A messenger relates how Ægisthus has been cut down by Orestes in the midst of a religious service; the avengers return with the body, over which Electra gloats.   Clytæmnestra is seen approaching, lured by a story that Electra has given birth to a child.   Orestes feels remorse, but is hardened by his sister, who awaits her mother alone.   A dispute follows about the queen's past, but Clytæmnestra refuses to quarrel, and goes within to perform the birth-ritual. Soon her cries are heard, and Orestes and Electra re-enter, filled with grief and shame.   In the sky appear Castor and Polydeuces (Pollux), brothers of Clytæmnestra, who blame the matricide, which they attribute to Apollo ; then they depart to the Sicilian sea to save mariners who are righteous and unperjured.

Special interest clings to this play, because here only can we see Euripides traversing precisely the same ground as Æschylus (in the *Choephoræ*) and Sophocles (in the *Electra*).   This similarity of subject long damaged Euripides' play in the eyes of critics.   It was assumed that the youngest poet was imitating his forerunners, and it needed small acumen to observe that the imitation was bad.   Whereupon, instead of wondering whether perhaps Euripides was after all not copying others, critics proceeded to write cheerful nonsense about " frivolity " and " a profound falling off in art and taste ".[1]   The fact simply is that each of these three

---

[1] Bernhardy, *Geschichte der griechischen Poesie* II, ii. p. 490.

tragedians discussed the story from a different viewpoint. Æschylus treated it as a religious fact, Sophocles as an emotional fact, Euripides as an ethical fact. Æschylus is on the side of Apollo, Sophocles on the side of Electra, Euripides on the side of no one. He asks himself what circumstances, what perversions of character, can result in this matricide.

Hence his careful study of Clytæmnestra, Electra, and Orestes, so careful that a reader at first supposes the poet a partisan of Clytæmnestra. Not so ; he has merely tried to understand her. A placid woman of quick but shallow affections, she was abandoned by her husband for ten years to the memory of a murdered daughter. Delightfully characteristic is her argument : " Suppose Menelaus had been stolen from home ; would it have been right for me to slay Orestes that Helen might regain her husband ? " [1] Vigorous and damaging, this is yet tinged with comedy by its raw novelty and precision. One almost overhears the *commèrages* of the street-corner. When Agamemnon brought back openly a concubine to his home, Clytæmnestra assisted [2] her lover in anticipating the king's revenge by murdering him. From this act she has drifted into condoning cruelty against her unoffending children ; throughout she has acted wickedly and acquiesced in worse conduct by others. Nevertheless, she is no figure of tragedy ; she only suggests tragedy because she is the mother of her executioners. Her chief love is placid domesticity ; if this can be obtained only by murdering those who threaten it, that is very terrible, but the world is notoriously imperfect. Clytæmnestra cannot, and will not, meet Electra on the tragic plane. Her daughter's great outburst and threat of murderous vengeance she meets in this comfortable fashion : " My child, it was always your nature to love your father. It often happens so. Some favour the male side, while others love their mother rather than their father. I forgive you : for

---

[1] vv. 1041-3.   [2] vv. 9-10.

in truth I rejoice not greatly, child, in the acts that I have done. . . . But you!—unwashed and shabby in attire!" . . . And so forth. Clytæmnestra is almost as ill-tuned to the atmosphere which Electra constantly and deliberately creates as Sancho Panza to the high converse of his master. The queen has been summoned to her daughter's cottage by report of a newly-born infant. She shows her natural goodness of heart by hurrying thither at once (though of course she has not the taste to leave her gorgeous retinue behind) and doing all she can to comfort and help her daughter. By this time she has all unconsciously "taken the wind out of the sails" of the avengers. But Electra can maintain her grimness and actually utter black hints of a wedding-bed in the grave![1] We turn next to her; what manner of woman can this be?

Electra is one of Euripides' most vivid and successful female characters. She has strong claims on our pity and sympathy, but fails to win them. Her mother is a ready victim of any emotion which breathes upon her; Electra has settled her position emotionally, intellectually, morally, years ago. Nothing can alter her; she is the victim and the apostle of an *idée fixe*. The crimes of love are no less frightful than the crimes of hate; in Electra affection for Agamemnon has become the basis of cold ferocity against Clytæmnestra. It is Orestes who shrinks when the deed is to be done, Electra who braces his resolution. She has borne no child. Instead of beginning a new life in her children, looking to the future, she has fed morbidly upon memories, stiffening natural grief and resentment into permanent inhuman morosity. Clytæmnestra has blandly outlived two murders in her own family, and remains neither unamiable nor uninteresting; but it is impossible to imagine what Electra will do, say, or think, after the events of to-day. This unnatural self-concentration, which means not only her mother's death

[1] 1142-6.

but her own spiritual suicide, is mainly the result of her childlessness. And it is on this that Euripides lays his finger. "Announce that I have given birth to a male child . . . . Then, when she has come, of course it is her death."[1] This plot of Electra is possibly the most brilliantly skilful and most terrible stroke in all the poet's work. It indicates the source of her heartlessness, it provides an excellent dramatic motive for the queen's arrival, and it shows, as nothing else could show, the fiendishness of a woman who can use just this pretext to the very woman who gave her birth. She relies upon the sanctity of motherhood to aid her in trampling upon it. Her first words, as she slips forth to join her husband beneath the star-lit sky, show how the heavens themselves remind her that she has had no infant at her breast during the night-watches : " Black Night, thou *Nurse* of golden stars ".[2] Moreover, not only does she feel her sorrows, she enjoys the sense of martyrdom. Her wrongs and present trials she is capable of exaggerating ;[3] at every opportunity she exploits them for purposes of self-pity, as her husband hints more than once.[4]

Orestes, living in exile, has escaped the blight of Electra only to become a criminal with no illusions, proud of his worldly experience, witness the blundering disquisition on "the true gentleman,"[5] and his cynical comments on his humble brother-in-law.[6] His onslaught upon Ægisthus from behind proves him at the best deficient in gallantry, and on the matricide itself nothing need be said. We can pity Orestes for his fearful position, but he is a poor creature. The *Electra*, in fact, is a clear-sighted attack upon the morality of blood-feuds. The poet feels that Ægisthus and Clytæm-

---

[1] vv. 652-60.   [2] v. 54.

[3] The peasant tells us that Electra's banishment to the country is due to her mother's efforts when Ægisthus wished to kill her (vv. 25 *sqq.*). Electra puts the matter very differently (vv. 60 *sq.*). The horrible story in vv. 326 *sqq.* is probably untrue ; cp. ὡς λέγουσιν.

[4] vv. 77-8, 354 *sq.*   [5] vv. 367 *sqq.*   [6] vv. 255 *sqq.*

nestra, left so long unmolested, should have been left alone still; if Apollo at Delphi, and the peasant in his Argive cottage, had estimated human nature more wisely, this horror would have been escaped, and no harm done. To punish the guilty is not always a virtue; often it is a debauch of self-glory, and sometimes the worst of villainies.

As always, the poet regards the " oracle," which commanded matricide, as an offence to civilization. But there is novelty in the extreme candour with which this is put forward. The Dioscuri repeatedly stigmatize its murderous command as " foolishness " or worse.[1] Equally outspoken are the chorus, who devote the last stanza of their lovely song on the Golden Lamb and Thyestes' crime to a brilliant denial of its truth. . . . " But legends that fill men with dread are profitable to divine worship "[2]—it is admirably put, and may rank with the epigrams of Ovid[3] and Voltaire.[4] As for the Dioscuri, it is impossible to speak without affection of such quaint and charming figures. Their converse with Electra and the chorus is an irresistible combination of dignity and a breezy contempt for official reticence. In his first long *ex cathedra* speech Castor is on the verge of saying what he really thinks of Phœbus Apollo, remembers himself just in time, and then—gives a broad hint after all.[5] In the less formal talk which follows, these bluff naval deities show a soundness of heart and a simplicity as to the meaning of great affairs which recall delightfully the traditional nautical character of modern literature. The anguish of brother and sister who after long years meet for a few frightful hours only to part for ever awakes their instant deep sympathy.[6] On the other side these subordinate deities are assuredly in a maze as to the theological problem into which they have strayed. " How was it," ask the Argive women,

---

[1] vv. 1294, 1296 *sq.*, 1302. [2] vv. 737-45.
[3] Expedit esse deos.
[4] " If God did not exist, it would be necessary to invent Him."
[5] vv. 1245 *sq.* [6] vv. 1327 *sqq.*

very pertinently, "that you, being gods and brothers of the woman that hath perished, did not repel destruction from the house?" Electra, too, would know why she was involved in the matricide. In answer the Brethren offer a bundle of reasons some one of which ought surely to be right : "the fate of necessity," "the guidance of doom," "the foolish utterances of Phœbus' tongue," "a partnership in act and in destiny," "the ancestral curse".[1] Even if traditional phrases could solve the problem of human sin, these simple souls are not qualified to use or expound them.

One incident in the *Electra* is of particular interest to the historian of literature. The pædagogus seeks to convince Electra that the mysterious visitor to Agamemnon's tomb is her brother. He offers certain evidences which she contemptuously rejects. There can be no doubt that this scene is a criticism of the Recognition in Æschylus' *Choephorœ*. The severed lock of hair, the footprint, and the embroidered cloth, appear in both scenes. Electra rejects all these clues. How can the hair of an athletic man resemble the soft tresses of a woman? Is not a man's foot larger than a woman's? Will the full-grown Orestes wear the same garment as an infant? But Euripides' attack is probably mistaken.[2] We may suppose that Æschylus could have seen these objections ; and it is quite possible that tradition told of physical peculiarities in the Pelopid family. As for the embroidered garment, Æschylus does not call it so. It may well have been a cloth preserved by Orestes. However this may be, we have here the most distinct example of Euripides' criticism of an earlier poet.

HELEN [3] ('Ελένη), or *Helena*, was produced in 412 B.C. The scene represents the palace of Theoclymenus, the

---

[1] vv. 1301-7. The first line, μοῖρά τ' ἀνάγκης ἦγ' ᾗ τὸ χρεών, is an exceptionally fine instance of misty verbiage.

[2] See Verrall's discussion in his edition of the *Choephorœ* (Introd. pp. xxxiii-lxx).

[3] *Probable Arrangement* : protagonist, Helen, the god (whether Castor or Pollux); deuteragonist, Teucer, Menelaus, Egyptian messenger ; tritagonist, old woman, Greek messenger, Theonoe, Theoclymenus.

young Egyptian king, with the tomb of his father Proteus. Helen relates that Hera gave Paris a phantom
in place of the true Helen. While Greeks and Trojans
fought for a wraith, she herself has lived in Egypt, waiting for Menelaus. Theoclymenus now seeks her hand;
she has taken sanctuary in Proteus' tomb. Teucer
enters to consult Theonoe, the king's prophetess-sister.
On seeing Helen he barely refrains from shooting her,
but realizing his " mistake " talks with the stranger, revealing that Menelaus and " Helen " have apparently
been lost at sea. Helen sends him off and breaks into
lamentation for Menelaus, but is advised by the chorus
of captive Greek maidens to consult the omniscient
Theonoe. She agrees, and they accompany her into
the palace. Menelaus enters, a pitiable shipwrecked
figure. He has left " Helen " and his comrades in
hiding, and is looking for help. When he knocks at the
palace-door the portress repels him with the warning
that the king is hostile to Greeks because Helen is
within his house. Menelaus is thunderstruck, but determines to await Theoclymenus. The chorus and
Helen return in joy, for Menelaus, they learn, still lives.
Menelaus comes forward; after a moment his wife recognizes and would embrace him, but he repels the
stranger. One of his companions arrives announcing
that " Helen " has vanished. As he ends his tale he
sees the true Helen, who he supposes has played a
practical joke; but Menelaus falls into her arms. They
plot escape, but realize that all depends upon the omniscient Theonoe; she comes forth, and, explaining that
she has a casting-vote in a dispute which to-day takes
place in Heaven between Hera and Aphrodite, decides
to aid the suppliants. When she has withdrawn it is
arranged that Menelaus shall pretend he is the sole
survivor, Menelaus being drowned; Helen is to gain
permission to offer funeral-rites at sea. The chorus
raise a beautiful song concerning Helen's woes and
the Trojan war. Theoclymenus enters and is easily
hoodwinked. After an ode on Demeter's search for

Persephone, the plotters are sent on their way by the king. The chorus sing of Helen's voyage and pray the Dioscuri to convoy their sister. A messenger hurries in and tells of the escape ; the Egyptian crew has been massacred by Menelaus' followers. Theoclymenus would take vengeance upon his sister, but is checked by the Dioscuri, who explain that all has occurred by the will of Zeus.

Two aspects of this play are unmistakable and apparently incompatible. The plot closely resembles that of the *Iphigenia in Tauris ;* the style and manner of treatment are curiously light. What can have been Euripides' purpose in repeating, after so short an interval, a copy of that grim masterpiece, and to execute it in this light-hearted fashion ? The *Helen* is in no possible sense a tragedy. At the point where the audience should be spell-bound by suspense and dread—the cajoling of the king—we are relieved from all oppression by the facility with which the captives succeed. Theoclymenus is an imbecile who gives them all they need with his eyes shut. The earlier action is robbed of all power by the superhuman attributes of Theonoe. How can, or need, Helen have any doubts concerning her husband with an all-knowing friend at hand? The central *datum*, that only a phantom fled to Troy and returned therefrom with Menelaus, is utterly destructive of tragic atmosphere. In the Recognition-scene the possibility of pathos is drowned in absurdity : the messenger suddenly turns to find his mistress smiling at his elbow and greets her with relief : " Ah, hail, daughter of Leda, here you are after all ! " [1] Teucer's scene, besides providing a palmary instance of bad construction (for his function is merely to cause Helen anxiety about her husband's fate, which one might have expected to arouse her curiosity earlier in the course of these seventeen years), is in itself absurd. After coming all this distance to consult Theonoe about his route, he is sent away

---

[1] v. 616 : ὦ χαῖρε, Λήδας θύγατερ, ἐνθάδ᾽ ἦσθ᾽ ἄρα ;

happy (without seeing the prophetess) by Helen's suggestion, "You will pick out your way as you go along".[1] Equally curious is the diction. Brilliantly idiomatic as are the iambics, they are almost everywhere light, loose in texture, almost colloquial. Such things[2] as φέρ' ἦν δὴ νῶν μὴ ἀποδέξηται λόγους ;—ἦν γὰρ εἴχομεν θάλασσ' ἔχει—εἷς γὰρ ὅ γε κατ' οὐρανόν, and the silly jingle on λόγῳ θανεῖν, are typical of the whole atmosphere. Even the lyrics glow with prettiness rather than beauty ; lovely as are the Naiad[3] and the Nightingale[4] they mitigate in no degree the flimsiness of the whole.

Theonoe herself, in an outrageous passage,[5] brings the mockery to a climax : "This very day among the gods there is to be strife and conference concerning thee before the throne of Zeus. Hera, who was thine enemy before, is kindly to thee now, and would bring thee safe to thy home-country with this thy wife, so that Greece may learn how Paris' love, the gift of Cypris, was but a mockery. But Cypris would fain deny thee thy home-return, that it may never come to light how in Helen's case she bought the prize of beauty with bridals that were naught. *And the decision lies with me*, whether, as Cypris wishes, I shall destroy thee by revealing thy presence to my brother, or whether I shall join Hera and save thy life." We should be ill-advised to take this in all earnest as a ludicrous blasphemy. It is graceful trifling. But what is Theonoe—a dread goddess to whom the queen of Heaven sues for aid, or a kind-hearted woman whose strong common-sense might, perhaps, in a circle like that of the dolts and *poseurs* who fill the stage, raise her to the repute of superhuman wisdom ? She is not all playful. When the honour of her dead father is in question, she stirs the heart by her passionate solemnity :—

---

[1] v. 151.   [2] vv. 832, 1048, 491, 1050-2.
[3] vv. 183 *sqq.*   [4] vv. 1107 *sqq.*   [5] vv. 878 *sqq.*

Aye, all that lie in death must meet their bond,
And they that live ; yea, all. Beyond the grave
The mind, though life be gone, is conscious yet
Eternal, with th' eternal Heav'n at one.[1]

This stands, together with Hecuba's outburst[2] in the
Trojan Women, as the most explicit statement of
personal religion in the extant plays of Euripides. In
the midst of this farrago of fairy-tale and false sentiment,
it is doubly startling. The drama is neither tragedy,
nor melodrama, nor comedy, nor farce. What are we
to think of it ?

Dr. Verrall[3] would regard it as a burlesque, that
is, as a playful imitation of serious work, with ex-
aggeration of weak features or tendencies. From the
facts that one ode[4] has nothing whatever to do with
the plot, but with the Mother and the Maid, and
that Aristophanes parodies the play in his *Celebrants
of the Thesmophoria*, wherein Euripides is accused of
profaning that festival, it is inferred that *Helen* was
not written for public presentation, but for private
performance at a house on the island of Helene belonging to an Athenian lady. The occasion was a
gathering of women who had been celebrating the
Thesmophoria, and forms Euripides' playful answer
to the charge that he had never depicted a good
woman. To prove his zeal, he chooses Helen (the
least reputable of her sex) and completely rehabilitates
her character.[5] At the same time he amuses his
audience with a parody of his own work. The sanctuary
of Helen recalls that of Andromache, and the escape

---

[1] vv. 1013-6 :—

> καὶ γὰρ τίσις τῶνδ' ἐστὶ τοῖς τε νερτέροις
> καὶ τοῖς ἄνωθεν πᾶσιν ἀνθρώποις. ὁ νοῦς
> τῶν κατθανόντων ζῇ μὲν οὔ, γνώμην δ' ἔχει
> ἀθάνατον, εἰς ἀθάνατον αἰθέρ' ἐμπεσών.

The precision of the wording is remarkable.

[2] *Troades*, 884 *sqq.*

[3] See *Four Plays of Euripides*, pp. 43-133 (*Euripides' Apology*).

[4] vv. 1301 *sqq.*

[5] The idea is taken from the famous recantation of Stesichorus, which
asserted that Helen never went to Troy.

that of Iphigenia and her friends. The news of this *tour de force* spread, and at last, owing to public curiosity, it was exhibited at the Dionysia.

There is no doubt (i) that the *Helen* is not serious either in intention or execution ; (ii) that there is good evidence for supposing a connexion between the play and the festival of the Mother and the Maid, the Thesmophoria ; (iii) that Aristophanes' jokes about Proteus-Proteas and the rest do support the view that Euripides has in his mind the history of a family who have nothing to do with Menelaus and Helen ; (iv) that in the play there are points, such as " Eido " (the baby-name of Theonoe), which are irrelevant to the story. Are we, then, to accept Verrall's account ? The sound view would appear to be that Euripides offered to the Archon a work which for once was a burlesque. So sincere a thinker as Euripides was certain sooner or later to attack himself, at any rate to examine his position and methods with humorous detachment. So far we may, we must, go with Verrall ; the elaborate and delightfully detailed development we can hardly accept—the evidence is not sufficiently strong.

But the poet is making fun not only of himself. The false Helen and her disappearance at a crisis in the action, are not merely miracles of a type in which he utterly disbelieves ; they are features which even a believer would remove as far as possible into the background. In handling this fairy-tale with such *naïveté*, he is possibly laughing at some indiscreet fellow-dramatist ;[1] certainly he is ridiculing the popular belief in such legends. Helen herself cannot credit the tale of Leda and the Swan.[2] When given the choice between two accounts of her brothers' fate, she prefers the non-miraculous version.[3] Even the dramatist's own dislike of soothsayers is elaborately

---

[1] In the inflated affectation of such things as vv. 355-6 and 629 parody of some contemporary lyrist is quite possible.

[2] vv. 20-1, 256-9 (rejected by Murray, after Badham).

[3] vv. 138 *sqq.*, 205 *sqq.*, 284-5.

expounded by the Greek messenger and sympathetically echoed by the chorus,[1] absurdly enough in a play which contains Theonoe, whom the chorus themselves have induced Helen to consult, and with success; although of course Theonoe knows only what could be learned by listening to the talk of Menelaus.

The PHŒNISSÆ[2] (Φοίνισσαι), or *Phœnician Women*, was produced about the year 410 B.C. The action takes place before the palace of Thebes. Jocasta explains that the blind Œdipus is kept prisoner there by his sons Eteocles and Polynices, whom he has therefore cursed with a prayer that they may divide their inheritance with the sword. They have arranged to rule for a year by turns; but Eteocles, at the end of his term, has refused to retire and Polynices has brought an army against Thebes. Jocasta has arranged that the brothers shall meet. When she has gone, a pædagogus shows the Argive host to Antigone from the roof. Next the chorus appear, a band of Phœnician maidens who sing of their voyage and of Delphi, their destination. Polynices stealthily enters and is greeted rapturously by his mother; Eteocles follows, and the brothers quarrel bitterly and finally. The chorus sing of Cadmus and the harvest of warriors. Eteocles comes forth and is advised by Creon to post a champion at each of the seven gates. He agrees, ratifies the betrothal of Antigone to Hæmon, and bids Creon consult Tiresias as to the hope of victory; if Polynices falls he is not to be buried in Theban ground. The chorus sing to Ares who has filled the land with war in place of the delightful Dionysiac worship; they celebrate the wondrous history of Thebes. Tiresias enters with Creon's son Menœceus, and declares that victory can be won only if the youth is sacrificed. Creon arranges to send his son away, but Menœceus resolves to slay himself. The next ode celebrates the

---

[1] vv. 744-60.

[2] *Arrangement* (according to Croiset): protagonist, Jocasta, Creon; deuteragonist, Antigone, Polynices, Menœceus; tritagonist, pædagogus, Eteocles, Tiresias, messengers, Œdipus.

Sphinx, the tale of Œdipus, and Menœceus' nobility. A messenger brings to Jocasta tidings that her sons are about to engage in single combat ; she hurries to the spot with Antigone. After a brief ode of suspense, Creon returns mourning for his dead son, and another messenger tells at length how Polynices, Eteocles, and Jocasta have died. Thebes has won complete victory. The corpses are brought in, followed by Antigone, who summons the aged Œdipus. Together they bewail the dead till Creon breaks in and decrees that Antigone must marry Hæmon, Œdipus go into exile, and Polynices remain unburied. Antigone defies him : she will bury her brother, she will not marry Hæmon, but will share her father's exile. Œdipus as they depart asserts his greatness as the Conqueror of the Sphinx.

This work was immensely popular in antiquity.[1] It was repeatedly "revived" ; ancient authors quote from it often ; together with the *Hecuba* and the *Orestes* it formed the final selection of Euripides' work made in Byzantine times ; and the scholia are extremely copious. Because of its popularity, the play was considerably expanded by interpolation. It is no mere question of isolated lines inserted by actors or copyists, though such appear to be numerous ; considerable masses are due to a later poet or poets.

The following passages[2] are generally suspected :

(i) vv. 88-201, the scene of Antigone and her attendant upon the roof-terrace. To this it has been objected[3] that the entrance of Polynices should occur as the first event of the play after the closing words of the prologue which mention his expected arrival. This passage contains, moreover, a number of words otherwise unknown which is enormous considering the length of the scene, and several awkward or strained expressions.

(ii) vv. 1104-40, the description of the seven chieftains as they advance upon the gates. It is "full of

---

[1] Perhaps one reason was the great sweep of story which it covers.

[2] See Mr. J. U. Powell's careful and lucid account in his edition (pp. 7-32).

[3] Verrall, *Eur. the Rationalist*, pp. 236 *sq.*

obscurities and difficulties," [1] particularly two elaborate
yet frivolous descriptions of shields. Moreover, it practically repeats the terrace-scene; both passages can
hardly be genuine.

(iii) 1223-58 (or 1282), the messenger's account of
preparations for the single combat, followed by the
dialogue in which Jocasta calls Antigone to accompany
her to the field. Not only are there marked faults of
style; [2] it is impossible, considering the urgency [3] of
the news, that the queen should stay for this tedious
narrative. Jocasta's conversation with Antigone is by
no means so objectionable. It is very short, and the
style is not unworthy [4] of Euripides. Nevertheless, it is
strange that the queen should wait for her daughter at
so urgent a time.

(iv) the end of the drama, though at what point
the addition begins is not agreed. The last address of
Œdipus which opens thus [5]:

> ὦ πάτρας κλεινῆς πολῖται, λεύσσετ', Οἰδίπους ὅδε,
> ὃς τὰ κλείν' αἰνίγματ' ἔγνω καὶ μέγιστος ἦν ἀνήρ,

unmistakably recalls part of the finale in *Œdipus Tyrannus:* [6]

> ὦ πάτρας Θήβης ἔνοικοι, λεύσσετ', Οἰδίπους ὅδε,
> ὃς τὰ κλείν' αἰνίγματ' ᾔδει καὶ κράτιστος ἦν ἀνήρ.

If we accept the customary date of Sophocles' play
(405 B.C.), it was produced after Euripides' death.
Further, the whole scene of Œdipus, Antigone, and
Creon has evidently been expanded and distorted.
According to one version, that followed by Sophocles
in the *Antigone*, the maiden remained in Thebes after
the battle and buried Polynices; according to the

---

[1] Mr. J. U. Powell, whose edition should be consulted.
[2] vv. 1233 *sq.* :—

> ὑμεῖς δ' ἀγῶν' ἀφέντες, Ἀργεῖοι, χθόνα
> νίσεσθε, βίοτον μὴ λιπόντες ἐνθάδε,

are out of the question as work of Euripides. There are several other
faults.
[3] vv. 1259 *sqq.*
[4] Mr. Powell, however, rightly remarks that vv. 1265-6 are "strained".
[5] vv. 1758 *sq.*   [6] vv. 1524 *sq.*

Œdipus Coloneus she accompanied her father into exile.
Here the two versions are combined. Moreover, from
the entrance of Œdipus onwards the play abounds once
more in unnatural or unusual turns of speech. And it
may be thought a serious mistake to bring the aged
sufferer forth at all,[1] thus creating a new interest at the
last moment of a play crowded with incident. But
though this portion contains much unauthentic work, it
appears to be intermingled with the genuine.

Certain other passages are open to suspicion, especially Jocasta's prologue and the remainder—hitherto
unmentioned—of the first messenger's speech.[2] We appear to have Euripides' prologue, padded out by another
hand. The same kind of recurrent weakness and flatness marks the messenger's speech. Above all, when
the speaker seeks to rise to the occasion, his efforts result
in this :[3] " From the scaling-ladder his limbs were hurled
asunder like sling-stones—his hair to Heaven, his blood
to earth; his arms and legs whirled round like Ixion's
wheel ". This imbecile bombast is fortunately without
parallel in Attic tragedy.

It seems likely that Euripides' work was in quite early
times (probably the fourth century) expanded by another
poet, whose main contribution was a large addition to
the messengers' speeches at a date when Æschylus was
little enough known to allow such things as the description of the hostile champions a good degree of novelty.
The new text was in its turn enlarged by accretions due
to actors.[4]

---

[1] So the scholiast : ὅ τε ἐπὶ πᾶσι μετ' ᾠδῆς ἀδολέσχου φυγαδευόμενος
Οἰδίπους προσέρραπται διὰ κενῆς.

[2] vv. 1090-1199 (the ῥῆσις containing the description of the Seven).

[3] vv. 1182 sqq.

[4] Verrall (*Eur. the Rationalist*, pp. 231-60) believed that those parts
which introduce Antigone are un-Euripidean. The terrace-scene has already been discussed. In the body of the play, as he argues with much
point, wherever mention of Antigone occurs, it is obtrusive and embarras-
sing. Her lament with Œdipus at the close contains many inappropriate
features. He concludes that Œdipus is an allegory of Euripides himself,
leaving Athens in sorrow at the end of his life, and that Antigone represents his literary offspring, the plays. The Sphinx is "the spirit of

Euripides' own work is vigorous and interesting,[1] a stirring scene of warfare, patriotism, and strong passions, which, in its present expanded form, reminds one by its spirit and its popularity of Kyd's *Spanish Tragedy*, the first favourite of Elizabethan audiences.[2] The two brothers are well distinguished, Polynices by his pathetic sense that intolerable wrong is urging him against his will into crime, Eteocles by a dark fervour of ambition which has grown upon his soul like religion ; and their terrible altercation in the sweeping trochaic metre is equal to anything of the kind in Euripides for terse idiomatic vigour. Jocasta's passionate joy when she sees her exiled son,[3] joy which stirs her aged feet to trip in a dance of fond rapture,[4] provides the one light-hearted moment. And her noble speech of reconciliation[5] is the single great achievement of the drama.

The ORESTES[6] ('Ορέστης) was produced in 408 B.C. and again in 341.[7] It was extremely popular, and formed with the *Phœnissæ* and the *Hecuba* the final selection of Euripides' work made in Byzantine times ; but the later interpolations are probably few. The scene is laid before the palace at Argos. Orestes and Electra, having slain Clytæmnestra and Ægisthus, are imprisoned in their own house by the Argive state, which will to-day decide whether they are to be stoned to death. Orestes

mystery and darkness," which the poet has fought and quelled. All this was composed by a poet of the Euripidean circle to commemorate the master ; it includes a compliment—the quotation from the *Œdipus Tyrannus*—to Sophocles, who had shown public respect to his rival when the news of his death reached Athens.

[1] One notices the criticism (vv. 751 *sq.*) of Æschylus, *Septem* (vv. 375 *sqq.*) when Eteocles declares that to give a list of his champions would be waste of time.

[2] The "popular" character of the *Phœnissæ* is brought out by the relish with which the *Argument* enumerates its murderous happenings.

[3] In this passage an allusion has by some been supposed to Alcibiades' return to Athens (411 B.C.).

[4] Cp. vv. 302 *sq.* (γηραιὸν πόδ' ἕλκω) with v. 316 (περιχορεύουσα).

[5] vv. 528 *sqq.*

[6] Croiset gives the probable *arrangement:* protagonist, Orestes, messenger ; deuteragonist, Electra, Menelaus, Phrygian ; tritagonist, Helen, Tyndareus, Pylades, Hermione, Apollo.

[7] See Murray's text.

has been tormented by madness and is now seen asleep, watched by Electra ; she hopes that they may yet be saved by Menelaus, who has come home with Helen. The latter enters and requests Electra to go for her to Clytæmnestra's tomb with drink-offerings ; she is persuaded to send her daughter Hermione instead. The chorus of Argive ladies now enter, and their voices awaken Orestes. Then follows a wonderful scene of affectionate tendance and a sudden paroxysm of the sufferer ; the chorus sing of the Furies and the agony through which the house is passing. Menelaus enters and Orestes passionately implores his aid. Tyndareus (father of Helen and Clytæmnestra) arrives and denounces the cowering Orestes : why did he not invoke the law against his mother ? The youth's long speech of exculpation further incenses Tyndareus. When he has departed, Orestes again appeals to Menelaus, who points out that the only hope lies in the Argive Assembly. Orestes watches him go with contempt, but is cheered by the arrival of Pylades, who throws in his lot with his friend, and the two walk off to the Assembly. The chorus sing the story of the house and lament the matricide. A messenger brings to Electra an account of the debate, which ended with permission to the criminals to die by their own hand. Electra pours forth a lyric of painful beauty until the two youths return. Pylades declares that he too will die, but suggests vengeance on Menelaus : let them slay Helen. Electra proposes that Hermione be held as a hostage whereby Menelaus may be induced to save them. The two men go within to despatch Helen, whose shrieks are soon heard. Meanwhile Electra receives Hermione, who is dragged within. A Phrygian slave flings himself in terror from a hole high up in the housefront ; in a strange lyric narrative, he tells how amid the confusion Helen has vanished. Orestes rushes forth in pursuit, but he is now insane and the slave contrives to escape. Orestes goes back, and in a moment the house is on fire. Menelaus rushes in distraught, and sees

Orestes on the battlements with his sword at Hermione's
throat. A frantic altercation arises, until Menelaus cries
to the citizens for a rescue. Apollo appears and bids
the quarrel cease. Helen is to become a sea-goddess;
Electra shall marry Pylades, and Hermione Orestes,
who is to stand his trial at Athens; Apollo will reconcile
him to the Argive state.

To appreciate this masterpiece, we must realize that
Euripides, who so often insists on considering tradition
in the light of his own day, has here insisted on that
principle even more definitely than elsewhere. Certain
legendary data are, to be sure, retained. Troy has fallen
but a few years ago; Iphigenia was offered by her father
as a sacrifice at Aulis. Otherwise the events described
might have occurred in the fifth century. Agamemnon,
though a noble of great eminence, was not a king[1];
Argos is ruled by an Assembly not distinguishable from
the Athenian Ecclesia. The youth who exacts vengeance with his own hand is told in language which
might have been employed by Pericles, that the vendetta
is an outrage upon law and society; punishment for
crime rests with the State alone.[2] The behest of Apollo,
all-important in the *Choephorœ*, is not even mentioned
in the discussion which decides the fate of Orestes.
The oracle is indeed treated with scant courtesy even by
those most concerned to uphold it; Electra complains
of the god's "wickedness,"[3] and her brother "blames
Loxias" for urging him to a villainous deed and then
giving no aid.[4] The atmosphere is one in which the
slaughter of Clytæmnestra must be regarded with horror
and the traditional defence of Orestes as unthinkable.
This is not a theological study, but a dramatic essay in
criminal psychology.

In Orestes the playwright has given us one of his
most terrible portraits. Highly sensitive, weak-minded,
over-educated in a bad school, he is unbalanced by the
horror of his father's death and by the oracular com-

[1] vv. 1167 *sqq*.   [2] vv. 491-525.   [3] vv. 28 *sqq*.
[4] vv. 285 *sqq*. Menelaus (v. 417) casually calls Apollo "stupid".

mand which has blasted his life. In the magnificent
sick-bed scene he, like his sister, fills us with nothing
but pity. But the calmer he becomes the more are we
filled with loathing for this pedant of eighteen, with his
syllogisms justifying murder, his parade of rhetoric,
his hopeless inability to grasp a situation. Rich as is
the world's drama in villains, Orestes occupies a place
conspicuous. He has little heart and no sense. Both
failings are common. But that both heart and brain
should be replaced by a factitious perverse cleverness,
an incredibly superficial passion for scoring logical points
against opponents who have in hand urgent interests of
real life—this grips us irresistibly. He is an example
of the wreck produced by a highly specialized mental
training which has ignored character. His first address
to Menelaus strikes the note :—

> Freely will I divulge my woes to thee.
> But *as the first-fruits of my plight*, I touch
> Thy knees, a suppliant, *tying prayer* the while
> To thy *unleafèd lips*. . . .[1]

This affected and obscure exordium is followed by
verbal subtleties at every opportunity : "through my
sorrows I live not, yet see the light"[2]—"my deeds, not
my appearance, ravage me"[3]—"my body's gone, my
name alone remains".[4] But all this is nothing to the
detestable exhibition wherewith he answers the aged
Tyndareus. To the vital point—that Clytæmnestra
should have been brought before a legal tribunal—he
makes no reply whatever. His only difficulties are that
Tyndareus is wounded to the soul by his daughter's
death, and that he is far older than Orestes. What is
to be done? Simply to "contract out of" natural feelings so that the way may be clear for pure logic :—

> True, matricide doth taint me, yet again
> Pure am I, for my sire I did avenge.
> Therefore let thy great age be set aside

---

[1] vv. 380 *sqq.*   [2] v. 386.   [3] v. 388.   [4] v. 390.

From this our conference, for it puts me out ;
And let me on—'tis but thy hair I dread.[1]

There follows a frigid "statement" — "balance two
against two"[2]—of his father's claim and his mother's
offences, and of his own glorious achievement in puri-
fying social life.   The original sinner is Tyndareus
himself who begot so vile a daughter!   He ends by an
appeal to Apollo's behest, and a pompous comment on
the importance of marriage.

The aged Spartan having given his grandson over
to justice as irreclaimable, the youth turns to Menelaus,
whom he insists on regarding as his real hope, in spite
of Menelaus' plain reluctance and extreme unpopu-
larity in Argos.   He is, moreover, unwilling to endure
another display : " Let me be ; I am reflecting. . . ."[3]
At all times he is impatient of subtleties ; in the first
moments of their meeting he asks his accomplished
nephew : " What mean you ?   Wisdom is shown not
by obscurity, but by plain speech."[4]   But now that
Orestes has his chance, he refuses to suffer Menelaus'
" reflections," and with a warning that " a long address
is better than a short one, and easier for the auditor to
follow"[5] produces a masterpiece of metallic cleverness which presses Seneca himself very hard ; perhaps
the finest gem is the offer of Hermione as a kind of
discount.[6]   Before the Assembly he succeeds in combining several insanely tactless insults to the Argives :
they are " possessors," not original citizens, of the land ;
they were Pelasgians at first, but later " Danaidæ," descendants of the women who slew their husbands ; and
he has killed his mother as much for their sake as his
father's.[7]   But Euripides' most frightful satire on "advanced education " is reserved for the nightmare of the
close, where the raving Orestes leans down over the

---

[1] vv. 544 *sqq.* The flatness of the translation given above is not, I
think, inappropriate. νῦν δὲ σὴν ταρβῶ τρίχα (v. 550), is merely hideous,
μαστοῖς τὸν ἔλεον θηρώμεναι (v. 568), is even worse.

[2] v. 551.   [3] v. 634.   [4] v. 397.
[5] vv. 640 *sq.*   [6] vv. 658-61.   [7] vv. 932 *sqq.*

battlement to the grief-maddened Menelaus and begins by a lunatic reminiscence of the "Socratic method": "will you be the questioner or the respondent?"[1]

Prig as he is, Orestes has nevertheless some elements of nobility at the first. He can tell his uncle plainly that his disease is "conscience, which convicts me for a criminal";[2] he shows real regard for Electra; the splendidly selfless friendship between him and Pylades stirs every one. As the play advances, however, we are lost in the loathing and breathless wonder wherewith we gaze upon the increasing insanity of the wretched prince.[3] Each moment he becomes more vigorous and more lost to sense of right; when Electra suggests the vilest part of the plot—the seizure of Hermione—he breaks forth into a cry like Macbeth's: "Bring forth men-children only!"[4]

Electra has been the chief definite cause of Orestes' fall. Amazingly vivid, she fills the whole drama with a thin acrid fume of malice. Her ruling passion is not mere hatred against Clytæmnestra. That bitterness has spread until (saving her tenderness for Orestes) there is nothing in her but a narrow viperishness. When an innocent like Hermione draws near, the fang strikes by instinct. Her intensity of feeling and her years have made her Orestes' monitor long before he returned home, and it is she to whom Tyndareus points, in searing language, as the more guilty.[5] Another influence has soured her, that lack of husband and children on which Helen, with the brutality so frequent in shallow natures, insists at their first meeting.[6] But Electra has vastly more common-sense than her brother

---

[1] v. 1576: πότερον ἐρωτᾶν ἢ κλύειν ἐμοῦ θέλεις;

[2] v. 396.

[3] His "progression, upward in strength and downward in reason, is visible throughout," says Dr. Verrall (*Four Plays*, p. 245), whose eloquent and vivid essay on this drama should be carefully studied.

[4] vv. 1204 sqq.: ὦ τὰς φρένας μὲν ἄρσενας κεκτημένη . . .

[5] vv. 615 sqq.

[6] vv. 72-92. Compare the amusing little passage-of-arms, vv. 107-11 (see Verrall, *Four Plays*, pp. 219 sq.).

or Pylades, and it is to her that the delightful comment
on Helen is given : [1]

> Ah, Nature ! . . .
> Saw ye how tiny was that tress she cut,
> Sparing her beauty ? 'Tis the old Helen still !

But her sense of humour cannot sustain her heart
long :

> Heaven's hatred seize thee ! Thou hast wrought the fall
> Of me, and this my brother, and of Greece.

These two women, so pungently contrasted in one
brief scene, share, however, one attribute—that nerveless
theology which Euripides detested as rotting the moral
fibre. Electra muses upon " suffering and disaster sent
by Heaven ".[2] Helen attributes her elopement with
Paris to the " maddening doom of Heaven," [3] which has
also " destroyed this hapless pair " [4]—her nephew and
niece. The latter in her lyric outcry explores [5] all the
legends of her line to discover the cause of the present
disaster, a method which the chorus, for all their sympathy, indeed complicity,[6] seem to parody by the
ludicrous baldness of their reflection that this horror of
fiends and bloodshed has fallen upon the house " because
Myrtilus fell out of the chariot " ! [7]

All the minor characters are skilfully drawn—
Pylades, the warm-hearted scatter-brained ruffian who
conceives the murder of Helen as soon [8] as he learns
that she is in his friend's house ; Tyndareus, the hot-
tempered, affectionate old king ; Menelaus, the vulgar
and successful, who has no other ambition than to let
bygones be bygones [9] and who has actually expected to
find Orestes and Clytæmnestra sharing the same home,

---

[1] vv. 126 *sqq.* [2] vv. 1-3. [3] vv. 78 *sq.*
[4] v. 121. [5] vv. 960 *sqq.*
[6] At v. 1539 (very late in the day) they discuss whether it is their
duty to inform the State of the murderous plot against Helen and
Hermione. Even then they decide to do nothing.
[7] vv. 1547 *sqq.*
[8] Note vv. 743, 745, 747, 749, and the excitement in the last two
verses.
[9] vv. 481 *sqq.*

quite comfortable after the death of Agamemnon ;[1]
Helen, that faded, facile creature, who cannot abstain
from conversation, even with murderesses if there is no
one else. Hermione, minute as is her part, commands
our affection, not only because of the vile complot which
centres round her, but for the shy graciousness of the
little she does say, ἥκω λαβοῦσα πρευμένειαν[2] and the
rest ; she seems to have strayed from some sunlit lost
drama by Sophocles.

The religious sanction which for Sophocles had
been the background of Orestes' story and which for
Æschylus provided the most vital part of the action,
has in Euripides' hands become, as it were, a small,
rather shabby stage-property hung upon the back-scene.
Those Avenging Spirits who hunt the matricide are
now called " frenzies "[3] by his sister, and in the
anxiously precise account[4] which Menelaus elicits from
his nephew, it becomes plain that the three "maidens
like night" are an hallucination ; any unfettered
intercourse between them and ordinary men is
out of the question. Traditional belief itself tells
rather against their divinity than for it.[5] Another
stage property is the incidental miracle. Menelaus
at Malea was addressed by the "prophet of Nereus,
Glaucus, truthful god," who told him of his brother's
death.[6] When we learn that at Nauplia he heard of
Clytæmnestra's death but from "some mariner,"[7] we
surmise that "Glaucus" too was human.[8] The second
miracle is that related[9] by the Phrygian slave ; Helen
vanished, "either by spells or the tricks of wizards or

---

[1] vv. 371 sqq.   [2] v. 1323.   [3] vv. 37 sqq.   [4] vv. 395 sqq.
[5] Contrast v. 420 : μέλλει· τὸ θεῖον δ' ἐστὶ τοιοῦτον φύσει ; with v. 423 :
ὡς ταχὺ μετῆλθόν σ' αἷμα μητέρος θεαί.
[6] vv. 360 sqq.   [7] v. 373.
[8] First Menelaus says that Glaucus spoke to him " from the waves "
(v. 362), but from v. 365 (ἐμφανῶς κατασταθείς) it seems that the person
is standing on the shore. Such inconsistencies are significant, and in
Euripides common. They indicate how much accuracy the narrator
commands.
[9] vv. 1493 sqq.

stolen by Heaven ". Helen has only hidden herself ; the
Phrygian is crazed by excitement and terror. But the
miracle of Helen is vouched for by a more august
witness, Apollo, who asserts that he has saved her from
Orestes' sword. Thus we arrive at the final triumph of
orthodox religion, the epilogue in which the Delphian god
stays at a word the vengeance of Argos and the quarrel
between Menelaus and Orestes. In the reality of this
epilogue we shall believe according as we find it credible
that Euripides could destroy all the effect of his own
play. All the action, all the atmosphere, which the
dramatist has created, are rent by an utter breach. The
objection is not so much that Apollo and his speeches
are in themselves absurd, though the consolation offered
to Menelaus, that Helen throughout their married life
has given him endless trouble,[1] is (however true) dis-
tasteful. What jars hopelessly is the monstrous dis-
continuity of event and emotion. As elsewhere, this
orthodox Olympian and his epilogue are a sham,
devised to suit the demands of an audience which
"knew" how Orestes went forth from Argos to Athens.
The real drama ends with the wild breakdown of
Menelaus, and for the three criminals and their victim
the doom falls which sin and bitter madness have made
inevitable.[2]

But the Orestes is not remarkable as a study in
scepticism, like the *Ion*. Even the psychology, superb
as it is, cannot be regarded as the cause of the immense
popularity which the play won in antiquity.[3] It is pre-

---

[1] vv. 1662-3.

[2] Professor Gilbert Murray (*Euripides and his Age*, pp. 160 *sqq*.) has
some beautiful and striking observations on the epiphany of Apollo and its
effect on the raving mortals below : a trance falls upon them from which
they awake purged of hate and anger. But could Euripides, can we,
attribute this to a god who has commanded matricide ? And the effect is
largely spoiled by Orestes (vv. 1666 *sqq*.) : " Prophetic Loxias, what oracles
are thine ! Thou art not, then, a lying prophet, but a true. Yet had I
begun to dread lest, when I heard thy voice as I thought, it was that of a
fiend." . . . These are not the tones of blissful faith.

[3] Paley says that this play is more frequently quoted by ancient
writers than all the works of Æschylus and Sophocles together.

eminent for magnificent situations. The sick-bed scene
is unforgettable, especially that marvellous hushed song [1]
of Electra beside her sleeping brother:—

> Holy night, outpouring ever
>   Slumber's boon on souls that mourn,
> From thy midmost deep dominion
> Hither bend thy sweeping pinion,
>   Where, 'neath woes that leave it never
>   Lies a princely house forlorn.

The whole progress of the later scenes is splendidly
exciting, and in the midst Euripides has set the audacious
scene of the Phrygian slave who replaces the conventional messenger's speech with his wild lyrical narrative,
incoherent and baffling. Equally brilliant is the finale
in which actual lunacy confronts the delirium of despair
and grief, with the frail victim flung upon the parapet,
the knife brandished in the madman's grasp, and the
flames which are to end the horror already rising behind.

The BACCHÆ [2] (Βάκχαι), or *Bacchantes* (female
votaries of the god Bacchus or Dionysus), was produced
in 405 B.C., soon after the poet's death in Macedonia,
and with its companion-plays obtained the first prize.

Dionysus, standing before the palace of Thebes, tells
how, disguised as a prophet, he has brought his religion
into Greece. His purpose in Thebes is to punish the
sisters of his mother Semele for declaring that their
sister had united herself not with Zeus but with some
mortal, and to crush the young king Pentheus, who
opposes his worship. Already the Theban women are
revelling upon Mount Cithæron, filled with the Bacchic
ecstasy. He departs to join them, and the chorus of
Phrygian votaresses throng in uttering a rapturous
eulogy of their religion. Tiresias and Cadmus are next
seen preparing to join the revels, when Pentheus enters
and reproaches them. Their answers enrage him
further and he orders the arrest of the stranger-prophet.
The chorus appeal to Holiness against the oppressor,

---

[1] vv. 174 *sqq.*

[2] *Arrangement:* Protagonist, Pentheus, Agave; deuteragonist,
Dionysus, Tiresias; tritagonist, Cadmus, guard, messengers,

reciting the blessings of Dionysus and the doom of
pride ; they yearn to revel unchecked. The Stranger is
brought in ; Pentheus questions and insults him, finally
haling him away to the stables. The chorus sing their
indignation and desire for the aid of Dionysus in person
when the prophet is heard summoning fire and earth-
quake ; the women in frenzy greet the overthrow of
the palace. Their leader comes forth and relates how
Pentheus in vain sought to bind him and how the god
has thrown the house into utter ruin. Pentheus rushes
out in fury, but is met by a rustic who relates the
revels and miracles performed by the Theban votaresses.
This excites the king still further, but the Stranger dissuades him from the use of armed force ; let him go
disguised as a woman to witness the revels. Pentheus
retires into the palace with the prophet, who reveals
the king's coming doom to the chorus ; they rejoice in
their future freedom and the fate of the ungodly. Pentheus re-appears, dressed as a female reveller and utterly
under the Stranger's influence. The two depart for
the mountains, the king being now practically imbecile.
The chorus fiercely call for bloody vengeance, then
praise the humble endeavour after all that is beautiful
in life. A messenger returns with the story of Pentheus' death : he has been torn to pieces by his mother
Agave and her companions. Agave enters in mad
triumph with her son's head, followed by Cadmus, who
bears the mangled remains of his grandson and gradually brings Agave back to her senses. He laments [1] the
prince who was the comfort of his old age.[2] Dionysus
appears in the sky, foretells the future of Cadmus and his
wife, and explains that the present sorrows are due to
the will of Zeus. Agave turns away, repudiating the
new religion.

[1] Before Cadmus' speech, a passage has been lost in which the
mourners adjusted the torn fragments.
[2] There is another gap at this point. A considerable number of
Dionysus' lines are missing, and no doubt also further conversation between
Cadmus and Agave.

Intoxicatingly beautiful, coldly sordid, at one moment baffling the brain, at the next thrilling us with the mystic charm of wood and hillside, this drama stands unique among Euripides' works. Its wonderful effect flows from three sources : primitive dramaturgy, lyrical beauty, the enigma of its theological import. As for the first of these, there is a marked simplicity both of plot and characters. A god brings a strange worship into the land of his birth ; the king rejects and scorns him ; whereupon the god turns his people to madness so that they avenge him upon the king. It is the simplest possible dramatic concept. If we consider the personages, comparing Agave with Phædra or Medea, Pentheus with Ion or Hippolytus, we find an equal simplicity. The characters of the *Bacchæ* impress us less by their subtle truth to nature than by the situation in which they stand. In this sense the *Bacchæ* is the most Æschylean work of Euripides. Like his predecessor when he composed the *Choephoræ*, he is studying directly a great religious fact, which submerges the refinements of individual psychology, leaving somewhat stark figures, the God, the Old Man, the King, the Prophet, and the Woman.[1] In technique we are not far from that primitive stage of modern drama which exhibits the interplay of Avarice, Lovingkindness, and the rest. This imparts an even greater attractiveness to the amazing literary excellence of the whole. This excellence is of two distinct kinds. The episodes are not filled with romantic beauty—only a few splendid passages in the long narratives of messengers exhibit this ; they show the same mastery of a brilliant half-prosaic idiom which is familiar elsewhere. But the lyrics are the poet's finest achievement in this field. Nothing that he had created hitherto can be compared with them, save the praises of Attica in the *Medea*[2] and the song of

[1] See Professor Murray (*Euripides and his Age*, pp. 183 *sq.*). I now think that what I wrote about the psychology of Dionysus and Pentheus (*The Riddle of the Bacchæ*, pp. 66 *sq.*, 87-101) is over-elaborated.
[2] vv. 824-45.

escape in the *Hippolytus*.[1] The profound beauty of their musings on the life of serene piety, the startling vividness wherewith they express the secluded loveliness which haunts bare peaks or remote woodlands, the superb torrent of glowing song[2] which celebrates the religious ecstasy of Dionysiac votaries, where the glorious diction is swept along by a tempest of ever more tumultuous rhythm—all these contribute to make the *Bacchæ* something precious and alone.

It is with regard to the third feature, the theological purport, that disagreement begins among critics. Is the playwright commending the Bacchic religion to his fellow-countrymen or is he not? If not, why this magnificent and intense proclamation of the glory conferred by belief? But if he supports it, why this dreary aching scene at the end, when Dionysus hears no voice raised in loyalty, only the despairing accents of the woman who repudiates his worship? It may be objected that perhaps we should not hope for definite interpretation, that since "like a live thing it seems to move and show new faces every time that, with imagination fully working, one reads the play,"[3] perhaps there is no core of central fact to find. Here lurks a dangerous confusion of thought. Every work of art springs from a definite concept held by the artist, some piece of reality clearly understood and sincerely felt, insisting on expression at his hands precisely because it affects him emotionally. The elusiveness of the final expression is not in the least degree any proof that no definite doctrine, or experience, or passionate wish, was its origin ; a fern has a physical centre of gravity as truly as an apple, though more difficult to locate. Rather, the luxuriant freedom is the proof that there is deep down something definite, else the freedom would be

[1] vv. 732-51.
[2] Professor Murray's beautiful translation of these lyrics will be familiar to most readers.
[3] Murray, *Euripides and his Age*, p. 196. My quotation, of course, does not imply that Professor Murray is guilty of the confusion of thought in question.

anarchy. We conclude that however enigmatic is the *Bacchæ*, yet Euripides had a definite opinion about the two questions : Does the god Dionysus exist ? Is his religion a blessing to humanity ? His opinion could have been written down in a few lucid sentences. Had this not been so, he would have postponed beginning his play until it was. This clear concept may itself indicate "doubt" (if we insist on the word) or rather a bifurcation of truth, as may be observed in the dramaturgy of Sophocles.

There is, then, a secret to be discovered. Is it lost for ever, or not ? It appears to some [1] that the drama contains evidence, unmistakable but long overlooked, which conveys Euripides' opinion concerning Dionysus. The chief, the only certain, clue is contained in the "Palace-Miracle". The facts are, that the chorus cry aloud at the tottering of the building ; that Dionysus a moment later when relating what has happened within, adds, "And this further evil hath Bacchus wrought upon him : he hath flung his dwelling to the ground, where it lies all in ruin" ; [2] that, finally, the palace is as a fact uninjured. This latter point is proved by the complete silence of all the personages, except Dionysus and the chorus. Neither Cadmus nor Agave, nor the two messengers, at their several entrances make the least remark about it. Above all, Pentheus, who was

---

[1] The view mentioned in this paragraph will be found worked out in the present writer's *Riddle of the Bacchæ*. This theory has met with much scepticism, but received the honour of almost entire acceptance by the late Dr. Verrall in *The Bacchantes of Euripides*. Dr. Verrall improved the statement of the theory, in particular by rejecting the supposition of a plot between Tiresias and the Stranger. Mr. W. H. Salter, in his delightful *Essays on Two Moderns*, also accepts this view of the play in the main (pp. 50-68). Dr. R. Nihard, in *Le Problème des Bacchantes d'Euripide* (Louvain, 1912), a useful study, rejects it.

[2] vv. 632 *sq.* :—

πρὸς δὲ τοῖσδ' αὐτῷ τάδ' ἄλλα Βάκχιος λυμαίνεται·
δώματ' ἔρρηξεν χαμᾶζε. συντεθράνωται δ' ἅπαν . . .

συντεθράνωται, however, is elsewhere only known to us by the explanation of Hesychius, συμπέπτωκε, and Verrall points out that it ought to mean "it has all been put together again",

within the house when the overthrow is alleged to have occurred, says nothing about it. Later the prince and his enemy enter the palace before proceeding to Cithæron, again with no hint that the building has been destroyed. It follows that the statements made by the chorus and by Dionysus are untrue.[1] The women believe what their leader cries out from within and what he tells them later. That is, they accept what their own eyes tell them is false. Only one power can work this marvel of belief—hypnotism, or, as earlier ages would call it, magic. The Dionysus of this play is precisely what Pentheus calls him, a " foreign wizard,"[2] no god at all, but a human hierophant of the new religion. Brought up in Western Asia, he combines a profound feeling for natural religion with an un-Greek leaning to orgiastic ecstasy and an instinct for fiendish cruelty; so that in spreading the gospel of joy and simple surrender to the mystic loveliness of Nature he crushes those who reject him, not destroying them in passion, but working their misery with a horrible cold relish : he is Shakespeare's Richard the Third with religious instead of political ambitions. As for the Dionysiac religion itself, the poet feels its vast emotional appeal—feels it so strongly that he has drawn the most wonderful picture of ecstatic religion to be found in literature ; but if it is proposed to him as " a way of life " for civilized men he condemns it as firmly as unwillingly. To give free rein to passions and instincts hitherto unconscious or starved, this is a path, perhaps the only path, towards strangely

---

[1] To this view no complete answer has yet been made. All that can possibly be said is what Professor Gilbert Murray (*Euripides and his Age*, pp. 186 *sq.*) and (in a letter to the present writer) Professor U. von Wilamowitz-Moellendorf suggest, that the palace is in the main destroyed, but the façade is more or less undamaged. This does away with the testimony to Dionysus' imposture which the audience receive from their own eyes, but it leaves untouched the incredible silence of Pentheus. Moreover, Dionysus' words as they stand mean that the building is utterly destroyed. That they do not mean this is only suggested in despair, because, if they do mean this, they are absurdly and patently false.

[2] v. 233 *sq.* : ξένος, γόης ἐπῳδός,

beautiful experience, the thrill of communion with non-human life; but it is not the path for man. Here Euripides stands at one with the great European tradition. If man is to attain the height of his destiny he will seek not the gold of joy but the silver of happiness, not the blazing rapture of absorption in strange beauty, but the calm glow of self-understanding and self-expression. He will not seek to destroy the instinct for ecstasy, but will harness it, and work it into the fabric of a sound coherent life. He may be a spectator, it is true, if not of all time, yet of all existence; his eyes will shrink from nothing, but his heart is not to be reft from him. He must prove all things, but hold fast only that which is good—a moral being, not the slave of sound and colour. In this drama, where Euripides seems to voice like some pagan archangel the glory of a non-moral absorption in the torrent of raw life, he is fundamentally as moral as at any moment in life. As Tannhäuser after his sojourn in the Venusberg is at length won back by the urgency of his own soul into the Roman Church, so does Euripides unflinchingly present, to an audience still breathing hard after the glories of Cithæron, Agave and Cadmus bowed over Pentheus' mangled body, and the rejection of a god whose unmitigated demands imply the wreckage of sound human life.

What, then, are we to believe of Dionysus? If we refuse him we are liable like Pentheus to be destroyed; if we surrender ourselves, what of Agave? Here is a dilemma which Euripides himself did not foresee. By θεός ("god") he often means something widely different from the concept of an ordinary Athenian, but he never intends all the associations of our word "God". For us belief in "God" implies that the universe holds a personal Governor, all-powerful and all-wise, who stands to us in a relation emotional as well as metaphysical. To accept Him is to believe that His purpose embraces the existence and history of the universe and of the humblest creature therein, and

because of that belief to merit His love by loving service
of our own.   These thoughts are to us tremendous
commonplaces ; they would have bewildered any fifth-
century Greek save Æschylus.[1] θεός means a power,
usually but not necessarily personal, which is outside
ourselves and affects our life in a manner which cannot
be affected by any wish or act of ours, save possibly
to a small degree by ritual submission.   Dionysus, like
the other "gods," is a permanent fact of life personified.
We must give him respect, take account of him in
our conduct and judgment of others.   To ignore him
is not so much sin as utter blindness.   If we insist on
the personality of Dionysus we find him attractive but
deadly, a deity who employs his might to entangle
the threads of life, crushing hearts better than his own.
In so far as he is a person he is unthinkable.   But as
a fact of life, with no more purpose or will than the
force of gravitation, he is neither good nor bad, simply
a profound reality, one of the elements we must consider in building our lives.   Cadmus expresses this
lesson : " If anyone despises the supernatural powers,
let him look on the death of this man and believe in
the gods ".[2]

Then why does the poet dwell on the personal
existence of Dionysus?   Even if we refuse to believe
the theory outlined already, that this person is a human
hierophant, we can still answer the question.   Euripides is concerned not merely to tell us the truth about
ethics, but to discuss the current theology of his day.
The majority of his fellows believed in a personal Zeus,
a personal Athena and Dionysus.   He wishes to convince them of the falsity, the pernicious falsity, of such
a creed.   Take this play in its superficial meaning
and you find a person who is detestable—a god who
does wrong, and who is, therefore, no god at all.[3]   Away

[1] The attachment between Artemis and Hippolytus is a remarkable
exception.   The stories concerning the "loves " of gods and goddesses for
mortals are evidently beside the question.

[2] vv. 1325 sq.

[3] *Bellerophon, fr.* 294, 7 : εἰ θεοί τι δρῶσιν αἰσχρόν, οὐκ εἰσὶν θεοί.

with him; purify your theology. And when this is done, we find, not that the drama has fallen to pieces, but that now it is coherent and forcible. There is in the human soul an instinct for ecstasy, for a relinquishment of self in order to feel and bathe in the non-human glory of Nature. Trample this instinct ruthlessly down as did Pentheus, and your life is maimed and shrivelled.

IPHIGENIA AT AULIS [1] ('Ιφιγένεια ἡ ἐν Αὐλίδι) was produced soon after the poet's death in 406 B.C. by his son, together with *Alcmæon at Corinth* and the *Bacchæ*.

The scene shows Agamemnon's tent at Aulis, where the Greeks are encamped ready to sail for Troy, but delayed by contrary winds. Before they can set out Agamemnon's daughter Iphigenia must be sacrificed to Artemis. The king has written to his wife bidding her send the maiden—to marry Achilles. We now see him in agony beneath the night-sky and entrusting to an aged slave a letter revoking the first. The chorus (women of Colchis) enter and describe the pastimes of various heroes. Menelaus intercepts the letter and reproaches his brother with treachery. After a vigorous dispute they learn that Clytæmnestra and Iphigenia are approaching. Menelaus relents, but they realize that the sacrifice must proceed. The chorus sing Aphrodite's power and the judgment of Paris. Agamemnon greets his family with half-concealed distress, and in vain attempts to send his wife back forthwith. A choric ode describes the impending doom of Troy. Achilles, seeking Agamemnon, meets Clytæmnestra, who to his amazement greets him as a son-in-law. In the midst of their embarrassment the old slave comes forward and reveals Agamemnon's purpose. The queen in agony appeals to Achilles, who promises to defend Iphigenia. The chorus sing the bridals of

---

[1] *Arrangement:* Croiset gives: protagonist, Agamemnon, Achilles; deuteragonist, Old Man, Iphigenia, messenger; tritagonist, Menelaus, Clytæmnestra.

Peleus and Thetis, Achilles' parents. Then mother
and daughter pitiously beg Agamemnon to relent; he
is heart-broken but determined. Iphigenia utters a
lyric lament, after which Achilles tells how the army
maltreated him for championing Iphigenia. He and
the queen are excitedly debating, when Iphigenia proclaims her readiness to die for the cause of Greece,
and departs, singing her farewell to life. A messenger
brings a description of the sacrifice : at the last moment
the princess miraculously disappeared, and a hind
was substituted for her by the goddess. Agamemnon
returns and takes leave of Clytæmnestra.

The text of this drama presents curious features.[1]
There are two prologues, and the last fifty or sixty
lines of the whole are corrupt. It seems that Euripides
died before the work was finished; the gaps were
filled by his son Euripides who produced the trilogy
(*Iphigenia, Alcmæon, Bacchæ*) soon after 406 B.C.
The original prologue, of the ordinary narrative kind,
delivered by Agamemnon in iambic metre, is embedded
in the later prologue, which takes the form of a dialogue
in anapæsts between the king and his aged retainer.
This later work is extremely charming, filled with the
quiet beauty of night overhanging the feverish ambition
and misery of men. But though the younger Euripides
probably wrote an ending also, this has been displaced
by extremely bad[2] work of a much later time. It is
not easy to understand why such inferior matter was
allowed to eject the composition of the younger Euripides. Perhaps the explanation is that the concluding
lines were known from the first not to be by the master,
that the play was often produced, and that for these
two reasons rival endings were very early before the
public. They would destroy one another's prestige,
so that in later centuries none survived, and some
scribe filled up the gap as best he could.

A noteworthy contrast exists between the *Iphigenia*

---

[1] For these see Professor Murray's text, especially his preface.

[2] It contains, for instance, unmetrical verses.

and the *Bacchæ*, though they were no doubt composed at almost the same time. In this play the chorus has practically no concern with the action, whereas the Asiatic women form the soul of the *Bacchæ*. Instead of the wild loveliness or serene spirituality which thrill us in the lyrics of that drama, we find here nothing more profound than graceful complications of phrase and facile emotion. In compensation, while the *Bacchæ* is primitive in psychology, its companion is superior to many Greek tragedies in the masterly freedom and subtlety of its character-drawing.

The play is a study of five ordinary characters under the stress of an extraordinary crisis. This common-place quality of the personages conveys the whole purport, giving it a momentous position even among such works as we have been discussing. In this latest tragedy no sincere reader can fail to detect himself under the thin disguise of names. Many men were pointed at as the original of Meredith's Sir Willoughby Patterne, and for the same good reason most Athenian husbands must have stirred a little on their benches in the presence of this unheroic Agamemnon. There is nothing heroic in any of the persons. Menelaus is an ordinary man—artlessly selfish at one moment, artlessly and uselessly kind-hearted at another, and a master of fluent invective which reveals his own failings. Clytæmnestra is an ordinary woman, showing indeed a queenly dignity in the normal relations of life, but when puzzled or alarmed revealing herself a thorough *bourgeoise*, and when confronted by the doom which threatens her daughter forgetting all her pride, clutching at even the most pitiful means[1] of gaining a respite, and utterly broken when her hope dies away. Agamemnon is an ordinary man, thrown by circumstances into a position where both generalship and statesmanship are needed, attempting to rule his army by diplomacy and his family by military discipline, with ruin as the result. Fatally open

---

[1] vv. 1366 *sq.*

to suggestion, he makes and remakes subterfuges, seeking to spare every one's feelings until at last he drifts into the necessity of slaying his own child. Even Iphigenia is an ordinary girl. It is precisely because she is a common type that we grieve for her anguish and triumph in her exaltation. Macaria in the *Heraclidæ* is almost unknown save to professed students of Euripides. She knows no fear or hesitation and lives on the heights ; we recognize in ourselves no kinship with her. But Iphigenia we meet every day. She is no heroine, but a child. Her delight at seeing her father again shows all a child's amiable abandon ; her pitiful cries and shrinking at the prospect of death are those of the ordinary happiness-loving girl. When finally the agony of her father, the empty clamour of Achilles, her mother's undignified tremors, nerve her to trample her own dread under foot, we rejoice precisely because what we witness is the triumph of common human nature. Even Achilles, son of a goddess as story reported him, is a common-place person too. This is not the hero who flames through the *Iliad*, but a young noble led into the extreme of folly by this very legend that his origin is divine. Perhaps nothing even in the deadly Euripides is quite so fatal to the traditional halo than the incredible speech [1] wherewith Achilles comforts Clytæmnestra. Of vast length, full of spurious, jerky rhetoric and contradictory comments on the situation—which, however frightful, appeals to him mostly as an atmosphere in which he can pose—this oration reveals him as a sham. Fortunately for him, he is never undeceived. This man is not the Achilles of tradition ; he is spiritual brother of the mad prince in the *Orestes* and the ancestor of Mr. Shaw's Sergius Saranoff.

In his last work, then, Euripides, so far from showing any exhaustion of power, appears on the verge of new developments. [2] He has drawn still nearer to the

[1] vv. 919-74.
[2] For what follows cp. Professor Murray, *Euripides and his Age*, pp. 173-5.

new comedy of Menander.   The suddenness with which,
after the quarrel between Agamemnon and Menelaus,
the crisis is precipitated by the entrance of the messenger
announcing Iphigenia's arrival—the man breaks into the
middle of a line [1]—is a remarkable novelty.   The altercation itself shows a brilliant freedom of idiom which
even this poet has hardly reached hitherto.   There is
at least one unprecedented license of metre.[2]   And the
complete change of spirit which comes upon Iphigenia
was novel enough to offend Aristotle.[3]

The CYCLOPS [4] (Κύκλωψ) is the only complete [5] satyric
play now extant.   No indications of date [6] seem available.

The background is a cave on Mount Etna, wherein
dwells the Cyclops, or one-eyed giant, Polyphemus.
Silenus tells how he and the satyrs have become the
ogre's slaves.   He is sweeping out the cavern when the
chorus of satyrs drive in their flocks.   Odysseus and his
men arrive, seeking provisions, which Silenus eagerly
sells for a skin of wine.   The conversation is interrupted
by Polyphemus who decides to devour the intruders.
Odysseus eloquently appeals to him, but receives a
brutal and blasphemous reply.   The giant drives the
Greeks within, and the chorus express their disgust at
his cannibalism.   Odysseus tells how two of his men
have been eaten ; he himself has gained favour by the
gift of wine, and proposes that they all escape, after
blinding Polyphemus with a red-hot stake.   The chorus
joyfully assent.   Polyphemus comes forth drunk and
intending to visit his brethren, but Odysseus dissuades
him.   The Cyclops asks Odysseus his name and is told
"Noman" ; he promises to eat his benefactor last.   The
revel proceeds until Polyphemus retires, whereupon

---

[1] v. 414.   [2] The elision of αι in v. 407.   [3] *Poetic*, 1454a.
[4] *Arrangement :* protagonist, Odysseus ;   deuteragonist, Silenus ;
tritagonist, Polyphemus.
[5] The *Detectives* ('Ιχνευταί) of Sophocles is now known to us by
extensive fragments, see pp. 175 *sq.*
[6] Murray puts it " perhaps even before 438 ".

Odysseus calls for action, but the chorus all offer ridiculous excuses. The hero goes within to perform the task with his comrades. Soon the giant reappears, blind and bellowing with pain, while the satyrs joke about "Noman," and give him false directions so that the Greeks escape from the cave. Odysseus reveals himself, and Polyphemus recognizes the fulfilment of an oracle. He threatens to wreck the ship, but the others depart unconcernedly to the beach.

This brief play—it has hardly more than seven hundred lines—is invaluable as being the only complete work of the satyric type which we now possess. Considered in itself, it is of small value,[1] though it must have formed an agreeable light entertainment. The lyrics are short and trifling. Of characterization there is little, and that little traditional and obvious—Odysseus is pious, valiant, resourceful ; Polyphemus brutally sensual, the satyrs cowardly and frivolous. Though there are passages of tension, the audience can never have felt any marked excitement, as the whole story, except that the satyrs are imported by the dramatist, is taken from a well-known episode in Homer[2] ; even such things as the joke on the name Outis[3] (" Noman ") and the comparison[4] between the spit which blinds Polyphemus and the auger of a shipwright, are borrowed from the epic. The nature of satyric drama in general is discussed elsewhere.[5] Here it will be enough to note that there are "tragic" features in this play ; Odysseus throughout speaks and acts in a manner as dignified, perhaps more dignified, than in certain tragedies of our poet. The farcical scenes provided by the rascally Silenus, the obscene jests and cowardice of the chorus, and a certain approximation[6] to comedy in the iambic metre

[1] It attracted little attention from ancient scholars. There are no scholia, and the hypothesis is incomplete.

[2] *Odyssey IX.* 105-566.

[3] Cp. vv. 549, 672-5, with *Od. IX.* vv. 366, 408-12.

[4] Cp. vv. 460-3 with *Od. IX.* 384-8.   [5] See p. 2.

[6] Anapæsts in other feet than the first, and occasional violations of the rule of the final cretic (see Chapter VI).

used by them or by Polyphemus, are marks of a satyric play. It should be noted, however, that even without them, the *Cyclops* would be no tragedy. Polyphemus is no tragic antagonist of the hero. His exposition of his philosophy of life,[1] such as it is, must not persuade us that there is here any valid moral antagonism as foundation of the drama. Odysseus contends with him and eludes him as one might escape the violence of a ravening animal.

The RHESUS [2] ('Ρῆσος) is a drama of uncertain date and authorship. The action is founded on the Tenth Book of the *Iliad*, and takes place at night in the Trojan camp. Hector has defeated the Greeks and hopes to destroy them at dawn. The drama opens with a song by the chorus of sentinels, come to warn Hector that the Greeks are astir. He is ordering instant attack when Æneas urges that a spy be first sent. Dolon volunteers, and sets forth disguised as a wolf, followed by the admiration and prayers of the chorus. A herdsman announces the approach of the Thracian prince, Rhesus, with an army to aid Troy, but Hector is displeased with his tardiness, and, despite the joyful ode of the chorus, greets his ally with reproaches. Rhesus offers excuses, promising to destroy the Greeks without Trojan help, and to invade Greece; Hector takes him away to bivouac. The chorus depart to rouse the Lycians, whose watch comes next. Odysseus and Diomedes steal in, intending to slay Hector. They have met Dolon and learned from him the position of Hector's tent and the watchword, " Phœbus ". Athena appears, bidding them slay Rhesus and take his wondrous steeds. They depart, and, seeing Paris draw near, she calms his suspicions under the guise of his protectress Aphrodite. Next she recalls the Greeks, who have slain

---

[1] vv. 316-41.

[2] The *arrangement* of the cast is not clear ; perhaps : protagonist, Hector, Odysseus ; deuteragonist, Æneas, Rhesus, Diomedes, charioteer ; tritagonist, Dolon, herdsman, Athena, Muse. The brief part of Paris may have been taken by Diomedes or Odysseus, possibly by a fourth actor.

Rhesus.   An exciting scene follows, in which the chorus
seize Odysseus, who escapes by using the pass-word.
The chorus sing the daring of Odysseus.   A wounded
charioteer of Rhesus staggers in, proclaiming his
master's death, of which he accuses Hector, who sends
him away for tendance.   As the chorus lament, a Muse
appears in the sky, bearing the body of her son Rhesus.
She sings a dirge and curses Odysseus and Diomedes.
Next she tells of her union with the river-god, father of
Rhesus, and upbraids Athena.   Hector promises glorious
obsequies, but she declares that her son shall live on
in the Thracian mountains as a spirit half-divine.[1]
Hector orders an assault upon the Greeks, and the
chorus sing a few courageous words.

This admirable drama stands quite by itself.   There
is a minimum of psychology ; the lyrics are mostly of
slight value.   But the writer has not aimed at a tragedy
of the usual type.   Its excellence lies in the vigour
and excitement of the action.   Almost all the scenes,
especially the debate at the opening, and the escape of
the Greeks, are written by a master of vivid realism,
who is less concerned with character-drawing.   The
unwearied Hector, the cautious Æneas, the vaunting,
splendid, barbarian prince, the fiercely loyal charioteer—
these are all obvious types.   The only really fine stroke
of psychological insight occurs where Hector, himself
reckless at first, is by the absurd presumptuousness of
Rhesus forced into discretion.[2]   What really stirs one
is the thrilling atmosphere of danger and the magical
little lyric [3] which falls half-carelessly from the wearied
sentries when the night begins to wane :—

> Hark ! Hark !
> That voice, as of a thousand strings !
> The nightingale, where Simois moves along
> 'Mid corpses stark !
> Upon the listening air she flings
> Her grief transfused into song.

[1] ἀνθρωποδαίμων (v. 971).   [2] vv. 474-84.   [3] vv. 546-56.

E'en now on Ida graze the sheep.
One distant pipe through darkness cries
          Over the upland lawn.
Now layeth velvet-footed sleep
Enchantment on my drooping eyes,
          Sweetest at hush of dawn.

Some ancient critics denied that Euripides wrote
the *Rhesus*, and the great majority of modern scholars
have accepted this view.[1]   The evidence for Euripidean
authorship is as follows : (i) The play comes down to us
in the manuscripts of that poet.   (ii) That Euripides
wrote a *Rhesus* is known from the *Didascaliæ* or
Dramatic Records.   (iii) Early Alexandrian writers
quote passages from our text as from "the *Rhesus* of
Euripides ".   On the other side are (i) a statement in
the *Argument* :[2] "Some have suspected this drama to
be spurious, and not the work of Euripides, for it reveals
rather the Sophoclean manner" ; (ii) various features
of the work which modern critics have regarded as
suggesting an inferior playwright : (*a*) the plot is superficial ; (*b*) there is no prologue ;[3] (*c*) four actors are
needed ; (*d*) Æneas and Paris have practically nothing
to do ; (*e*) the chorus is employed in a manner foreign
to Euripidean plays ; (*f*) there is a lack of force and
pathos ; (*g*) there is no rhetoric ; (*h*) there is no sen-
tentiousness ; (*i*) we have here the beginning of historical
drama, which is later than the fifth century ; (*j*) the
style is eclectic : imitations of Æschylus, Sophocles, and
Euripides are to be observed.[4]

Several of these objections are plainly unfounded.
Four actors are not clearly necessary, as was shown

[1] An excellent summary of the evidence (to which I am indebted) is
to be found in the *Introduction* to Professor Murray's verse-translation.

[2] Its author, however, is by no means convinced by them.   He gives
also interesting information on other points.

[3] That is, the two prologues mentioned in the *Argument* were added
for later performances.

[4] Another argument on this side, which is perhaps new, lies in the fact
that almost all the action takes place at night—an unique feature.   The
ancient theatre, of course, could not be darkened.   It might be urged that
the drama was meant for readers only, and so comes from one of the
ἀναγνωστικοί of the fourth century (see p. 32).

above. Pathos, of a kind quite Euripidean, is to be found in the scene where the Muse laments her glorious son. And how deny rhetorical force to a poet who can write such brilliantly vigorous things as :—

> Aye, friends in plenty shall I find, now Heaven
> Stands firm for us, and Fortune guides my sword.
> I need them not ! Where hid they those long years
> When Troy, a galleon with her canvas rent,
> Reeled onward through war's shrieking hurricane ? [1]

The high-hearted defence [2] of Rhesus is full of the same tingling rhetoric. Yet many critics [3] of the highest rank have denied Euripidean authorship to the *Rhesus*. On the other side stands [4] the testimony of the almost contemporary record. One consideration, obvious yet too often ignored, may help us. The earliest work of Euripides to which we can assign a date—the *Alcestis* —belongs to the year 438. The poet was then at least forty-two years old. Is it beyond belief that twenty years before the *Alcestis* the youthful dramatist composed a stirring tale of war and hair-breadth escape, which owed much to the manner of Æschylus, especially in his handling of the chorus ? During the period for which we have evidence, he was constantly testing the possibilities of his art. Need we assume that until the *Alcestis* he had not advanced ?

The soundest view appears to be that we have here a very early work of Euripides. This is confirmed by the critic Crates, an Academic philosopher of the second century before Christ, who asserted that Euripides was still young when he wrote the *Rhesus*.[5] To this should be added whatever help may be drawn from contemporary history. It is natural to suppose that when this drama was composed Athenian politics were closely concerned with Thrace. An Athenian colony at Nine Ways, afterwards called Amphipolis, was destroyed by

---

[1] vv. 319-23.   [2] vv. 422-53.
[3] It suffices to mention Scaliger, Böckh, Hermann, Valckenaer, and Wilamowitz-Moellendorff.
[4] Upheld, *e.g.* by Christ and Murray.
[5] Schol. on v. 528.

the Thracians in 465 B.C. In 436 the place was re-
settled under the new name by Hagnon, who brought
the bones of Rhesus from the Troad back to Thrace.
The later year, as connected with the hero, would seem
the more suitable, were it not for the words[1] of his
mother who refuses burial for her son and proclaims
his strange life after death : " hidden in caverns of the
silver-yielding soil he shall lie as a human spirit, still
living ". Such language would rather be avoided after
the bones themselves had been visibly committed to
Thracian earth. On the whole, one thinks the situation
more suitable to some period, anterior to Hagnon's expedition, when Thracian politics were in the air, perhaps
quite soon after the disaster of 465 B.C.[2]

Of the lost plays we have about eleven hundred fragments. Few of these comprise more than three or four
lines, but a fair conception of several dramas can be
formed from reports of the plot, parodies by Aristophanes,
and the remains themselves.

The TELEPHUS was acted in 438 B.C., together with
The Cretan Women, Alcmæon at Psophis, and *Alcestis.*
Sophocles won the first prize, Euripides the second.
Telephus, King of Mysia, was wounded by Achilles when
the Greeks invaded Mysia in mistake for Troy. His
wound would not heal, and he entered his enemies'
country disguised as a beggar, to consult the Delphic
oracle, which declared that "the wounder would heal
him". Meanwhile the Greek heroes were deliberating
at Argos about a second expedition. Agamemnon
refused to set forth again, and uttered to Menelaus the
celebrated words : Σπάρτην ἔλαχες · ταύτην κόσμει—
" Sparta is thy place : make thereof the best ". While
the council was in progress Telephus begged audience.
His disguise was penetrated by Odysseus, and he was

---

[1] vv. 962-73.
[2] On the whole question see Mr. W. H. Porter's excellent paper,
" The Euripidean *Rhesus* in the Light of Recent Criticism " (*Hermathena,*
xvii. pp. 348-80), and his useful edition of the play.

about to be slain when he snatched up the infant Orestes,
threatening to kill the child if the Greeks molested him.
He was given a hearing and justified his action in fight-
ing the Greeks when they invaded his country. His
hearers were won over, but it was found that Achilles
had no knowledge of medicine. Odysseus suggested
that the real " wounder " was Achilles' spear. Telephus
was thus healed, and in his gratitude consented to guide
the Greeks to Troy.

We possess in the *Acharnians* of Aristophanes an
elaborate and brilliant parody of the interview granted
to Telephus. Dicæopolis, an Athenian farmer who
has made peace on his own account with Sparta, is
attacked by his fellow-citizens, the charcoal-burners of
Acharnæ, and only obtains leave to plead his cause by
threatening to slay their darling—a coal-basket. Then
he begs from Euripides the beggar's outfit of Telephus,
and, returning, delivers a clever harangue denouncing
the war. The baby-hostage idea Aristophanes used
again in the *Thesmophoriazusæ*, where Mnesilochus, in
great danger from the infuriated women, seizes the
infant which one of them is carrying, only to find it a
concealed wine-skin.

PHILOCTETES was produced in 431 B.C. with the
Medea, *Dictys*, and *Harvesters* (Θερισταί), when both
Euripides and Sophocles were defeated by Euphorion,
the son of Æschylus. Our knowledge is derived almost
wholly from Dio Chrysostom[1] who compares the three
plays called *Philoctetes* by Æschylus, Sophocles, and
Euripides. He offers interesting comments on the differences in plot. In Euripides, as in Æschylus, the
chorus consists of Lemnian men, but the later poet
anticipates criticism by making his chorus apologize for
not visiting the sufferer earlier. One Lemnian, by name
Actor, takes part as a friend of Philoctetes. The "prologue" is spoken by Odysseus (here working with Diomedes, not Neoptolemus, as in Sophocles) who explains

[1] Cp. pp. 119 *sq.*, 165 *sq.*

that he would not have undertaken this present task for fear of being recognized by Philoctetes, had not Athena changed his appearance. (Here, as in the apology offered by the chorus, we have implied criticism [1] on Æschylus.) The Trojans are sending an embassy in the hope of gaining Philoctetes. Later in the drama, no doubt, occurred a set dispute between the Greek and the Trojan envoys.

In the BELLEROPHON Euripides seems to have gone to the extreme in depicting the passionate atheism inspired by the sight of prosperous wickedness. " If the gods do aught base," he exclaims in a famous line, "they are not gods." Another vigorous fragment begins :—

> Then dare men say that there are gods in Heaven ?
> Nay, nay ! There are not. Fling the tale away,
> The ancient lie by human folly bred !
> Base not your judgment on these words of mine—
> Use but your eyes.

Bellerophon ascended to Heaven on his winged steed Pegasus in order to remonstrate with Zeus. This idea is used farcically in Aristophanes' *Peace*, where Trygaeus ascends on a monstrous beetle.

ERECHTHEUS was a beautiful picture of patriotism. Athens being attacked by the Eleusinians and Thracians, King Erechtheus was told by the Delphic oracle that he could secure victory for Athens by sacrificing his daughter. His wife Praxithea, in a speech of passionate patriotism, consented to give up her child ; Swinburne has used this fragment in his own *Erechtheus*. Another long fragment contains the advice which Erechtheus gives to his son, and which in its dry precision curiously resembles the farewell of Polonius to Laertes. While the issue of battle remains uncertain, the chorus of old Athenians sing a lyric which charmingly renders their yearning for peace :

---

[1] Euripides revises even the diction of his predecessor. Æschylus wrote φαγέδαινα δ' ἥ μου σάρκας ἐσθίει ποδός ; Euripides repeats the line with the verb altered to θοινᾶται (Aristotle, *Poetic*, 1458b).

Along my spear, at last laid by,
　　May spiders weave their shining thread ;
May peace and music, ere I die,
　　With garlands crown my whitening head.

I'd deck Athene's cloistered fane
　　With shields of Thracian mountaineers,
And ope the well-loved page again
　　Where poets sing across the years.

Another popular play was the ANTIOPE. It dealt
with the persecution of Antiope by Lycus, King of
Thebes, and his wife Dirce. She was rescued from
death by her two sons, Amphion and Zethus, whom she
had been compelled to abandon at birth, and who discovered the relationship in the critical hour. The chief
interest of the play was the contrast between the brothers
—Zethus a man of muscle, devoted to farming ; Amphion, a musician and lover of the arts. Euripides developed this contrast in a long debate wherein culture
was upheld against the " Philistine ". We still read
one criticism of myth which recalls a blunt passage of
the *Ion*.[1] Story said that Antiope's sons were the offspring of Zeus, but Amphion has the hardihood to express doubt to his mother herself.

With the *Helen* (B.C. 412) was produced a work of
the first importance—the ANDROMEDA, a charming love-
story full of romance and poetical loveliness. It was
immensely popular ; Aristophanes gives in his *Thesmophoriazusæ* a parody as elaborate as that of *Telephus* in
the *Acharnians*, and it was a perusal of this drama which
excited Dionysus in the *Frogs* to descend to Hades
for the purpose of fetching back the dead playwright.
Lucian[2] tells how Archelaus, the tragic actor, came to
Abdera and performed the *Andromeda*. The whole
town grew crazy over it. "They used to sing the solo
from the *Andromeda* and recite Perseus' speech from beginning to end. The town swarmed with these actors

---

[1] vv. 1520-7.
[2] *Quomodo historia conscribenda*, § 1.

of a week's standing, pale and lean, shouting with all the strength of their lungs

> O Love, of gods and men tyrannic Lord,

and all the rest of it. This went on for a long time, in fact till winter, when a severe frost cured them of their nonsense." The *Andromeda* points forward to the novel, and it is interesting to note that in the best Greek novel—the *Æthiopica* of Heliodorus, who wrote about eight hundred years after Euripides' death—the heroine's father, like Andromeda's, was an Æthiopian king.

Scanty as are the remnants of this drama, we can still form some idea of its structure.[1] " It is the crowning virtue of all great art that, however little is left of it by the injuries of time, that little will be lovely."[2] The country of Cepheus, the Ethiope king, was ravaged by a sea-monster, and the only help lay in sacrificing to the creature Andromeda, the king's daughter, who was bound to a rock and left as his prey. At this point the action begins. It is still night and from the cliff rises the lament of the captive :—

> O solemn night,
> How slow thy coursers trace,
> Amid the holy Heaven star-bedight,
> Their pathway through the deeps of space !

At each pause in her song comes the voice of Echo repeating the sad syllables, till Andromeda is joined by the maidens who form the chorus. The lyric dialogue concluded, it seems[3] that the father and mother, Cepheus and Cassiopeia, enter and that there is some talk of attacking the monster ; Phineus, brother of the king and the affianced of Andromeda, shrinks from the risk. But now comes unlooked-for aid. Perseus, fresh from his slaughter of the Gorgon, arrives, borne through the air

---

[1] See Hartung's masterly treatment in *Euripides Restitutus*, II, pp. 344-60.

[2] Ruskin, *Mornings in Florence*, I, 14.

[3] The statements in this sentence are taken from Hartung, who bases his conception here upon other authors ; there are no Euripidean fragments to this effect.

on his winged sandals.　Though Zeus is his father, in this play he figures as the lowly hero familiar in our own fairy-tales.　Certainly he appears to be contrasted with the rich but cowardly Phineus, and the helpless despairing king.　His first words have been preserved :—

> Gods !　To what alien kingdom am I come
> On sandals swift, between the earth and Heaven
> Journeying homewards on these wingèd feet ? . . .
> But soft !　what crag is that by tossing foam
> Surrounded ?　Lo, the statue of a maid
> Hewn from the living rock by patient art,
> Its craftsman's master-work !

Drawing near, he perceives that this thing of beauty is a living maiden, and at once longs to make her his bride. When she asks his name, instead of proudly claiming Zeus as his father, he mentions his own name, his journey's end, and his achievement :—

> Περσεύς, πρὸς Ἄργος ναυστολῶν, τὸ Γοργόνος
> κάρα κομίζων.

But he is no mediæval knight ; he does not forbear to state his claim before addressing himself to the task : "And if I save thee, maid, wilt give me thanks?" Andromeda, on her side, feels and speaks without subtlety :—

> Stranger, have pity on my sore distress :
> Free me from bonds,

and again

> Take me, O stranger, for thy handmaiden,
> Or wife, or slave.

Before encountering the monster Perseus comes to an understanding with Cepheus and goes forth to the conflict, calling upon Eros to aid his chosen :—

> O Love, of gods and men tyrannic Lord,
> Either teach Beauty to unlearn her power,
> Or speed true lovers, through th' adventurous maze
> That in thy name they enter, to success.
> So shall all men to thee pay reverence.
> Refuse, and lo ! thy glories fade to naught
> E'en through thy very boon of wakened hearts.

Two or three lines picture the grateful crowd of rustics who surrounded the victor : "all the shepherd-folk flowed around him, one bringing an ivy-bowl of milk for his refreshing, another the joyous grape-juice ". Phineus sought to assert his claim upon Andromeda, but was repulsed by her father. Later the maiden's parents themselves begged her not to leave them desolate. In a thrilling[1] reply she declared that she would cleave to her husband. Then follows mention of a wedding-feast, and at the close it seems probable that Athena foretold the future.

Of the PHAETHON we are fortunate in possessing two unusually long fragments of seventy and seventy-five lines respectively. It is an exciting and romantic story —the legend of Phaethon, child of the Sun-god, who called upon his father to prove their relationship by permitting him for one day to drive the chariot of the Sun. This conception, gorgeous with the spirit of adventure and an un-Greek yearning for what transcends mortal power, seems to have filled the whole play with glow and rushing movement. A fragment of the prologue marks this at once: it tells how Clymene is wedded

> To Merops, lord of this our land
> Which first of all the earth the Sun-God smites
> With golden radiance of his risen car,
> Nam'd by black-visaged folk that dwell around
> The gleaming stable of the Sun and Dawn.

From Strabo,[2] to whom we owe this extract, we learn that the palace of Merops is close to the abode of the Sun-god. This notion that the youth's home is only an hour's walk from the palace of the Sun, gives a sense of delightful verisimilitude.[3] It appears that Phaethon in this prologue tells how his father Merops plans to marry him to a goddess, but that he himself is unwilling.[4]

---

[1] Eratosthenes (*Catast.* 15, quoted by Nauck) says: οὐχ εἵλετο τῷ πατρὶ συμμένειν οὐδὲ τῇ μητρί, ἀλλ᾽ αὐθαίρετος εἰς τὸ Ἄργος ἀπῆλθε μετ᾽ ἐκείνου εὐγενές τι φρονήσασα. The last three words suggest a scene of irresolution followed by a speech of high resolve, as in the *Iphigenia at Aulis.*

[2] I, 33.

[3] See Goethe's enthusiastic and brilliant discussion, *Altgriechische Literatur* (Works, Vol. V, p. 127, edition of 1837).

[4] Hartung's brilliant sketch of Phaethon's character (*Eur. Restitutus*, II, pp. 192 *sq.*), however imaginary, will be read with interest.

Clymene, his mother, to persuade her son that he will not
be distastefully united to one vastly his superior, reveals
that he is the son not of Merops but of the Sun-god,
Helios, who promised her long ago that he would grant
her child one wish. Let Phaethon approach Helios with
some request, and prove her story. The prince resolves
to do so. The chorus of female attendants enter with
a lovely song in honour of Phaethon's wedding ; they
picture the whole earth awakening to daily activities.
Next appears the king, who describes the brilliant future
which awaits his son.[1] Phaethon views with distaste
this life of easeful splendour ; to him at this moment may
well be attributed the vigorous words [2]

> Each nook of earth that feeds me is my home.

Goethe has indicated, with splendid insight, the dramatic
power which must have filled this scene : the aged king
offering the easy joys of riches and a royal home to this
youth already burning in secret for the high enterprise
of seeking his real and divine father.

Later the interview was described between Phaethon
and Helios, who after seeking to dissuade him, granted
his request and added anxious instructions :—

> "Let not thy steeds invade the Afric sky :
> Its temper hath no moistness, and thy wheels
> Downward must sink. . . .
> Direct thy path toward the Pleiads Seven."
> Impatient of the rest, he snatched the reins
> And smote the wingèd coursers till they flew
> Unchecked thro' opening vistas of the heaven.
> His father, mounted on a blazing star,
> Rode after, warning him : " Drive thither, boy ! "
> "Wheel yonder ! "

The messenger seems to have continued with a
picture of Phaethon's fall. The body, still giving off the
smoke of destruction, is next brought in, and we possess
part of Clymene's frantic speech. Her grief is mingled
with terror : the strange manner of her son's death may

---

[1] This is an acute suggestion of Goethe.
[2] ὡς πανταχοῦ γε πατρὶς ἡ βόσκουσα γῆ.

provoke her husband Merops to inquiry and reflexion and so her long-past union with the Sun-god may come to light. She bids them hide the body in the treasure-chamber, of which she alone holds the keys. Soon the king enters amid lyric strains celebrating the marriage-day of Phaethon. He is giving orders for merry-making when a servant hurries out to inform him that the treasure-chamber is giving forth clouds of smoke. Merops hastens within, and the chorus bewail the disclosure which is imminent. In a moment the stricken father is heard returning with lamentation. The course of the last scene is not certain, but probably a god reconciled the king and his wife, giving directions for the disposal of Phaethon's body; a beautiful but obscure fragment,[1] redolent with the charm of breezes and murmuring boughs after all this blaze and splendour, seems to point to the story of Phaethon's sisters, who mourned him beside the western waters and were transformed into poplars. This god was probably Oceanus,[2] the father of Clymene. He alone (deity of the world-encircling water) could give unity to these two pictures, the radiant eastern land of Phaethon's youthful enterprise, and the distant western river where his sorrows and his end are bathed in dim beauty.

This sketch allows us to realize how much we have lost in the *Phaethon*. The romantic events and setting recall the *Andromeda*. Clymene's sorrow and shame mingle strangely with the gallant enterprise and bright charm of the whole, somewhat as Creusa's story is contrasted with the fresh cheerfulness of Ion. Above all, the noble simplicity and high-hearted adventurousness of Phaethon, inspired by his new-found kinship with a god and chafing at the placid programme of domestic honour and luxury which his supposed father sets before him—this is a concept of boundless promise.

---

[1] δένδρεα φίλοισιν ὠλέναισι ψυκτήρια λέξεται.

[2] The chorus in their terror bid the queen seek refuge with her father Oceanus.

The HYPSIPYLE,[1] which was produced late[2] in Euripides' life, is specially interesting through the discovery in 1906 of extensive fragments at Oxyrhynchus in Egypt. Previously it was known by scanty quotations of no great interest, though apparently much prized in ancient times.[3] The plot is now in the main clear. Hypsipyle, grand-daughter of the god Dionysus and daughter of Thoas, King of Lemnos, was exiled because she refused to join in the massacre of the Lemnian men by their women. Previously she had borne twin sons to Jason. These she lost when expelled from her home. She is now slave to Eurydice, Queen of Nemea in the north of the Peloponnese, and nurse to her infant son Opheltes. Her own sons come in quest of her, and without recognizing their mother are entertained in the palace. Hypsipyle is quieting the child with a song and a rattle when the chorus of Nemean women enter. Next certain soldiers arrive from the host which the seven chieftains are leading against Thebes. Their commander, the prince Amphiaraus, explains that the army is in need of water, and Hypsipyle consents to show them a spring. Later she returns in anguish : during her absence the child has been killed by a great serpent. Eurydice is about to slay her, when she appeals to Amphiaraus, who pleads her cause and promises Eurydice that the Greeks shall found a festival in honour of the child. (This festival is that of the famous Nemean Games.) He sees that this fatal accident is a bad omen for the enterprise of the Seven, and names the child Archemorus[4] instead of Opheltes. Eurydice is appeased. Later we find Hypsipyle and her sons made known to one another, and the god Dionysus appears, apparently to arrange future events.

[1] See *Oxyrhynchus Papyri*, VI, pp. 19-106.
[2] The scholiast on *Frogs*, v. 53, which was performed in 405 B.C. (the year after Euripides' death) mentions the *Hypsipyle* among recent plays.
[3] The critic Didymus, for instance, knew the *Hypsipyle* better than the *Bacchæ*. For "Achelous" as a synonym for "water" he quotes the former play rather than *Bacchæ*, 625. See Macrobius, V, xviii. 12.
[4] That is, "the beginning of doom".

Though there is one difficulty as to the plot, namely, that we do not know what function was assigned to Hypsipyle's sons—they cannot have been introduced merely for the recognition-scene—the whole conception strikes one as simple and masterly. It has been well remarked [1] that while a modern dramatist would have omitted the Theban expedition, "nothing seemed to the Greeks worthy of contemplation in the theatre by a great people, unless it had some connexion with the exploits and the history of nations. . . . On the same canvas the death of one little child and the doom of the seven chieftains with their crowding battalions are depicted in a perspective which sets the former fatality in the foreground."

The captive princess, even through the ruins of the text, shines forth with great charm. Her whole life centres round her lost children and the brief magical time of her union with Jason. The chorus reproach her with her indifference to the exciting presence of Adrastus' great army—she will think of nothing save Argo and the Fleece. When at point to die her spirit flashes back to those old days in a few words of amazing poignancy :—

$$\text{ὦ πρῷρα καὶ λευκαῖνον ἐξ ἅλμης ὕδωρ}$$
$$\text{Ἀργοῦς, ἰὼ παῖδ' . . .}$$

" Ah, prow of Argo and the brine that flashed into whiteness! ah, my two sons!" Her talk with them towards the end is a pathetic and lovely passage equal to anything Euripides ever wrote in this kind.

MELANIPPE THE WISE [2] appears to have been a drama of unusual personal interest. Æolus espoused Hippe, whose daughter Melanippe became by Poseidon mother of twin sons. The god bade her hide them from Æolus, and they were discovered by grooms in the care

---

[1] Hartung, *Eur. Rest.* II, p. 442.

[2] Μελανίππη ἡ σοφή, so called to distinguish it from M. δέσμωτις, or *Melanippe in Prison.* The latter play seems to have been much less important. Unfortunately there is often a doubt, when authorities quote the " *Melanippe*," from which of the two the quotation comes.

of a bull and a cow. They, supposing the children miraculous offspring of these animals, reported their discovery to Æolus, who decided to expiate the portent by burning the infants alive. Melanippe was instructed to shroud them for death. In order to save her children without revealing her own secret she denied the possibility of such portentous births, but seems to have found herself forced at length to confess in order to prove the natural origin of the infants. Æolus condemned her to be blinded and imprisoned, her offspring to be exposed. Her mother Hippe appeared as *dea ex machina*[1] and saved her kin.

The great feature of this play was the heroine's speech in which she sought to convince her father that such a portent was impossible. Lines from the opening of this argument are preserved : " The story is not mine —from my mother have I learned how Heaven and earth were once mingled in substance ; when they separated into twain they engendered and brought into the light of day all creatures, the trees, birds, beasts, nurslings of the sea, and the race of men ". The speech was an elaborate scientific sermon to disprove the possibility of miracles. Similarly, according to a famous story, the drama opened originally with the line : " Zeus, whoever Zeus may be, for only by stories do I know of him . . . " ; but this open agnosticism gave such offence that Euripides produced the play again with the words : " Zeus, as Truth relates. . . . " A different but closely-connected source of interest is the fact that here Euripides veiled his own personality less thinly than usual. That Melanippe was only his mouthpiece appears to have been a recognized fact. Dionysius of Halicarnassus[2] observes that it presents a double character, that of the poet, and that of Melanippe ; and Lucian[3] selects the remark on Zeus in the prologue as a case

---

[1] See pp. 313-5.
[2] ἔχει δὲ διπλοῦν σχῆμα, τὸ μὲν τοῦ ποιητοῦ, τὸ δὲ τοῦ προσώπου τοῦ ἐν τῷ δράματι, τῆς Μελανίππης (quoted by Nauck).
[3] *Jupiter Tragœdus*, 41.

where the poet is speaking his own views. The "mother" from whom "Melanippe" learned her philosophy has been identified with the great metaphysician and scientist Anaxagoras, who was banished from Athens in 430 B.C.; and it is natural to suppose that this *Melanippe* is not much later than that year, perhaps much earlier [1] in view of the strongly didactic manner.[2] Hartung refers to this play the splendid fragment:—

> ὄλβιος ὅστις τῆς ἱστορίας
> ἔσχε μάθησιν, μήτε πολιτῶν
> ἐπὶ πημοσύνῃ μήτ' εἰς ἀδίκους
> πράξεις ὁρμῶν,
> ἀλλ' ἀθανάτου καθορῶν φύσεως
> κόσμον ἀγήρω, πῇ τε συνέστη
> καὶ ὅπῃ καὶ ὅπως.
> τοῖς δὲ τοιούτοις οὐδέποτ' αἰσχρῶν
> ἔργων μελέτημα προσίζει.

"Happy is he who hath won deep learning. He setteth himself neither to hurt his fellow-citizens nor towards works of iniquity, but fixeth his gaze upon the ageless order of immortal Nature, the laws and methods of its creation. Unto such a man never doth there cling the plotting of base deeds." If these lines point at Anaxagoras and belong to our play, the two significant clauses which defend the moral character of the philosopher in question indicate the year 430 itself.

The CRESPHONTES had immense success as a powerful melodrama. Polyphontes, having slain his brother Cresphontes, King of Messenia, seized his throne and married his widow Merope, who sent her infant son Cresphontes away to safe keeping in Ætolia. When he grew up he returned to avenge his father. At this point the action begins. Cresphontes seems to have delivered the prologue; since Polyphontes fearing his return has offered a reward to whoever shall slay him, he has determined to win the usurper's confidence by claiming to have destroyed his enemy. Meanwhile, Merope, alarmed by the proclamation of the king, has sent an aged slave to find whether Cresphontes is well;

---

[1] Hartung assigns it to 448 B.C.
[2] Cp. Aristotle's criticism, *Poetic*, 1454a: τοῦ δὲ ἀπρεποῦς καὶ μὴ ἁρμόττοντος (παράδειγμα) . . . ἡ τῆς Μελανίππης ῥῆσις.

he returns with tidings that the prince has disappeared from Ætolia.   Merope gives her son over for lost, and observing the youthful stranger who is received with joy by the king, she becomes convinced that he is the murderer of her son.   While he lies asleep she steals upon him with an axe, when the old slave recognizes the stranger and stops her arm.   Mother and son are united, and at once plot to slay Polyphontes.   Merope pretends to be reconciled to the king, who in his joy goes to sacrifice, accompanied by the youth, who takes advantage of a suitable moment to slay his enemy.

Plutarch, nearly six centuries later, testifies[1] to the sensation which the Recognition caused in the audience. Merope herself seems to have been a figure ranking with Hecuba in the *Troades*.   The tidings of her son's death draw from her words which in their quiet dignity of grief have something of Wordsworth :—

> Children have died ere now, not mine alone,
> And wives been widow'd.   Yea, this cup of life
> Unnumber'd women have drain'd it, as do I. . . .
>   . . . Insistent Fate,
> Taking in fee the lives of all I lov'd,
> Hath made me wise.

Probably it was Merope again who uttered the famous lines which advise lament over the newly-born and a glad procession to accompany the dead.   The recognition-scene is singled out for especial praise by Aristotle.[2]

The fragments of this tragedy include a perfect jewel of lyric poetry, a prayer to Peace :—

> Εἰρήνα βαθύπλουτε καὶ
> καλλίστα μακάρων θεῶν,
> ζῆλός μοι σέθεν, ὡς χρονίζεις.
> δέδοικα δὲ μὴ πρὶν πόνοις
> ὑπερβάλῃ με γῆρας,
> πρὶν σὰν χαρίεσσαν ὥραν προσιδεῖν
> καὶ καλλιχόρους ἀοιδὰς
> φιλοστεφάνους τε κώμους.
> ἴθι μοι, πότνα, πόλιν.
> τὰν δ' ἐχθρὰν στάσιν εἴργ' ἀπ' οἴ—
> κων τὰν μαινομέναν τ' ἔριν
> θηκτῷ τερπομέναν σιδάρῳ.

[1] *Moralia*, 110 D, 998 E.   [2] *Poetic*, 1454a.

A paraphrase might run thus :—

O Peace, thou givest plenty as from a deep spring : there is no beauty like unto thine, no, not even among the blessèd gods.

My heart yearneth within me, for thou tarriest ; I grow old and thou returnest not.

Shall weariness overcome mine eyes before they see thy bloom and thy comeliness ? When the lovely songs of the dancers are heard again, and the thronging feet of them that wear garlands, shall grey hairs and sorrow have destroyed me utterly ?

Return, thou Holy One, to our city : abide not far from us, thou that quenchest wrath.

Strife and bitterness shall depart, if thou art with us : madness and the edge of the sword shall flee away from our doors.

Matthew Arnold's *Merope* has the same plot and includes a recognition-scene which probably resembles the lost original closely. His conception of Polyphontes is thoroughly Euripidean.

Of the other lost plays little can be said here. Still amid this faint glow of star-dust many marvellous things are to be discerned—words of tremulous tenderness from the *Danae* describing the charm of infancy ; a line from *Ino* which in its powerful grimness recalls Æschylus, " like a lone beast, he lurks in caves unlit " ;[1] out of the *Polyidus* the celebrated query,

> Who knows of life that it is aught but death,
> And death aught else than life beyond the grave ?[2]

From an unknown drama comes a line which owes its preservation to St. Paul[3] :

$$\phi\theta\epsilon\acute{\iota}\rho o\upsilon\sigma\iota\nu\ \mathring{\eta}\theta\eta\ \chi\rho\acute{\eta}\sigma\theta'\ \acute{o}\mu\iota\lambda\acute{\iota}\alpha\iota\ \kappa\alpha\kappa\alpha\acute{\iota},$$

" evil communications corrupt good manners ". Euripides' cosmopolitan sympathy nowhere finds finer expression than in the distich

> Where'er spreads Heaven the eagle cleaves his path ;
> Where'er lies earth the righteous are at home.[4]

But the student must at his leisure explore the

---

[1] κοίλοις ἐν ἄντροις ἄλυχνος ὥστε θὴρ μόνος (*fr.* 425).

[2] τίς δ' οἶδεν εἰ τὸ ζῆν μέν ἐστι κατθανεῖν,
τὸ κατθανεῖν δὲ ζῆν κάτω νομίζεται ;

[3] 1 Cor. xv. 33.

[4] *Fr.* 1034 :—

ἅπας μὲν ἀὴρ ἀετῷ περάσιμος,
ἅπασα δὲ χθὼν ἀνδρὶ γενναίῳ πατρίς.

marvels of these rock-pools left by the retiring ocean. One majestic passage[1] from the *Cretans* shall suffice to close this survey. The lines are from a march sung by the Curetes or priests of the Cretan Zeus, and show that even in the Hellenic world the monastic spirit was not unknown :—

Thou whom the Tyrian princess bare
  To mighty Jove, thou Lord of Crete,
To whom her hundred cities bow,
  Lo, I draw near thy judgment-seat,

Quitting my home, yon hallowed place
  Where beams of cypress roof the shrine,
By far-brought axes lopped and hewn,
  Close knit by oxen's blood divine.

Pure is my life's unbroken calm
  Since Zeus to bliss these eyes unsealed ;
The feast of quivering flesh I shared
  While through the dark strange thunder pealed.

The Mountain-Mother heard my vows,
  And saw my torch the darkness ride ;
The Hunter named me for his priest,
  A mail-clad Bacchant sanctified.

Now robed in white I keep me pure
  From food that e'er has throbbed with breath ;
I shun the new-born infant's cry,
  And gaze not on the couch of death.

It now remains for us to attempt a synthesis—to set before ourselves as clearly as may be the whole personality of Euripides. We are studying not the programme of a politician, but the spirit and method of a great artist, the inspiration of a great teacher. An artist has other things to heed than a superficial consistency of presentation ; and a teacher of permanent value shows his followers not what to think, but how to think—not opinions, but the reasoned basis of opinion. Euripides is a man not of dogmas, nor indeed of negations ; he is the apostle of a spirit which blows whither it lists, setting up a healthful circulation of tingling life throughout regions

[1] *Fr.* 475.

which have languished in the heavy air of convention. His work forces us to think and feel for ourselves, not necessarily to think and feel with him.

The briefest description of his special quality is that he is in the same moment a great artist and a great rationalist—a man profoundly conscious of the beauty and value of all life, all existence, all energy, and yet an uncompromising critic of the vesture which man throws around those parts of the Universe which are subjected to him.   No man has ever loved and expressed beauty with a mind less swayed by illusion.   These two instincts, the instinct to study life in all its unforced manifestations, and the instinct to question all conventions, lie at the root of his work.   It is in virtue of these that he has been called enigmatic.   Like Renan he was ἀνὴρ δίψυχος, a man of two souls[1]; but he is no more an enigma than others.   His peculiarity lies herein, that the duality of nature often found in ordinary men was by him exhibited at the heights of genius.   That is why he so often seems labouring to destroy the effect he has created; he is "inconsistent" because he is equally at home in the two worlds of feeling and of thought.   Precisely for this reason he created a new type of drama.   Horace Walpole wrote that "Life is a comedy to those who think, a tragedy to those who feel"; thus, when a genius of Euripides' type addressed itself to the theatre, the result was drama which could not but shock people who, bred in the school of Æschylus, had no conception of "tragedy" which could be witty, light, modern, destructive.   Menander is the successor of Euripides, not of Aristophanes.

Anyone who follows out these two strands of instinct will understand much that might seem strange, much that gave offence, in his work.   It will be well therefore to bring together the faults which have been found with him in ancient and in later times.   Leaving on one side, since it is by no means certainly a reproach, the

---

[1] Mr. F. Manning, *Scenes and Portraits* (*Preface*, p. viii).

celebrated remark [1] of Sophocles, " I represent people as
they should be, Euripides as they are," we find our chief
material in Aristophanes and Aristotle. The *Frogs*
contains an elaborate attack upon the tragedian which,
whether fair or not, has a *prima facie* reasonableness.
Euripides is twitted with moral and literary offences.
In the first place, his predilection for depicting the power
of love, especially the adulterous or incestuous passions
of women [2] and the sophistical restlessness of mind which
he inculcates,[3] mark him as a corrupter of Athens. On
the technical side, his music [4] is affected and decadent,
the libretto [5] of his choruses is both elaborate and
jejune, the style of his iambics [6] lacks weight and dignity,
his prologues [7] are tiresome and written in a mechanical
fashion. Aristotle in his turn objects to certain weaknesses of characterization : Menelaus in the *Orestes* is
particularly bad, the speech of Melanippe—no doubt
that celebrated oration on miracles—is indecorous and
out of character ; in the Aulid *Iphigenia* the heroine is
inconsistent.[8] He gives two examples [9] of the irrational,
Ægeus in the *Medea* and Menelaus once more in the
Orestes. Euripides' use of the *deus ex machina* is also
often bad ; he instances Medea's miraculous chariot.
Lastly there is the famous mixture [10] of praise and
blame : " Euripides, faulty as he is in the general
management of his subject, is yet felt to be the most
tragic of the poets." If we pass now to modern de-
tractors, we find one fault overshadowing all the
rest—bad construction, what Aristotle calls "episodic"
plots, namely, plays the several scenes of which are
more or less accidentally combined and form no organic
whole.

---

[1] Aristotle, *Poetic*, 1460*b* : Σοφοκλῆς ἔφη αὐτὸς μὲν οἵους δεῖ ποιεῖν,
Εὐριπίδην δὲ οἷοί εἰσιν.

[2] *Frogs*, vv. 850, 1043 *sq.*   [3] *Ibid*. 954-8.
[4] *Ibid*. 1304-8, 1314, 1348.   [5] *Ibid*. 1309-63.
[6] *Ibid*. 1378-1410.   [7] *Ibid*. 1198 *sqq*.
[8] *Poetic*, 1454*a*.   [9] *Ibid*. 1461*b*.
[10] *Ibid*. 1453*a*. ὁ Εὐριπίδης εἰ καὶ τὰ ἄλλα μὴ εὖ οἰκονομεῖ ἀλλὰ
τραγικώτατός γε τῶν ποιητῶν φαίνεται.

There is truth in some of this fault-finding ; whether we are to regard such features as actually blemishes is another matter.   Two certainly are defects of the gravest possible description—" episodic " plots and the *deus ex machina*.   If a man produces plays which have no organic unity, or which at the close of the action are in such a tangle that a being of superhuman informa- tion and power is necessary to " cut the knot," he is no "unskilful dramatist" but merely a blockhead, for he can always fling his rubbish into the fire.   So hopelessly damaging are these two accusations that one really cannot believe Euripides obnoxious to them.   One might as well allege that Alexander did not understand tactics, or that Pericles believed Byzantium was in Sicily.   The charge of faulty construction has been considered earlier in connexion with the plays which are supposed examples thereof.   But the *deus ex machina* needs a few words.   " The god out of the machine " is a phrase of two applications.   It may mean a deity brought in to round off the play by giving information about the future history of the personages.   Or the god may be introduced when the plot, owing to the human limitations of the characters, has become knotted and progress is impossible ; then a being who miraculously knows all the facts appears and " cuts " the knot.   In the first case the epiphany is practically outside the drama ; in the second it is only too vital to it.   Of the first case there are five[1] instances in the extant plays : to these, of course, our grave objection cannot apply. Of the second type there are seven[2] examples if we regard the miraculous car of Medea as a "deus". *Granted the story which is known to the audience*, such interventions are necessary.   Medea cannot escape the vengeance of Corinth, Orestes the verdict of the Argive

---

[1] *Andromache, Electra, Bacchæ, Rhesus,* and the original text of the *Iphigenia at Aulis* (see Murray's *Apparatus* at the end of the play). Aristotle naturally allows such as these (*Poetic,* 1454*b*) : μηχανῇ χρηστέον ἐπὶ τὰ ἔξω τοῦ δράματος, κτέ.

[2] In the extant plays.   Of course there were others, which we cannot discuss with knowledge, *e.g.* the close of *Melanippe the Wise.*

State, without supernatural aid ; Theseus would, it might seem, never have been persuaded by mortal witness that Hippolytus is innocent; in the Tauric *Iphigenia* and the *Helena*[1] nothing but a miracle can save from death the fugitives who as a matter of "history" reached home in safety : the *Supplices* would end without the formal compact between rescuers and rescued if the goddess did not intervene; as for the *Ion*, Euripides' contemporaries knew that Delphi still flourished, so that the annihilating investigation of Ion must, it appeared, have been somehow arrested.   For these seven plays, then, we can choose between two theories of the *deus ex machina* (in that second sense of a pseudo-dramatic expedient).   The first theory is that the poet wishes to end with "historical" truth, but in the course of his action has so blundered that he cannot naturally do so; therefore he puts forward a god who asserts that the action *shall* continue as "history" asserts that it did; so might a competitor in a match of archery employ a confederate who, whenever his arrow missed the target, should pick it up and plant it in the white.   The other theory is that Euripides intended to work out an interesting situation of legend as a study in natural psychology and social development.   The situation according to story came to a certain end; according to Euripides that was not the natural end.   And he emphasizes this legendary distortion by pointing out clearly that to square nature and the story nothing less than a miracle is required. To assert that he needed the supernatural intervention to save his play is absolutely to reverse the facts. Can we doubt which of these theories is sound ?

Two further questions at once arise.   Why did he select situations from misleading legends ?   And, is there then no pseudo-dramatic *deus ex machina* at all?   The first question is of vital importance.   It is

[1] For the *Iphigenia* carries the *Helena* with it (see the discussion of the latter, pp. 260 *sqq.*).   As a matter of cold fact, to be sure, Theoclymenus could never have overtaken the Greeks,

incorrect to say that he was bound by convention to the traditional stories ; Phrynichus, Agathon, and Moschion all defied this "convention". Euripides was a student of human thought, of the development of belief, as well as a dramatist. Convinced that his contemporaries held false beliefs about the gods and that the myths were largely responsible for this, hypnotizing thought by their beauty and paralyzing logic by their authority, he sets himself to show, not only that they are untrue, but also how, though untrue, they ever won credence. As for the *deus ex machina* the truth is that he does not exist (save, of course, in the rôle of a non-dramatic narrator). He is, like the three unities, a figment based on uncritical and hasty reading. Outside this poet the only possible case is that of the *Philoctetes*, which has been shown no genuine instance.

We may now return to the objections raised by Aristophanes and Aristotle. They are all due to the two instincts we have described—his interest in every manifestation of life, and his stern rationalism. Most of the technical flaws, for instance, alleged against him are proofs that he was attracted by the possibilities of his own art ; he is constantly testing the limits to which development can go. The iambics of the *Orestes*, for example, are extraordinarily full of resolved feet ; after that play he restrains himself more. In music too he appears to have been an explorer ; at any rate the fault found with the words of his choruses points to a development like the modern, in which libretto was becoming subservient to music. The comic poet, again, fastens eagerly upon the prologues, and puts into the mouth of Æschylus a famous jest :—[1]

Æsch. : And now, by Jove, I'll not smash each phrase word by word, but with heaven's aid I'll ruin your prologues with—a little oil-flask.

Eur. : An oil-flask ? You . . . my prologues ?

[1] *Frogs*, 1198-1247.

Æsch.: Just one little flask. You write so that anything will fit into your iambics—a little fleece, a little flask, a little bag. I'll show you on the spot.

Eur.: Oh! you will?

Æsch.: Yes.

Dion.: Now you must recite something.

Eur.: " Ægyptus, as the far-spread story tells,
          With fifty sons in voyage o'er the deep
          Landing at Argos . . ."

Æsch.: (interrupting) . . . "lost his flask of oil ".
Several other absurd instances follow.

This celebrated jest means (i) that Euripides constructs the early sentences of his prologue in such a way that a subordinate clause (usually containing a participle) leads up to a short main clause at the end of the sentence ; (ii) that his prologues descend to trivial details ; (iii) that the *cæsura* occurs always in the third foot ; (iv) that he is viciously addicted to resolved feet. The tragedian can be defended from these charges, such as they are, but the idea at the back of Aristophanes' mind is true, namely, that these prologues are often dull performances. Probably the poet did not intend much more. He wishes to put his hearers *au fait* with the precise legend and the precise point with which he is concerned ;[1] as is often said, these passages take the place of a modern playbill.

Later in the *Frogs* Dionysus produces a huge pair of scales ; each is to utter a line into his scale-pan, and the heavier line wins. Euripides declaims into his pan the opening line of the *Medea*, εἴθ' ὤφελ' Ἀργοῦς μὴ διαπτάσθαι σκάφος, and his rival Σπερχειὲ ποταμὲ βουνομοί τ' ἐπιστροφαί. Dionysus absurdly explains that the latter wins because he has put in water like a fraudulent woollen-merchant, while Euripides has offered

_____
[1] He seems in private conversation to have maintained the necessity of this ; compare the criticism of Æschylus which he utters in the *Frogs*, 1122 : ἀσαφὴς γὰρ ἦν ἐν τῇ φράσει τῶν πραγμάτων. φ.τ.π. is precisely "prologue " in the Euripidean sense.

a "word with wings". Underlying this nonsense is
the truth that the Æschylean line is ponderous and
slow, that of Euripides light and rapid; it is like con-
trasting Marlowe and Fletcher. The difference is not
between good and bad, but between old and new.
Æschylus' iambic style is fitted most admirably for his
purpose. But Euripides has not the same purpose—
that is all. It is one of his most remarkable innovations
that he practically invented the prose-drama. A very
great deal of his "verse" is simply prose which can be
scanned. To compare such a passage[1] as :

> ἥξει γὰρ αὐτὸς σὴν δάμαρτα καὶ τέκνα
> ἕλξων φονεύσων κἄμ' ἐπισφάξων ἄναξ·
> μένοντι δ' αὐτοῦ πάντα σοὶ γενήσεται,
> τῇ τ' ἀσφαλείᾳ κερδανεῖς· πόλιν δὲ σὴν
> μὴ πρὶν ταράξῃς πρὶν τόδ' εὖ θέσθαι, τέκνον,

or a hundred others, with the beacon-speech in *Agamemnon* or Athena's charge to the Areopagite court, is to
ignore the whole point of a literary revolution. Who
would set a page of Hedda Gabler's conversation against
an extract from *Macbeth*, and affirm that Ibsen could
not write dialogue ?

Ibsen, indeed, it is particularly instructive to bear in
mind here. According to him "the golden rule is that
there is no golden rule".[2] Dr. Stockman's nobility
consists in telling the truth at all costs. Gregers Werle
insists on that course, and is seen to be a meddlesome
prig who ruins his friend's home. Here the Greek and
the Norwegian agree heartily ; for the "sophistry"
with which many at Athens were disgusted is only
Euripides' way of putting his conviction that there is no
fixed rule of conduct, still less any fixed rule for our
self-satisfied attempts to praise or blame the abnormal.
An impulse of pity ruins Creon in the *Medea ;* Lycus
in the *Heracles* turns his back on mercy, and is
destroyed also. The pride of glorious birth nerves
Macaria to heroism ; of Achilles it makes merely
a pathetic sham. Consciousness of sin wrecks and

---

[1] *Herc. Fur.*, 601 *sqq.*   [2] Mr. G. B. Shaw.

tortures Phædra, while to Helen in *Orestes* it means
little more than a picturesque melancholy.   Hermione
in *Andromache* and Creusa both go to all lengths in
their passionate yearning for domestic happiness; one
destroys her husband and her own future, the other
reaps deeper bliss than she dared to hope.   Iphigenia
and Hippolytus serve the same goddess, but amid what
different atmospheres and diverse destinies!   This consciousness that effort brings about results different from
its aims, that chance, whatever chance may be, is too
potent to allow any faith in orthodox deities, only in
moods of despair wrings from the poet such outcry as
Hecuba's, that Fate is "a capering idiot".[1]   But it has
planted surely in his mind the conviction that there is
no golden rule of conduct.   And hence that "love of
forensic rhetoric" of which we hear so much—each case
must be considered on its own merits.

To this agnosticism we owe not only that treatment of religious legend which we have already studied
but the poet's greatest achievement.   Socrates, because,
as he said, he could not understand metaphysics or
astronomy, gave his attention to man.   His friend
because he despaired of a satisfying theology threw his
genius into psychological drama.   The centre of his
interest is the human heart.   Only one fact about
destiny can be stated as consistently held by him,
namely, that the spring of action and the chief factor in
happiness or misery is, not the will of Heaven or dog-
matic belief, but the nature ($\phi\acute{\upsilon}\sigma\iota\varsigma$) of the individual.[2]
Because he studies sin, not to condemn but to under-
stand, he has earned that reproach of Aristophanes who
rages at his predilection for Phædras and Sthenebœas.
What attracted him was not a desire to gloat or even to
pardon; it was the fact that the sinners he depicts are

---

[1] *Troades*, vv. 1204-6.   Cp. *Helena*, 1140-3.
[2] See Mr. W. H. S. Jones, *The Moral Standpoint of Euripides*, pp.
28 *sq.*   This view is also set forth by Jebb, *The Growth and Influence of
Classical Greek Poetry*, p. 218, and by Nestle, *Euripides der Dichter der
Gr. Aufklärung*, p. 174.

so intensely alive. A being dead in virtue engaged his
interest less than one who, however evilly, existed with
vigour. To this passionate interest in human life can
be referred as basis all the other themes on which he
spent study. Religion, as we have found, only attracts
him because it guides or misleads conduct. His political
studies have little concern with ethnology or economics;
they are only an expansion to a wider field of this same
interest in sheer humanity. Philosophy and natural
science are of value for him, as for Lucretius, in that
they provide an escape from paralyzing superstition.
If they are presented as a refuge from the facts of life,
he will have none of them. When Electra [1] seeks in her
knowledge of astronomy a far-fetched consolation for
self-fostered misery, she strikes us not as heroic but as
own kin to the febrile "intellectuals" of Tchekov's
Cherry Orchard or the novels of Dostoevsky.

His dislike of convention in morals is answered by
his originality in portraiture as well as in dramatic
situations. Nothing is more thrilling than to observe how
in the hands of a great realist whole masses of human
beings come to life. What was the background of one
novelist suddenly begins in the pages of another to stir,
to articulate itself, to move forward and discover a
language. "The men" commanded by Captain Os-
borne in *Vanity Fair* become Private Ortheris or
Corporal Mulvaney in the pages of Kipling. So in
Euripides the dim and familiar background of "barbarians" who existed merely to give colour and outline
to Achilles and Odysseus, the women who bore the
necessary children and ground the needed flour, the
henchmen without whom horses would not be groomed
or trees felled, suddenly awake and reveal passions of
love and hatred, pathetic histories, opinions about
marriage and the grave. In every age the man who
points to the disregarded, the dormant, hitherto supposed securely neutral and plastic, who cries "it is

[1] *Orestes*, vv. 982 *sqq.*: μόλοιμι τὰν οὐρανοῦ κτέ.

alive, watching you and reflecting, waiting its time "—
such a man is met in his degree with the reception
given to Euripides by the elder generation of Athenians.
The clamour of "crank!" "faddist!" "this is the thin
end of the wedge," and kindred watchwords, may be
found translated into brilliant Attic by Aristophanes.
But in virtue of these same interests Euripides became
the Bible of later Greek civilization.   He would have
passed into a fetish had it not been that the destruc-
tively critical side of his genius prevented the most
narrow-minded from reducing him to a system.   To
the last he remains inconclusive, provocative, refreshing.

On the other side his sensitiveness to all aspects of
life—his " feeling for Beauty " to use the familiar phrase
—held him back from mere cynicism.   The *Hippolytus*
remains as perhaps the most glorious support in literature
for unflinching facing of facts—it shows triumphantly
how a man may feel all the sorrow and waste which
wreck happiness, yet declare the endless value and
loveliness of life.   We may detect two aspects in which
this joy in life shows itself most markedly—his romance
and his wit.

Romance is not improperly contrasted with "classic-
ism," but as few Greek or Roman writers are classical
in the rigid sense it is not surprising to find romantic
features outcropping at every period of their literature.
Euripides himself is the most romantic author between
Homer and Appuleius, whatever our definition of
romance may be.   R. L. Stevenson's remark that
"romance is consciousness of background," Hegel's
doctrine that "romantic art is the straining of art to go
beyond itself," [1] and a more recent *dictum* that "romance
is only the passion which is in the face of all realism," [2]
each of them definitely recalls some feature of Euripides'
work already discussed.   A modern writer with whom
he can be fruitfully compared, at this point especially,
is Mr Bernard Shaw.   In many characteristics these

[1] See Mr. E. F. Carritt, *The Theory of Beauty*, p. 156.
[2] *Ibid.* p. 89.

two dramatists are notably alike : their ruthless insistence
upon questioning all established reputations, whether of
individuals, nations, or institutions ; their conviction that
there is no absolute standard of conduct ; their blazing
zeal for justice ; their mastery of brilliant lithe idiom.
But in their feeling about romance they diverge violently.
Perhaps the largest ingredient in Mr. Shaw's strength
is his hatred and distrust of emotion and of that spirit,
called romance, which organizes emotion and sees in
it a basic part of life. But Euripides appreciates it all
the more highly that he is not enslaved by it. Even in
such ruthless dramas as the *Medea* and the *Iphigenia in
Tauris* one remarks how the thrill and beauty of life
gleams out, if only as a bitter memory or a present pain
of contrast—the magic fire-breathing bulls and the heapy
coils of the glaring dragon in the remote land where
Jason won his quest, the strange seas, deserted beaches,
and grim savages among whom Iphigenia cherishes her
thoughts of childhood in Argos. The same sense of
glamour which inspires early in his life such a marvellous flash as the description of Rhesus' steeds :

στίλβουσι δ'ὥστε ποταμίου κύκνου πτερόν,[1]

and indeed the whole dashing buoyant drama—this
passion survives the shames and disillusionment wrought
by twenty-five years of tyranny and war ; it persists
even in those black but glorious hours when he wrote
the *Troades* and at the close of his life culminates in the
splendours of the *Bacchæ*. No attentive student of his
work can ignore this effect, but if we possessed all his
plays we should be in no danger of accepting the idea
that Euripides is beyond all other things a bitter realist.
The *Andromeda* and the *Phaethon* would have redressed
the balance.

The wit of Euripides cannot easily be discussed ; it
often depends upon idiomatic subtlety, and must almost
disappear in translation. But frequently, again, it consists in the method of handling a situation. Just as

[1] v. 618.

the playwright often makes of his drama, among other things, an elaborate *reductio ad absurdum* of myth, so is he capable of writing a whole scene with a twinkle in his eye. The clearest example is the *Helena;* Menelaus' stupefaction at learning that Egypt contains an Helen, daughter of Zeus, is indeed definite comedy :

> Διὸς δ' ἔλεξε παῖδά νιν πεφυκέναι.
> ἀλλ' ἦ τις ἔστι Ζηνὸς ὄνομ' ἔχων ἀνήρ
> Νείλου παρ' ὄχθας; εἰς γὰρ ὅ γε κατ' οὐρανόν.[1]

"And she told me that the lady was a daughter of Zeus! What! is there some person called Zeus living beside the Nile? There's one in Heaven, to be sure, but that's another story." Such a translation gives perhaps the intention of the words and colloquial rhythm of the last sentence. Here is comedy, but that of Congreve, not of Aristophanes. The distinction is important. Euripides is less comic than witty. As we turn his pages we rarely laugh, but a thousand times we break into the slight smile of intellectual enjoyment; one delight in reading an Euripidean play—tragedy though it be—is the same as that aroused by the work of Meredith. Euripides' sense of the ludicrous is a part of his restlessness in conception. Again and again he startles us by placing at some tragic moment a little episode which passes the pathetic and becomes absurd. When Clytæmnestra and Achilles bring each other into awkward perplexity over the espousal of Iphigenia the effect is amusing, and the intervention of the old slave who puts his head out of the tent-door must provoke a smile, even though we realize that he has misery and death on his lips.[2] After Creusa has given her instructions for the assassination of Ion, it is, though natural, yet quaint for the prospective murderer to reply : " Now do you retire to your hotel ".[3] In the *Medea* the whole episode of Ægeus, to which Aristotle objected as " irrational," is tinged with the grotesque. That the horrible story of Medea's revenge must hang upon a slow-witted

---

[1] *Helena*, vv. 489 *sqq.*   [2] *Iph. Aul.*, vv. 819 *sqq.*   [3] *Ion*, v. 1039.

amiable person like Ægeus is natural to the topsy-turviness of life as the dramatist saw it. In fact, just as Euripides on the linguistic side practically invents the prose-drama, so in the strictly dramatic sphere he invents tragicomedy. Nothing can induce him to keep tears and laughter altogether apart. The world is not made like that, and he studies facts, depicting the phases of great happenings not as they "ought to be" but "as they are". He would have read with amused delight that quaint sentence of Dostoevsky : "All these choruses sing about something very indefinite, for the most part about somebody's curse, but with a tinge of the higher humour".[1] It is indeed significant that sparkles of incidental mirth are (so far as a modern student can tell) commonest in that most heartbreaking play *Orestes*. One dialogue between Orestes and Menelaus, to take a single passage, is a blaze of wit—it exemplifies every possible grade of witticism, from the downright pun[2] to subtle varieties of iambic rhythm. Perhaps the most light-hearted and entertaining example[3] is provided by Helen who (of all casuists!) evolves a theory of sin as a method of putting her tigerish niece into good humour and so inducing her to perform for Helen an awkward task. Even more skilful, but ghastly in its half-farcical horror, is the dialogue between Orestes and the escaped Phrygian slave.

Later ages of Greek civilization looked upon Euripides as a mighty leader of thought, a great voice expressing all the wisdom of their fathers, all the pains and perplexities familiar to themselves. After generations had passed it was easy to dwell upon one side only of his genius, and for Plutarch or Stobæus to regard him as the poet of sad wisdom :—

> Amongst us one,
> Who most has suffer'd, takes dejectedly
> His seat upon the intellectual throne ;

---

[1] *The Possessed*, Ch. I.   [2] v. 674 : ὦ πατρὸς ὅμαιμε θεῖε.
[3] *Orestes*, vv. 71-111.

And all his store of sad experience he
Lays bare of wretched days ! [1]

But his own contemporaries, living in the days before
Ægospotami and knowing the many facets of his spirit,
could not so well accept a man of such contradictions,
who was in strange earnest about things they felt to
be indifferent, and who smiled at such odd moments.
Euripides must often have felt himself very lonely in
Athens. " My soul," he cries, " lay not hold upon words
of subtlety.   Why admit these strange high thoughts,
if thou hast no peers for audience to thy serious musings? " [2]   And again :—

Though far beyond my ken a wise man dwell,
Across the earth I greet him for a friend.[3]

It may be that Europeans of our own day are better
fitted to estimate him aright than enthusiasts under the
Empire or his companions who saw him too close at
hand.   During the last half-century we have witnessed
great changes which have their counterpart in the Athens
for which he wrote.   Hopes have been realized only
to prove disappointments and the source of fresh perplexities.   In England the spread of knowledge has
resulted not in a cultivated, but in a mentally restless
people.   Universal ability to read has for its most obvious
fruit not wider knowledge of literature, but more news-
papers and a rank jungle of " popular " writing.   Similarly at Athens the sophists had produced mental avidity

---

[1] M. Arnold, *The Scholar-Gipsy*.   Cp. Mrs. Browning's well-known
lines on " Our Euripides the human ".

[2] *Fr.* 916 :—

μή μοι
λεπτῶν θίγγανε μύθων, ψυχή ·
τί περισσὰ φρονεῖς, εἰ μὴ μέλλεις
σεμνύνεσθαι παρ' ὁμοίοις ;

[3] *Fr.* 894 :—

σοφὸν γὰρ ἄνδρα, κἂν ἑκὰς ναίῃ χθονός,
κἂν μήποτ' ὄσσοις εἰσίδω, κρίνω φίλον.

And Nestle (p. 368) aptly quotes from Schiller's *Don Carlos* (III, 10) :

Das Jahrhundert
Ist meinem Ideal nicht reif.   Ich lebe
Ein bürger derer, welche kommen werden.

where there was no quickening of spiritual vigour to correspond. Another fact of vital import has been the rise of our working-class to solidarity and political power : it probably resembles that "demos" which Cleon led more closely than "the masses" with which Peel or Russell had to deal. Again, experience of war has shown how small is the effect which settled government, social reform, and education have exercised upon the raw, primitive, human instincts, both base and noble. In Greece, the empire of Athens, with its tyranny and selfishness, and the Peloponnesian war which had produced a frightful corruption of conduct and ideals,[1] tainted society with that cynicism (ἀναίδεια) of which Euripides so often speaks. Just as we are severed by a wide gulf from the crude but not ignoble certainty, the superficial worship of progress which marked the Victorian era, so was Euripides severed from the "men of Marathon" for whom Æschylus wrote.

So it is that we can judge the poet of "the Greek enlightenment"[2]—or rather of the Athenian disillusionment —better than most generations of his readers. To aid us, there have naturally arisen writers to voice, in a manner often like his, our own disappointment and our renewed interest in parts of life and the world which we had ignored as unmeaning or barren. The disinherited are coming into their own. Mr. Thomas Hardy has written of the English peasant with a richness and profundity unknown since Shakespeare. He offers indeed another interesting analogy with Euripides : while the critics are concerned with his "pessimism" he remains for an unsophisticated reader a splendid witness to the majesty and charm of the immense slow curves of life, the deep preciousness which glows from the gradual processes of nature and that dignity of mere existence which survives all sin and effort. *Tess of the D'Urbervilles* is

---

[1] See the celebrated sketch of progressive degradation in Thucydides (III, 82, 83).

[2] Dr. W. Nestle's work is entitled *Euripides der Dichter der griechischen Aufklärung.*

the best modern parallel to *Hippolytus*. Meanwhile M.
Anatole France has given us many an example of that
ironical wit of which the Greek poet is so consummate
a master. Another Frenchman, Flaubert, has set as
the climax to his dazzling phantasy, *La Tentation de
St. Antoine*, an expression in un-attic vehemence and
elaboration of that passionate sympathy with all existence
which blazes in the lyrics of the *Bacchæ*—a yearning
which Arnold in the *Scholar-Gipsy* has uttered in milder
and still more haunting language.

There is no final synthesis of Euripides. Throughout his life he held true to those two principles, the
worship of beauty, and loyalty to the dry light of intelligence. Glamour never blinded him to sin and folly ;
misery and coarse tyranny never taught his lips to for-
swear the glory of existence. One of his own noblest
songs sets this triumphantly before us [1] :—

οὐ παύσομαι τὰς Χάριτας
　　Μούσαις συγκαταμειγνύς,
ἁδίσταν συζυγίαν.
μὴ ζώην μετ' ἀμουσίας,
αἰεὶ δ' ἐν στεφάνοισιν εἴην.

"I will not cease to mingle the Graces with the Muses
—the sweetest of fellowships. When the Muses desert
me, let me die ; may the flower-garlands never fail me."
The Graces and the Muses—such is his better way of
invoking Beauty and Truth, the two fixed stars of his
life-long allegiance.

[1] *Herc. Fur.*, 673 *sqq.*

CHAPTER VI

METRE AND RHYTHM IN GREEK TRAGEDY

§ I. Introduction

POETRY is illuminating utterance consisting of words the successive sounds of which are arranged according to a recurrent pattern. The soul of poetry is this illumination, its body this recurrent pattern of sounds; and it is with the body that we are now to deal. At the outset we must distinguish carefully between rhythm and metre. Rhythm is the recurrence just mentioned—the structure; metre is the gathering together of sounds into masses upon which rhythm shall do its work. Metre, so to put it, makes the bricks, while rhythm makes the arch.

Greek metre is based, not upon stress-accent,[1] but upon quantity—the length of time needed for the pronunciation of a syllable. In English the line

My bosom's lord sits lightly in his throne

is "scanned" (that is to say, marked off into "feet"— the metrical units) as a series of five iambi; the iambus being a foot which consists of an unaccented, followed by an accented, syllable. The word "bosom's" can stand where it does because the stress of the voice naturally falls upon the first syllable of "bosom"; to begin a line with "my seréne bosom" would clearly be wrong. The *length* of the syllables has no effect on the scansion. That "sits" needs as long a time for its

---

[1] A totally different thing from the written Greek accents ′, ` , and ˆ, which refer to pitch, not stress.

utterance as the first syllable of "lightly" does not alter the fact that "sits light-" is an accentual iambus.

Greek words, on the other hand, as metrical material, are considered only from the quantitative point of view, not the accentual. The voice-stress in the word λόγους rests upon the first syllable, but the word is an iambus, a "short" followed by a "long" (marked respectively thus ‿ –). Whereas an English blank verse consists of five accentual iambi, *e.g.*

To éntǀertaín ǀ divíne ǀ Zenócrǀaté,

the corresponding verse of all the Greek dramatists is composed of six feet each of which is theoretically a quantitative iambus, and most of which actually are such. Thus *Andromache*, v. 241 is to be scanned

$$\breve{} \; \bar{} \; \ | \; \breve{} \; \bar{} \; \ | \; \breve{} \; \bar{} \; \ | \; \bar{} \; \breve{} \; \bar{} \; \ | \; \breve{} \; \bar{}$$
τι δ ου ǀ γυναιξǀι ταυτǀα πρωτǀα παντǀαχου.

When is a syllable long and when short? A few rules will settle all but a minority. *All* syllables are long—

(i) Which contain a necessarily long vowel (η or ω), *e.g.* μην, των.

(ii) Which contain a diphthong or *iota* subscript, *e.g.* οινος, αινουμεν, ραδιως, save that the first syllable of ποιω̂ and τοιου̂τος (and their parts) is often short.

(iii) Which end with a double consonant (ζ, ξ, ψ), *e.g.* οζος, εξω, εψαυσα.

(iv) Which have the circumflex accent, *e.g.* ὑμι̂ν, μυ̂ς.

Most syllables are long the vowel of which is followed by two consonants. But there is some difficulty about this very frequent case. It can arise in three ways :—

(*a*) Both consonants may be in the same word as the vowel. Then the syllable is long, save when the consonants are (i) a voiced stop (β, γ, δ) followed by ρ ; or (ii) a voiceless stop or spirant (κ, π, τ ; θ, φ, χ) followed by a liquid or nasal (λ, ρ, μ, ν)—in both of which cases the syllable can be counted long or short at pleasure. Thus εσμεν, ομρφη, ανδρος ; but the first syllables of ιδρις, τεκνον, ποτμος are "doubtful"—they can be either long or short as suits the poet.

(*b*) One of the consonants may end its word and the other begin the next. Such syllables are *all* long. Thus, τηκτός μολυβδος, ανδρές σοφοι, although both these long syllables are "short by nature" (see below).

(*c*) Both consonants may occur at the beginning of the second word. If the vowel is naturally short, the syllable is almost always short, though such scansions as σέ κτενω are occasionally found. But if the second word begins with a double consonant or σ followed by another consonant, the syllable is always long. Thus ὁ ξενος, τι ζητεις, ταυτα σκοπουμεν.

A vowel, naturally short, when thus lengthened is said to be "lengthened by position".

The following types of syllable are *always* short :—

(i) Those containing a naturally short vowel (ε or ο) not lengthened by position, *e.g.* ἑκων, ὁλος.

(ii) Final *a* of the third declension neuter singular (σωμᾰ), third declension accusative singular (ελπιδᾰ, δρασαντᾰ), and all neuters plural (τᾱ, σωματᾱ, τοιαυτᾱ).

(iii) Final ι (*e.g.* εστι, τι), save, of course, when it is part of a diphthong.

(iv) The accusative -ας of the third declension (ανδρας, πονουντᾱς). But μουσᾱς (first declension). The quantity in both cases is that of the corresponding nominative.

Hiatus is practically unknown. That is, a word ending in a vowel is not to be followed by a word beginning with a vowel, unless one vowel or the other disappears. Almost always it is the first vowel which is thus cut off, the process being called "elision". In verse one would not write πάντα εἶπε, but πάντ' εἶπε; not ἔτι εἶναι, but ἔτ' εἶναι. When the first vowel is long and the second short, the latter is cut of by "prodelision," a much rarer occurrence. Thus τούτῳ ἀνεῖπε would become τούτῳ 'νεῖπε. Two long vowels, as in καλὴ ἡμέρα, are not used together at all. But the rule as to hiatus does not normally apply at the end of a verse; usually one can end a verse with an unelided vowel and begin the next with a vowel. If in any metrical scheme this liberty is not allowed, it is said that "synapheia [1] prevails".

We are now in a position to discuss the various metres to be found in Greek Tragedy.

§ II. THE IAMBIC METRE

Practically all the dialogue and speeches are written in this metre. The student would do well to grow thoroughly accustomed to reading these aloud with correct quantities before he attempts the others.

The iambic line consists of six feet, any one of which may be an iambus. But a "pure" iambic line, one in which every foot is an iambus, as in *Andromache*, v. 241 (see above), is very rare. A speech written solely in such feet would be highly monotonous and far too rapid. Other feet are therefore allowed, under restrictions, to take the place of the iambus.

By far the commonest of these is the spondee, which consists of two long syllables (λόγχη, πάντων). This can occur in the first, third, or fifth places—one, two, or all three. Thus :—

$$\bar{\ } \bar{\ } \mid \smile \bar{\ } \mid \smile \bar{\ } \mid \bar{\ } \bar{\ } \mid \smile \bar{\ } \mid \bar{\ } \bar{\ }$$
δῆσαι | βίᾳ | φάραγγ|ι πρὸς | δυσχείμ|ερῳ (*Prom. Vinctus*, 15).

$$\bar{\ } \bar{\ } \mid \smile \bar{\ } \mid \bar{\ } \bar{\ } \mid \smile \bar{\ } \mid \bar{\ } \smile \mid \bar{\ } \smile$$
ὦ τέκν|α Κάδμ|ου τοῦ | παλαι | νέα | τροφή (*Œd. Tyr.*, 1).

Next, the lightness and variety is often greatly increased by the use of "resolved" [2] (or broken-up) feet. Each long syllable being regarded as equal to two "shorts," it follows that the iambus can be "resolved" into ᴗᴗᴗ, the spondee into ‾ᴗᴗ, ᴗᴗ‾ (and ᴗᴗᴗᴗ, but this last is not employed in iambics).

---

[1] συνάφεια, "connexion," "continuity".
[2] These cause almost all the difficulty of scanning iambics. Till one is quite familiar with them it is a good plan to begin at the end. Nearly all resolved feet occur in the third or fourth place.

Of these three the tribrach (◡◡◡) is much the most frequent.   As it corresponds to the iambus, it can occur in any place, save the sixth ; it is exceedingly rare in the fifth place :—

$$- - | - - ◡ ◡◡ - - | - - - | - -$$
φαιδρωπ|ον εδιδ|ον τοισ|ιν Αιγ|ισθον | φιλοις (*Orestes*, 894).

$$◡ - | ◡ - | ◡ ◡◡ - | - - ◡ | - ◡ -$$
περιξ | εγω | καλυψ|α βοτρυ|ωδει | χλοη (*Bacchæ*, 12).

The dactyl (-◡◡) is allowed in those places to which the spondee is admitted, save the fifth (just as the tribrach is excluded from the sixth).   Thus :—

$$◡ - | - - ◡ ◡◡ - ◡ - - | - ◡ -$$
ου φασ|ι πρωτ|ον Δανα|ον Αιγυπτ|ῳ | δικας (*Orestes*, 872).

$$- ◡◡ | - - ◡ | ◡◡ - | - ◡ | - ◡ -$$
λογους | ελισσ|ων οτι | καθιστ | αιη | νομους (*Ibid.*, 892).

It is rare in the first foot.

Least common of all is the anapæst (◡◡-), which appears only in the first foot, unless it is contained entirely in a proper name, when it can occur in any place save the sixth.   This license is due to necessity : such a name as 'Αντῐγόνη could not otherwise be introduced into iambics at all.   Examples :—

$$◡ ◡ - | - - - ◡ ◡| - ◡◡ - | ◡◡ -$$
στεφανους | δρυος | τε μιλ|ακος τ|ανθεσφ|ορου (*Bacchæ*, 703).

$$- - - - | - ◡| - - | ◡◡ - | - ◡ -$$
δεσποιν|α γαρ | κατ οικ|ον Ερμ|ιονην | λεγω (*Androm.*, 804).

Occasionally a line is to be found with two or even three resolved feet :—

$$- ◡ - ◡◡ - ◡◡ - ◡◡ - | - ◡◡| - ◡ -$$
λουτροισ|ιν αλοχ|ον περι|πεσων | πανυστ|ατοις (*Orestes*, 367).

$$◡◡ - | - ◡◡ - ◡ - ◡ ◡◡ - ◡ -$$
μητερα | το σωφρ|ον τ ελαβ|εν αντ|ι συμφ|ορας (*Ibid.*, 502).

$$◡◡ - | ◡◡ - ◡ ◡◡ - | - ◡ | - ◡ -$$
αναδελφ|ος απατ|ωρ αφιλ|ος ει | δε σοι | δοκει (*Ibid.*, 310).

Two licenses should be noted.   The last syllable of the line may be short ; no doubt the pause [1] at the end

---

[1] Sophocles sometimes neglects this pause.   Not only does he occasionally end a line with a word (such as the definite article) which belongs closely to the first word of the next line ; in a few places he elides a vowel at the end before a vowel in the following line.   See, for instance, *Œd. Tyr.*, 29.

was felt to help it out. Lines of this kind are innumerable, *e.g.* :—

$$\text{Κρατος Βια τε σφῳν μεν εντολη} \mid \overset{\smile\smile}{\text{Διος}} \textit{ (Prom. Vinctus., 12)}$$

(which is followed by a vowel—ἔχει). It matters little
whether such syllables are marked as short, as long, or
with the sign of doubtful quantity (◡). Next, synizesis
(συνίζησις, "collapse") occurs now and then—two
syllables coalesce and are scanned as one, *e.g.* μη ου,
πολέως :—

$$\overline{\alpha\lambda\lambda} \; \underline{\epsilon\alpha} \mid \overline{\mu\epsilon} \; \overset{\smile}{\kappa\alpha\iota} \mid \overline{\tau\eta\nu} \; \overset{\smile}{\epsilon\xi} \mid \overline{\epsilon\mu\upsilon\upsilon} \mid \overset{\smile\smile}{\delta\upsilon\sigma\beta\upsilon\upsilon\lambda}\overset{\smile}{\iota\alpha\nu} \textit{ (Antigone, 95)}.$$

$$\overline{\omega\varsigma \; \mu\eta} \; \overset{\smile}{\epsilon\iota\delta}\overline{\upsilon\theta} \; \overset{\smile}{\eta\tau}\overline{\iota\varsigma} \; \mu \; \overset{\smile}{\epsilon\tau\epsilon\kappa}\overline{\epsilon\nu} \; \overset{\smile}{\epsilon\xi} \mid \overline{\upsilon\tau\upsilon\upsilon} \; \overset{\smile}{\tau}\overline{\epsilon\phi\upsilon\nu} \textit{ (Ion, 313)}.$$

$$\overline{\sigma\phi\alpha\zeta} \; \overset{\smile}{\alpha\mu}\overline{\mu\alpha\tau\upsilon\upsilon} \mid \overline{\theta\epsilon\alpha\varsigma} \; \overset{\smile}{\beta\omega\mu}\overline{\upsilon\nu} \; \eta \mid \overline{\mu\epsilon\tau\epsilon\iota\varsigma}\overset{\smile}{\iota} \; \overline{\sigma\epsilon} \textit{ (Andromache, 260)}.$$

(Synizesis is specially common in the various cases of
θεός and θεά.)

Finally, two important rules of rhythm remain to be
stated.

First, there must be a "caesura"[1] in either the third
or the fourth foot. A caesura is a gap between words
in the middle of a foot. Either the third foot, then,
or the fourth must consist partly of one word, partly of
another. It is indicated in scansion by the sign ‖.
Many verses have this necessary caesura in the third
foot only, *e.g.* :—

$$\overset{\smile}{\alpha}\overline{\pi\alpha\nu\theta} \mid \overset{\smile}{\upsilon} \; \overline{\mu\alpha\kappa\rho}\overset{\smile}{\upsilon\varsigma} \parallel \overline{\kappa\alpha\nu}\overset{\smile}{\alpha\rho\iota\theta}\overline{\mu}\overset{\smile}{\eta\tau\upsilon\varsigma} \mid \overline{\chi\rho\upsilon\nu\upsilon\varsigma} \textit{ (Ajax, 646)}.$$

Many show it in the fourth only :—

$$\overline{\pi\rho\upsilon\varsigma \; \tau\eta\sigma\delta}\overset{\smile}{\epsilon} \; \overline{\tau\eta\varsigma} \mid \overset{\smile}{\gamma\upsilon\nu\alpha\iota\kappa}\overline{\upsilon\varsigma} \parallel \overline{\upsilon\iota\kappa\tau}\overset{\smile}{\epsilon\iota\rho\omega} \mid \overset{\smile}{\delta\epsilon} \; \overset{\smile}{\nu\iota\nu} \textit{ (Ibid., 652)}.$$

A still larger number have caesura in both places :—

$$\overline{\phi\rho\upsilon\upsilon\rho\alpha\varsigma} \mid \overset{\smile}{\epsilon\tau\epsilon\iota}\overline{\alpha\varsigma} \parallel \overline{\mu\eta\kappa}\overset{\smile}{\upsilon\varsigma} \parallel \overline{\eta\nu} \mid \overset{\smile}{\kappa\upsilon\iota\mu\omega\mu}\overline{\epsilon\nu\upsilon\varsigma} \textit{ (Agamemnon, 2)}.$$

This usage is essential to rhythm. It is of course possible for every foot in the line to exhibit a caesura, but

---

[1] Latin, *caesura* "a cutting".

one in the midst is necessary to prevent the line from falling into pieces. That coextension of word and foot which is naturally frequent must at one point be emphatically excluded, so that the whole line may be felt as a single rhythmical whole. Such "lines" as

$$- \; - \; \cup \; - \; - \; \cup \; - \; - \; \cup \; - \; \cup \; \cup$$
ταυτην αναξ λεγει καλην ειναι πολιν,

or

$$\cup \; \cup \; - \; \cup \; - \; \cup \; - \; \cup \; - \; \cup \; \cup$$
Οδυσσεως δουλοι μαχουμενοι ταχα,

are utterly impossible.[1] The first falls into six scraps, and the second into two mere lumps, of equal length. If a breach of the rule ever occurs, it is for a special reason. When Sophocles (*Œd. Tyr.*, 738) writes

ὦ Ζεῦ, τί μου δρᾶσαι βεβούλευσαι πέρι;

the dragging rhythm well represents the dawning dread of Œdipus. But the main caesura may be dispensed with if the third foot ends with an elision, apparently because, if the word could be written in full, the fourth foot would be divided between two words. Thus :—

χαῖρ'· οὐ γὰρ ἐχθαίρω σ'· ἀπώλεσας δ' ἐμέ (*Alcestis*, 179).

ζητοῦσι τὸν τεκόντ'· ἐγὼ δὲ διαφέρω (*Heracles*, 76).

The other rule is that generally called "the rule of the Final Cretic".[2] It is most simply stated thus: if there is a caesura in the fifth foot, that foot must be an iambus, *e.g.* :—

μη μὲ στυγησῃς· ουχ εκων | γαρ || αγγ|ελω (*Troades*, 710).

τον τουδε νεκρον ουκ αθαπτ|ον || αν | λιποις (*Ibid.*, 738).

---

[1] No such lines are extant in Greek, but an analogy can be found in Ennius' hexameter :

Sparsis hastis longis campus splendet et horret.

In the *Peruigilium Veneris*, the trochee is much too often contained in a single word, *e.g.* :

Hybla totos funde flores, quotquot annus adtulit.

[2] It is so called because the second half of the fifth foot *plus* the sixth will obviously have the metrical form $- \cup -$, which sequence of syllables, when it forms a single foot (as, of course, it does not in iambics), is called a cretic. The rule is therefore often thus stated : "When the final cretic extends over a whole word or whole words, it must be preceded by a short syllable".

This rule does not exclude from the first half of the foot long *monosyllables* which are in meaning and syntax closely connected with the "cretic" word or words. Thus τῶν σωμάτων is a quite correct ending, but not τούτων σωμάτων.

Subjoined is a scheme of the iambic verse as written by the tragedians. The writers of comedy allowed themselves licenses with which we are not here concerned. Euripides is much fonder of resolved feet than Æschylus or Sophocles.

§ III. The Trochaic Tetrameter

Under this head we shall deal only with trochees as used in dialogue. Originally all dialogue was written in this metre,[1] and they sometimes appear in extant plays when the situation is too hurried or excited for iambics though not agitated enough for lyrical dialogue. These passages are not usually long, and it is interesting to note that the longest are found in the two most melodramatic plays, *Orestes* and *Iphigeneia at Aulis*.[2] The metre is always the trochaic tetrameter catalectic [3] (sometimes called the trochaic

---

[1] Iambics were adopted because nearer to the rhythm of everyday speech. It has been held, for instance by Dr. J. H. H. Schmidt, that iambics are nothing but trochaics with "anacrusis" (for this term see below, p. 342). So near is the iambic metre to ordinary talk that one now and again finds accidental "lines" in prose. Thus Demosthenes (*Olynth.*, I, 5) writes δῆλον γάρ ἐστι τοῖς Ὀλυνθίοις ὅτι. . . . George Eliot, early in *Middlemarch*, actually produces two consecutive "lines": "Obliged to get my coals by stratagem, and pray to heaven for my salad-oil".

[2] Euripides is much fonder of this metre than the other two masters. Sophocles in particular is very sparing of it. That passage (*Philoctetes*, 1222 sqq.), where Odysseus and Neoptolemus hurry upon the scene in violent (iambic) altercation, would infallibly have been put into trochaics by Euripides.

[3] From καταλήγω, "to stop short".

octonarius), that is, a line consisting of eight feet, mostly trochees, with "catalexis". Catalexis occurs when the last foot of a line has not its full number of syllables, the remainder being filled by a pause in delivery.

Pure trochaic verses are occasionally to be found :—

κατα | πως αφ|ικομ|εσθα | δευρο | ταυτ αμ|ηχαν|ω, | (*Ion*, 548).
1   2   3   4   5   6   7   8

The mark ⌃ means that there is a pause equivalent in length to a short syllable. It is often found in the scansion of lyrics, and there one also at times uses ⌃ ⌃ ⌃, which mean pauses equivalent to two, three, and four short syllables respectively. As in iambics, the last syllable may be short by nature :—

ουχι | σωφρον|ειν γ επ|εμψε | δευρο σ | η Δι|ος δαμ|αρ, (*Heracles*, 857).

This metre is plainly analogous to Tennyson's

> Dreary gleams about the moorland flying over Locksley Hall.

But such purely trochaic lines are rare. Other feet are usually admitted, especially the spondee :—

βλεψον | εις ημ|ας ιν | αρχας | των λογ|ων ταυτ|ας λαβ|ω, (*Iph. Aul.*, 320).

Spondees may occur only in the second, fourth, or sixth foot.

The tribrach also is often employed by Euripides :—

ψηφον | αμφ ημ|ων πολ|ιτας | επι φον|ῳ θεσθ|αι χρε|ων, (*Orestes*, 756).

ευτυχ|εις δ ημ|εις εσ|ομεθα | ταλλα δ | ου λεγ|ουσ ομ|ως, (*Iph. Taur.*, 1232).

The fifth foot is the favourite place for the tribrach, and next to that the first :—

χρονιος | αλλ ομ|ως ταχ|ιστα | κακος εφ|ωραθ|η φιλ|οις, (*Orestes*, 740).

Euripides, late in his career, introduced a good deal of license, here as elsewhere. Firstly, tribrachs become far more frequent and occur in unusual places :—

ανοσι|ος πεφ|υκας | αλλ ου | πατριδος | ως συ | πολεμι|ος, (*Phœnissæ*, 609).

To place a resolved foot practically at the end of the
line is bold—the metre is shaken almost to pieces.
Here, as in other respects, Euripides points forward to
the conversational manner of the New Comedy. But
he goes further, and allows feet hitherto not found in
trochaics: the anapæst and the dactyl. The latter,
however, is extremely rare[1] and employed only with
proper names:—

$$- \; \cup \; - \; \cup \; - \; \cup \; - \; \cup \; - \; \cup \; - \; \cup \; -.$$
συγγον|ον τ εμ|ην Πυλαδ|ην τε | τον ταδ|ε ξυνδρ|ωντα | μοι‚ (*Orestes*, 1535).

$$- \; \cup \; - \; \cup \; \cup \; \cup \; - \; \cup \; - \; \cup \; - \; \cup \cup$$
εις αρ | Ιφιγεν|ειαν | Ελενης | νοστος | ην πεπρ|ωμεν|ος‚ (*Iph. Aul.*, 882).

The anapæst is commoner (there is a proper-name
instance in the line just quoted):—

$$- \; \cup \; - \; \cup \; \cup \; \cup \; - \; - \; \cup \; - \; \cup \; \cup \; - \; \cup \;$$
ως νιν | ικετευσ|ω με | σωσαι | το γε δικ|αιον | ωδ εχ|ει‚ (*Orestes*, 797).

$$- \; \cup \; - \; \cup \; \cup \; \cup \; - \; - \; \cup \; - \; \cup \; -$$
και συ | μητερ | αθεμιτ|ον σοι | μητρος | ονομαζ|ειν καρ|α‚ (*Phœn.*, 612).

There is no rule as to caesura. The end of the
fourth foot regularly coincides with the end of a word;
such an arrangement is named diaeresis.[2] In all extant
tragedy only one certain exception to this rule is found:—

$$- \; \cup \; - \; \cup \; - \; \cup \; - \; - \; - \; \cup \; -$$
ει δοκ|ει στειχ|ωμεν | ω γενν|αιον | ειρηκ|ως επ|ος‚ (*Philoctetes*, 1402).

Since diaeresis is practically always found in so many
hundreds of lines, being preserved even in the loosest
writing of Euripides, why should we regard the recognized trochaic verse as an unity? Why not write,
e.g.:—

> οὐ γὰρ ἂν ξυμβαῖμεν ἄλλως
> ἢ 'πὶ τοῖς εἰρημένοις,
> ὥστ' ἐμὲ σκήπτρων κρατοῦντα
> τῆσδ' ἄνακτ' εἶναι χθονός (*Phœnissæ*, 590 *sq.*).

If the line falls into two clearly marked halves, why not
show this to the eye? There is no unanswerable
objection to doing so—the passage above corresponds
exactly in rhythmical form to much English verse,
e.g.:—

---

[1] The two instances given are, in fact, all that I have found.
[2] διαίρεσις, "division".

> Art is long, and Time is fleeting,
> And our hearts, though stout and brave,
> Still, like muffled drums, are beating
> Funeral marches to the grave.

The practice in English is to break up the long trochaic "line" into two when the words at the diaeresis rhyme (as in the above passage from Longfellow), but not to do so when the only rhymes occur at the catalectic foot. We print the opening of another poem by Longfellow thus :—

> In the market-place of Bruges stands the belfry old and brown ;
> Thrice consumed and thrice rebuilded, still it watches o'er the town.

In Greek there is, of course, no rhyme-scheme to settle this, but the regular catalexis is felt to mark off separate units. The entire question depends upon personal fancy,[1] though the instance from the *Philoctetes* shows that Sophocles at any rate regarded the whole octonarius as the unit.

Subjoined is the scheme :—

1	2	3	4	5	6	7	8
‾ ◡	‾ ◡	‾ ◡	‾ ◡	‾ ◡	‾ ◡	‾ ◡	‾ ‸
◡ ◡ ◡	‾ ‾	◡ ◡ ◡	‾ ‾	◡ ◡ ◡	‾ ‾	◡ ◡ ◡	
	◡ ◡ ◡	[‾ ◡ ◡]	◡ ◡ ◡		◡ ◡ ◡		
	◡ ◡ ‾		◡ ◡ ‾		◡ ◡ ‾		
	[‾ ◡ ◡]						

§ IV. The Anapæstic Metre

Whereas iambics and trochaics were declaimed by the actors, anapæsts were used mostly by the chorus, and were chanted in recitative. They are found when the chorus move into the orchestra, or salute the entrance of a new character. Most tragedies end with a brief anapæstic system, executed by the singers as they depart.

The most usual line is a tetrapody—that is, a verse of four feet :—

$$\overset{\smallsmile\smallsmile\ -}{τι\ συ\ προς} \mid \overset{\smallsmile\smallsmile\ -}{μελαθροις} \mid \overset{\smallsmile\ \cdot\ \smallsmile\ -}{τι\ συ\ τηδ|ε} \overset{\smallsmile\ -}{πολεις} ; \quad (Alcestis, 29).$$

[1] For example, the splendid poem by Anacreon beginning πῶλε Θρηκίη is printed by some in long lines, by others in short, even though the first, third, etc., long lines are not catalectic.

But lines consisting of anapæsts alone are very uncommon.   The spondee is often found :—

$$\text{–} \ \text{–} \ \cup\cup \ \text{–} \ \cup\cup \ \text{–} \ \text{–} \ \text{–}$$

ουκ ηρκ|εσε σοι | μορον Αδμ|ητου (Alcestis, 32).

Dactyls also are frequent :—

$$\text{–} \ \text{–} \ \cup\cup \ \text{–} \ \text{–} \ \cup\cup \ \text{–}$$

σφηλαντ|ι τεχνη | νυν δ επι | τηδ αυ (Ibid., 34).

No other foot is admitted, but each of these three may
occur at any place in the line.

Besides the tetrapody, we find now and then a
dipody, or verse of two feet.

Anapæstic systems are invariably closed by a catalectic verse :—

$$\text{–} \ \text{–} \ \cup\cup \ \text{–} \ \text{–} \ \cup\cup \ \text{–} \ \text{–}$$

αυτη | προθανειν | Πελιου | παις_κ (Ibid., 37).

In systems of considerable length such lines occur at
intervals.   They are called "paroemiacs".[1]

§ V. Lyrics

The metres of Greek songs form a difficult and
complicated study.   So long as we do not know the
music composed for them, the scansion of lyrics must
remain a more difficult and doubtful question than that
of the iambics, episodic trochaics, and anapæsts.

The best preparation for their study is the habit of
reading iambics and trochaics with correct quantities
and natural emphasis.   Let us, so prepared, address
ourselves to the following passage[2] from the *Agamemnon*
(975 *sqq.*) :—

<blockquote>
Τίπτε μοι τόδ' ἔμπεδον
δεῖμα προστατήριον
καρδίας τερασκόπου ποτᾶται ;
μαντιπολεῖ δ' ἀκέλευστος ἄμισθος ἀοιδά,
οὐδ' ἀποπτύσαι δίκαν
δυσκρίτων ὀνειράτων
θάρσος εὐπειθὲς ἵζει φρενὸς φίλον θρόνον ;
χρόνος δέ τοι πρυμνησίων ξυνεμβολαῖς
ψαμμίας ἐξ ἀκτᾶς βέβηκεν, εὖθ' ὑπ' Ἴλιον
ὦρτο ναυβάτας στρατός.
</blockquote>

---

[1] The meaning of this term is uncertain.

[2] I have, here and later, printed the readings and arrangement best
suited to my purpose.

It soon becomes plain that the passage is, at any rate in the main, trochaic. The first two lines scan easily, ending with a catalectic foot. We note that the third seems to drag at the end :—

$$- \cup - \ \cup \ \cup - - \ \cup \ - -$$

καρδι|ας τερ|ασκοπ|ου ποτ|αται,

for we remember that in the trochaic octonarius the last complete foot is never a spondee. But in the fourth line we are quite baffled :—

$$- \ \cup \ \cup - \ \ \cup \cup \ -$$

μαντιπ|ολει δ | ακελευστ|ος . . . ?

Anapæsts are very rare in trochaics, iambi unknown. That the iambus should never replace the trochee is quite natural. It would be hideous rhythm, in the first line of *Locksley Hall*, instead of " Cómrades, leave me here a little . . . ," to write " Dragoóns, leave me . . . ". The foot ολει cannot be right. The line seems hopeless ; or rather, if we have any knowledge of Homeric and Virgilian metre, we recognize something like the dactylic hexameter :—

$$- \cup \cup \ - \ \ \cup \cup \ - \ \ \cup \ \cup \ - \ \ \cup \ \cup \ -$$

μαντιπολ|ει δ ακελ|ευστος αμ|ισθος α|οιδα.

But is such a passage possible in a trochaic passage written for Greek music? It is known that in Greek music the notes corresponded closely to the syllables; music composed for trochees will certainly be in three-eighths time, for dactyls in four-eighths time. All these feet should have three beats, not four.

The next two lines are plainly similar to the first and second. In the seventh line we first wonder why, though we are in the midst of a grammatical sentence, the words should begin farther to the right than is usual, as if for a new paragraph. When we try to scan, we find once more the iambus-difficulty :—

$$- \ \cup \ - \ - \ \cup \ -$$

θαρσος | ευπειθ|ες ιζ . . .

If we work backwards from the end, -ος φιλον θρονον gives the familiar trochaic-octonarius ending, $- \cup | - \cup | - {}_\wedge$.

But the middle of the line has fallen to pieces, and for the present we leave it.

The eighth line seems at first more familiar. Is it not the ordinary iambic senarius of § II? But where is the caesura? And can we suddenly insert an iambic line into a trochaic system? Is it then possible after all to scan it as some kind of trochaics? Begin at the end. . . . $\overline{\epsilon\mu\beta\overline{o\lambda}}\,\overline{ais}_\wedge$ suits excellently; and if we work backwards we soon find that the whole would fall readily into trochaics if only we could ignore the first syllable :—

$$\chi\rho o\nu os\ \delta\epsilon\ |\ \tau o\iota\ \pi\rho o\mu\nu|\eta\sigma\iota|\omega\nu\ \xi\upsilon\nu|\epsilon\mu\beta o|\lambda ais_\wedge$$

But why should we ignore it? And why does the line begin farther to the left?

The ninth line again offers perplexity in the first half, clearness in the second :—

$$\eta\kappa\epsilon\nu\ |\ \epsilon\upsilon\theta\ \upsilon\pi\ |\ \text{I}\lambda\iota|o\nu_\wedge .$$

Grown by this time bolder, we attack the first half in detail, working backwards. $\overline{as}\ \overline{\beta\epsilon}$ is easy. Then $\dot{\epsilon}\xi$ $a\kappa\tau$ . . . may be either $-\cup$ or $--$, both of which are admissible. We are left with $\psi a\mu\mu ias$. Reading the whole line over slowly, marking the trochees carefully, we find ourselves somehow dwelling on the last syllable of $\psi a\mu\mu ias$. Why should we? If that syllable were only $-\cup$, all would be well; but it is not. Finally, the tenth and last line is quite easy :—

$$\omega\rho\tau o\ |\ \nu a\upsilon\beta a\tau|as\ \sigma\tau\rho a\tau|os_\wedge.$$

The whole passage then is trochaic; but we have met four difficulties: (i) the necessity to dwell upon certain syllables, (ii) the irrational presence of dactyls, (iii) the temptation to ignore the first syllable of $\chi\rho\acute{o}\nu os$, (iv) the insetting of $\theta\acute{a}\rho\sigma os$. Understanding of these four facts will carry us a long way. We take them in order.

Our first point indicates that we must revise that division of all syllables into "longs" of equal value and "shorts" of equal value (each "long" being exactly equivalent to two "shorts") which obtains in iambics.

The lyric metres recognize syllables of greater length
than ∪∪. Most frequent is the length ∟, equal to ∪∪∪.
A syllable of this length is therefore admitted in lyric
trochaic systems as a whole foot, and investigations, such
as we have practised above, will generally show where
such a foot is to be postulated. We can now scan
certain portions which we found troublesome :—

$$\text{θαρσος} \mid \overset{-}{\text{ευπ}} \mid \overset{\cup}{\text{ειθες}} \mid \overset{-}{\text{ιζ}} \mid \dots$$

$$\overset{-}{\text{ψαμμι}} \mid \overset{\cup}{\text{εξ}} \overset{-}{\text{ακτ}} \mid \overset{\cup}{\text{ας}} \dots$$

Moreover, as we were suspicious of the final spondee
(replacing the expected trochee) in the third line, we
obtain at any rate a quasi-trochee by scanning thus :—

$$\text{καρδι}\mid\text{as} \; \text{τερ}\mid\text{ασκοπ}\mid\text{ου} \; \text{ποτ}\mid\text{ατ}\mid\text{αι}_\wedge .$$

This prolongation of a syllable is called τονή ("stretch-
ing"). Such a syllable may fill a foot, as in trochaics,
and this rhythm is said to be syncopated.[1]

Next comes the dactylic fourth line, which introduces
another vital rule. Trochaic systems admit, not genuine
dactyls, but "cyclic" dactyls. To the "long" of each
foot and to the first "short" is given less than their
usual length : the rhythm is accelerated, so that - ∪ is
equivalent to -, and the whole cyclic dactyl, marked ⌣∪ ∪,
is equivalent to a trochee.[2] Whenever we see a number
of apparent dactyls, we must examine the whole passage
to find whether it is trochaic or not. Trochaic systems
which contain cyclic dactyls are called "logaoedic".[3]
The present line, then, being trochaic, we feel the same

---

[1] Greek συγκοπή, "coalescence". But ∟ need not fill a foot : for
instance in a true *dactylic* system we find (*Œd. Col.*, 1082) :—

$$\text{αιθερι}\mid\text{ας} \; \text{νεφελ}\mid\text{ας} \; \text{κυρσ}\mid\text{αμ} \; \text{αν}\mid\text{ωθ} \; \text{αγ}\mid\text{ωνων}.$$

Analogously to ∟ as a trochee, dactyls admit ⊔ (= ∪∪∪∪) as a foot.

$$\text{Θησεα} \mid \text{και} \mid \text{τας} \mid \text{διστολ}\mid\text{ους} \; \text{αδμ}\mid\text{ητας} \; \text{αδ}\mid\text{ελφ}\mid\text{ας}_{\overline{\pi}} \mid (\textit{Œd. Col.}, 1055).$$

[2] Before condemning this statement as a mere evasion, the student
should reflect that all such poetry is written for music, which would in
performance make the rhythm "come right".

[3] λογαοιδικός, "mingled of prose and verse".

doubt of the final spondee (which would equal ⌣⌣⌣⌣,
not ⌣⌣⌣, as it should) which we felt in the third line,
and scan the whole :—

$$\bar{\ }\ ⌣\ ⌣\quad \bar{\ }\ ⌣\ ⌣\quad \bar{\ }\ ⌣\ ⌣\quad \bar{\ }\ ⌣\ ⌣\ L\ \bar{\ }$$
μαντιπολ|ει δ ακελ|ευστος αμ|ισθος α|οιδ|α‸.

Our third question touched the first syllable of χρόνος
in the sixth line. It is, as a fact, to be regarded as
standing outside the metrical line—a kind of prelude,
called "anacrusis".[1] It is plain that neglect of anacrusis
will often throw our scansion out completely. A useful
rule can be given : in almost [2] any line, whatever comes
before the first long syllable forms an anacrusis. The
reason is that the first syllable of a foot must have an
"ictus" (see below) or stress-accent, and the foot-ictus
normally falls on long syllables. It becomes natural then
to pronounce the first short or shorts (if any) quickly,
and to give the first long the ictus ; in this way the short
is felt as a mere preliminary to the line. The anacrusis,
however, can be of three forms, ⌣, ⌣⌣, ‾. Its length
must be that of the second part of the characteristic foot,
⌣ for trochees, ‾ or ⌣⌣ for dactyls, and so forth. It is
marked off from the first foot by the sign : .

The fourth point was the insetting of θάρσος.
It happens in the middle of a grammatical sentence,
so that there can be no question of an ordinary paragraph. But if it does not point to a break in sense,
its only reference can be rhythmical. The whole passage
must fall into two distinct rhythmical paragraphs. Let
us scan them separately and endeavour to find a reason
for this break. Take the first, scanning, marking, and
numbering the feet :—

$$\bar{\ }\ ⌣\quad \bar{\ }\ ⌣\quad \bar{\ }\ \bar{\ }$$
τιπτε | μοι τοδ | εμπεδ|ον‸||
　1　　　2　　　3　　4

$$\bar{\ }\ ⌣\quad \bar{\ }\ ⌣\ ⌣\bar{\ }$$
δειμα | προστατ|ηρι|ον‸||
　1　　　2　　　3　　4

---

[1] ἀνάκρουσις, "striking up".

[2] Not all, for the first short syllable may be part of a resolved foot.

```
        -  ᴗ   -  ᴗ  -  ᴗ  -  ᴗ L -
καρδι|ας τερ|ασκοπ|ου ποτ|ατ|αι‸||
    1     2       3      4     5 6

        -  ᴗ ᴗ  -  ᴗ ᴗ  -  ᴗ  -  ᴗ L -
μαντιπολ|ει δ ακελ|ευστος αμ|ισθος α|οιδ|α‸||
      1       2        3      4    5 6

        -  ᴗ   -  ᴗ  -  ᴗ  -
ουδ απ|οπτυσ|αι δικ|αν‸||
   1     2     3    4

        -  ᴗ   -  ᴗ  -  ᴗ  -
δυσκριτ|ων ον|ειρατ|ων‸||
    1     2    3     4
```

If we examine this to find structural unity, it soon
appears. The first pair of lines answers to the last, and
line three to line four, in the number of their feet: 4 + 4,
6, 6, 4 + 4. The correspondence is indicated thus:—

$$\left(\begin{matrix} \{4 \\ \{4 \\ (6 \\ (6 \\ \{4 \\ \{4 \end{matrix}\right.$$

Each of these masses, it will be noticed, is marked off
by the sign ||. Such a mass is named a "sentence" or
"colon" (κῶλον, "limb"), and such a balanced structure
of cola is named a "period" (περίοδος, "circuit"). It
happens that in the passage just examined the "sentence"
division always occurs at the end of a word, but this
is not invariably so. We proceed now with the second
paragraph[1]—the second period as we shall now call it.

```
        -  ᴗ   L -  ᴗ  -  ᴗ  -  ᴗ  -
θαρσος | ευπ|ειθες | ιζ||ει φρεν|ος φιλον | θρον|ον‸||
    1     2    3      4      1     2       3    4

    ᴗ    -  ᴗ  -  >  -  ᴗ ᴗ  -  ᴗ  -  ᴗ  -
χρον : ος δε | τοι πρυμν|ησι|ων ξυν | εμβολ|αις‸||
   1     2     3       4      1     2    3   4 5 6

        -  ᴗL  -  ᴗ  -  ᴗ  -  ᴗ  -  ᴗ  -
ψαμμ|ιας | εξ ακτ|ας βεβ||ηκεν | ευθ υπ | Ιλι|ον‸||
   1     2     3    4      1     2    3   4

        -  ᴗ   -  ᴗ  -  ᴗ  -
ωρτο | ναυβατ|ας στρατ|ος‸||
   1     2       3    4
```

[1] The first syllable of πρυμνησίων in the second line, though long, is
musically equivalent to a short. Such syllables are marked with the sign >,
and the foot τοι πρυμν- may be called an "accelerated spondee". Syllables which carry a musical length different from their metrical length are
named "irrational".

That is : 4 + 4, 6, 4 + 4, 4. This would be an obviously well-balanced structure but for the last colon, to which nothing corresponds. Such an extra sentence is called a "postlude" (ἐπῳδικόν). Non-corresponding sentences like this are far from rare.[1] They may occur at the beginning of the period ("prelude," προῳδικόν), in the middle ("mesode," μεσῳδικόν), or at the end. This very period supplies an example of a mesode as well as of a postlude. The scheme is :—

The whole passage, then, consists of two periods connected by meaning and grammar, but—for us—by no more intimate musical bond than the common use of trochees. But the dance and music which accompanied the whole would clearly demonstrate its unity. The end of a period is indicated by]].

It is necessary now to consider briefly the passage which immediately follows (vv. 988 sqq.) :—

> Πεύθομαι δ' ἀπ' ὀμμάτων
> νόστον, αὐτόμαρτυς ὤν ·
> τὸν δ' ἄνευ λύρας ὅμως ὑμνῳδεῖ
> θρῆνον Ἐρινύος αὐτοδίδακτος ἔσωθεν
> θυμός, οὐ τὸ πᾶν ἔχων
> ἐλπίδος φίλον θράσος.
> σπλάγχνα δ' οὔτοι ματάζει πρὸς ἐνδίκοις φρεσίν
> τελεσφόροις δίναις κυκλούμενον κέαρ.
> εὔχομαι δ' ἐξ ἐμᾶς τοι[2] ἐλπίδος ψύθη πεσεῖν
> ἐς τὸ μὴ τελεσφόρον.

This is an exact counterpart in syllables, feet, cola, and periods, of the first passage. The first is called the "strophe" (στροφή, "turn"), the second the "antistrophe" (ἀντιστροφή, "counter-turn"). The chorus,

[1] The existence of these cola forms (to us who have not the music written for Greek lyrics) one of the greatest obstacles to a clear and easy perception of periodic structure.

[2] In lyrics a long syllable (if it does not end with a consonant) may be shortened—instead of disappearing by elision—before a vowel.

while singing the one, performed various evolutions about the orchestra, and these were repeated exactly, but in reversed order, while they sang the antistrophe. All these lyrics are so constructed ; the normal tragic "chorus" consists of one or more such pairs, though occasionally the antistrophe is followed by a passage called an "epode".[1] The epodes correspond to each other, not to the strophes. This equivalence of strophe and antistrophe is often of value in determining the quantities or the text in one of them.

We have now gained some insight into the nature of a Greek choric song. But before proceeding further it will be well to deepen our impression by taking from the *Agamemnon* (vv. 160 *sqq.*) another, and a simpler, pair of strophes :—

> Ζεύς, ὅστις ποτ᾽ ἐστίν, εἰ τόδ᾽ αὐτῷ φίλον κεκλημένῳ,
> τοῦτό νιν προσεννέπω.
> οὐχ ἔχω προσεικάσαι, πάντ᾽ ἐπισταθμώμενος,
> πλὴν Διός, εἰ τὸ μάταν ἀπὸ φροντίδος ἄχθος
> χρὴ βαλεῖν ἐτητύμως.

> οὐδ᾽ ὅστις πάροιθεν ἦν μέγας, παμμάχῳ θράσει βρύων,
> οὐδὲ λέξεται πρὶν ὤν ·
> ὃς δ᾽ ἔπειτ᾽ ἔφυ τριακτῆρος οἴχεται τυχών.
> Ζῆνα δέ τις προφρόνως ἐπινίκια κλάζων
> τεύξεται φρενῶν τὸ πᾶν.

> ∪ | L | L | –∪ | –∪ | –∪ | L ‖ –∪ | –∪ | –∪ | –ᴧ‖
> –∪ | –∪ | –∪ | –ᴧ‖
> –∪ | –∪ | –∪ | L ‖–∪ | –∪ | –∪ | –ᴧ‖
> –∪∪ | –∪∪ | –∪∪ | –∪∪ | L | –ᴧ‖
> –∪ | –∪ | –∪ | –ᴧ‖

$$\left(\begin{cases} 6 \\ 4 \end{cases} \right.$$
$$\left(\begin{cases} 4 \\ 4 \end{cases} \right. \text{—mesode.}$$
$$\left. \begin{cases} 4 \\ 6 \\ 4 \end{cases} \right.$$

---

[1] ἡ ἐπῳδός. The masculine word, ὁ ἐπῳδός, has a different meaning, with which we are familiar from the *Epodes* of Horace—a poem which repeats from beginning to end the same period, each period being usually two cola "which either have equal length, or the second of which is catalectic or 'falling' or is even shortened by an entire measure" (see Schmidt's *Introduction*, Eng. tr. by Prof. J. W. White, pp. 93 *sqq.*).

The chief interest of this subject is the art wherewith
the Greek masters accompanied variations of emotion
and the like with variations of rhythm. This passage
affords a simple and stately example. The heavy open-
ing ($\llcorner\llcorner$) is followed by the more confident trochees till,
at the last line but one, religious rapture (in the strophe)
and the ardour of triumph (in the antistrophe) burst
forth with the leaping cyclic dactyls.

We have now become acquainted with three rhythmical masses : the colon, the period, the strophe. Are
there others? What is a "verse" in lyrics? There
is no such thing.[1] One must, of course, distinguish
between a "line" and a "verse". Lines there must
be—that is an affair of the scribe and the printer ; verses
are rhythmical units, and there is no rhythmical mass in
Greek lyrics between the colon and the period. How
then are we to arrange our periods, there being no verse-
division? The most obvious way is to write each colon
as a separate line. The difficulty is that we shall often
be compelled to break words :—

> θάρσος εὐπειθὲς ἵζ-
> ει φρενὸς φίλον θρόνον . . .
> ψαμμίας ἐξ ἀκτᾶς βέβ-
> ηκεν . . .

Another method is to let each line run on until we reach
a colon-ending which coincides with a word-ending.
Here is no new rhythmical rule : it is purely a question
of convenience for the eye. Next, shall we ever write
lines of (say) two cola the first of which does close with
a word-ending? It is natural so to do when to the two
cola in question there correspond (whether periodically
or strophically) two cola which *must* on this system fill
one line only. For instance, in Æsch., *Supplices*, 656,
we shall write—

$$-\cup- \ \cup-\ \ -\cup-\ \cup-\ \ -\cup-\ \ -\cup-\cup \ -\cup$$
> και γαρ υποσκιων ‖ νυν στοματων ποτασθ‖ω φιλοτιμος ευχα ‖,

[1] Though my obligations to Dr. J. H. H. Schmidt's volumes, especially *Die Eurhythmie in den Chorgesängen der Griechen*, are very great,
I cannot see in his verse-pause—according to him (*Eurhythmie*, p. 89) the
foundation of his system—anything but a delusion. Dr. Schmidt's own
appendices show a good minority of "verses" which end with no pause.

though the first colon ends at the end of ὑποσκίων, because the corresponding passage of the antistrophe runs—

$$\smile\smile\,\smile\,-\,\smile\,\llcorner\quad-\smile\smile\,-\,\smile\,\llcorner\quad-\smile\smile\,-\,\,\smile\,-\,\smile$$

καὶ γέραροι δὲ πρεσβ||υτοδόκοι γέμοντ||ων θυμέλαι φλεγόντων ||,

where the first colon ends inside a word. It is purely a matter of taste whether we give a line to each colon, in which case the drawback is the breaking of words, or continue our line till breaking of words is excluded, the trouble about which method is the reader's difficulty in seeing where some of the cola begin.

We must now consider the most vital and difficult portion of our subject. How are we to determine the cola? The colon is the very soul of the rhythm. The period is generally too long for the ear to receive it as one artistic impression. The foot is too short; moreover, the mere foot too often tends to play us false: irrational syllables and τονή are against us. But the colon is neither too long nor too short. The colon-division serves the same purpose as non-commissioned officers in a regiment, or the determination of watersheds in geography—it gives a sense both of grouping and of control.

What precisely *is* a colon? It is as much of a strophe as can be uttered without making a new start. It is the embodiment of rhythm, as the foot is the embodiment of metre. In other words, it is a series of feet bound into a rhythmical unity by the presence of one main ictus. Three questions, then, arise. (i) What is an ictus? (ii) Which is the main ictus of a series? (iii) Can we with certainty determine the beginning and end of a colon when we have identified the main ictus?

(i) Ictus is stress-accent. The ictus of any single word is usually obvious. In the word "maritime" it falls upon the first syllable, in "dragoon" upon the second, in "cultivation" upon the third. In πάντων, λυσαμένοις, and κατάπαστος, it falls upon the first, second, and third respectively. Greek metre is based upon quantity, but Greek rhythm (like all other rhythm) is based upon ictus. A strophe can, and must, be scanned foot by foot on quantity alone ; but when we go beyond the foot-division to exhibit the structure of the whole, we must refer to ictus and nothing but ictus—for structure is an affair of cola, and the colon is created by the main ictus.

(ii) Among the many word-ictuses of a considerable passage, a few will be found which are heavier than the rest. These are simply the ictuses of the most important words. Each of these prominent ictuses gathers the neighbouring minor ictuses into a group round itself. We should begin then by fixing some obvious example, one (that is) where the main ictus is unmistakable, and on this basis attempt, by the help of the correspondences which we expect, to determine other main ictuses. The strophe will thus gradually fall into cola. This leads us at once to our third question.

(iii) Can we with certainty determine the extent of each colon ? Unfortunately no simple invariable rule can be given for the settlement of this vital point. But certain useful principles may be mentioned.

(*a*) A well-trained ear is the chief guide. Intelligent and careful reading aloud of an English prose-passage will show this. Take first (the best-known version of) a famous sentence of John Bright :—

> The Angel of Death is abroad in the land : you may almost hear the beating of his wings.

It is plain that this falls into two rhythmical parts, though we shall not expect them to correspond, since this is prose, not verse. If we set a dash for each syllable and mark the ictuses by one or more dots according to their strength, we find this scheme :—

$$\_\ \overset{.}{\_}\ \_\ \_\ \overset{.}{\_}\ \_\ \_\ \overset{.}{\_}\ \_\ \_\ \overset{..}{\_}\ \parallel$$
$$\_\ \_\ \overset{..}{\_}\ \_\ \overset{.}{\_}\ \_\ \overset{.}{\_}\ \_\ \_\ \_\ \overset{.}{\_}\ \parallel$$

(It will be noticed that in this superb passage the two periods do, as it happens, correspond in length.)

Who hath believed our report?   And to whom is the arm of the Lord revealed? (*Isaiah* liii. 1).

⏑ – – ⏑ – ⏑ ‖ – – ⏑ – – ⏑ – ⏑ ‖

So with longer passages, where, however, we shall find at times that our voice quite naturally makes a colon-ending in the midst of a grammatical sentence.

Therefore let us also, ‖ seeing we are compassed about ‖ with so great a cloud of witnesses, ‖ lay aside every weight, ‖ and the sin which doth so easily beset us, ‖ and let us run with patience ‖ the race that is set before us ‖ (*Hebrews* xii. 1, R.V.).

⏑ – – ⏑ + –
⏑ – – ⏑ – – ⏑
– – ⏑ – ⏑ – ⏑ –
⏑ – – ⏑ – ⏑
– – ⏑ – – ⏑ – – – ⏑ –
– ⏑ – ⏑ – ⏑ –
– ⏑ – ⏑ – ⏑ – –

(Observe how, in the last two cola, first the mounting and then the declining emphasis provide a splendid close.)

Let us now attempt so to catch the rhythm of a passage from Sophocles (*Antigone*, 582 *sqq.*) if set out as prose.

εὐδαίμονες οἷσι κακῶν ἄγευστος αἰών. οἷς γὰρ ἂν σεισθῇ θεόθεν δόμος, ἄτας οὐδὲν ἐλλείπει, γενεᾶς ἐπὶ πλῆθος ἕρπον· ὅμοιον ὥστε ποντίαις οἶδμα δυσπνόοις ὅταν Θρῇσσαισιν ἔρεβος ὕφαλον ἐπιδράμῃ πνοαῖς, κυλίνδει βυσσόθεν κελαινὰν θῖνα, καὶ δυσάνεμοι στόνῳ βρέμουσιν ἀντιπλῆγες ἀκταί. ἀρχαῖα τὰ Λαβδακιδᾶν οἴκων ὁρῶμαι πήματα φθιτῶν ἐπὶ πήμασι πίπτοντ’, οὐδ’ ἀπαλλάσσει γενεὰν γένος, ἀλλ’ ἐρείπει θεῶν τις, οὐδ’ ἔχει λύσιν. νῦν γὰρ ἐσχάτας ὑπὲρ ῥίζας ὃ τέτατο φάος ἐν Οἰδίπου δόμοις, κατ’ αὖ νιν φοινία θεῶν τῶν νερτέρων ἀμᾷ κονίς, λόγου τ’ ἄνοια καὶ φρενῶν Ἐρινύς.

If we first mark the quantities (ignoring, as we must at first, the possibility of ⌣ and ⌣⌣) and go over the whole carefully, we soon find that it falls into two corresponding portions : εὐδαίμονες . . . ἀκταί is the strophe, ἀρχαῖα . . . Ἐρινύς the antistrophe.   Next we look for rhythmical units.   On the one hand, there is the great difficulty that, since we must have both periodic and strophic equivalence, certain cola may take in words not belonging to the same sense-groups or grammatical clauses. On the other hand, the fact that we have two great masses which correspond exactly will help us. First, then, we note that εὐδαίμονες . . . αἰών looks promising, and observing that this points to ἀρχαῖα . . . ὁρῶμαι as a colon also, and that this is in itself likely, we mark off both these groups. Conversely, at the end of the antistrophe, λόγου . . . Ἐρινύς attracts us, and this is supported by the naturalness of στόνῳ . . . ἀκταί at the end of the strophe. Working backwards, and seeing a pause in the punctuation at precisely the same place in both halves, namely, after πνοαῖς and δόμοις, we assume that κυλίνδει . . . δυσάνεμοι and κατ' αὖ . . . κονίς are correspondent masses. But each is too long—sixteen syllables—to be pronounced as a unit. We soon perceive that κυλίνδει . . . κελαινάν, θῖνα . . . δυσάνεμοι, κατ' αὖ . . . τῶν, νερτέρων . . . κονίς, are all separate cola. Going backwards again, we find that ἐπιδράμῃ [1] πνοαῖς and Οἰδίπου δόμοις, ὕφαλον . . . πνοαῖς and φάος . . . δόμοις, Θρήσσαισιν . . . πνοαῖς and ῥίζας . . . δόμοις, and indeed longer masses still, all give a metrical correspondence. Which pair are we to select? οἶδμα . . . πνοαῖς (= νῦν . . . δόμοις) is too long; ἐπιδράμῃ πνοαῖς (= Οἰδίπου δόμοις) is too short. For we seek the longest unit which is convenient. We therefore mark off οἶδμα . . . ὅταν, νῦν . . . ὑπέρ, Θρήσσαισιν . . . πνοαῖς, ῥίζας . . . δόμοις as cola. The same method will give us ὅμοιον . . . ποντίαις and θεῶν . . . λύσιν. Then we find ourselves left with οἷς γάρ . . . ἕρπον and πήματα . . . ἐρείπει, which we divide after ἄτας and πίπτοντ'.

At last we can set out the passage according to its structure. The strophe runs thus :—

$$\text{ευ : δαιμονες } | \text{ οισι κακ}|\text{ων α}|\text{γευστος } | \text{ αι}|\text{ων}_{\wedge} ||$$

$$\text{οις γαρ } | \text{ αν σεισθ}|\text{η θεο}|\text{θεν δομος } | \text{ ατ}|\text{ας}_{\wedge}]]$$

$$\text{ουδεν } | \text{ ελλειπ}|\text{ει γενε}|\text{ας επι } | \text{ πληθος } | \text{ ερπον } ||$$

[1] The first two syllables (⌣ ⌣) correspond to the first (–) of Οἰδίπου.

ὀ : μοιον | ωστε | ποντι|αις‸||

οιδμα | δυσπνο|οις ορ|αν‸||

Θρησσ : αισιν | ερεβος | υφαλον | επιδραμ|η πνο|αις‸||

κυ : λινδει | βυσσο|θεν κελ|αιναν ||

θινα | και δυσ|ανεμ|οι‸||

στον : ῳ βρεμ|ουσιν | αντιπλ|ηγες | ακτ|αι‸]]

There are two periods :—

I

$\left(\begin{matrix} 6 \\ 6 \end{matrix}\right.$

II

$\left(\begin{matrix} \left\{\begin{matrix} 6 \\ 4 \\ 4 \end{matrix}\right. \\ \quad 6\text{—mesode.} \\ \left\{\begin{matrix} 4 \\ 4 \\ 6 \end{matrix}\right. \end{matrix}\right.$

To this the antistrophe of course corresponds, though here and there an irrational long corresponds to a short (*e.g.* -ειπει to ερπον); the last syllable of πήματα is lengthened by the following φθ.

It should be noted that this scheme differs somewhat from that given in Jebb's edition of the *Antigone* (pp. lxi. *sq.*). One reader's ear differs from that of another : hence the frequent divergencies to be observed between editors in the arrangement of many lyrics.

(*b*) The ancient writer Aristoxenus gives certain rules as to the maximum length of cola. They may be stated as follows :—

(i) There are three types of colon, the equal, the un-equal, and the quinquepartite. The equal cola are the dipody of 1 + 1 feet, the tetrapody of 2 + 2 ; the unequal are the tripody of 2 + 1, and the hexapody of 4 + 2 ; the quinquepartite is the pentapody of 3 + 2.

(ii) Equal cola must not be of greater length than sixteen "shorts". Therefore we may have a dipody of any foot, and a tetrapody of any save those of more than four shorts in value ; that is (*e.g.*) a dipody of cretics (- ◡ -) is allowed, but not a tetrapody of that foot, which would give 5 × 4 = 20 "shorts".

(iii) Unequal cola may have the length of eighteen "shorts". A tripody, therefore, of any foot is allowed, but a hexapody of trochees only : a hexapody of spondees would give 4 × 6 = 24 "shorts".

(iv) Quinquepartite cola may extend to the value of twenty-five "shorts". Pentapodies are therefore possible of trochees, dactyls, spondees and five-time feet.

(*c*) Certain detailed hints may be added :—

(i) The tetrapody is the most frequent length, the pentapody the rarest.

(ii) The end of a colon is often indicated in dactyls by a spondee, in trochees by a single long syllable (whether ∟ or - ᴧ).

(iii) In any one period there is a tendency to conformity in length. If 6 + 5 + 4 and 6 + 6 + 4 are *prima facie* equally possible, the latter is as a rule to be preferred. In spite of the difference in sum-total (6 + 6 + 4 = 16 ; 6 + 5 + 4 = 15), this question often arises, because of the possibility of τονή. It has to be decided[1] whether (*e.g.*) παντός at the close of a colon is to be scanned as two feet or one : παντ|ος ᴧ ‖ or | παντος ‖.

It is now time to offer an account of the various feet used in lyrics.

(*a*) *Trochees.*—With these we are now familiar. This foot is often called a choree, chorees with anacrusis

---

[1] How? By examination of the whole period. If we look at the seventh line of the strophe from *Antigone*, scanned above, it may seem arbitrary to write | αιναν ‖ rather than | αιν|αν ᴧ ‖. But the former method is suggested by the corresponding fourth line, which cannot possibly be scanned otherwise than as above, and which therefore has four feet ; hence we scan -αιναν so as to give the seventh line also four, not five, feet altogether.

being iambi,[1] without anacrusis trochees.   The trochee
is the most frequent foot in lyrics.   Such systems express
ordinary strong interest.   Whenever more definite
emotion is to be conveyed, either cyclic dactyls are
introduced, or a change is made to some other metre:—

> Κολχίδος τε γᾶς ἔνοικοι
> παρθένοι, μάχας ἄτρεστοι   (*Prom. Vinctus*, 415).
>
> $-\cup\,|-\cup\,|-\cup\,|-\cup\,||$
> $-\cup\,|-\cup\,|-\cup\,|-\cup\,||.$

So in English :—

> Then, upon one knee uprising,
> Hiawatha aimed an arrow.—(Longfellow.)

Resolution into tribrachs is frequent :—

> $\cup\cup\cup-\quad\cup-\cup\quad-\cup$
> Ἀραβι|ας τ αρ|ειον | ανθος || (*Prom. Vinctus*, 420).

Anacrusis is common.

(*b*) *Dactyls.*—These are found pure, or mingled with
spondees or quasi-trochees ($\llcorner\,\cup$).   They are often employed to express excitement and awe :—

> ὦ Διὸς ἀδυεπὲς φάτι, τίς ποτε τᾶς πολυχρύσου[2]
> Πυθῶνος ἀγλάας ἔβας ;   (*Œd. Tyr.*, 151).
>
> $-\cup\cup\,|-\cup\cup\,|-\cup\cup\,||-\cup\cup\,|-\cup\cup\,|--||$
> $-\,\vdots\,\llcorner\cup\,|\,\llcorner\cup\,|\,\llcorner\cup\,|-_{\pi}||.$

Anacrusis is found, as in the second line above and in
Medea, 635 :—

> $-\quad-\cup\cup\quad-\cup\cup\quad-\quad-\,\llcorner\cup\quad--\,\llcorner\,\cup\,-$
> στεργ ; οι δε με|σωφροσυν | α δωρ||ημα | καλλιστ|ον θε|ων $_\pi$ ||.

The tetrapody without spondees or catalexis gives an
exquisite heaving effect in Soph. *Electra*, 147-9 :—

[1] It is therefore possible to scan the ordinary iambics of dialogue as
trochees :—

> $\cup\quad-\cup\quad-\,\rangle\quad-\cup-\,\rangle\quad-\cup-$
> ειθ ; ωφελ | Αργους | μη δι|απτασθ|αι σκαφ|ος $_\wedge$ (*Medea*, 1).

This is the method followed by Dr. J. H. H. Schmidt, and of course
changes altogether the rules given above (§ II), but will hardly perplex the
student.   It has the advantage of bringing "iambic" dialogue closer to
lyric and to episodic trochees, but it has seemed more convenient to keep
the traditional statement.

[2] Printed as one line, though containing a colon which ends with the
end of a word, because the corresponding line of the antistrophe contains
a colon which does not :—

> πρῶτά σε κεκλόμενος, θύγατ||ερ Διός, ἄμβροτ' Ἀθάνα. . . .

ἀλλ' ἐμέ γ' ἁ στονόεσσ' ἄραρεν φρένας,
ἁ Ἴτυν αἰὲν Ἴτυν ὀλοφύρεται,
ὄρνις ἀτυζομένα, Διὸς ἄγγελος.

Ariel's lines in *The Tempest* (V. i.) :—

Merrily, merrily, shall I live now,
Under the blossom that hangs on the bough,

are dactylic tetrapodies with catalexis.

(*c*) *Spondees.*—It is not certain that these are used as a base, though as a variant in anapæstic and dactylic metre they are common. *Iph. Taur.*, 123-5, may be taken as spondees :—

εὐφαμεῖτ' ὦ
πόντου δισσὰς συγχωρούσας
πέτρας Ἀξείνου ναίοντες.

-- | -- |
-- | -- | -- | -- |
-- | -- | -- | -- |

But they may be quasi-anapæsts. the whole passage which they introduce being an anapæstic entrance-march, though heavily spondaic. *Ion*, 125-7 :

ὦ Παιάν, ὦ Παιάν,
εὐαίων, εὐαίων
εἴης, ὦ Λατοῦς παῖ,

is scanned by Dr. J. H. H. Schmidt as molossi, a molossus being - - -.

Spondaic systems are scarcely to be found in English.[1]

(*d*) *Cretics.*—This foot (- ᴗ -) is rare; it generally expresses piteous agitation :—

φρόντισον, καὶ γενοῦ πανδίκως
εὐσεβὴς πρόξενος ·
τὰν φυγάδα μὴ προδῷς,
τὰν ἔκαθεν ἐκβολαῖς
δυσθέοις ὁρμέναν   (Æsch., *Supplices*, 418 *sqq.*).

- ᴗ - | - ᴗ - | - ᴗ - ||
- ᴗ - | - ᴗ - ||
- ᴗ ᴗ ᴗ | - ᴗ - ||
- ᴗ ᴗ ᴗ | - ᴗ - ||
- ᴗ - | - ᴗ - ||.

---

[1] Because spondaic *words* are lacking. It is sometimes said that the only spondee in English is "amen". The peculiar pronunciation of this word is due to the fact that it is so often sung to music where each syllable is given a whole bar. The name of Seaford in Sussex is undoubtedly pronounced by its inhabitants -- ; but one may perhaps therefore argue that it should be written "Sea Ford".

Few cretics are found in English, though Tennyson's brief poem *The Oak* is written entirely in this metre, *e.g.* :—

> All his leaves
> Fall'n at length,
> Look, he stands,
> Trunk and bough,
> Naked strength.

Most English verse of cretic appearance is shown by the context to be trochaic with alternate τονή. So in *A Midsummer Night's Dream*, II. i. :—

> Over hill, over dale,
> Thorough bush, thorough brier,
> Over park, over pale,
> Thorough flood, thorough fire,

which is followed by

> I do | wander | every|where ∧ |
> Swifter | than the | moones | sphere ∧ | etc.

We are forbidden to view the Greek cretics given above in the same way, by the resolved feet. If we scan φρόντισον καὶ γενοῦ πανδίκως as - ∪ | ᴸ | - ∪ | ᴸ | - ∪ | - ∧ ∥, this method will give us in the fourth line - ∪ | ∪ ∪ | - ∪ | - ∥, where the second foot is impossible. ∪ ∪ can take the place of -, but never of ᴸ.

(*e*) *Bacchiacs.*—This curious foot consists of - - ∪, the system being invariably introduced by anacrusis. Bacchiacs are regularly associated with dochmiacs (see below). They express strong emotion, generally mingled with perplexity or vacillation; resolved feet are therefore often found :—

> τίς ἀχώ, τίς ὀδμά
> προσέπτα μ' ἀφεγγής; (*Prom. Vinctus*, 115).
>
> ∪ ⋮ - - ∪ | - - ∧ ∥
> ∪ ⋮ - - ∪ | - - ∧ ∥.
>
> στενάζω; τί ῥέξω; γελῶμαι πολίταις.
> ἔπαθον ὣ δύσοιστα (*Eumenides*, 788 *sq.*).
>
> ∪ ⋮ - - ∪ | - - ∥ - - ∪ | - - ∧ ∥
> ∪ ⋮ ∪ ∪ - ∪ | - - ∧ ∥.

> Ye storm-winds of Autumn !
> Who rush by, who shake
> The window, and ruffle
> The gleam-lighted lake.—(M. Arnold.)

∪ ː − − ∪ | − − ⌃ ||
∪ ː − − ∪ | − ᵗ⌄ ||
∪ ː − − ∪ | − − ⌃ ||
∪ ː − − ∪ | − ᵗ⌄ ||·

But it should be noted that, though bacchiac scansion seems soundest for the above—"storm-winds" for instance has two ictuses—the poet probably meant the lines for dactylic dipodies with anacrusis : "storm-winds of" thus would be an accentual dactyl. But that would slur "winds" unduly.

(*f*) *Ionics.*—These are formed by − − ∪ ∪. When anacrusis is found—the usual form—the foot is often called *Ionicus a minore* (*i.e.* ∪ ∪ − −) ; otherwise it is called *Ionicus a maiore :*—

> κυανοῦν δ' ὄμμασι λεύσσων φονίου δέργμα δράκοντος
> πολύχειρ καὶ πολυναύτας Σύριόν θ' ἅρμα διώκων (*Persæ*, 81 *sq*.).

∪ ∪ ː − − ∪ ∪ | − − ∪ ∪ || − − ∪ ∪ | − − ⌃ ||·

A strange variant is − ∪ − ∪ ; the variation is called "anaclasis" ("breaking-up"). Thus the above passage proceeds—

> ἐπάγει δουρικλύτοις ἀνδράσι τοξόδαμνον Ἄρη.

∪ ∪ ː − − ∪ ∪ | − − ∪ ∪ || − ∪ − ∪ | − ⌃ ||·

Ionics are employed to express strong excitement governed by confident courage. The first lyric of the *Persæ* begins with a splendid example. It is sung by the Persian counsellors in expectation of Xerxes' triumph, and makes a strong contrast with the piteous rhythms of the close. This poem should be studied carefully in comparison with another in the same metre—the opening of the first chorus in the *Bacchæ* (vv. 64 *sqq*.) :—

> Ἀσίας ἀπὸ γαίας
> ἱερὸν Τμῶλον ἀμείψασα θοάζω
> Βρομίῳ πόνον ἡδύν
>   κάματόν τ' εὐκάματον, Βάκχιον εὐαζομένα.
>   τίς ὁδῷ; τίς ὁδῷ; τίς μελάθροις; ἔκτοπος ἔστω,
> στόμα τ' εὔφημον ἅπας ἐξοσιούσθω·
> τὰ νομισθέντα γὰρ ἀεὶ Διόνυσον ὑμνήσω.

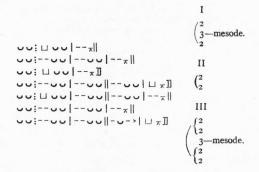

This song of the Bacchantes, like that of the Persians, expresses both excitement and confidence; both are magnificent, and the *metre* is the same. But the difference is unmistakable; it lies in the *rhythm*. In Æschylus the practically unvaried rhythm and the gorgeous language give to such a passage as πολύχειρ καὶ πολυναύτας Σύριόν θ᾽ ἅρμα διώκων an almost intolerable weight and austere pomp. Euripides, by use of the doubly-lengthened syllable, by varying the extent of his cola, and by the irrationality of the penultimate foot, has, within the limits of the same metre, produced a sense of exotic beauty and urgency, a thrill of wildness as well as of awe.

(*g*) *Choriambics.*—These consist of -‿‿-. Anacrusis is not found :—

δεινὰ μὲν οὖν, δεινὰ ταράσσει σοφὸς οἰωνοθέτας
οὔτε δοκοῦντ᾽ οὔτ᾽ ἀποφάσκονθ᾽ · ὅ τι λέξω δ᾽ ἀπορῶ (*Œd. Tyr.*, 483 *sq.*).

    -‿‿-|-‿‿-||-‿‿-|-‿‿-||
    -‿‿-|-‿‿-||-‿‿-|-‿‿-||

This measure expresses great agitation and perplexity. In the passage just cited they pass into ionics, which indicate a gradual comparative calming of mind. For example, the antistrophe reads :—

ἀλλ' ὁ μὲν οὖν Ζεὺς ὅ τ' 'Απόλλων συνετοὶ καὶ τὰ βροτῶν
εἰδότες· ἀνδρῶν δ' ὅτι μάντις πλέον ἢ 'γω φέρεται
κρίσις οὐκ ἔστιν ἀληθής· σοφίᾳ δ' ἂν σοφίαν
παραμείψειεν ἀνήρ.

- ∪∪ - | - ∪∪ - || - ∪∪ - | - ∪∪ - ||
- ∪∪ - | - ∪∪ - || - ∪∪ - | - ∪∪ - ||
∪∪ : - - ∪∪ | - - ∪∪ || - - ∪∪ | ⌣ x̄ ||
∪∪ : - - ∪∪ | ⌣ x̄ ||.

The late Rupert Brooks left some exquisite *Experiments*
in this metre, *e.g.* :—

> Ah! Not now, when desire burns, and the wind calls, and the suns
>   of spring
> Light-foot dance in the woods, whisper of life, woo me to wayfaring.

That is—

∟ ∟ | - ∪∪ - | - ∪∪ - || - ∪∪ - | ∟ ∟ ||

(*h*) *Dochmiacs.*—It is convenient to discuss these
here, though the dochmius is not a foot, but a colon.
The rule both of metre and music is that all feet or bars
should have the same time-value; a trochaic colon may
contain ∟ or -∪∪ as well as -∪, but not -∪∪. Dochmiacs are generally regarded as an exception to this rule.
The dochmius is a colon of which the simplest form [1] is
∪ - - ∪ -, to be divided ∪ : - - ∪ | - ∧ ||, *e.g.* κακορρημόνων.
The dochmius is always catalectic, but the anacrusis of one
serves to complete the trochee of the preceding colon :—

> φανήτω μόρων ὁ κάλλιστ' ἐμῶν
> ἐμοὶ τερμίαν ἄγων ἀμέραν (*Antigone*, 1329 *sq.*).

∪ : - - ∪ | - ∪ || - - ∪ | - ∧ ||.

But this simplest form is not the most frequent, and a
considerable sequence is rare. Resolution of one or
more long syllables is very common. The favourite
form is ∪ : ∪∪ - ∪ | - ∧ || :—

> περίβαλον γάρ οἱ πτεροφόρον δέμας (*Agamemnon*, 1147).

∪ : ∪∪ - ∪ | - ∪ || ∪∪ - ∪ | - ∧ ||.

This metre is frequent in passages of lamentation, and
as these are extremely numerous the dochmiac measure
is one of the most important. It is also perhaps the
most difficult, because of the many varieties admitted.
In all, twenty-two [2] forms are said to be found, though

----

[1] This important sequence may be conveniently memorized—if we
substitute accent for quantity—by the sentence "Attack Rome at once".

[2] I take this figure from Schmidt's *Introduction* (English Translation,
p. 76).

several of these are rare; this great number is due to resolution and irrational long syllables. Thus—

> ἰὼ σκότου
> νέφος ἐμὸν ἀπότροπον, ἐπιπλόμενον ἄφατον
> ἀδάματόν τε καὶ δυσούριστον ὄν (*Œd. Tyr.*, 1313).

> ∪ː ⎵ ∪ ⎮ - ᴧ ‖
> ∪ː∪∪∪∪∪ ⎮ ∪∪∪ ‖ ∪∪∪∪∪ ⎮ ∪∪ᴧ ‖
> ∪ː∪∪-∪ ⎮ -∪ ‖ --∪ ⎮ -ᴧ ‖·

The second line of course would by itself have no rhythm at all, being so completely broken to pieces, in order to express the extreme limit of agitation possible in articulate speech. But it gains rhythm from the clearer lines of the context. The antistrophe shows a further variety —an irrational syllable in the last line :—

> ἰὼ φίλος,
> σὺ μὲν ἐμὸς ἐπίπολος ἔτι μόνιμος· ἔτι γάρ
> ὑπομένεις με τὸν τυφλὸν κηδεύων.

(κηδεῦων). Evidently it is important to accustom one's ear thoroughly to the basic form ∪--∪- and to ∪∪∪-∪-. Another instance may be of use :—

> ἆρα πύλαι κλήθροις χαλκόδετ' ἔμβολά τε
> λαΐνεοισιν 'Αμφίονος ὀργάνοις
> τείχεος ἥρμοσται; (*Phœnissa*, 114 sqq.).

> ˃ː∪∪- ˃ ⎮ - ˃ ‖ ∪∪-∪ ⎮ ∪∪ᴧ ‖
> ∪ː∪∪-∪ ⎮ - ˃ ‖ ∪∪-∪ ⎮ -ᴧ ‖
> ˅ː∪∪- ˃ ⎮ -ᴧ ‖·

The last division of our subject is the different types of period, the various ways in which cola are combined and correspond. It should be noted that a colon with anacrusis can correspond to one without; so of catalexis and τονή.

(i) The simplest form is the *stichic* (στίχος "a row"), in which the cola are of the same length. The scheme is (^a_a—that is ($^2_2$ or ($^4_4$ or ($^6_6$, etc.—or $\begin{cases} a \\ a \\ a \end{cases}$, and so forth :—

> πᾶς γὰρ ἱππηλάτας
> καὶ πεδοστιβὴς λεώς (*Persæ*, 126 sq.).

> -∪ ⎮ ∟ ⎮ -∪ ⎮ -ᴧ ‖
> -∪ ⎮ -∪ ⎮ -∪ ⎮ -ᴧ ‖·

Where correspondence is indicated by $\binom{4}{4}$. It makes no difference that ∟ is answered by - ◡ in the second foot.

(ii) To the stichic corresponds the *palinodic* period (παλινῳδία, "repetition"), in which not a single colon but a group of cola is repeated so far as length is concerned :—

> μείξουσιν ἢ πρὸς Πυθίαις ἢ λαμπάσιν ἀκταῖς,
> οὗ πότνιαι σεμνὰ τιθηνοῦνται τέλη (*Œd. Col.*, 1047 *sq.*).

$$-\vdots\, \llcorner\,\cup\,|\,--\,|\,\llcorner\,\cup\,|\,--\,\|\,-\,\cup\,\cup\,|\,--\,\|\qquad \binom{4}{2}$$
$$-\vdots\, \llcorner\,\cup\,|\,\sqcup\,|\,-\,\cup\,\cup\,|\,--\,\|\,\llcorner\,\cup\,|\,-\,\overline{\wedge}\,\rrbracket.\qquad \binom{4}{2}$$

This type of period is frequent in English poetry, where the use of rhyme and the absence of τονή make the cola perfectly plain, *e.g.* :—

> Love still has something of the sea $\qquad\quad\ \binom{4}{3}$
> From whence his Mother rose ;
> No time his slaves from care sets free, $\qquad \binom{4}{3}$
> Or gives their hearts repose.—(Sedley.)

(iii) *Antithetic* periods are formed by the inverted repetition whether of different cola or of different groups of cola.

(*a*) The simplest type is that in which a series of un-grouped cola is repeated in inverse order :—

> διανταίαν λέγεις δόμοισι καί
> σώμασιν πεπλαγμέναν
> ἀναυδάτῳ μένει
> ἀραίῳ τ᾽ ἐκ πατρὸς διχόφρονι πότμῳ (*Septem*, 895 *sqq.*).

$$\cup\vdots\, \llcorner\,|\,\llcorner\,|\,-\,\cup\,|\,-\,\cup\,|\,-\,\cup\,|\,-\,\wedge\,\|\qquad 6$$
$$-\,\cup\,|\,-\,\cup\,|\,-\,\cup\,|\,-\,\wedge\,\|\qquad\qquad\quad 4$$
$$\cup\vdots\, \llcorner\,|\,\llcorner\,|\,-\,\cup\,|\,-\,\wedge\,\|\qquad\qquad\qquad 4$$
$$\cup\vdots\, \llcorner\,|\,\llcorner\,|\,-\,\cup\,|\,-\,\cup\,|\,-\,\cup\,\cup\,|\,-\,>\,\rrbracket.\qquad 6$$

(*b*) In a similar manner groups may be repeated antithetically. Each group retains its internal order; hence such periods are called "palinodic-antithetic" :—

> δι᾽ αἰῶνος μακροῦ πάνολβον ·
> ἔνθεν πᾶσα βοᾷ χθών,
> " φυσιζόου γένος τόδε Ζηνός ἐστιν ἀληθῶς ·
> τίς γὰρ ἂν κατέπαυσεν Ἥρας νόσους ἐπιβούλους ; "
> Διὸς τόδ᾽ ἔργον καὶ τόδ᾽ ἂν γένος λέγων
> ἐξ Ἐπάφου κυρήσαις (Æsch., *Supplices*, 582 *sqq.*).

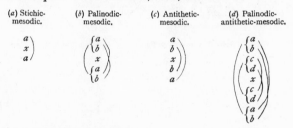

(iv) Any of the three periods just described, the stichic, the palinodic, the antithetic (whether simple or palinodic-antithetic) may be "mesodic," that is, it may be grouped round a central colon (the mesode), to which no colon corresponds, save of course the mesode of the other *strophe*. The schemes, then, are :—

(*a*) Stichic-mesodic.	(*b*) Palinodic-mesodic.	(*c*) Antithetic-mesodic.	(*d*) Palinodic-antithetic-mesodic.
$\left.\begin{array}{l}a\\x\\a\end{array}\right\rangle$	$\left(\begin{array}{l}\{a\\b\\x\\\{a\\b\end{array}\right)$	$\left.\begin{array}{l}a\\b\\x\\b\\a\end{array}\right\rangle$	$\left(\begin{array}{l}\{a\\b\\\{c\\d\\x\\\{c\\d\\\{a\\b\end{array}\right)$

(*a*) The stichic-mesodic :—

ἀμηχανῶ φροντίδος στερηθείς
εὐπάλαμον μέριμναν
ὅπα τράπωμαι, πίτνοντος οἴκου (*Agamemnon*, 1530 sqq.).

ᴗ:-ᴗ|∟|-ᴗ|-ᴗ|∟|-ʌ‖   6
-ᴗᴗ|-ᴗ|∟|-ʌ‖   4
ᴗ:-ᴗ|∟|-ᴗ|-ᴗ|∟|-ʌ‖.   6

(*b*) The palinodic-mesodic :—

ἐμοὶ χρῆν συμφοράν,
ἐμοὶ χρῆν πημονὰν γενέσθαι,
Ἰδαίαν ὅτε πρῶτον ὕλαν
Ἀλέξανδρος εἰλατίναν
ἐτάμεθ᾽, ἅλιον ἐπ᾽ οἴδμα ναυστολήσων (*Hecuba*, 629 sqq.).

ᴗ:∟|∟|-ᴗ|-ʌ‖   4
ᴗ:∟|∟|-ᴗ|-ᴗ|∟|-ʌ‖   16
->|-ᴗᴗ|-ᴗ|->‖   4
ᴗ:∟|-ᴗ|-ᴗᴗ|-ʌ‖   4
ᴗ:ᴗᴗᴗ|ᴗᴗᴗ|-ᴗ|-ᴗ|∟|-ʌ‖.   6

(*c*) The antithetic-mesodic :—

> σύ τοι σύ τοι κατηξίωσας,
> ὦ βαρύποτμε, κοὐκ
> ἄλλοθεν ἔχει τύχᾳ
> τᾷδ᾽ ἀπὸ μείζονος ·
> εὖτέ γε παρὸν φρονῆσαι . . . (*Philoctetes*, 1095 *sqq.*).

$$\cup\hspace{-2pt}:\hspace{-2pt}-\cup\mid-\cup\mid-\cup\mid-\cup\parallel \qquad\qquad 4$$
$$-\cup\mid\cup\cup\cup\mid-\wedge\parallel \qquad\qquad 3$$
$$>\hspace{-2pt}:\hspace{-2pt}\cup\cup\cup\mid-\cup\mid-\wedge\parallel \qquad\qquad 3$$
$$-\cup\cup\mid-\cup\mid-\wedge\parallel \qquad\qquad 3$$
$$>\hspace{-2pt}:\hspace{-2pt}\cup\cup\cup\mid-\cup\mid\llcorner\mid-\wedge\parallel\cdot \qquad 4$$

(*d*) The palinodic-antithetic-mesodic :—

> μή μοι μὴ προδίδου ·
> μόνος μόνῳ κόμιζε πορθμίδος σκάφος.
> χαιρέτω μὲν αὔλις ἥδε, χαιρέτω δὲ θυμάτων
> ἀποβώμιος [1] ἅν ἔχει θυσίαν
> Κύκλωψ Αἰτναῖος ξενικῶν κρέων κεχαρμένος βορᾷ.
> νηλής, ὦ τλᾶμον
> ὅστις δωμάτων ἐφεστίους . . . (*Cyclops*, 361 *sqq.*).[2]

$$->\mid-\cup\cup\mid-\wedge\parallel$$
$$\cup\hspace{-2pt}:\hspace{-2pt}-\cup\mid-\cup\mid-\cup\mid-\cup\mid-\cup\mid-\wedge\parallel$$
$$-\cup\mid-\cup\mid-\cup\mid-\cup\parallel-\cup\mid-\cup\mid-\cup\mid-\wedge\parallel$$
$$\omega\hspace{-2pt}:\hspace{-2pt}-\cup\cup\mid-\cup\mid-\cup\cup\mid-\wedge\parallel$$
$$->\mid->\mid-\cup\cup\mid-\cup\parallel-\cup\mid-\cup\mid-\cup\mid-\wedge\parallel$$
$$->\mid->\mid-\wedge\parallel$$
$$\llcorner\mid\llcorner\mid-\cup\mid-\cup\mid-\cup\mid-\wedge\,\rrbracket\cdot$$

Most of the periodic structures which have been dis-cribed are by no means obvious to the ear. A trained sense of rhythm, attention to quantity, and careful prac-tice, will reduce the difficulties. But in any case Greek periods are far less easy to grasp than English. Their variety and length, the frequent occurrence of prolonga-tion, resolution, and irrational syllables, the possibility of preludes or postludes—all these are formidable to modern students, who lack the help of the music. We may perhaps work out the period with ease on paper,

---

[1] The first two syllables of this word form the anacrusis, though the metre is trochaic ; that is, we find ⏑⏑ instead of ⏑. In such cases the two "shorts" are given the length of one only, and this is indicated by the sign ω.

[2] I have taken Schmidt's readings and arrangement for the sake of an example. Murray's arrangement is quite different.

but our ear often cannot appreciate the balance and contour of the whole as it can in English lyrics, where we have the immense assistance of a rhyme-scheme. But it is no sound deduction that the study of Greek lyric metre and rhythm is therefore useless. We cannot always hear the period—that is a question of music; but we can always hear the colon—that is a question of language. To utter the cola correctly is easy after a little practice; and it is these "sentences" which, by their own internal rhythmical nature and by the identities or contrasts existing between them, reinforce and more pungently articulate the sense of the words wherefrom they are moulded.

INDICES

I. GREEK

Names of plays, etc., in capitals

II. PLACES, Etc.

A. = Aristophanes, Æ. = Æschylus, E. = Euripides, S. = Sophocles, Sh. = Shakespeare.

Abdera, 298.
Acharnæ, in *Acharnians*, 296.
Achelous, in *Trachiniæ*, 160.
— 304 n.
Acropolis, 14, 49, 239.
— in *Eumenides*, 113.
Ægospotami, 13, 182, 324.
Æthiopia, in *Andromeda*, 299.
Ætolia, in *Cresphontes*, 307-8.
Alexandria, Library of, 39.
— Pleiad of, 39.
— Theatrical activity in, 3rd century B.C., 39.
Amphipolis, 294.
Arachnæus, Mount, in *Agamemnon*, 101.
Arden, Forest of, 63.
Areopagus, in *Eumenides*, 112 ff., 128 n.
Argolid plain, in S.'s *Electra*, 63.
Argos, in *Agamemnon*, 99 ff.
— — *Choephoræ*, 106.
— — *Eumenides*, 112.
— — *Supplices* of Æ., 84.
— — E.'s *Electra*, 253.
— — — *Heracleidæ*, 200 ff.
— — — *Orestes*, 268 ff.
— — — *Supplices*, 234 n., 235.
— — — *Telephus*, 295.
— 316, 321.
Asia Minor, Græco-Roman theatres in, 59 n.
Asopus, plain of, in *Agamemnon*, 124.
Athens, 228-9, 244, 252 n., 307, 312, 324-5.
— Agathon of, 21.
— and drama, 3, 5.
— — Euripides, 317 ff.
— Athena's temple in, 63.
— in *Eumenides*, 111 ff.
— — *Œd. Coloneus*, 168 ff., 185.
— — E.'s *Erechtheus*, 297.
— — — *Hippolytus*, 205 ff., 213.
— — — *Ion*, 236 ff.
— — — *Supplices*, 234 n., 235.
— local cults of, in Æ., 128.

Athens, Phrynichus of, 6.
— Sophocles of, 12.
Athens' war with Eleusis, 119.
Athos, Mt., in *Agamemnon*, 101.
Attica, 4, 279.
— and Furies, 131.
— E.'s cenotaph in, 18.
— in *Eumenides*, 113.
— — *Heracleidæ*, 200.
— — *Medea*, 194.
Aulis, 247, 270.
— in *Iph. at A.*, 285 ff.

Bradfield College, Gk. plays at, 55.
Byzantium, 313.
— Homer, the tragedian of? 40.
— Python of? 39.

Caria, Mausolus, k. of, 38.
Catana, Python of? 39.
Chæronea, battle of, 31.
Chapel, Sistine, 102.
Chios, Ion of, 21 ff.
— Sophocles in, 15.
Chrysé, in S.'s *Philoctetes*, 161.
Cithæron, Mt., in *Œd. Tyr.*, 147 ff.
— — — E.'s *Bacchæ*, 277 ff.
Colchis, Mt., in E.'s *Medea*, 192 ff.
Colonus, Eumenides at, 172.
— in *Œd. Coloneus*, 168 ff.
— Sophocles' home, 172.
— — song, 71.
Congo, Upper, 248.
Corinth, 22.
— and drama, 3.
— in *Œd. Tyr.*, 147.
— — *Medea*, 192 ff., 313.
Crete, in *Hippolytus*, 206 ff.
Cynthus, 249.
Cyzicus, 167.

Delium, 234 n.
Delphi, 257.
— in *Choephoræ*, 108, 110.

367

III. PERSONS AND WORKS

A. = Aristophanes, Æ. = Æschylus, Ar. = Aristotle, E. = Euripides, S. = Sophocles, Sh. = Shakespeare. Names of authors in small capitals, of works in italics.

IV. METRE

LINES QUOTED IN CHAPTER VI.

V. GENERAL

DRAMABOOKS

WHEN ORDERING, please use the Standard Book Number consisting of the publisher's prefix, 8090-, plus the five digits following each title. (Note that the numbers given in this list are for paperback editions only. Many of the books are also available in cloth.)

For a complete list of plays (including the New Mermaids and Spotlight Dramabooks series), please write to Hill and Wang, 72 Fifth Avenue, New York, New York 10011.

AMERICAN CENTURY SERIES

DATE DUE